A Theory of Ordered Liberty

William J. Zanardi
St. Edward's University

Second, revised edition. 2011
Published in the USA by
Forty Acres Press
2214 San Antonio, Ste 101
Austin, Texas 78705
www.fortyacrespress.com

ISBN-13: 9781610430036

Formatting and cover design: Carlos Velasco

TABLE OF CONTENTS

PREFACE i

INTRODUCTION iv

CHAPTER ONE: What Does It Mean to Pay Attention?

    Introduction 1
    From Description to Explanation 5
    Applications of Categories of Neuroscience 18
    Neurochemistry and Acts of Attention 27
    The "Turn" to Top-Down Ordering 33
    Libet's Puzzle 51

CHAPTER TWO: How Do Emotions and Images
                Affect Human Action?

    Introduction 57
    Versions of the Puzzle 58
    What Sense Can We Make of
        These Dependencies 70
    Shifting the Puzzles into a
        Theoretical Context 78
    Summary 96
    A Puzzle from Neuropathology 101

CHAPTER THREE: What Is Creative Understanding?

    Introduction 107
    Descriptions of Creative Understanding 110
    Approximations to the Meaning of Creative
        Understanding 120
    Introducing a Dialectical Notion of Liberty 143

CHAPTER FOUR: How Do Institutions Affect
                Decision-Making?

    Introduction 157

What Is Decision-Making?..161
Decisions and Institutions..170
A Dialectical Account of Liberty
    and Institutions..186
Liberty and the Anarchist Dream............................206

CHAPTER FIVE: Economics and Liberty

Introduction 213
A Normative Understanding of Liberty....................215
Implications for Economic Practices........................230
A Puzzle about Consumer Responsibility................241

CHAPTER SIX: Political Liberty

Introduction 265
Descriptive Context and
    Contemporary Puzzles.......................................266
Explanatory Context..275
Case Study...296

EPILOGUE: Book(s) Not Written

Anamnesis 311
Prolepsis 323
Future Studies of Liberty 342

BIBLIOGRAPHY 361

INDEX 367

Preface

Twentieth-century debates over freedom and order assumed the choices were between liberal democracies and fascist states, between market economies and command economies, between an atomistic model and an organic model of social relations. With the demise of fascist regimes and command economies, the question of freedom and order today is less about government regulation and more about persons making responsible use of their increasingly available liberties. In his last years Milton Friedman supposedly changed his economic mantra from "Privatize! Privatize! Privatize!" to "Rule of Law! Rule of Law!" Apparently privatization increased liberties but also gave rise to new threats to social order.

If efforts to impose order from the "top down" have failed, what new measures are compatible with preserving liberty? For some the impersonal, even "mechanistic," operations of free markets (accompanied by the regulations of a minimal state), afford the best hope of harmonizing liberty and order. Some naysayers liken this hope to a nineteenth-century belief in the beneficence of Nature, i.e. a secular version of an earlier trust in divine providence.[1] The bloody deeds of the last century eroded confidence in both beliefs, and every new environmental catastrophe or global economic crisis further undermines trust in markets. Still, the hope that open markets and the minimal state are the way forward has survived previous crises of confidence. Economic revivals and returns to prosperity restore the shaken faith of many. Future economic contractions and political upheavals will undoubtedly test that faith again. But what will ultimately sustain such a faith?

---

[1] René Girard's description of this belief is succinct: "the beneficence of Nature (that good angel of complacent humanism, the last relic of those optimistic theologies engendered by the deterioration of historical Christianity)." <u>Violence and the Sacred</u> (Baltimore: The Johns Hopkins University Press, 1989), 221.

This text is blunt in asserting that there is no substitute for individuals acquiring ordered liberty. If there are widespread abuses of liberty, then "Nature," Providence or the impersonal workings of open markets will not rescue persons and entire societies from dire consequences. To paraphrase an author whose works have shaped this text: history is not run as a kindergarten where children are protected from their own follies.[2]

It is one thing to assert that ordered liberty is indispensable to the preservation of open markets and democratic political orders; it is another to explain what ordered liberty is and how it emerges and endures. An explanation of any phenomenon should be on the level of the best science of the day. Thus, the first two chapters of this study of liberty survey what the neurosciences and experimental psychology have discovered about the basic conditions for exercises of liberty. This beginning asks readers to move beyond the descriptive and popular literature on liberty. A serious understanding or "science" of liberty is not yet part of that literature. However, the question of ordered liberty can be a meeting ground for researchers in the natural and human sciences. Of course the meeting need not take place. Many scientists proceed on the assumption that conscious acts are reducible to preconscious events and processes. At the same time, many of their counterparts in the humanities speak of conscious acts as if they had no connection to neurochemical and organic processes. Both proceed with blind spots.

Identifying some of these blind spots and bridging the divides between scientific and humanistic discourses on liberty are purposes of this work. Changes in vocabulary may bridge some of the gaps. If today neuroscientists are uneasy with an eighteenth-century vocabulary of "mechanisms" in the brain, humanists should be equally uneasy with their debts to an

---

[2] Bernard Lonergan. Insight: A Study of Human Understanding. Vol.3 in Collected Works (Toronto: University of Toronto Press, 1992), 474.

obsolete faculty psychology when they talk of "free will" and "volitional control." But what new terms is either group to use? An alternative vocabulary appears in this text, one that may make talk of free will and determinism obsolete.

Detecting blind spots is a trickier business. How can anyone pay attention to what they cannot see? The first chapter surveys findings from the neuroscience of attention to answer this question, but the subtle maneuvers there are proleptic. An explanatory account of the basic intentional act of attending has implications for understanding more complex intentional acts dependent on it. The strategy is a slow assembling of research data, insights and generalizations that can support increasingly more complex approximations to the meaning of ordered liberty.

An Introduction is the conventional place to find a more specific overview of what is to follow in a text. A Preface conventionally announces broad purposes and acknowledges debts. If the general purpose is to offer an explanatory notion of ordered liberty, there are secondary purposes. Identifying blind spots and changing the vocabulary of discourse about liberty are means to an end, namely, understanding how ordered liberty emerges and endures. A single text is unlikely to evaluate every means or to achieve every end. All the same, the issues at stake are too central to the survival of liberal democracies to delay until authors have answered every question, anticipated every objection and formulated a complete theory of ordered liberty. So this text makes a beginning and takes the first steps. The Epilogue imagines further steps. But even the initial steps are following traces left by many others. Most noticeably this text follows in the footsteps of two remarkable thinkers: Bernard Lonergan and Philip McShane. Their works inspired this inquiry. Needless to say, its limits and deficiencies are due not to those in the lead but to a much slower climber lagging behind them.

INTRODUCTION

Since the publication of <u>The Idea of Freedom</u>[3] over fifty years ago, developments in neuroscience, biochemistry and cognitive psychology have vastly expanded the materials relevant to any new theory of liberty. This book makes use of these materials in pursuing several purposes: (1) to identify problems with how we understand and talk about liberty, (2) to advance a hypothesis about how to solve some of these problems, (3) to outline a future collaborative project that could produce an explanatory account of ordered liberty.

The problems first appear as a series of questions. How do advances in neuroscience alter how we understand and talk about liberty? How do we break our dependence on the residual language of faculty psychology, e.g. talk of free will, volition, reason or rational intellect? For that matter, how do we break free of the metaphors of an eighteenth-century mechanistic worldview, e.g. talk of determinisms and of mechanisms in the brain? By default must we adopt new metaphors about brain-maps, neurons presenting arguments, neural pathways sending messages or information to different brain locales?[4] Are these metaphors attributing psychological acts to neurochemical and organic processes?

One hypothesis in response to these questions proceeds with two assumptions. First, liberty is a property of acts of intentionality; and, second, it is manifest in every type of intentional act. Contrary to conventional views that limit liberty to human operations of deciding and acting, the hypothesis is that liberty extends "all the way down" to even the most basic intentional act, namely, the act of attention. Thus, Chapter One reviews recent literature on the neuroscience of attention and relates its findings to

---

[3] Mortimer J. Adler (Garden City, N.Y.: Doubleday, 1958).
[4] Debates over the legitimacy of such metaphors appear in the lively exchanges among Maxwell Bennett, Daniel Dennett, Peter Hacker and John Searle in <u>Neuroscience and Philosophy</u> (New York: Columbia University Press, 2003).

intentionality theory. But why do we pay attention to one thing rather than another? This question shifts the focus from neuroscience to psychology, and so Chapter Two explores the roles emotions and images play in action.

A puzzle recurs throughout the first two chapters: How are we to understand and to talk about the relations between neurochemical processes that condition intentional acts ("bottom-up conditioning") and deliberate acts of attention that condition which neurochemical and biological events occur ("top-down conditioning")? Chapter Three experiments with talk of "dialectical relations" as an improvement over recent talk of "interactive systems" and the even older language of volitional control. Acts of understanding that integrate "lower-order materials" into new syntheses provide a model for understanding both types of conditioning.

The dialectical alternative assumes that liberty is at first only a capacity for deliberate control over lower-order conditions. The development of this capacity is dependent on the "orientation" of a person. But this orientation is, in turn, dependent on impersonal conditions ranging from neurochemical processes, organic states and psychological make-up to sociohistorical contexts. This mix of internal and external conditions and the dialectical relations among them constitute a complex web of variables for understanding liberty.

For liberty to develop, some set of these variables must be favorable. That is, this indeterminate capacity requires that, amid the range of variables conditioning intentional acts, some of them make it more probable that deliberate intentional acts occur. Assumed here is that non-systematic processes occur as part of cognitive development. As a result, it is a matter of probability whether populations can focus attention or suffer from extreme forms of ADHD, can recognize friends' faces or have brain lesions that prevent the making of memories, can meet challenges or suffer from phobias that new challenges exacerbate. Generalizing to a sociohistorical perspective, we can recognize that progress and regress, civic mindedness and forms of sociopathology are always empirical possibilities.

Chapter Four shifts from psychology to sociology. The title of the chapter is, "How Do Institutions Affect Decision-Making?" As a matter of historical antecedents, patterns established by prior choices narrow the range of possibilities for the development of liberty-as-capacity. Such patterns form a context out of which individuals operate, not just as a matter of personal dispositions (habits) but also as a matter of institutional design.

Chapter Four pursues the discussion of liberty within an explanatory framework, the basic categories of which are drawn from intentionality analysis. These categories, plus the conclusions of the preceding chapters, provide the framework for talking about the "structure of the good" in which liberty-as-capacity becomes liberty-in-act through the mediation of personal orientation and social relations. The remaining chapters apply this understanding of liberty to questions about ordered liberty in economic and political contexts.

Chapter Five shows the relevance of the categories "orientation," "displacement" and "personal relations" to understanding the origins of different moral stances regarding economic exchanges and their consequences. Chapter Six investigates a series of questions about political liberty. Why do we endorse liberty as freedom from interference? When contemporary writers mention "ordered liberty," to what ends do they think liberty should be ordered and why do they find it so difficult to specify more than the general end of pursuing "one's interests"? The same difficulty reappears when contemporary authors talk about liberty as self-determination. Why do they have so much trouble identifying a normative "content" that would distinguish it from the pursuit of "interests"?

Finally, an Epilogue offers fantasies about future scholarly practices that would yield more efficient and productive studies of liberty. Why end on a note of fantasy? In prosaic terms, philosophical reflection on liberty should have some "street value." That is, after writing books, delivering conference papers and publishing articles, scholars might ask what these conventional academic practices are about, where they are heading? Particularly when writing about liberty, we might expect the inquiry to have some relevance to improving practices.

There is a historical rationale for the breadth of this study. While Aristotle used metaphysical categories to describe intellectual motions leading to deliberate acts, Descartes, in separating the *res extensa* and the *res cogitans*, generated an epistemological question about how motions occurred between the two. Cognitive psychology "brackets" the epistemological question, but twentieth-century depth psychology suggested that cognitive acts themselves were the playthings of a Cartesian "evil genius." Intentionality theory corrected Descartes' flawed wording of the puzzle, but new puzzles arose about the neurochemical and biological antecedents of intentional acts. Since liberty is a property of intentional acts, a contemporary study of it should proceed from an adequately informed historical perspective. Beginning a study of liberty with a review of what neuroscientists are saying about basic intentional acts of attention acknowledges these historical shifts from metaphysics to epistemology and on to cognitive and depth psychology and, more recently, to neuroscience.

What is the evidence that this inquiry and its fantasy warrant attention? The first test is whether the chapters supply insights and terminology that improve upon the problematical usages noted above regarding faculty psychology, brain mechanisms and newer metaphors attributing psychological acts to neurochemical and organic processes. The chapters gradually introduce a new vocabulary of operators, integrators and their varied demands that evoke responses conditioned by but capable of altering prior neurochemical and organic patterns.

The second test is whether the chapters show ways of evading intellectual impasses that appear in contemporary discussions of liberty. Accordingly, the final part of each of the first four chapters describes a specific impasse and then suggests how preceding materials in the chapter can help circumvent it. Chapter One, for example, takes up Libet's famous puzzle about the relation between neural activity and conscious acts of choice. Chapter Two presents a puzzle from neuropathology: covert face recognition in prosopagnosia. Chapter Three puzzles over how persons are able to overcome latent, emotionally weighted dispositions that block some images from reaching consciousness and so prevent unwanted insights from occurring. (A dialectical understanding of liberty, first appearing in this chapter, explains how overcoming such psychological barriers is possible.) Chapter Four ends with a section entitled " Liberty and the Anarchist Dream." The puzzle there is to analyze the anarchist dream of a society without political authority, i.e. one without any executive power that could legitimately coerce the acts of its competent members.

The last two chapters shift from puzzles to case studies. Chapter Five applies a notion of ordered liberty to a current issue in social economics: Under what conditions, if any, should consumers as "indirect employers" think they are responsible for unintended harms occurring to anonymous others as a result of their economic exchanges? The case study at the end of Chapter Six diagnoses psychological obstacles embedded in consumer societies that are barriers to politically responsible uses of economic liberty.

This overview of the chapters, their puzzles and case studies is a clue to the meaning of the Epilogue's subtitle: "Book(s) Not Written." Although this text cites numerous historical and contemporary thinkers, it is not a comparative study of different theories of liberty. While the author has exploited the results of inquiries in diverse fields for this study of liberty, he makes no claim to thorough familiarity with the empirical findings of any of those fields. The Epilogue identifies further questions, any one of which could be the focus of some future dissertation or research project. For example, the text makes repeated references to conscious intentional acts, but what is consciousness? The text remarks on the neurochemical conditions for acts of attention, but what similar types of conditions make possible images, experiences of curiosity and acts of deciding? And what about the language of "conditioning," either from the bottom up or from the top down? Scholars and scientists routinely use such terminology, but is there any theoretical understanding, formulated as explanatory correlations, supporting these terms? Then there are the standard references to liberty as "self-determination." But what do we mean by "self"? Can a serious study of liberty go forward without answering this question? Finally, there are more routine grounds for embarrassment regarding commonly used terms. Words such as "development," "progress," "decline" and "creativity" regularly appear in contemporary works on liberty, but how often do we find a sustained effort to puzzle out an explanatory understanding of any of them?

So much for a few of the omissions in this work and in others like it. The promise of the Epilogue is that functional specialization offers an alternative to contemporary academic practice and will eventually remedy some of its deficiencies. But the promise is about future collaborative projects and their results. This present work falls far short of the promise, and a reader might well wonder why it deserves any attention. If current practice is defective and if we allow ourselves to fantasize about a better way, then we need to make a beginning. One option is to produce a text that exhibits the ambitions and the weaknesses of current academic practice. The weaknesses, particularly if they are explicitly noted, will underline the need for collaboration among specialists and a clear differentiation of just which tasks each is performing. Perhaps this text will serve to focus attention on both the lack of collaboration and the confusion of tasks that mar current practice. But even more, imagine collaborators "circulating" their individual works among other collaborators for their criticisms. Each produces a new text in response to the criticism and, in turn, circulates it through the group for further criticism. What might come of all this?

CHAPTER ONE

What Does It Mean to Pay Attention?

I Introduction

While this first chapter focuses on acts of attention, it serves a more general purpose, namely, exploring how liberty can be part of even this most basic type of intentional act.[5] In assembling an explanatory account of acts of attention, Part II begins with descriptive examples and then identifies the requirements of an explanatory account. Parts III and IV draw upon recent findings in the neuroscience of attention to provide evidence for the correlations among three "elements" of any act of attention. These findings are far from complete. For instance, they leave a crucial question unanswered: How do deliberate acts of attending and understanding exercise an "executive function" over neurochemical and organic processes? Part V emphasizes the need for a "turn" in future research projects to this question of a top-down ordering of lower-order conditions. Descriptive examples and research results on feedback processes between biochemical and conscious acts help to specify just what the puzzle is about and how adopting a dynamic notion of interacting schemes of recurrence might solve it. Finally, Part VI reviews Libet's famous experiment that some have read as proof that intentional acts (and by extension, liberty) are epiphenomenal. An alternate reading makes use of the previous explanatory

---

[5] As will appear below, a first, provisional meaning of liberty is the capacity for higher-order operations to integrate lower-order materials. A question for this chapter, then, is how acts of attention integrate more rudimentary materials. This simple beginning anticipates a later focus on ordered liberty as dialectical in nature, i.e. both an ordering or integrating and a being ordered or integrated. The medieval formula for this correlation will appear below: *et motus et movens*.

account of attention to solve the puzzle of the "time lag" occurring in Libet's experiment.

To differentiate acts of attention from other types of intentional acts, we can employ a simple pattern among distinct but related acts leading to decision-making. Four questions distinguish the components of this overly simplified pattern. First, there is the question of diagnosis: What is the situation, the problem or the challenge we face? Next is the question of motivation: Why do we find it significant, of interest to us, worth our attention? Third is the question for deliberation: What are our options, the realistic possibilities for improving the situation, the actions we could take? Finally, there is the question for decision: What should we do? What is worth doing? Which is the best option?

This simple pattern of questions has certain common-sense merits. To begin with, we should diagnose a problem before attempting some remedy. Physicians who prescribed treatments without first examining patients would keep the undertakers busy. But being careful in diagnosing and deliberating over options presupposes we find a problem worth our attention. If we are indifferent to a problem, we lack the motivation to give it careful thought. Think of how casually we can scan a newspaper report of some distant tragedy that leaves us unfazed and uninterrupted in our routines. But if the motivation to pay attention is present, we focus on details and begin to wonder not just why this problem has occurred but what we can do about it. When the situation evokes our strong interest, identifying realistic options may consume our time and energy. On occasion this labor yields not just imagined courses of action but choices as to what we need to do.

The process of decision-making seems to begin with an act of attention to some situation, an act that a question of diagnosis makes explicit. Perhaps, then, a good place to begin an analysis of decision-making and the role of liberty in it is to ask what goes on in acts of attending, what does it mean to pay attention? Descriptive responses to this question are easy to make.[6] However, what if the aim is an explanatory response? We will begin with descriptive remarks about paying attention but then go on to ask what an explanatory answer to the question requires.

To anticipate these requirements, we need: (1) a deliberate shift from talk of acts of attending as we experience them to such acts in relation to other classes of mental acts, states-of-mind and their nonconscious preconditions; (2) an identification of basic categories and correlations among them as the "outer words" for insights into acts of attending relative to their preconditions and their results; (3) an increasingly complex series of images or diagrams to "track" insights into complex relations among acts of attending, their preconditions and results.

It helps to begin by acknowledging the limits of such an ambitious inquiry. This inquiry will raise more questions than any one person can answer. Answering the seemingly simple question about what it means to pay attention will depend on answers to related questions in the neurosciences,[7] biochemistry and cognitive psychology. This complexity points to the need for a division of labor among specialties and also underlines just how limited expectations should be of any

---

[6] Perhaps the most famous common-sense account or description is the one provided by William James. "Every one knows what attention is. It is the taking possession by the mind, in clear and vivid form, of one out of what seem several simultaneously possible objects or trains of thought. Focalization, concentration, or consciousness are its essence. It implies withdrawal from some things in order to deal effectively with others, and is a condition which has a real opposite in the confused, dazed, scatterbrained state...." The Principles of Psychology (1890) quoted in Maria Ruz. "Let the Brain Explain the Mind: the Case of Attention," in Philosophical Psychology. Vol.19, No.4 (August 2006), 498-499.

[7] In subsequent pages "neurosciences" will be used in the singular for the sake of convenience though cited evidence will be drawn from specialized fields of neuropathology, neuroanatomy, neurophysiology and neuropsychology.

writer's foray into the horizon of theory, even if the focus seems quite narrow.[8]

Finally, since writers should acknowledge at least some of their assumptions, this author accepts the following generalizations about intentional acts, their preconditions and objectives.

1. To speak of actual, as opposed to possible, data or stimuli independent of a relation to a conscious subject is to overlook how actual data are correlates of conscious acts. They are defined in relation to such acts as what evoke responses of surprise, questioning, fearing and so on.
2. To distinguish between being conscious and being attentive avoids confusion. The difference is empirically available by asking persons if they are aware of the chairs they are sitting on. The question makes the chairs objects of attention whereas they previously were taken for granted and used without standing out as objects of attention.[9]

---

[8] These remarks anticipate the self-criticism and the fantasy of a future academic practice that appear in the Epilogue.

[9] This distinction shows up in neuroscience. For example, "awareness facilitates rapid scanning of an array of information, while attention is associated with a higher probability of learning and memory encoding." Richard C. Deth et al. "Attention- Related Signaling Activities of the D4 Dopamine Receptor" in <u>Cognitive Neuroscience</u> of <u>Attention</u>. Michael I. Posner, ed. (New York: Guilford Press, 2004), 274. The distinction is useful in understanding how selective attention, in blocking irrelevant stimuli, must also allow for "background-monitoring" of potential threats or new opportunities for reaching goals. See Oliver Gruber and Thomas Goschke, "Executive Control Emerging from Dynamic Interactions between Brain Systems Mediating Language, Working Memory and Attentional Process" in <u>Acta</u> <u>Psychologica</u> Vol. 115 (2004), 113.

3. An explanatory account of intentional operations should range from relations among conscious acts to relations: (1) among underlying nonconscious events in biological organs (e.g. parts of the brain), (2) among chemical processes (e.g. neurotransmitters affecting changes within parts of the brain), and (3) among genetic substrates supporting the chemical processes.[10] Such an account ideally includes both a bottom-up detailing of how lower-level conditions make possible higher-level operations and a top-down analysis of how the latter can effect changes in the former.

II From Description to Explanation

As promised above, some descriptive claims about being attentive provide a beginning.

- Being attentive is not the presuppositionless inquiry of the nineteenth-century positivists; it is not a blank staring. Once past the earliest months of infancy, we bring to any act of attending accumulated insights that form the initial context for responding to stimuli, for example, broadly classifying data as disturbing sights or sounds. Over time such a context can become the refined sensibilities of the artist, the detective, the medical diagnostician.
- Since initial responses can mislead an inquiry, the ideal way of being attentive is to be open and critically receptive to whatever data are available. Letting the

---

[10] One study that exhibits concern for the full range of underlying conditions for conscious acts is James M. Swanson et al. "Clinical and Cognitive Definitions of Attention Deficits in Children with Attention-Deficit/Hyperactivity Disorder" in Posner, 430-445. The study of acts of attention in this chapter is limited to the biological and neurochemical processes undergirding them.

phenomena "show themselves" can be an art learned through years of training and careful observation.[11]
- The standards for being critically attentive will be dependent on variables, e.g. one's prior training in the conventional practices of some art or science. Thus, the novice hunter learns from others to read signs of tracks on the forest floor while the graduate student in history learns how to detect signs of forgeries.[12]
- Initial habits in attending are not fixed and incorrigible. Further growth in attentiveness is possible, especially when surprises disrupt our conventional assumptions and draw our attention to new data and prompt new questions. Jerome Bruner remarked on how surprises are a "window on presupposition" or conventional expectation.[13] But our expectations are patterned results of prior attending.[14]

---

[11] The distinction between automatic or reflex responses and trained responses to data will appear below. The latter are instances of higher-order control over lower-order materials and so examples of the first meaning of liberty.

[12] These examples anticipate insights in Chapter Four regarding the dialectical role of institutions in shaping the capacities of individuals.

[13] "Possible Castles" in <u>Actual Minds, Possible Worlds</u> (Harvard University Press, 1986), 46.

[14] "If the first time we have an injection it hurts, we are more likely to feel pain the second time, which in turn strengthens the likelihood of our feeling it the third time. Eventually the expectation of pain will be so strong that even if the needle enters our skin without touching a nerve we will flinch. If, however, the first experience of an injection happens not to be painful, we will be less likely to feel the pain the second time." Rita Carter. <u>Exploring Consciousness</u> (Berkeley: University of California Press, 2002), 207. As will become apparent in later chapters, "patterned results" can be neurochemical, biological, psychic and intellectual integrations that are liable to disruptions from external sources (e.g. disturbing and

The preceding generalities about being attentive do not necessarily reflect results from operating within an <u>explanatory</u> context. This becomes evident when further questions arise. For example, how is attending dependent on prior understanding? Why do "surprises" evoke our attention? Moreover, is attending ever the result, not of one's being surprised, but of deliberate intentional acts? If so, how do such conscious acts "order" the neurochemical conditions for attending? In addition, how do acts of attending focus on some data to the neglect of others? What parts of the brain are engaged when we focus on specific objects and ignore others?

What is required to answer these further questions? One author offered a complex set of clues in a long paragraph opening with, "Study of an organism begins from the thing-for-us...."[15] To begin with the "thing-for-us" is to begin with

---

dissonant data) and from internal sources (e.g. new questions that find no adequate answers in prior integrations of meaning).

[15] <u>Insight</u>, 489. To quote the text in its entirety: "Study of an organism begins from the thing-for-us, from the organism as exhibited to the senses. A first step is a descriptive differentiation of different parts, and since most of the parts are inside, this descriptive preliminary necessitates dissection or anatomy. A second step consists in the accumulation of insights that relate the described parts to organic events, occurrences, operations. By these insights, the parts become known as organs, and the further knowledge constituted by the insights is a grasp of intelligibilities that (1) are immanent in the several parts, (2) refer each part to what it can do and, under determinable conditions, will do, and (3) relate the capacity-for-performance of each part to the capacities-for-performance of the other parts. So physiology follows anatomy. A third step is to effect the transition from the thing-for-us to the thing-itself, from insights that grasp described parts as organs to insights that grasp conjugate forms systematizing otherwise coincidental manifolds of chemical and physical processes. By this transition one links physiology with biochemistry and biophysics. To this end, there have to be invented appropriate symbolic images of the

descriptive examples (things in relation to us or the medievals' *priora quoad nos*), and only later might we pursue explanations (things in relations among themselves or the medievals' *priora quoad se*). Another set of clues, particularly relevant to the question of attention, is found in William Mathews' biography of the same author. Mathews reviews how his subject understood Aquinas on the question of abstraction.

> Lonergan's main argument is that for Aquinas formative abstraction or concept formation is the outcome of the prior stages of objective and apprehensive abstraction. In objective abstraction our questioning selects some datum out of the entire world of sense or of consciousness and becomes interested in it.[16]

Lonergan's interest was in explanatory accounts, and so he pushed beyond the descriptive categories of "selecting" and "becoming interested" in some datum. The following quote exemplifies how explanatory accounts rely on correlations among terms.

> In the Contra Gentiles the actual intelligibility of phantasm is clarified: in the dark colors are visible in potency; in daylight they are visible in act but seen in potency; they are seen in act only inasmuch as sight is in act; similarly, prior to the illumination of agent

---

relevant chemical and physical processes; in these images there have to be grasped by insight the laws of the higher system that account for regularities beyond the range of physical and chemical explanation; from these laws there has to be constructed the flexible circle of schemes of recurrence in which the organism functions; finally, this flexible circle of schemes must be coincident with the related set of capacities-for-performance that previously was grasped in the sensibly presented organs."

[16] Lonergan's Quest (Toronto: University of Toronto Press, 2005), 196.

intellect, phantasms are intelligible in potency; by that illumination they become intelligible in act but only understood in potency; they are understood in act only inasmuch as the possible intellect is in act.[17]

How is this use of metaphysical categories (potency and act) a clue to operating in an explanatory context? First, the writer identifies a set of relations among descriptive terms, i.e. objects, conditions and operations; so we have (1) colors, (2) under conditions of darkness or daylight, and (3) the operation or act of seeing. Then the variable "state" of each term is linked to the "state" of another term, e.g. colors are potentially visible relative to darkness but actually visible relative to the daylight and actually seen relative to someone looking. Similarly, images or phantasms are potentially intelligible prior to someone attending to them.[18] They are actually intelligible (though only potentially understood) relative to someone attending to them as puzzling or interesting objects, i.e. someone engaging in objective abstraction. They are understood in act relative to someone having a preconceptual understanding of them, i.e. someone engaging in apprehensive abstraction.

Since the focus of this chapter is on "attention," the question is whether Aquinas' views on abstraction can advance our understanding of what it means to pay attention

---

[17] Verbum : Word and Idea in Aquinas, Vol.3 in Collected Works, (University of Toronto Press, 1997), 174.

[18] Since phantasms are not something independent of minds, how can they be even potentially intelligible when no one is attending to them? The answer may depend on distinguishing between something being an object for consciousness and something being an object of attention. We are conscious of far more than what we are attending to, and the evidence is found everyday in driving a familiar route to work when routine processing of sights and sounds requires little attention to details. See as well the second assumption listed in the Introduction to this chapter.

to something.[19] The preceding remarks on types of abstraction do offer some general guidelines for pursuing further questions in an explanatory or theoretical context. First of all, we can anticipate the _form_ explanatory or theoretical responses must take, i.e. they will take the form of correlations among classes of objects, states or operations. For example, consider how one shifts from describing rain to explaining why it rains. The change is from talk of rain as we sense it to talk of how classes of events are correlated among themselves in the familiar hydrological cycle. Since the focus of this chapter is on the intentional act of attending, we can go on to ask what correlations among types of mental acts, states-of-mind and their preconditions and results might someday yield a similarly familiar explanation of "attention."

The first step in arriving at such correlations is to identify basic categories as the terms to be correlated. Doing so is initially dependent on a process of trial and error.[20] But

---

[19] Mathews translates the meaning of "objective abstraction" into descriptive terms: "Subjectively, this constitutes the awakening of our mind's desire to a problem in the world. Objectively, it involves a particular realm in the universe being selected out as interesting or even fascinating by our minds. In the initial stages of the opening up of a problem there is no question of our being able to understand it in depth or converse about it." (196) The absence of understanding "in depth" does not mean that selecting does not require a minimal determination of the object of interest, for example, classifying it as a sight or a sound. Seth A. Herd et al. investigate how attentional control makes use of prior categories (e.g. a general category of color) in responding to tasks. See "Neural Mechanisms of Cognitive Control: An Integrative Model of Stroop Task Performance and fMRI Data" in Journal of Cognitive Neuroscience Vol. 18, No.1 (2006), 22-32.

[20] "Out of the endless classificatory possibilities analysis selects not the one sanctioned by ordinary speech nor again the one sanctioned by facility of measurement but the one that most rapidly yields terms which can be defined by the relations in which they stand to one another. To discover such terms is a lengthy and tedious process of

there are shortcuts in what researchers have already discovered about "attention." For example, neuroscience offers clues to understanding acts of attending. "Attention requires three elements: arousal, orientation, focus."[21] Arousal seems to occur in either of two ways: as an "automatic engagement of the senses or as a deliberate turning of the mind" toward something.[22] Suppose "orientation" is the term or category for the state-of-mind preceding either of these possibilities, i.e. a person is first orientated to an indeterminate range of possible sensations either by "automatic" (reflex) reactions or by "deliberate" (trained) responses. This understanding of orientation permits us to speak of (1) a flexible range of possible responses to (2) what is "potentially sensible."

What accounts for "arousal," i.e. for the shift from potentially sensible data to what is actually sensible? This is a question about the terms or correlates of "objective abstraction." The findings of neuroscience indicate two ways

---

trial and error. To justify them, one cannot reproduce the sequence of blind efforts that ultimately chanced upon them. One can only appeal to the success, be it great or small, with which they serve to account systematically for the phenomena under investigation." Bernard Lonergan. Macroeconomic Dynamics: An Essay in Circulation Analysis. Vol. 15 in Collected Works (Toronto: University of Toronto Press, 1999), 19.

[21] Rita Carter. Mapping the Mind, (Berkeley: University Of California Press, 1998), 186. Rita Carter's popular summary of the clues still leaves us operating on the fringes of a theoretical context. The three categories are repeated in her Exploring Consciousness, 148-149.

[22] Carter, Mapping, 192. The distinction between automatic and controlled or deliberate processing of stimuli is challenged by some researchers. See Jonathan D. Cohen et al. "A System-Level Perspective in Attention and Cognitive Control" in Cognitive Neuroscience of Attention, 74-75. The meaning of "automatic" as used in the literature is probably descriptive. An explanatory account of it remains elusive.

in which this shift occurs. First, out of an indeterminate field of sensations, the mind's variable orientation is disposed to select part of that field for attention.[23] For example, some sights, sounds and smells routinely evoke reflex responses of fight, freeze or flight. But attention may also be "automatically" aroused on a wider basis. "Attention is automatically triggered by more or less anything that stands out against its background either because it is unusual, emotionally salient (a familiar face, say) or exceptionally 'noisy' (e.g. it excites sensory neurons by its colour, motion or size)."[24] So a variety of types of sensory data can have a priority status when it comes to "arousing" attention. How is this possible? One hypothesis is that "memories" stored in the amygdala allow for quick responses to some types of data, e.g. signs of danger.[25] But a broader hypothesis is that whatever goes contrary to expectation evokes or arouses attention.

But do we mean more by "expectations" than "patterned results of prior attending"? Carter offers some help:

---

[23] Recasting talk of "automatic responses," "expectations" and "orientation" into talk of probabilities seems a promising shift toward a more explanatory account of how all three are related to to sensitive presentations and images.

[24] Exploring Consciousness, 150. Recall Jerome Bruner's observation that surprises offer windows on our presuppositions.

[25] Mapping the Mind, 94-95. Aquinas appears to support the idea that sensory data already associated with emotional responses have priority in arousing us. He wrote: "An image or imagined form of an object without some appraisal that it is beneficial or harmful leaves the sensitive appetite unmoved. It is the same with the apprehension of a truth apart from its being good and desirable. Accordingly Aristotle observes that we are moved, not by the theoretical, but by the practical reason." Summa Theologiae Ia, 2ae, 9,1 ad 2. (Blackfriars 1970), 67. Chapter Two will explore this linkage between emotions and images.

Millions of neurons must fire in unison to produce the most trifling thought. [...] New neural connections are made with every incoming sensation and old ones disappear as memories fade. Each fleeting impression is recorded for a while in some new configuration, but if it is not laid down in memory the pattern degenerates.... Patterns that linger may in turn connect with, and spark off, activity in other groups, forming associations (memories) or combining to create new concepts. In theory, each time a particular interconnected group of neurons fires together it gives rise to the same fragment of thought, feeling or unconscious brain function...[26]

So the electrochemical roots of expectations are in linked or associated groupings of neurons. Is it plausible to assume that, when some "part" of a grouping "fires," our conscious, but prereflective, tendency is to anticipate the "whole"? Evidence for this shows up in a clinical case in which a son was convinced his parents were both imposters.[27] The thirty-year old son, Arthur, suffered serious head trauma in a car accident and was in a coma for three weeks. Following rehabilitation and with no evidence of memory loss, he seemed back to normal except for a delusion regarding both parents. He would admit the couple taking care of him looked exactly like his parents but insist they really were not his parents. Curiously, when his contact with his parents was over the phone, he would recognize them as his real parents; it was only when face-to-face with them that he was convinced they were imposters.

The authors diagnosed his illness as Capgras' delusion[28] and assumed the problem had to do with the distinct "pathways concerned with visual recognition and

---

[26] Mapping the Mind, 19.
[27] V.S. Ramachandran and S. Blakeslee. Phantoms in the Brain (New York: William Morrow and Company, 1998), 158-173.
[28] Ibid. 161.

emotions in the brain."²⁹ As Ramachandran reports his diagnosis:

> After thinking about Arthur's symptoms, it occurred to me that his strange behavior might have resulted from a disconnection between these two areas (one concerned with recognition and the other with emotions). Maybe Arthur's face recognition pathway was still completely normal, and that was why he could identify everyone, including his mother and father, but the connections between this "face region" and his amygdala had been selectively damaged. If that were the case, Arthur would recognize his parents but would not experience any emotions when looking at their faces. He would not feel a "warm glow" when looking at his beloved mother, so when he sees her he says to himself, "If this is my mother, why doesn't her presence make me <u>feel</u> like I'm with my mother?" Perhaps his only escape from this dilemma – the only sensible interpretation he could make given the peculiar disconnection between the two regions of his brain – is to assume that this woman merely resembles Mom. She must be an imposter.³⁰

In short, "Arthur's problem...was neither his ability to recognize faces nor his ability to experience emotions; what was lost was his ability to <u>link</u> the two."³¹ In this case, the "expectation" was for a linkage of image and affect. When the expected "whole" was not experienced (or "aroused"), the son suspected deception.³² In effect, his expected feeling trumped his seeing.

---

²⁹ Ibid. 162.
³⁰ Ibid. 166.
³¹ Ibid.
³² The authors pursue related questions and learn even more about the "normal" linking of facial recognition and emotional response. For example, the father asks why Arthur experienced no problem in

Expectations seem to play a decisive role in how one detects and responds to familiar data, e.g. the sensitive presentations of faces.[33] But what is the relation between expectations (which predispose persons in objective abstraction) and the third category "focus"? What are some steps toward an explanatory account of how expectations focus attention?

As a preliminary answer to how expectations focus attention, suppose "focus" is a variable dependent (1) on prior developments (e.g. patternings of neural impulses) and (2) on sensations arousing interest. For something to be an object

---

recognizing his parents over the phone? In replying to the father, Ramachandran hypothesized:

> '…there is a separate pathway from the auditory cortex, the hearing area of the temporal lobes, to the amygdala. One possibility is that this hearing route has not been affected by the accident – only the visual centers have been disconnected from Arthur's amygdala.' (168)

Granted the visual pathways alone have been affected, why do the visual cues from his parents' faces evoke a delusional response but not the cues from faces of former acquaintances? The authors respond:

> It may be that when any normal person (including Arthur, prior to his accident) encounters someone who is emotionally very close to him – a parent, spouse or sibling – he expects an emotional "glow," a warm fuzzy feeling, to arise even though it may sometimes be experienced only very dimly. […] On the other hand, when one sees the mailman, one doesn't expect a warm glow and consequently there is no incentive for Arthur to generate a delusion to explain his lack of "warm fuzzy" response. (166)

[33] Damasio investigates how memory of an object (e.g. an image of a face) is "stored in dispositional form" and provides a basis for processing similar images in the future. This sort of implicit record is one way of thinking descriptively about expectations. See Antonio R. Damasio, The Feeling of What Happens (New York: Harcourt, Brace and Co., 1999), 160-161 and 331-332.

"in focus," i.e. to be <u>actually</u> observed (an instance of apprehensive abstraction), there must be a latent patterning of prior data allowing acts of recognition as well as some new datum arousing curiosity. What "completes" an act of attention, then, is twofold: an operation of minimal understanding (i.e. recognizing an object as something determinate) and an object evoking the minimal understanding of, for example, a puzzling noise, a colorful object, a strange smell, a novel taste.[34]

To review the relations among the set of three categories: we began by suggesting Aquinas' distinctions among types of abstraction could offer a clue on how to treat the question of attention in an explanatory way. Recall that images are <u>potentially</u> intelligible prior to someone attending to them. The corresponding understanding of "orientation" is of a capacity to respond, first, to an indeterminate range of possible data, but, second, a capacity gradually given determinate content ("training") by the forming of expectations as "patterned results of prior acts of attending."

Next, objects are <u>actually</u> intelligible relative to someone attending to them, i.e. engaging in objective abstraction. The subsequent understanding of "arousal" (or objective abstraction) is of either automatic or trained responses to data. The corresponding understanding of "focus" is of an act of recognition (i.e. apprehensive abstraction) of a determinate something due both to prior patternings of neural impulses and to the data that evoke a response.

How well do these categories fit the requirements mentioned in the Introduction?[35] First, how are the terms

---

[34] Chapter Three will introduce a "principle of completion" to explain the dynamic structure of cognitive operations, but there is evidence of its "demands" in even basic acts of attending.

[35] Recall the first two goals: (1) a deliberate shift from talk of conscious acts of attending as we experience them to such acts in relation to other classes of mental acts, states-of-mind and their nonconscious preconditions; (2) an identification of basic categories

used descriptively? "Orientation" refers to an understanding of a general capacity to attend made determinate by actual acts of attending, thereby increasing the probability that some sensations or images will be noticed rather than others. "Arousal" refers to an understanding of how the exercise of this capacity may occur in various ways, i.e. as reflexive, surprised or deliberate responses to data. Finally, "focus" refers to an understanding that the capacity activated in any of the various ways results in conscious attending to a determinate object.

Can the three categories be parts of an explanatory correlation? Following the model above of Aquinas' account of abstraction, we begin with descriptive terms: (1) a general capacity malleable by experience; (2) possible objects of attention (a field of potential data); (3) three possible ways of responding to the possible objects; (4) an act of attending to a determinate object. Next, we need to link the variable state of each term to that of another. For example, the general capacity (orientation) has its correlate in the field of potential data; but the capacity is actually exercisable and so potentially determinate relative to some potentially determinate subset of that field. The capacity is actually exercised (aroused) relative to one of the three ways of responding to an actually determinate (focused on) subset of the field. These relations can be reversed such that one begins with the field as what sets the range for any possible exercise of the general capacity (orientation) and goes on to define a potentially determinate subset of the field as what can evoke (arouse) a potentially determinate exercise of the capacity. An actually determinate subset will be the correlate of a specific act of attention, i.e. what it focuses on. This at least is an initial effort to fix the meanings of some basic categories.

But the Introduction promised more. One of the requirements of an explanatory account of attention is "an increasingly complex series of images or diagrams to 'track'

---

and correlations among them as the "outer words" for insights into acts of attending relative to their preconditions and their results.

insights into complex relations among acts, their preconditions and results." The following serves as the first of such diagrams.

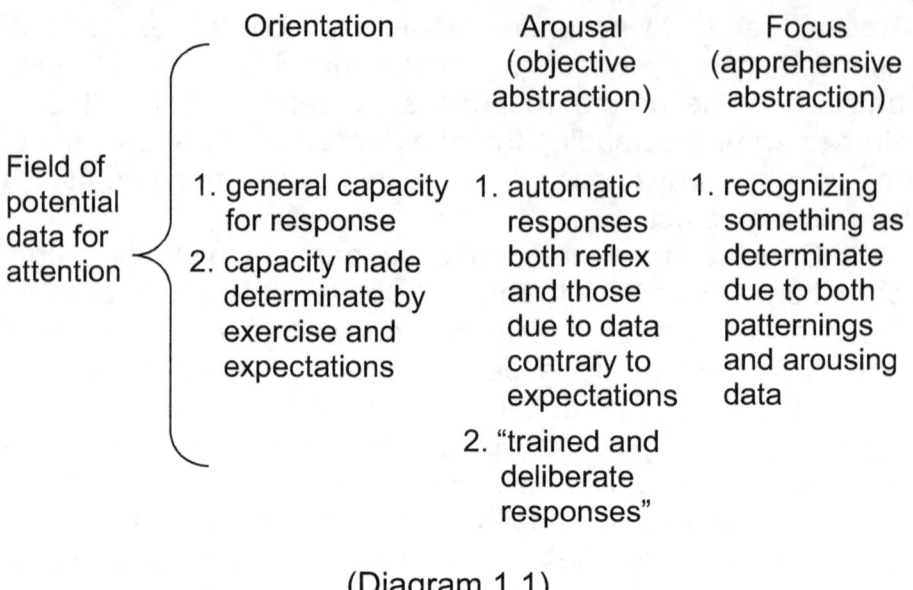

(Diagram 1.1)

III Applications of the Categories in Neuroscience

Can the preceding three categories and their relations to preconditions and results begin to "map" the findings of neuroscience regarding attention? The proof lies in the doing, so this section "tests" the capacity of these correlated terms to "integrate" some of the recent conclusions in the neuroscience of attention.

First, there is the puzzle of how selectivity occurs within an indeterminate field of possible objects of attention. How do some objects become selected for attention? Recall the general hypothesis that whatever goes contrary to expectation (an instance of previously exercised orientation) evokes or arouses attention. Expectations are patterns arising from previous acts of attention and understanding, but there can be an asymmetry between expectations and surprising events. While surprises can "disorient" expectations, still in some

18

cases expectations can suppress what we actually perceive. Recall the case Ramachandran cites of a son who believed both parents were imposters. Earlier I wrote, "his expected feeling trumped his seeing." Now I would add, "expectation can invent perception." Carter remarks along the same lines:

> The perception of pain…is influenced not just by attention, but also by how bad you think the pain is going to be. In one experiment, students who signed a consent form which suggested they would be subjected to discomfort reported a 'stinging' or 'burning' feeling when their hands were stimulated by a vibrator. Those who had been told the experiment would feel pleasant reported a pleasant 'tingling' when they were given the same stimulus, while those who had been led to expect a neutral sensation described just that.[36]

Here expectations clearly focus attention to the extent that the recognition of whatever content is received in sensation can vary relative to what is expected. The "arousing" data or stimuli seem wholly secondary to the perceiver's expectations. Are there to be no variables independent of expectations in accounting for attention, e.g. a pure datum that will limit what persons can select as the focus of their puzzling? Perhaps no. Selection seems to be dependent on orientation; to select and to focus on any arousing sensation will have an a priori component in the "patterned results of prior acts of attending and understanding."[37]

---

[36] Exploring Consciousness, 203.

[37] Lonergan took a middle position between the terms of this puzzle: Do sensible data or expectations have priority in determining what becomes an object of attention? In his language, neural demands and how they are met are subject to preconscious control and selection. "Perceiving is a function not only of position relative to an object, of the intensity of the light, of the healthiness of the eyes, but also of interest, anticipation, and activity. Besides the demands

However, the unqualified dependence of the <u>actually</u> observable data on prior patterns of learning seems at odds with the role of "surprise" in arousing attention. Sufficiently disconcerting sights and sounds can override expectations and force their own "selection." Still, when something evokes surprise, responders will draw upon prior understanding to classify an arousing datum as, for example, a noise or a color or a smell. In other words, a datum will be actually observable as already something partially determinate, i.e. something classified according to prior understanding.[38]

Have we arrived at an impasse? Do stimuli evoke responses independently of expectations or do expectations set limits on what stimuli get noticed? Which has priority? Perhaps the earlier distinction between objective and apprehensive types of abstraction suggests how to approach this puzzle. While objective abstraction provides an object to be understood, apprehensive abstraction is of an object actually understood to a limited degree. Thus, expectations may bias what one attends to as something to be understood, but there is room for revising initial responses if apprehension

---

of neural processes, there also is the pattern of experience in which their demands are met; and as the elements that enter consciousness are already within a pattern, there must be exercised some preconscious selection and arrangement. (…) Since, then, the demands of neural patterns and processes are subject to control and selection, they are better named demand functions. They call for some psychic representation and some conscious integration, but their specific requirements can be met in a variety of different manners. (…) Still, there are limits to this versatility and flexibility. The demand functions of neural patterns and processes constitute the exigence of an organism for its conscious complement; and to violate that exigence is to invite the anguish of abnormality."
<u>Insight</u>, 213-214.

[38] See Herd et al. on the use of a general category of color by test subjects in the Stroop task, especially 22-23.

is open to surprises. In short, expectations guide selection, but misleading expectations are corrigible.[39]

Such puzzling about the dependence of actually noticed data on prior understanding is a secondary matter when the purpose of an inquiry is to correlate conscious acts with nonconscious neural events in parts of the brain.[40] Contemporary neuroscience aims in part at correlating determinate conscious operations with distinct and localized electrochemical events in the brain. Research shifts from describing observable behavior to using the results of anatomy and neuroimaging to link parts of the brain to psychic events and operations.[41] Carter provides examples of parts-related-to-parts and of their varied "capacities for performance."

> Attention occurs when several areas of the brain lock in a circuit. One area is the cluster of neurons which process the object of attention. In the case of a visual image, for example, the neurons in the visual processing area at the back of the brain would be activated. Another area is the thalamus, which directs attention to the relevant processing area. A third is the part of the frontal lobes which deals with short-term

---

[39] Chapter Three will revisit this question about revising prior understanding and initial guesses when it takes up the distinction between questions for understanding and questions of judging.

[40] An example of such numerous studies is research on momentary lapses of attention and recovery from them. "Lapses of attention were associated with decreases in sensory-related processing in the inferior occipital cortex, so that on trials with slower reaction times, both prefrontal and occipital regions showed reduced activation." Trey Hedden and John D.E. Gabrieli. "The Ebb and Flow of Attention in the Human Brain" in Nature Neuroscience. Vol.9, No.7, July 2006, 864.

[41] This shift from descriptive accounts of behavior toward explanatory correlations is a specific case of what is outlined in Insight, 489. See above at footnote 11.

memory. Attention also involves activation in the parietal lobe where we encode 'maps' of our bodies and our relationship to things in space.[42]

How are these "parts" related such that together they provide the underlying conditions for conscious acts of attention? At a more general level, this question asks how the insights of biology can be useful in expanding psychological accounts of conscious events. As a provisional answer, suppose that lower-level conditions make possible higher-level operations.[43] To investigate the former is to begin to understand what makes the latter possible. Study of these conditions accelerates with advances in the technical means for collecting data. So the improving technology of neuroimaging, positron emission tomography (PET) and functional magnetic resonance imaging (fMRI), provides greater access to brain data. These data in turn provide the "material" for more complex theorizing about the conditions for the higher-level cognitive operations that neuroscientists are themselves employing when trying to explain the relevant data.[44] In tracking these relations, researchers will need

---

[42] Exploring Consciousness, 148.

[43] This formulation is "provisional" since it continues to use the descriptive categories of hierarchy theory, i.e. talk of "levels" at higher and lower elevations.

[44] This comment anticipates the "turn" outlined in Part IV of this essay. The challenge to cognitive sciences in this century is to account for both the underlying conditions for conscious acts and the capacity of such conditioned acts not only to understand but even to alter those conditions. While neuroscience focuses on the first half of the challenge (often leaving the second half to cognitive psychology?), an explanatory account of attention needs to synthesize the best available insights of both fields. Despite academic boundaries, science aims at complete explanation. Among the data to be explained are the intentional operations, e.g. deliberate acts of attention, that neuroscientists employ to study the data of acts

increasingly complex "mappings between cognitive functions and brain structures."[45] But any complete mapping or correlation is a long-range task. The first steps are to study how some nonconscious neurochemical processes in localized parts of the brain coincide with fairly basic conscious acts.

A limited review of the literature on basic acts of attention reveals that even the first steps in mapping are not without their naysayers. Some critics consider the entire mapping effort to be misguided, either as a waste of time (akin to eighteenth-century phrenology) or as irrelevant to cognitive psychology because the same mental operations can be carried out by very different parts of the brain (so correlating those operations with brain parts will add little to an understanding of those operations).[46] Ruz offers a moderate third option: "Theories and taxonomies of the mind proposed today are only in their early stages; they are not definitive but, rather, subject to continuous revision."[47]

One of the most influential typologies for distinguish-ing the anatomical and functional components of attention is that associated with the work of Posner and his colleagues. They write of three distinct systems or networks comprising attention: an orienting network, an alerting network, and an executive network.[48]

---

of attention. Their own performance makes them specimens of the very operations they are studying.

[45] Ruz, 495.

[46] Works by Uttal reflect the first criticism; works by Fodor the second. See ibid. 496-498.

[47] Ibid. citing studies by Bechtel and Hubbard, 498.

[48] An earlier version of "three attentional systems in the brain" was proposed by Posner and Petersen in 1990, and has been widely discussed in subsequent studies. See Cohen, 76-77. However, the version above appears to be the most recent. See Ian H. Robertson, "Examining Attentional Rehabilitation" in <u>Cognitive Neuroscience of Attention</u>, 409.

Do these three networks parallel the three categories of orientation, arousal and focus? A provisional parallelism is possible despite some differences among the labels. The parallel between our category of "orientation" and Posner's orienting network is clear. For instance, we assume that attending is conditioned by anticipatory dispositions that orientate and rely on, sometimes quite deliberately, acquired habits in processing data. But accounts of the orienting network seem to make the same assumption.[49] However, those writing of such networks make an advance in linking expectations not only with parts of the brain but also with chemical events. For example, anatomically, the orienting network "comprises areas of the right parietal and frontal hemispheres, and it is mainly related to the neurotransmitter norepinephrine (NE) that arises from the locus coeruleus."[50]

What parallel is there between our category of "arousal" and the alerting network? Ruz summarizes some early findings:

> Voluntary changes in the allocation of attention are mediated by areas in the superior parietal lobe, together with the frontal eye fields, superior colliculus, and some nuclei in the thalamus. Reflexive or automatic changes in attention generated by the appearance of unexpected stimuli at novel locations seem to be resolved by activations in the temporo-parietal junction (TPJ). The neurotransmitter acetyl-

---

[49] "Attentional orienting can be defined as the set of processes by which neural resources are deployed selectively toward specific attributes of events on the basis of changing motivation, expectation, or volition in order to optimize perception and action." Anna C. Nobre, "Probing the Flexibility of Attentional Orienting in the Human Brain" in ibid. 157.
[50] Ruz, 499.

choline (Ach) originating in the basal frontbrain is the main chemical regulating the ... function....[51]

Note that the previous listings under "Arousal" (1. automatic responses both reflex and those due to data contrary to expectations, and 2. "trained" and deliberate responses) correspond to reflexive or automatic changes "due to unexpected stimuli" as well as to "voluntary changes." The category of arousal seems to include both parts of the alerting network.

How well does the executive network line up with the category of focus? Ruz, again drawing on the findings of Posner and others, associates the executive network with the "classic selective nature of attention." The usual situation is supposedly one of competition for attention among different stimuli. Ruz writes of the selective function as most in evidence in "decision making, error detection, novel or difficult situations, or when overcoming a habitual response is needed."[52] Above "focus" was understood as recognition of something determinate due to both prior patternings of neural impulses and to the data which evoke their response. The key parallel between focus and the executive network is in the developed patterns that weight or select some data among a

---

[51] Ibid. 499-500. Ruz uses labels for the networks that seem to be at odds with Posner's latest, revised model. For example, her orienting network seems to correspond to the alerting network in the revised model and her alerting network to the orienting network in the revised model. So what she labels "the orienting network" parallels in its functions what above was understood under the category of arousal.

[52] The author goes on to link the process of selection with brain parts and chemical substrates. "Research using the Stroop task has shown the relevance of lateral prefrontal regions, the anterior cingulate cortex (ACC) and basal ganglia in mediating executive attention. The neurotransmitter most relevant in this case is dopamine (DA) from the ventral tegmental system, and its imbalances are known to affect executive functions." Ibid. 500.

field of potential competitors for attention.[53] Problem solving and "difficult situations" initially evoke habitual responses. Since initial responses may be inadequate, focus should be understood as an ongoing conscious processing of determinate clues, one that may over time "complete" the cycle by altering orientation.[54]

---

[53] The effects of such competition are described in a study of inattentional blindness. "Attending to an event in the visual world improves its processing. However, this benefit is likely to come at a cost; namely the inability to detect other events in that same visual scene. [...] Inattentional blindness is thought to result from the inability of unexpected, task-irrelevant stimuli to attract attention, thereby preventing them from reaching awareness. Although attentional engagement in a primary task is thought to be crucial for the generation of [inattentional blindness], it is much less clear how such engagement prevents awareness of the unexpected stimulus." (96) The study ends by offering a number of possible answers. "One possibility is that executive load reduces activity in the visual cortex. Alternatively, executive processes could suppress the neural circuit involved in attentional orienting, so as to prevent task-irrelevant stimuli from interfering with ongoing behavioural goals. A final possibility is that the neural substrates underlying [a particular task] are also involved in the perception of task-irrelevant stimuli." In other words, the former's engagement in one task may "prevent its simultaneous involvement in other cognitive functions, such as the reorienting of attention." (98-99) Daryl Fougnie and René Marois, "Executive Load in Working Memory Induces Inattentional Blindness" in Visual Cognition, Vol. 14, No. 1 (June 2006), 96-99.

　　　Does talk of "executive processes" preventing "task-irrelevant stimuli from interfering with ongoing behavioural goals" anticipate the "turn" to top-down control by intentional acts (the focus of the next section of this chapter)?

[54] Understanding the three dependent variables of orientation, arousal and focus as elements of a scheme of recurrence in attending to clues is a promising innovation in explaining acts of attention. See Part IV for a sketch of such an innovation. Understanding "focus" as a dynamic process that may alter orientations and

These conclusions have broadened the initial meanings of the three "elements" of an act of attention. Recall that orientation was first understood as a capacity to attend to potentially recognizable objects; arousal was understood as the automatic or the trained response to actually recognizable objects; focus was the apprehending of actually recognized objects. In part, the expanded meanings are due to the correlation of the elements with distinct brain locales and chemical regulators.

Categories/Networks	Brain Locales	Main Chemical Regulators
Orientation/Orienting Network	Right Parietal and Frontal Hemispheres	Norepinephine (NE)
Arousal/Alerting Network	Superior Parietal Lobe, Frontal Eye Fields, Superior Colliculus, Nuclei in Thalamus, Temporo-Parietal Junction	Acetylcholine (Ach)
Focus/Executive Network	Lateral Prefrontal Regions, Anterior Cungulate Cortex, Basal Ganglia	Dopamine (DA)

(Diagram 1.2)

IV Neurochemistry and Acts of Attention

The preceding section largely focused on relating the three elements of attending to locations in the brain. A few

---

expectations is part of the evidence for a principle of completion that first appears in Chapter Three.

references were made to the neurotransmitters or chemical regulators of the relevant brain activities. What further understanding of the "chemical and physical processes" that support organic processes does an explanatory account of attention require? Again, we have some clues. To make the transition that "links physiology with biochemistry and biophysics" is

> ...to effect the transition from the thing-for-us to the thing-itself, from insights that grasp described parts as organs to insights that grasp conjugate forms systematizing otherwise coincidental manifolds of chemical and physical processes. [...] To this end, there have to be invented appropriate symbolic images of the relevant chemical and physical processes....[55]

What might all this mean? An example of the cited transition is found in inchoate form in research exploring questions about the electrochemical preconditions for attending to or selecting some objects or events over others. One of these questions is the old puzzle about how we are able to recognize objects as coherent unities perduring through a variety of changes.[56] The question was put this way in a relatively recent article: "An enduring controversy in neuroscience concerns how the brain 'binds' together separately coded stimulus features to form unitary representations of objects." The authors found that

---

[55] Insight, 489.

[56] This recognition puzzle is as old as Aristotle's comments in the second and third books of the De Anima on the soul's faculty ("common sense") to unify the data it apprehends. The medievals went on to distinguish a number of inner senses to account for the sensible soul's ability to retain forms, combine them, estimate their importance and remember such prereflective estimates. Averroes and Aquinas were aware that we not only combine sense data in recognizing objects, we also make prereflective estimates of an object's importance.

"oscillatory neural circuits play a key role...in the process." More precisely, their experiments, and those of others, found evidence correlating the "binding process and 40-hertz (gamma band) oscillations generated by localized neural circuits."[57] In tests with adults involving the recognition of illusory objects, the 40-hertz oscillations occur "at about 250 to 300 ms after stimulus onset."[58] In tests with infants the researchers found similar brain activity by the time the test subjects were eight months old.[59]

The "binding process" seems to be one electro-chemical condition for focusing on "bound" objects.[60] What other conditions might there be? In other words, once "bound" how does a recognized object become the center of conscious focus, the center of attention? Suppose we limit ourselves to visual attention. Integrating visual data involves a complex process occurring in the brain of neurochemical feedforwarding (of sensory data), feedback (of responses to

---

[57] G.Csibra et al. "Gamma Oscillations and Object Processing in the Infant Brain" in Science Vol. 290 (Nov. 24, 2000), 1582.

[58] Ibid. This time gap between recognition and "stimulus onset" is relevant to understanding standard puzzles in cognitive psychology. For example, test subjects report that an event and their consciousness of it seem synchronous, yet the evidence of "backdating" indicates a half second delay between the two. (Exploring Consciousness, 29) Similarly, Libet's experiments regarding decision-making show that, prior to an act of conscious choosing, preparatory neural events are occurring suggesting that conscious choice is not the discrete or "independent" event we think it is. (Ibid. 84-85) Finally, puzzles generated by Kolers' experiments in apparent motion produced debates over "retrospective construction theory" [see Nelson Goodman. Ways of Worldmaking, (Indianapolis: Hackett, 1978), 78-83] which could be resolvable given more recent findings in neuroscience about time gaps.

[59] Csibra, 1583.

[60] Damasio identifies further features of this "binding process" and cites a half dozen or so contributors to research on this puzzle. See The Feeling of What Happens, 333 and 335.

the former from latent patterns of prior sensing and understanding), and lateral integration of the preceding (since different parts of the brain contribute to the "binding" of an object of attention).[61] On the one hand, visual attention will often be predominantly a top-down process involving "feedback" since established patterns or expectations are more receptive to the familiar sensitive presentation than to the unfamiliar sight. On the other hand, dramatic and extremely salient data, e.g. surprising sights, will have an advantage in becoming objects of attention.[62] So on occasion "bottom-up" processing will override familiar patterns.

How does either type of process happen? Some experimental evidence supports the claim that, "Attention modulates the sensory-driven activation of cells...such that activity in response to an attended stimulus is increased in amplitude and duration."[63] But why this "increase in amplitude and duration"? Using the metaphor of "competition," two neuroscientists suggest that attention operates like a biased referee on a playing field.

> For neurons in the ventral pathway the response to a stimulus that generates strong neural activation when presented in isolation is reduced by the introduction of a second nonpreferred stimulus within the receptive field. [Then] multiple stimuli within the same receptive field appear to compete in a mutually suppressive manner. If attention is directed toward one stimulus [,] then the response becomes more similar to the response that would be generated by that stimulus

---

[61] M. W. Spratling and M. H. Johnson. "A Feedback Model of Visual Attention" in Journal of Cognitive Neuroscience. Vol.16 No.2 (2004), 219.

[62] "Perception will be influenced both by bottom-up biases, such as stimulus saliency, and by top-down influence such as familiarity." Ibid. 226.

[63] Ibid. 219.

in isolation. [....] Hence, attention appears to bias the competition in favor of the attended stimulus.[64]

Even if attention favors certain data and suppresses other claimants,[65] how is such selectivity possible within neural processing? Spratling and Johnson cite numerous studies indicating that "training has been observed to increase the apparent salience of a stimulus. [....] This effect is explained because training is likely to enhance the neuronal representation of the training stimulus and hence provide that stimulus with a competitive advantage."[66] The claim here seems uncontroversial. Think of how training and years of practice distinguish the veteran detective from the rookie at a crime scene. Prior training yields a complex array of stored patterns that allow the veteran to anticipate relevant sensory clues and more readily to integrate them laterally. But what does "anticipate" mean here and do we really have an explanation for how "training is likely to enhance the neuronal representation of the training stimulus"?

Spratling and Johnson offer a series of surmises: "Nodes learn to become selective to frequently reoccurring patterns within the input data."[67] What does "learning" mean here? Presumably "higher level knowledge about previous events stored in the feedforward synaptic weights can provide top-down information to enable familiar stimuli to be represented more strongly than unfamiliar stimuli or

---

[64] Ibid. 222.

[65] Shifting from talk of "competition" and "competitive advantage" to talk of probability would be an advance in providing an explanatory account of selection. A precedent occurs in accounts of biological evolution which drop descriptive references to competition for limited resources in a struggle for survival in favor of talk of schemes of recurrence and probabilities of emergence and survival. See Joseph Flanagan. Quest for Self-Knowledge (Toronto: University of Toronto Press, 1997), 102-103.

[66] Spratling and Johnson, 223.

[67] Ibid. 227.

background noise."[68] In sum, training disposes some nodes to be more responsive to certain perceptual data. Top-down feedback will favor some data in subsequent processing, i.e. the favored data are more likely to receive attention. In feedforwarding the same favoritism appears when bottom-up processing is disposed to weight some sensory data more heavily insofar as they correspond to familiar patterns.[69]

The preceding fragments from neuroscience leave unanswered questions about the metaphors of "learning" and about "higher level knowledge" stored in nodes.[70] These fragments do, however, help answer an earlier question about how a person's "orientation" can be both automatic and deliberate in attending to sensory presentations. Studies of attention routinely mention feedback and feedforward connections, top-down and bottom-up processing. An adequate account of what occurs in paying attention will, therefore, have to acknowledge both types of responses to

---

[68] Ibid. 229.

[69] "Training causes a node to become selective to a certain stimulus. This node subsequently generates a stronger response to this stimulus, which can bias processing of perceptual data via feedback. Such bias can modulate the responses of nodes in the previous region. It could also be transmitted via feedforward connections, to increase the strength (or saliency) of the bottom-up signal corresponding to the familiar item in subsequent processing stages." Ibid. 232.

[70] Consider the further questions suggested by the following: "A cell will generate a range of different firing rates when its response is measured across a range of different stimuli. For example, a cell with selectivity for stimulus orientation will generate its maximum response at one stimulus orientation and progressively weaker responses to stimuli at orientations that increasingly deviate from the preferred one." (Ibid. 224.) As a matter of fact intensity of firing rates varies and the rates can be correlated with certain stimuli. However, how does one account for "preferences" among stimuli? How do cells store "knowledge" allowing for selectivity? Just what do we mean by "selection"?

"salient" data as well as anticipatory dispositions that, sometimes quite deliberately, orientate and rely on acquired patterns in processing data.

V The "Turn" to Top-Down Ordering

The preceding section has emphasized how electrochemical events make possible brain functions that, in turn, make possible conscious acts of attention. Currently neuroscience is a sustained inquiry into the lower-level conditions that support both localized brain functions and basic intentional acts. Study of the dependency of conscious acts on organic functions and of the latter on chemical transmitters and genetic substrates is an attempt to understand the more complex in terms of the simpler. However, might these relations of dependency also go in the other direction? That is, might deliberate acts of attending and understanding exercise an "executive function"[71] over "simpler" conditions?

---

[71] The analogy here is to the "executive network" in Posner's taxonomy cited in Part III. Various definitions of "executive control" are offered in the literature. For example, Gruber and Goschke propose "a neurocognitive model of executive control according to which the human ability to flexibly adapt to changing behavioral requirements, i.e. executive control, depends on dynamic and context-sensitive interactions between… brain systems." (105) Regardless of the definition, most subsequent research into executive functioning focuses on brain locales and neural activities. "The involvement of the prefrontal cortex in the ability to engage executive control constitutes one of the fundamental results of cognitive neuroscience. Current research focuses on the respective roles of frontal lobe structures such as anterior cingulate cortex (ACC), dorso-lateral prefrontal cortex (DLPFC), or orbito-frontal cortex (OFC) in this general process of control." Lionel Naccache et al. "Effortless Control: Executive Attention and Conscious Feeling of Mental Effort are Dissociable" in Neuropsycholgia, Vol. 43, No. 9 (2005), 1318.

The literature on such top-down ordering is sparse. Posner and Synder detected the problem in 1975. Over thirty years ago they speculated about the future of attention studies suggesting a "kind of research schizophrenia" with one focus being on "mechanisms that subserve" neural processing and conscious attention and the other being on conscious strategies that "modify and build upon 'automatic processes.'"[72] Most of the current literature reflects an opting for the first focus, so their original question remains unanswered.

> To what extent are our conscious intentions and strategies in control of the way information is processed in our minds? This seems to be a question of importance to us both as psychologists and as human beings. Yet...most theorists in psychology have avoided consideration of the relationship between conscious and unconscious mental events.[73]

However, at least one author wrote twenty years earlier of something like top-down ordering and its correlation with lower-level conditions.

> Human intelligence and reasonableness function as the higher integration of the sensitive flow of percepts and images, emotions and feelings, attitudes and sentiments, words and deeds. It follows that as the cognitional and volitional appropriations of truth are

---

[72] "Attention and Cognitive Control" (1975), reprinted in Cognitive Psychology: Key Readings, A. Balota and Elizabeth J. Marsh, eds. (New York: Psychology Press, 2004), 221-222.

[73] Ibid. 205. Implicit here is a rudimentary form of the question of liberty. One way of expressing it is to ask how deliberate mental acts might exercise some "control" over or integrate lower-level conditions.

solidary with each other so also they condition and are conditioned by adaptations of human sensibility.[74]

First, what does it mean to say, "Human intelligence and reasonableness" integrate the lower-order "sensitive flow of percepts and images, emotions and feelings, attitudes and sentiments, words and deeds"? Persons are, for example, "integrating" when they understand sights and sounds, when they recognize their moods and then support or resist them, when they ponder possible words and actions and then choose or reject them.[75] But this top-down ordering is only half the story. The higher-order operations are themselves "conditioned by adaptations of human sensibility." Negatively, for example, a student's illness interferes with taking an exam; foul moods disrupt a writing schedule; anger undercuts a resolve to mend a relationship. Positively, "adaptations of sensibility" promote higher-order operations. For example, a love of dance helps the aspiring ballerina practice despite pain. The cultivated and discriminating eye of the painter sees variations in color and texture where the untrained eye sees none. The compassion of an attentive nurse allows patients to reveal fears they hide from family members lest they add to their worries.

So how are sensibility and intelligence mutually conditioning? From a "top-down" perspective, actual developments in understanding through professional training can alter sensitivity and alertness to the contents of sensibility. For example, engineers and physicians were less frequently fooled than other test subjects in Kolers' famous experiments

---

[74] <u>Insight</u>, 585. Chapter Three will supplant this residual terminology of faculty psychology with categories from intentionality theory.

[75] Chapter Three will introduce the notion of an "integrator" to suggest how sensible "materials" (e.g. ink marks on a page) may be unified into intelligible objects (e.g. words).

in apparent motion.[76] They saw the same images but made more careful inferences about what they were seeing.[77] Similarly, trained therapists detect deceit in clients far more reliably than nonprofessionals talking with the same persons. Training in forensic science prepares investigators to be more alert for relevant clues. On the other hand, from a "bottom-up" perspective, we suppose that persons develop in understanding and improve deliberate acting by raising and answering questions prompted by sensitive presentations and imaginative representations. The bottom-up argument is cogent: we would have nothing to question without the lower-order contents of human sensibility, and without questioning intellectual and practical development would not occur. So training presupposes the lower-order data as the "material" for its own occurrence.

    Do the preceding claims about sensibility and intelligence make the case for a mutual conditioning of conscious acts and biological and neurochemical events? At most they provide a model of how conscious acts are conditioned by and, in turn, "order" some lower-level materials, e.g. sensations and images. But what does this model suggest about nonconscious processes in the brain? As noted above, when researchers are engaged in higher-level cognitive operations studying neurochemical conditions for intentional acts, they are studying conditions that make their own performance possible. That is, they are studying the lower-level conditions for their own conscious operations. What might be the benefit of shifting the focus of their inquiry to their own performance? What are the conditions for such performance, a performance that extends well beyond basic acts of attention? But in exploring those conditions, are the researchers "ordering" those very conditions in themselves?

---

[76] See the review of Kolers' experiments in apparent motion in Goodman, 71-89. The reference to the populations less frequently deceived occurs on page 92.

[77] Implicit here are distinctions among seeing, understanding and judging which will be more explicit in Chapter Three.

A simple example may help. Suppose the phone rings while you are counseling a troubled client and you choose to ignore it and to continue the conversation. Your deliberate attending to the client and not to the phone affects neural events, suppressing some and allowing others to occur. In the "competition" among stimuli for attention, the "winner" owes its victory to what some authors called a "higher level template."[78] Yet how is any such victory possible?

Serious attention to how conscious acts can affect lower-level neurobiological events is the "turn" referred to in the heading of this section. In one sense the turn is uncontroversial. Deliberate interventions in brain disorders through pharmacological means are evidence that conscious acts can indirectly alter neurobiological conditions. Experiments in bio-feedback produce evidence of test subjects deliberately altering patterns among neural activities. There are similar results associated with meditation techniques and hypnotism.[79] What was talk of an "executive network" modeled on if not the experience of conscious and deliberate acts controlling performance?[80] Consider how the following assumes such a model: "The executive network plays its main role when processing and/or responding requires any kind of control. For example, control is

---

[78] Cohen et al. in Cognitive Neuroscience of Attention, 76.

[79] "A number of human practices, including ingestion of drugs, meditation, and hypnotism, are known to alter attention." Michael I. Posner, "Progress in Attention Research" in ibid. 7.

[80] Perhaps the following quote manages to reflect both the implicit model of executive control and the explicit focus on organic and neurochemical conditions for it. "Flexible cognitive control over our behavior is a key part of human intelligence. In what we call here the top-down excitatory biasing (TEB) model of cognitive control…, the prefrontal cortex (PFC) is viewed as maintaining representations that guide control of tasks. These PFC representations provide an excitatory top-down bias to groups of neurons processing task-relevant information." Herd et al. (22) What is missing here is "equal time" for the second half of Posner and Synder's puzzle.

necessary when...a wrong response has been emitted and the subject has noticed it...."[81] Noticing a wrong response presupposes someone has made a <u>judgment</u>, an act which depended on but is more complex than acts of attention which had their own neurobiological preconditions. But once the judgment is made, once the higher-order operation occurs, a new series of acts is evoked and so a new set of neurobiological events occurs.

Further examples are plentiful. We have all experienced sustained attention, i.e. "the volitional maintenance of the current focus of attention. This may mean awaiting the change from red to green in traffic stoplights..." or simply waiting for water to boil.[82] But what does "volitional" control of conscious acts of attention mean? How can conscious acts effect nonconscious changes in brain activities? <u>Descriptively</u> we can all recount how, at some time or other, we deliberately shifted our attention away from disturbing sights or distracted ourselves from painful memories by staying busy. We were trying to control our emotional responses by controlling our attention.[83] In doing so, did our conscious acts have repercussions on our biochemical states?[84]

---

[81] Luis J. Funtes, "Inhibitory Processing in the Attentional Networks" in <u>Cognitive Neuroscience of Attention</u>, 46.

[82] Melinda Beane and Richard Marrocco, "Holinergic and Noradrenergic Inputs to the Posterior Parietal Cortex Modulate the Components of Exogenous Attention" in ibid. 318.

[83] Such deliberate acts to "control" attention are evidence that attention is not monolithic but occurs in gradations. Damasio provides support for talking about various levels or gradations of attention by citing cases of epileptic automatisms. During seizures patients are awake but exhibit only a low-level attention to the activities they carry out. After the seizure they have no recollection of their actions during it. <u>The Feeling of What Happens</u>, 96-99.

[84] Cf. Seth D. Pollack and Stephanie Tolley-Schell, "Attention, Emotion, and the Development of Psychopathology" in <u>Cognitive Neuroscience of Attention</u>, 359.

Perhaps there is no controversial "turn" if conscious executive acts are so commonplace. However, what do we make of the following?

> Given that a true understanding of the nature of cognitive function can only be derived from an understanding of its underlying mechanisms, an overarching theme of our research program has been to focus on the processes of attention in infancy....[85]

To interpret these remarks descriptively, the author envisions a one-way street leading to an understanding of intentional acts.[86] But why should "true understanding" only be possible through correlating cognitive functions with "underlying" conditions? If one assumes that any explanation must be "reductive," this view of serious understanding follows. However, the puzzle of the "turn" is how a complete explanation can include the data of cognitive functions altering their underlying conditions. Presumably a "true understanding" of the "nature" of something will leave out

---

[85] John Colombo, "Visual Attention in Infancy" in ibid. 329. What does "mechanism" mean here? Is it a descriptive category hiding the absence of explanatory understanding?

[86] While the preceding citation is evidence of a reductionistic stance not uncommon in contemporary sciences, an intermediate stance between it and the position taken in this essay may be the following: "'...no attempt is made to discard the notion that attentional selection is controlled by an intelligent agent, but a serious attempt is made to relieve the burden on the agent by placing a powerful mechanism at its disposal.'" C. Bundsen. "A Theory of Visual Attention," in Psychological Review, Vol. 97 (1990), 523. Quoted in Gordon D. Logan. "Attention, Automaticity, and Executive Control" in Experimental Cognitive Psychology and Its Applications. Alice F. Healy, ed. (Washington, D.C.: American Psychological Association, 2005). Does this talk of "mechanisms" reveal a tendency to dodge the complexity of what "intelligent agent" might mean?

nothing relevant, i.e. all the known variables will be taken into account.[87] References to the "nature" of something are initially anticipations of some unknown "x" much like that found in algebraic equations. To solve for it is to proceed from the known variables to an understanding of how relations among them reveal a correct solution. But are conscious acts of questioning, imagining, surmising, deliberating and deciding relevant variables in "controlled" acts of attention? They are if neurochemical events are ever dependent for their occurrence on such conscious acts. Most of the previous pages sketched the reversed order of conditioning. They summarized how some neurochemical events and organic functions were conditions allowing conscious acts to occur. Now the question is whether the "effects" can act back on their "causes."

How are we to understand this feedforward and feedback process between biochemical conditions and conscious operations? Much of the literature in neuroscience reflects an interest in model building. References to an "interactive model, which assumes that pattern recognition is not simply controlled by the stimulus but is aided by pre-existing memory representations" is one way of portraying both bottom-up and top-down processes in acts of attention.[88] How the interaction occurs is the neglected puzzle. Still, some features of the puzzle are well documented.

The feedforward processes include genetic, neurochemical and organic processes in the brain that make possible actual conscious acts. The routine occurrence of the latter makes possible neuroscientific inquiries that seek to trace psychological events back to organic, chemical and physical roots. The aim of the inquiries has been to move from descriptive studies of individual specimens (e.g. the test subjects of PET and fMRI) and static accounts of brain parts

---

[87] A comprehensive understanding of some object of inquiry will be what in later chapters appears as the "demand" of a principle of completion.

[88] Balota and Marsh, "An Overview" in Cognitive Psychology: Key Readings, 12.

to explanations of the dynamic processes investigators assume are occurring. The other side of the puzzle is less frequently visited. While neuroscientific explanations have to date been largely correlations between neurochemical events and brain locales, research is expanding into questions about how the brain operates in relation to both its inner components and its outer environment. There are numerous studies of how stimuli evoke attention but fewer studies of how practice or training alters attention. The latter are a promising focus for further research into top-down control of lower-level conditions.

Suppose that among the "outer" conditions for acts of attention is the training previously mentioned as sharpening alertness and refining one's capacity for focus, e.g. the training of detectives and forensic scientists. Educational institutions and their programs try to shift the probabilities that their graduates will be more alert and on target in attending to clues. But the educators usually declare their intent is not to modify brains but to redesign minds, i.e. to educate students to think more deliberately and effectively. This is not the place to debate the distinction between "brain" and "mind." The turn from lower-level conditions to higher-level conscious operations may circumvent that nest of puzzles by simply observing how brains not only integrate non-organic materials to achieve conscious outcomes (e.g. focused attention), they also adapt to external stimuli (e.g. tutoring rookies to detect clues at a crime scene).[89] Both teachers and students deliberately act back on the initial conditions of their "untrained" performance in a conscious effort to alter them. This much suggests that feedback processes from conscious

---

[89] An initial hypothesis is that "mind" refers to our recognition that higher integrations of the brain's capacities do occur as persons learn to alter deliberately both outer environments (caves become high rises) and the brain's own functioning (pharmacological interventions remedy neurochemical deficits).

operators modify underlying organic and biochemical conditions.[90]

To repeat an earlier question: How are we to understand these interacting feedforward and feedback processes? Posner provides a helpful clue in remarking: "...attention is the emergent property of the cognitive system that allows it to successfully process some sources of information to the exclusion of others, in the service of achieving some goals to the exclusion of others."[91] What might "emergent property" mean here?

The literature on emergence or "supervenience" has expanded in the past twenty years. In abbreviated form, the often divergent views on emergence are struggling to integrate two distinct types of processes. First, there are regularly occurring and continuous processes, e.g. the cycles of seasons and planetary motions. Second, there are processes that admit of irregularities and discontinuities, e.g. weather patterns and survival rates of species. Integrating both types of processes requires an understanding of how systematic and non-systematic processes are related. So neuroscientists study how various neurochemical events routinely generate localized brain activities associated with facial or spatial recognition. As a result, we get systematic correlations among chemical, organic and conscious events. However, clinical psychology cites its individual cases of departures from the "norm" (e.g. ADHD cases) and so presents the systematic view with irregularities. Subsequent research discovers both the ideal frequencies according to which correlations are expected to show up and the rates of departure from them in large populations, e.g. the incidence of ADHD.

---

[90] Experimental programs in treating dyslexic students by means of computer instruction have demonstrated how such instructional techniques can modify brain functions and improve reading skills. The notion of "operator" as a principle of development in thinking and deciding will appear in Chapter Three.
[91] Cognitive Neuroscience of Attention, 71.

What has this to do with "emergence"? One linkage between types of processes and emergence occurs in thinking about the evolutionary development of species. Initially genetic and chemical substrates are open to an indefinite number of organic possibilities, i.e. any number of biological phenomena could emerge from different combinations of those prior substrates or conditions. But in any range of possible combinations, some will be more probable than others because of existing resources in a given environment, and so some organic combinations, given enough time and enough numbers, will actually emerge. To emerge is one thing, to survive is another. In a given environment an emergent organism will interact with routinely available resources (those forming the initial conditions for its appearance) and with novel conditions occurring after its initial emergence. Survival then becomes a question of whether the systematic operations of the organism and the systematic relations among them and their initial conditions are sufficiently flexible to adjust to non-systematic variations occurring within and outside of the organism. So we find a range of animals flourishing in a given environment only to diminish in number and variety when physical and chemical resources change. Some animal types will exhibit greater flexibility in their "routines" and so adapt to changed conditions, i.e. to non-systematic variations.

How can we comprehend together both systematic processes and their flexible responses to non-systematic variations? The notion of "schemes of recurrence" may be of some help.[92] First, organisms interact routinely with available resources to meet their demands for nutrition, procreation and survival. Thus, the systematic processes of nitrogen and seasonal cycles supply conditions for an herbivore's cycles of foraging, mating and hibernation. Departures from regularly occurring conditions tend to disrupt cycles, so the schemes of

---

[92] The following comments on schemes of recurrence are indebted to Lonergan, Insight, 140-148.

recurrence through which a species exists need to be a flexible range of possibilities if a species is to survive.

To the notion of schemes of recurrence (incorporating both routine cycles and adjustments to variations in the conditions for their recurrence), we need to add an account of how higher-order schemes emerge from lower-order ones. The literature in cognitive psychology simply assumes this routinely happens. Thus, we find references to "volitional control" over acts of attention. Such comments assume: (1) in evolutionary history cognitive schemes have emerged from organic schemes; (2) the former depend on but also can, to some degree, order the latter. Now, in regard to both assumptions, scientific inquiries are in their infancy, i.e. explanatory theories remain remote possibilities. The barely recognized question is how development from one ordered series of schemes to a new series, not reducible to the former, can occur. For instance, cognitive operations form their own schemes (one roughly described example: deliberating over and choosing ends; deliberating over and choosing means; intending actions; carrying out specific acts; learning from actual outcomes and perhaps altering ends and/or means). But how do such routinely occurring conscious schemes emerge from organic schemes and, through further development (e.g. stages of infancy, adolescence and maturation), exercise increasing control over those organic schemes?

These questions, anticipated by Posner and Synder in 1975, are worth formulating even if answers remain elusive. As anticipations of possible answers, the questions can serve a heuristic function. That is, without specifying answers, they direct inquiry along certain lines. For example, questions about systematic or ordered processes anticipate that any answers will (ideally) take the form of invariant correlations among classes of events. Questions about non-systematic processes anticipate answers in terms of probabilities or ideal frequencies in the relations among such classes of events. The heuristic notion of schemes of recurrence integrates both of the preceding types of processes. How do systems adjust to novel conditions? The question of emergence anticipates answers in terms of developmental stages, i.e. when new systematic processes emerge from prior ones. For example, how does embryonic development in humans occur and give way eventually to the stages studied by child psychologists and the more elusive, and less studied, stages of adult self-control?

That emergence and development occur in plants and animals continues to be the focus of intense inquiry. The same is not yet true in regard to cognitive schemes and their organic and neurochemical conditions. At least the "turn" mentioned above has not become a routine line of inquiry. As previously noted, the focus has largely been on the underlying conditions for such cognitive schemes but not on the latter's emergence from and conditioning of those substrates. From an evolutionary perspective, most will agree that radical alterations in underlying conditions threaten existing schemes with extinction, but, to the degree that those schemes are "flexible," a range of alterations in underlying conditions may be not only survivable but a step toward novel developments. However, is there any agreement that variations in conditions make possible the emergence of novel combinations of antecedent resources yielding new, discontinuous life forms? How might this happen? An appeal to probability is common: what is possible, given enough time and enough numbers, becomes probable and, in the long run, becomes an almost guaranteed development. So in a very old universe, we should expect to find complex molecules, botanical species, biological species, patterns of psychological development and structured conscious acts that act back on their initial conditions.

Asserting the preceding is not the same as explaining how these processes of emergence and mutual conditioning occur. Why should explaining both be so remote from current inquiries? One author identifies the "foundational problem" behind this difficult challenge.

> On the one hand, there is the tendency to consider conscious activities as unconscious and to reduce them to lower-level conjugate forms; the other tendency is to consider conscious activities without any reference to the lower levels which set the conditions for the emergence and maintenance of these higher conscious schemes. Behind these two tendencies is the foundational problem of integrating the higher human sciences with the lower natural sciences.[93]

This "foundational problem" sets a cultural task far beyond the limits of a single chapter or even a single book. The task of integrating the intentional operations producing commonsensical, artistic, religious, scientific and scholarly meanings with the processes studied in neuroscience and biochemistry is a project spanning generations of researchers, a project more anticipated than actually underway. Still, what can be done now? Perhaps a first step is to acknowledge the need for the "turn" described in this final section.

To review what led up to this section: the intent was to sketch an explanatory response to the question of what it means to pay attention. The requirements for doing so were three: (1) a deliberate shift from talk of conscious acts of attending as we experience them to such acts in relation to other classes of mental acts, states-of-mind and their nonconscious preconditions; (2) an identification of basic categories and correlations among them as the "outer words" for insights into acts of attending relative to their preconditions and their results; (3) an increasingly complex series of images or diagrams to "track" insights into complex relations among acts of attending, their preconditions and results.

Identifying these requirements was followed by lists of assumptions about and descriptions of acts of attending. The first items on each list were: (1) actual data or stimuli are correlates of conscious acts, and (2) contrary to a nineteenth-century ideal of presuppositionless inquiry, conscious acts of

---

[93] Flanagan, 171.

attention occur within a context of prior insights, even so far as the refined sensibilities of artists and medical diagnosticians. Both positions are compatible with an "interactive" understanding of acts of attention, i.e. one not solely focused on bottom-up processing of stimuli. The strategy was to prepare for the "turn" from the beginning by including the results of prior acts of understanding in the subsequent account of attention. Thus, the category of "orientation" had priority over "arousal" and "focus" and so suggested how acts of attention occur in context. Or, as was asserted above: "Once past the earliest months of infancy, we bring to any act of attending accumulated insights that form the initial context for responding to stimuli, for example, broadly classifying data as disturbing sights or sounds."

This preparatory, strategic move is defensible. First, it evades an impasse in theories of cognitive psychology. The latter often describe "mechanisms" which produce and control conscious acts of attention. But what do we mean by "mechanisms" and how are they controlled?[94] One may focus on lower-level controls, e.g., "What are the neural mechanisms for the control of control."[95] Working out the implications of this question would be a massive undertaking. This chapter has focused on the neurochemical and organic conditions for acts of attention. Similar inquiries would need to be conducted regarding those same types of conditions for imagining, feeling, puzzling, understanding, judging, inventing and deciding.

At a minimum we can describe experiences of top-down control, e.g. the deliberate ignoring of a ringing phone while one is talking to a client. Then the hard question is how

---

[94] Does the language of "mechanism" reveal the hold imagination has over understanding? Machinery has imaginable parts; the whole can be imagined as disassembled. Inquiry becomes a matter of determining what each piece contributes to the whole. But how is this language about mechanical processes to handle questions about emergence and development?
[95] Herd, 29.

conscious, deliberate acts effect changes in neural events. Posner recognized the same question. While the prefrontal cortex appears to be the organic basis for cognitive control and its functions seem dependent on dopamine release, he asks how "the system knows when top-down control is needed in the first place."[96] One critical response is that formulating the question in terms of a "system" that "knows" may be part of the problem rather than a clue to the solution, especially if the relations among functions are non-systematic and "knowing" is a function of a set of operations higher than biochemical processes.[97]

Our hypothesis is that the higher-level operations, already contributing to the prior content of "orientation" (the partially determinate context which an inquirer brings to attending), are the promising sources of an answer. This stance is consistent with Posner's generic description of the process of orientation.

> Attentional orienting can be defined as the set of processes by which neural resources are deployed selectively toward specific attributes of events on the basis of changing motivation, expectation, or volition in order to optimize perception or action.[98]

But how do motivation, expectation, or volition effect changes in "neural resources"? That they do so is a commonplace within "folk psychology," but explanations still elude cognitive psychology, and the explanatory correlations of neuroscience largely focus on preconditions to and presumed results of

---

[96] Posner, Cognitive Neuroscience of Attention, 79.

[97] Again, the problem of language reappears. If "knowing" is attributed to organic or even neurochemical processes, is the usage deliberately metaphorical or are psychological phenomena (e.g. cognitive states and acts) being dismissed as epiphenomenal? My reading of Posner is that he rejects the second position.

[98] Ibid. 157.

such higher-level operations. When will similar correlations for the other half of the puzzle be the goal of research?

This chapter's minimal contributions to the entire puzzle are: (1) recognizing the need for the "turn" to this further question about higher-level controls, (2) suggesting a set of categories open to making the turn, (3) exploiting a dynamic notion of schemes of recurrence in hypothesizing how conscious, organic and neurochemical processes interact in producing acts of attention.

The diagram on the following page offers a summary of the preceding contributions and a sketch of future lines of research.

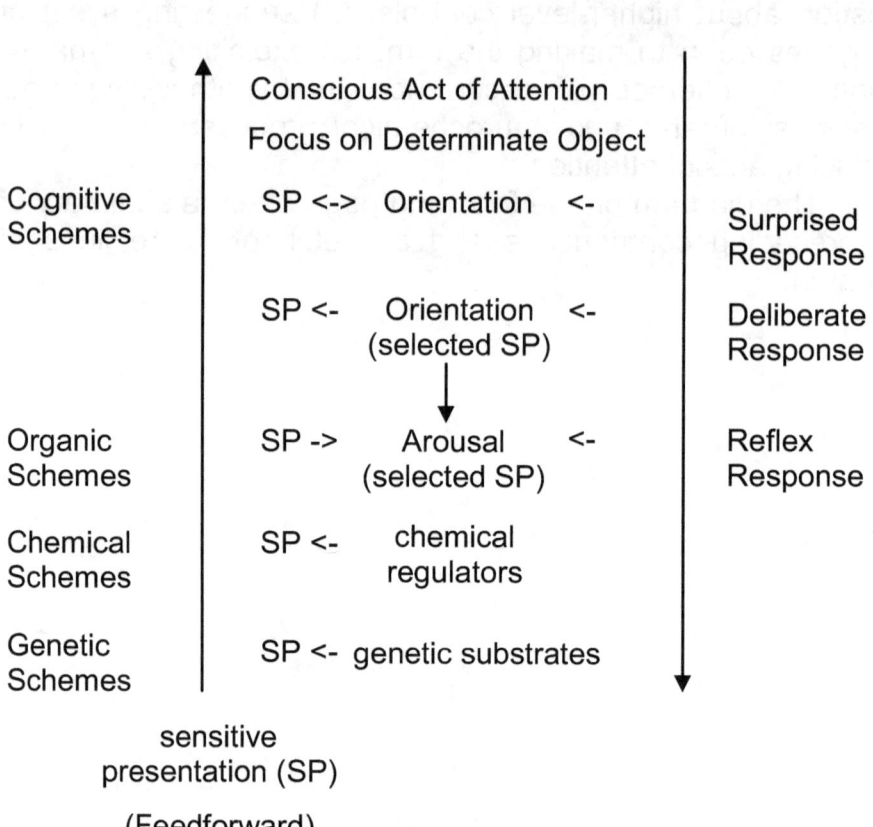

(Diagram 1.3)

VI Libet's Puzzle

The "turn" called for in the preceding section seems to presuppose that something like "deliberate control" is a real part of acts of attending. In other words, deliberate intentional acts can exercise "control" over brain activities such that, as ordinary language would have it, the conscious acts "cause" neurochemical events in the brain. Results from experiments conducted first by Benjamin Libet[99] nearly thirty years ago, and then by many others in the intervening years, raise doubts about this common-sense view. A variety of experiments instructed test subjects to make a gesture at a time of their own choosing within a fixed period. They were to indicate when exactly they decided to gesture. The findings were uniform. Nearly a half second before the test subjects reported their conscious decision to make a gesture, brain activity associated with such gesturing (labeled "readiness potential") was detected by monitoring devices. It seems that the brain "commands" the movement prior to any conscious decision. One conclusion was that the test subjects' conscious acts of deciding could not be the cause of the gestures. This priority of neural events over conscious acts was plausible evidence that popular notions of "free will" were illusory. Some read the test results as further proof that all conscious acts are epiphenomenal. The resulting puzzle is: if the subjects' reports of their conscious decisions are reliable, then the test data must be unreliable; but, if the latter are reliable, then the subjects must be deluded.

Rather than review the extensive literature spawned by these experiments, we can conclude this chapter by applying some of its findings to this puzzle. One goal of the preceding pages has been to outline a hidden complexity in what seems a rudimentary conscious act, namely, paying attention. The

---

[99] Benjamin Libet, "Timing of Cerebral Processes Relative to Concomitant Conscious Experience in Man," in <u>Advances in Physiological Sciences,</u> ed. G. Adam, I. Meszaros and E.I. Banyai (Elmsford, NY: Pergamon Press, 1981).

terms "orientation," "arousal" and "focus" first appeared along with descriptive accounts of attending, but the intent was to employ the terms as explanatory categories for understanding what makes an act of attending what it is. Doing so involved a shift from describing instances (for example, of arousal due to surprise) to understanding them in their relations to established neural patterns (i.e. expectations) and to sensitive presentations inconsistent with those patterns.

The shift from description to explanation is one clue to solving Libet's puzzle. Put another way, the puzzle may be due to an unnoticed mixing of descriptive and explanatory readings of the experimental results. On the one hand, there was the use of calibrated instruments to record and measure brain activities which prior studies had already correlated with biochemical events, brain locales and bodily gestures. The interpretation of the registered brain activities was, thus, dependent on an understanding of a series of correlations (including the measuring scales used in monitoring devices) among objects and events. On the other hand, the test subjects' reports of acts of deciding were self-descriptions of their intentional acts and conscious feelings.

The contrast here may not be immediately apparent. Suppose we begin with the metaphor of "perspective" and suggest the perspective of the test subjects is one of reporting or describing how their own inner states appear to them. However, the measured correlations among events (correlations which no one ever sees or feels) belong to a different perspective. Some precedents for this mixing of descriptive and explanatory perspectives may help clarify the contrast. Perhaps the two most famous precedents are Zeno's paradoxes and Eddington's two tables. In the former's example of an arrow flying toward its target but never reaching it, the paradox arises because of a mixing of an unimaginable geometric line composed of Euclidean points, having position but no dimensions, and imaginable objects (the moving arrow and fixed target) separated by a finite distance. If we imagine stopping the arrow after it has crossed some portion of the line stretching from archer to target and if we then imagine further halts at points along its line of flight, we can conceive of the remaining distance composed of geometric points as always having further halting points, and so the arrow never crosses all of them. The distance the arrow has yet to travel is always divisible.

In Eddington's case, the familiar desktop holding his books, pen and papers is a solid object, but the physicist's understanding of any material object is of largely empty space and rapidly moving particles. Which is the real desktop? Eddington was unable to supply an answer, but the puzzle begins to dissolve if one invokes and understands the distinction between a descriptive perspective (i.e. things in relation to us) and an explanatory perspective (i.e. things in relations among themselves).

What is the effect on Libet's puzzle if we apply the same distinction? Clearly the time differences are not illusory. As well, the correlations among calibrated instruments, detected and measured brain activities and self-reported conscious acts of decision-making are not fictive. However, are we talking about all these terms as correlates within a single explanatory perspective? My hypothesis is that the third term, "a deliberate, conscious act to gesture," belongs to a descriptive perspective, i.e. the test subjects are reporting how things seem in relation to them. We, like them, feel we are the agents of our own "willed" movements. However, we commonly believe and feel the same about the solidity of the tables we use and about imaginable objects moving toward imaginable targets.

To begin to dissolve Libet's puzzle requires retrieval of the medieval distinction between things *priora quoad nos* and things *priora quoad se*, but to resolve it actually would require "lifting" any terms about intentional acts into an explanatory perspective. The "turn" mentioned above calls for as much. This chapter tried to sketch an explanatory account of one basic type of intentional act, i.e. paying attention. Acts of decision-making are arguably far more complex, so Libet's puzzle is not resolved by the commentary on a more rudimentary type of act. However, the analysis of acts of attending does offer clues for future researchers. For example, if one's orientation is conscious but not attended to, it is part of conscious acts of attending without being what anyone would cite in response to being asked what it was they were focusing on. Conscious extroverted attention routinely does not register either neural patterns or expectations that guide acts of attending. For example, professional training may make habitual a deliberate attending to relevant clues and an ignoring of irrelevant sights and sounds (i.e. cases of objective abstraction), but these habits in focusing are conscious without being attended to. We should expect there to be measurable neural activity in skilled detectives' intelligent searching for clues and overlooking of irrelevant details <u>before</u> they report "deciding" what to examine at a crime scene.

Admittedly these are no more than preliminary steps toward understanding the "time delays" occurring in experiments inspired by Libet. The steps are incomplete since (1) an explanatory account of acts of deciding is an unmet challenge, and (2) the experiments for detecting relations among key classes of events occurring in such acts have yet to be conducted. Still, we have some clues as to how we might someday meet both challenges. First, just as the preceding pages treated acts of attending as correlates of intended objects, so the same approach may prove useful in regard to more complex intentional acts. Recall that orientation was first understood as a capacity to attend to potentially recognizable objects; arousal was the automatic or the trained response to actually recognizable objects; focus was the apprehending of actually recognized objects. How might these distinctions help in approaching the puzzle of time delays? A provisional response has three parts.

Insofar as the orienting network over time becomes a capacity with a determinate content (i.e. having neural patterns or expectations formed from previous experiences), it becomes a type of preparation for a flexible range of future acts of attending. Neural patterns become dedicated to certain types of tasks and so are predisposed to anticipate and to respond actively to signals, including those from the executive network.

Next, prior training makes arousal more probable in the presence of some types of stimuli. Recall, for example, how engineers in Kolers' studies of apparent motion were less frequently fooled than other test subjects. In contrast to the naïve expectations of the other test subjects, an engineer's alerting network was more "tutored" to control naïve responses and more disposed to detect misleading clues.

Finally, to focus is to recognize a specific object, state or event. Now it is such attention to something determinate that Libet's test subjects were asked to report, i.e. when exactly they consciously decided to make a gesture. However, the preliminary categories of orientation and arousal are relevant to explaining any complete act of attending. While expectations and predispositions are not what we attend to, they need not be unconscious. Again, the distinction between being conscious of something and attending to it is well founded. We manage to navigate through traffic while attending to our passengers' conversations or talking on a cell phone or planning what we will say at an upcoming meeting. Carter observed that conscious recognition requires neurons to "be active for a minimum period of time – anything from one-tenth to half a second – before the information they discriminate becomes conscious."[100] Perhaps we could adapt her remark to say: "Attending to and reporting choices requires neurons to be active before the conscious act of choosing is actually recognized." The time delays of Libet's experiment may not be so puzzling after all. Still, they will remain some of the data to be correlated in an explanatory account of conscious decision-making.

---

[100] Exploring Consciousness, 118.

CHAPTER TWO

How Do Emotions and Images Affect Human Action?

I Introduction

In slowly assembling an explanatory understanding of liberty, this chapter moves from neuroscience and its puzzles to psychology and its puzzles. A pattern within decision-making provides a framework for the inquiry: What is the problem? Why is it significant? What can we do about it? What decision should we make? This sequence of questions seems commonsensical. We should diagnose a situation before trying to find options. Doing so requires attention to the details of a specific situation. So Chapter One focused on what it means to pay attention. Far more, of course, is involved in diagnosis than attention to details. For instance, judging whether one's understanding of a problem is accurate requires more complex operations than acts of attending. However, even with the narrow focus on attention, there was no shortage of complexity and puzzles. To add to both we can wonder whether the sequence of the first two questions in the outline should be reversed. After all, we can ask why anyone pays attention to a problem in the first place, and the answer apparently is because the problem has some significance for the person. Even more obvious is that, unless persons feel strongly enough about a problem, they are unlikely to trouble themselves about closely observing a situation, imagining various options and carefully evaluating them. Feeling strongly about a problem seems to be a precondition to sustaining attention and to spending time and energy on the various tasks.

Why persons care about any number of things is a question inviting research that would prove probably inexhaustive and definitely exhausting.[101] So this chapter

---

[101] Still, in Part III a minimal answer about two types of caring (about understanding and about others) will appear. In Part IV

asks two narrower but related questions. First, assuming that most deliberate acts proceed from some prior caring,[102] we can puzzle about the roles of emotion and image (or symbol) in prompting such acts. Second, we can ask why there are relations of dependency among action, image and emotion. As in Chapter One, we begin with descriptive examples providing clues to answering both questions, but the goal is to reach for an explanatory understanding of the relations among these terms.

The inquiry unfolds in three stages. Part II cites various texts relevant to our two primary questions. The limited purpose of Part II is to record what a number of major thinkers have written about either question. Part III takes up the question of how to shift from descriptive accounts into a theoretical or explanatory context, and Part IV reformulates the puzzles in explanatory terms and so demonstrates how to operate in a theoretical context. Part V offers a summary of the chapter's content. Part VI concludes the chapter with a puzzling case from neuropathology that the preceding analyses of attention, emotion and image may help solve.

II Versions of the Puzzles

We all have our favorite literary works. We also develop a special affinity for a few of these favorites. Such has been this writer's experience with <u>The Education of Henry Adams</u>. In Chapter XXV, entitled "The Dynamo and the Virgin (1900)," Henry Adams asks a question that is useful in exploring puzzles about actions, images and emotions.

Speaking of how powerful the symbol of the Virgin Mary was for the medieval imagination, Adams writes: "…at the Louvre and at Chartres …was the highest energy ever known

---

caring will be a descriptive instance of what is meant by the basic category "demand."

[102] We are exempting reflex responses from this assumption since they are non-deliberative. This is not to say neural demands and emotions are not part of reflex responses.

to man, the creator of four-fifths of his noblest art, exercising vastly more attraction over the human mind than all the steam-engines and dynamos ever dreamed of...."[103] Commenting on the late nineteenth-century fascination with new technologies based on steam, he writes: "All the steam in the world could not, like the Virgin, build Chartres."[104] He adds: "Symbol or energy, the Virgin had acted as the greatest force the Western world ever felt, and had drawn man's activities to herself more strongly than any power, natural or supernatural, had ever done...."[105]

In his other classic, <u>Mont Saint Michel and Chartres</u>, he writes:

> Mary concentrated in herself the whole rebellion of man against fate; the whole protest against divine law; the whole contempt for human law as its outcome; the whole unutterable fury of human nature beating itself against the walls of its prisonhouse, and suddenly seized by a hope that in the Virgin man had found a door of escape. She was above the law; she took feminine pleasure in turning Hell into an ornament; she delighted in trampling on every social distinction in this world and the next.[106]

But, then, in that same work Adams pronounces his cadenced judgment on the once powerful symbol: "the Virgin in her majesty...looking down from a deserted heaven, into an empty church, on a dead faith."[107]

Now the pressing question for Henry Adams was whether any new image or symbol could do for the early twentieth century what the Virgin had done for the Middle

---

[103] <u>The Education of Henry Adams</u> (Boston: Houghton Mifflin, 1961), 384-385.
[104] Ibid. 388.
[105] Ibid. 388-389.
[106] (New York: Penguin Books, 1986), 260.
[107] Ibid. 186.

Ages. But in asking this question, he was assuming affirmative answers to more basic questions: (1) Is it the case that we proceed to act deliberately only if we feel an emotion moving us to do so?[108] (2) Is any emotion we feel dependent on symbols or affect-evoking images? Assuming we share Adams' affirmative answers, we can go on to ask our two questions: How do images or symbols evoke or inspire actions? Why are there relations of dependency among action, image and emotion?

Another text relevant to these questions comes from lectures given by Richard P. Feynman in 1963, but published only in 2005.[109] In those lectures he remarked:

> ...even the greatest forces and abilities don't seem to carry with them any clear instructions on how to use them. As an example, the great accumulation of understanding as to how the physical world behaves only convinces one that this behavior has a kind of meaninglessness about it. The sciences do not directly teach good and bad.[110]

Religion traditionally taught the difference between "good and bad." Feynman takes note of this ethical function of religion but goes on to talk of its metaphysical and inspirational roles. The metaphysical function is presumably to offer us plausible answers to our questions about the intelligibility of the universe and the worthwhileness of our lives in time. If the answers are persuasive, we may believe that our lives make sense and are worth living. In Feynman's

---

[108] The word "emotion" derives from the Latin *movere*, and the "turn" described at the end of Chapter One is part of a medieval puzzle about how a free act can be both moved and moving (*et motus et movens*).

[109] Herman E. Daly, "Feynman's Unanswered Question" in Philosophy and Public Policy Quarterly, Vol. 26 (winter/spring 2006).

[110] Ibid. 13.

words, "if you are working for God and obeying God's will, you are in some way connected to the universe, your actions have meaning in the greater world, and that is an inspiring aspect."[111] In short, the inspirational role serves living and acting but depends on the conviction or trust promoted by the metaphysical role.

Here, then, is Feynman's reading of the puzzle:

> [This] brings me to a central question that I would like to ask you all, because I have no idea of the answer. The source of inspiration today, the source of strength and comfort in any religion, is closely knit with the metaphysical aspects. That is, the inspiration comes from working for God, from obeying His will, and so on. Now an emotional tie expressed in this manner, the strong feeling that you are doing right, is weakened when the slightest amount of doubt is expressed as to the existence of God. So when a belief in God is uncertain, this particular method of obtaining inspiration fails. I don't know the answer to the problem, the problem of maintaining the real value of religion as a source of strength and courage to most men while at the same time not requiring an absolute faith in the metaphysical system.[112]

To word Feynman's difficulty more simply: the inspiration to do good needs more than the understanding provided by the sciences, but the understanding provided by the sciences undermines the traditional source of the needed inspiration.

There are older versions of Feynman's difficulty. For example, Plato may have weakened his political message by elaborating it in philosophical concepts and failing to provide the effective images and symbols that could inspire his audience to act. In his biography of Bernard Lonergan, William Mathews observed:

---

[111] Ibid.
[112] Ibid.

> ...in the time of Plato philosophy emerges and asserts its social significance. The function of the state is to teach virtue, but as only philosophers know what virtue is, there arises a need for a higher-order control. Involved is the problem of the shift from symbols to concepts, which illustrates at the time the impotence of philosophy.[113]

A diagnosis of the "impotence of philosophy" presupposes detection of deeply entrenched resistance to "higher-order control."[114] The most famous of Plato's accounts of such resistance is his parable of the cave in which those most in need of philosophy's care are those least likely to detect the need.

> Throughout the centuries there has rested upon Plato a heavy burden of proof. Most men presume they are wide awake to the realities of their world. For them seeing is believing. But Socrates' teaching concerning the *psyche* has loosed Plato forever from the tyranny of the obvious. [...] He knew that those who shared his viewpoint would agree, but he was fully aware, as stated in the *Republic* (527e), that those who had no first hand acquaintance with the powers of *nous* would necessarily regard his sketch of reality as incredible. Plato's task, therefore, was that of bringing men to the point of acknowledging that they were, in fact, asleep to the real nature of their world.[115]

---

[113] Lonergan's Quest, 75.

[114] Part III will pursue this issue of resistance in terms of the interdependence of human sensibility and intelligence. The temporal priority of the former in human development proves an obstacle to thinking in terms of things in relations among themselves, i.e. in terms other than those of "picture thinking."

[115] R. E. Cushman. Therapeia: Plato's Conception of Philosophy (Westport, CT: Greenwood Press, 1958), 44, quoted in Mathews, 256. Thoreau believed most of his contemporaries were also asleep,

Still, are there no effective images in any of Plato's works? Does the ring of Gyges in the Republic or the myth of the Judgment of the Dead in the Gorgias fail to move readers? Plato provides his own answer in the *Laws* where his argument invites readers to leave self-concern behind and his images presuppose detachment from personal interests. However, he expects few will accept the invitation or achieve the required detachment. In Eric Voegelin's terms:

> This argument [in the Laws] is climaxed by the vision of the creator-god as the player at the board who shifts the pieces according to the rules. When he observes a soul, now in conjunction with one body and then with another, undergoing changes through its own actions as well as through the actions of other souls, there is nothing left for the mover of the pieces but to shift the character (*ethos*) that has improved to the better place and the one that has worsened to the worse place, thus assigning to each the lot that is due its fate (903b-d).
>
> The Mover of the Pieces (*petteutes*) is the last and most awesomely intimate revelation of the Platonic God. [...] The Mover of the Pieces – this vision of the God who broods over the board of the cosmos and moves the particles of the Great Soul according to their relative merit ... is drawn from the cosmic depth in the soul of Plato.[116]

---

and he fabricated his images of life amid Nature to encourage an awakening. "To be awake is to be alive. I have never yet met a man who was quite awake." (65) "The commonest sense is the sense of men asleep, which they express by snoring." (216) Walden (New York: New American Library, 1960).

[116] Plato and Aristotle. Vol.3 of Order and History (Baton Rouge: Louisiana State University, 1983), 236.

Presumably the symbols drawn from such remote recesses will fail to appeal to most audiences whose own depths remain *terra incognita* and for whom self-concern and personal interests are the center of whatever cosmos they know. How then was Plato to reach such audiences?

Voegelin remarks on how Aristotle eventually responded to the problem.

> Aristotle recognizes both Myth and Philosophy as languages man equally can use to express the truth of reality, even though he accords to Philosophy the rank of the instrument that is better suited to the task. The historically earlier thinker who articulates his truth of reality by means of the Myth is the *philomythos*. He is in search of the same truth as the *philosophos*; and the *philomythos* is, therefore, to be considered something like a *philosophos*. The equivalence of Myth and Philosophy, of *philomythos* and *philo-sophos*, is stressed even more strongly in a late letter where Aristotle admits to becoming *philomythoteros* the older he becomes.[117]

After being a lover of philosophy, did Aristotle become a lover of myth because he learned that the latter inspires actions which the concepts of philosophy less readily evoke? Presumably myth with its images and dramatic stories is better able to effect changes in how people think and act.

Aquinas in his day referred to the dependency of action on emotionally loaded images. He wrote:

> An image or imagined form of an object without some appraisal that it is beneficial or harmful leaves the sensitive appetite unmoved. It is the same with the apprehension of a truth apart from its being good and

---

[117] "Equivalences of Experience and Symbolization in History" in Published Essays: 1966-1985. Vol. 12 of Collected Works (Baton Rouge: Louisiana State University Press, 1990), 125-126.

> desirable. Accordingly Aristotle observes that we are moved, not by the theoretical, but by the practical reason.[118]

Aquinas was asserting that affect-laden images are preconditions to assenting to truths and consenting to actions. He reaffirms this when he quotes favorably from John Damascene: "if a man judges without affection for the object of his judgment[,] there is no decision, that is, there is no consent."[119]

If an emotional response to images is a precondition to deliberate action or decisive "movement," just how do images evoke affects supporting actions? To remain with the medieval author and his faculty psychology, we can rephrase the question: How do images move the "will" toward certain acts rather than toward others? In Aquinas' works I found one intriguing passage suggestive of how an answer could be couched in terms of statistical probabilities.

> Now since the will, like the mind, is a certain non-material force, there corresponds to it one common reality, namely being good, as there corresponds to mind one common reality, namely being true and being real and so forth. This universal good embraces many particular goods, towards none of which is there a determinism within the will.[120]

What might this absence of "a determinism within the will" mean to a contemporary audience? First, we can translate "being good" and "being true" as indeterminate ranges of objects of possible choices and affirmations. That is, if we assume persons desire to understand and to do what is actually good, we can posit the intentional objects of such

---

[118] Summa Theologiae, Ia, 2ae, 9,1 ad 2. (Blackfriars 1970), 67.
[119] Ibid. 15, 1 (159).
[120] Ibid. 10, 1 (87).

desiring as anything whatever insofar as it is good and true.[121] However, we recognize that actual practices and beliefs vary widely. Without detouring into a debate about cultural relativism (and the subordinate issue of moral relativism), we can at least affirm that affect-laden goods have "moved" different peoples to believe and to act differently.[122]

Variations in the sources of such movement are sometimes quite improbable. Recall the case cited in Chapter One from the clinical work of V.S. Ramachandran and Sandra Blakeslee. The client, Arthur, was convinced his parents were both imposters. The authors diagnosed his illness as Capgras' delusion and surmised that, because of a severed connection to the son's amygdala, the sight of his parents' faces was not accompanied by the usual emotional response. This disconnect between image and emotion led to the improbable inference of imposture.

More troubling responses to images showed up in the same clinical case. The authors noted how Arthur exhibited "an almost obsessive preoccupation with Jews and Catholics." This prompted Ramachandran to comment:

> [There is] another rare syndrome called Fregoli, in which a patient keeps seeing the same person everywhere. In walking down the street, nearly every woman's face might look like his mother's or every young man might resemble his brother. (I would predict that instead of having severed connections from face recognition areas to the amygdala, the Fregoli patient may have an excess of such connections. Every face

---

[121] These "possible" objects, of course, may differ from what persons actually choose or affirm. Then we have the puzzles of how and why basic desires are frustrated. See the following footnote for a study of some of the frustrating limits.

[122] A survey of the sources of moral differences extends over three chapters (five through seven) in Michael Shute and William Zanardi. <u>Improving Moral Decision-Making</u> (Boston: McGraw-Hill, 2006).

would be imbued with familiarity and "glow," causing him to see the same face over and over again.)[123]

The indiscriminate linking of visual clues with determinate emotional responses would be one way of talking about the Fregoli patient but also for understanding racist stereotypes.

> Perhaps a single unpleasant episode with one member of a visual category sets up a limbic connection that is inappropriately generalized to include all members of that class and is notoriously impervious to "intellectual correction" based on information stored in higher brain centers. Indeed one's intellectual views may be colored (no pun intended) by this emotional knee-jerk reaction; hence the notorious tenacity of racism.[124]

In the Fregoli patient and with racist stereotypes, acquired links between images and emotions tend to override higher intellectual functions. In these cases Plato's call for "higher-order control" remains unanswered. Advocates of the priority of emotion over reasoning receive empirical support from such instances. However, as will appear below, there are other puzzles challenging this claim to priority.

What happens when a person is unable to feel any emotion no matter what images are presented? Rita Carter cites the work of Antonio Damasio with a patient named Elliott.

> 'He was always controlled, always describing scenes as a dispassionate, uninvolved spectator. Nowhere was there a sense of his own suffering ... he was not inhibiting the expression of internal emotional resonance or hushing inner turmoil. He simply did not have any turmoil to hush.'[125]

---

[123] Phantoms in the Brain, 171.
[124] Ibid.
[125] Antonio R. Damasio. Descartes' Error: Emotion, Reason and the Human Brain (London: Picador, 1995) quoted in Rita Carter.

Carter's diagnosis of Elliott's condition is relevant to the puzzles in this chapter.

> The reason that Elliott was referred to Professor Damasio was because after his operation he seemed unable to function efficiently in almost any capacity. [...] A battery of behavioural and neuropsychological tests...revealed the root of Elliott's problem: emotions no longer registered and without them he was unable to weigh up or evaluate one thing over another. Faced with a situation that called for decisive action he could generate a full range of appropriate responses – but none of them felt any more 'right' than any other. The result was that he could not choose between them. He had no 'gut feelings' to warn him away from dodgy enterprises and no instinctive sense of who [sic] to trust.[126]

The preceding clinical cases indicate a dependency of action on both sensitive presentations and their affect-laden associations. In partial contrast, we read in Chapter One that Lonergan affirmed how intelligence and deliberate action both condition and are conditioned by "adaptations of human sensibility."[127] If the Fregoli patient is constrained by a set of improbable links between image and emotion, what of the alternative of a higher-order deliberate manipulation of images to effect new adaptations? Political propaganda and commercial advertizing seem to have mastered the art of such manipulation. But what of more benign efforts to coordinate action and emotion?

> Here the basic problem is to discover the dynamic images that both correspond to intellectual contents,

---

Mapping the Mind (Berkeley: University of California Press, 1998), 81.
[126] Carter, 81.
[127] Cf. Chapter One, footnote 70.

orientations, and determinations yet also possess in the sensitive field the power to issue forth not only into words but also into deeds. [...] For the moment it must suffice to draw attention to the fact that, as intellectual development occurs through insights into sensible presentations and imaginative representations, so also the intelligent and reasonable control of human living can be effective only in the measure that it has at its disposal the symbols and signs by which it translates its directives to human sensibility.[128]

In this quotation we find a reprise of the main contents of the preceding citations. Lonergan implicitly asks a version of Henry Adams' pragmatic question: How do we "discover the dynamic images that both correspond to intellectual contents...[and] possess in the sensitive field the power to issue forth not only into words but also into deeds"? As Feynman reformulated the question to specify religion as the endangered source of action-inspiring images, so Lonergan's observation that control over human living needs symbols to direct cooperating emotions is a similar focusing of the question. It may seem that Plato's political question is an altogether different focus, yet for him politics is the art of soul-making. His problem is that those able to practice this art have left the darkness of the cave, and, when "forced to go back down," they find their new understanding of reality to be remote from the common sense of their audience. How, then, are they to persuade an audience still confined to a world of shadows? How can those who have left the cave effectively communicate their "directives" for living? Lonergan recognizes what is needed: "...the intelligent and reasonable control of human living can be effective only in the measure that it has at its disposal the symbols and signs by which it translates its directives to human sensibility."[129] Aristotle

---

[128] <u>Insight</u>, 585.

[129] The same author also remarked that "explanation does not give [us] a home. (...) [Our] explanatory self-knowledge can become

recognized the need for such symbols and signs, hence his late admiration for the power of myth. Similarly, Aquinas linked action (movement) to emotional responses to images.

In Ramachandran's case study, the generalized insight is that understanding, or recognizing, some sensible presentations (e.g. parents' faces) is dependent on, or conditioned by, emotional attachments or associations. Arthur expects to feel a certain way when he sees his real parents; so, when the expected feeling does not accompany the familiar sensible presentations, he judges the visual clues to be misleading. In this case, feeling trumps seeing. Such a possibility is presumably realized in Fregoli patients and racist stereotypes. Thus, some "adaptations of human sensibility" become impediments to intelligent acting. The case of Elliott points to a similar conclusion: in the absence of feeling, judgments and decisions can be difficult to make or, if made, go terribly awry.

III What Sense Can We Make of These Dependencies?

The purpose of Part III is to suggest how one can move from the descriptive materials of Part II to a theoretical or explanatory account of them. Recall the basic puzzles: (1) Assuming we act deliberately only if sufficient care is present, how is any emotion we feel dependent on symbols or emotion-evoking images? (2) What sense can we make of these relations of dependency among action, emotion and image? Part II assembled a few descriptive texts responsive to the puzzles. Adding texts, for example, from the writings of Jung, could easily expand the range of views.[130] A much shorter —

---

effective in [our] concrete living only if the content of systematic insights, the direction of judgments, the dynamism of decisions can be embodied in images that release feeling and emotion and flow spontaneously into deeds no less than words." Ibid. 570.
[130] Examples of relevant observations by Jung include the following. "But to live and experience symbols presupposes a vital participation on the part of the believer, and too often this is lacking in people

even more persuasive — case for relations of dependency could appeal to the billions of dollars spent each year on commercial advertizing. The verbal slogans and visual designs are products of mature craft and calculation. Those spending the billions know they are not wasting money. Years of manipulating consumer behavior by ever more carefully designed commercial images both presuppose and prove a link between action and image. The efforts to elicit emotional responses to a Golden Arch, a bottle of Coke or Krispy Kreme sign rest on the belief that affect-laden images can evoke prereflective responses from potential consumers.

But why do images play such a central role in evoking emotions and actions? So far we have indirect clues from Plato's cave and direct clues from Lonergan's remarks. Plato's hints are: (1) we all begin in the cave, deluded but self-confident that what we take to be obvious is what is true and real; (2) some may be "forced to turn around" *(periagogê)* and leave the cave (Augustine's *ex umbris et imaginibus*), but at first they will find themselves unfit for life above ground. Why "unfit"? In our beginnings lies our destiny; or, if that Freudian mantra is too strong a claim, what comes first tends to shape subsequent thinking and acting. So sensibility comes first, and soon after we make our first estimates of what is real in terms of what is sensible, in terms of what is imaginable. With priority comes privilege, and so our habits and first sense of

---

today. In the neurotic it is practically always lacking." (140) "To the extent that I managed to translate the emotions into images – that is to say, to find the images which were concealed in the emotions – I was inwardly calmed and reassured. Had I left those images hidden in the emotions, I might have been torn to pieces by them. There is a chance that I might have succeeded in splitting them off; but in that case I would inexorably have fallen into a neurosis and so been ultimately destroyed by them anyhow. As a result of my experiment I learned how helpful it can be, from the therapeutic point of view, to find the particular images which lie behind emotions." (177) <u>Memories, Dreams, Reflections</u> (New York: Vintage Books, 1989).

the "obvious" exert a power over our later thinking and acting and resist challenges.[131] Thus, even to escape from picture thinking, one must be "forced to turn around" and "go up," and even then one will at first be blinded, i.e. unfit to understand what is real. Now imagine the added difficulties of returning and, by relying solely on the "force" of persuasion, attempting to "turn around" those who have never left their cave and the realm of shadows. The philosopher may argue quite soundly against the old patterns of picture thinking, but emotions were early on associated with those pictures, and the philosopher's arguments will be ineffective if they fail to evoke equally strong emotions.

Lonergan's comments on this challenge are less metaphorical. "Human intelligence and reasonableness" integrate the lower-order "sensitive flow of percepts and images, emotions and feelings, attitudes and sentiments, words and deeds." So, for example, sights and sounds are understood; moods are recognized and then encouraged or resisted; possible words and actions are weighed and then chosen or rejected. But this top-down ordering is not the entire story. The higher-order operations are themselves "conditioned by adaptations of human sensibility." So Chapter One offered examples of interference from "below." Illness interferes with taking an exam; a foul mood disrupts a writing schedule; anger undercuts a resolve to mend a relationship. Still, "adaptations of sensibility" can also cooperate with and promote higher-order operations. So Chapter One provided examples of cooperation from "below." A love of dance helps the aspiring ballerina practice despite pain. The cultivated and discriminating eye of the painter sees variations in color and texture where the untrained eye sees none. The compassionate listening of a nurse allows patients to reveal

---

[131] See footnote 110 in this chapter.

fears they hide from family members lest they add to their worries.[132]

As part of the "sensitive flow," images can support or impede intelligent planning and acting. But there is more to the role of images in evoking emotion and action. As noted above, what comes first tends to shape subsequent thinking and acting, and with priority comes privilege. So the images we first experience tend to shape our subsequent orientations toward new objects and events. Thus, Chapter One discussed selectivity in attention as due to neural patterns or expectations arising from prior acts of attending. With the roots of expectations being in linked or associated groupings of neurons, it seems that, when some part of a grouping "fires," our conscious, but prereflective, tendency is to anticipate the whole. Also in Chapter One were remarks on how feelings are associated with images (e.g. the faces of Arthur's parents), and so similar images tend to evoke similar feelings. Thus, advertisers link their products with images widely associated with status and happiness. The part (the "product") becomes associated with the broader groupings that include, for example, feelings of achievement and pleasure. The commercial strategy, then, is to associate a product image with the recurrence of such positive emotions in consumers and thereby to increase the odds of "brand loyalty," i.e. what consumers will think of first when "feeling" the "demands" for a kind of product.[133] But what do we mean by "feeling" and by "demands"?

To this point in following the clues from Plato and Lonergan, the examples have reflected how "things are

---

[132] Chapter Three will describe this potential cooperation in terms of a dialectic between operator and integrator, a notion and a language somewhat remote from picture-thinking.

[133] A summary of research on the manipulation of consumer appraisals of products is available in S. Han, J.S. Lerner, D. Keltner, "Feelings and Consumer Decision Making: The Appraisal-Tendency Framework" in Journal of Consumer Psychology, Vol. 17 (2007), 158-168.

related to us." It is easy to begin the study of emotional responses to images from this familiar perspective. There is no shortage of descriptive examples of particular emotions routinely attached to determinate auditory and visual clues. We can imagine friends and family members casually and predictably interacting with one another. Individually and as a group, they are caring and intelligent in responding to one another. But what happens in a particular family if the teenage daughter exhibits symptoms of manic depression or her brother withdraws into drug-induced fantasies? Emotional responses to routine gestures are no longer predictable. Misunderstanding and confusion become more frequent; the earlier exchanges and familiar gestures become less casual and more guarded. All the family members struggle to adapt to the confusing and alarming responses; the expected links between determinate emotions and determinate sensitive presentations are no longer reliable. A new set of expectations is taking shape.

What will it take to shift talk of feelings, emotions, demands and actions into a theoretical context, i.e. into a study of how things are related among themselves? Ramachandran's and Damasio's clinical cases can point us toward a theoretical understanding of, for example, what the phrase "adaptations of sensibility" means. There is sufficient evidence to assert a reciprocal conditioning of sensibility and understanding. For good or ill, lower-order operations and their higher-order counterparts condition one another. Again, one of the opening questions was how we are to make sense of this mutual dependency. Let me suggest an initial answer in three steps.

At the beginning of this chapter, care was cited as a precondition to deliberate action. The ancient Romans had a maxim: "Care is the mother of all things." From our own experience (or from the case of Elliott), we know that, in the absence of care, not much happens. When we could not care less about something, our attention and efforts are at best halfhearted.[134] However, when care is present, we are more energized, focused and careful. But why do we care about anything?

One answer is that, as a matter-of-fact, we spontaneously care about understanding and about other people. Being around three-year olds will supply the proof of a native and affect-laden curiosity.[135] Less in evidence may be signs of caring about others, i.e. a child's emerging moral sensitivity. This is not the place for more than a few suggestions. Some hold that young children are egocentric and morally obtuse. In contrast, I suggest the following scenario. When doting grandparents arrive with a camera and the young child "hams it up," is the child delighting in being the center of attention? Could the child also be delighting in delighting others? So we have two possible readings of the same data. Even if we "buy" the second meaning of the child's behavior, we still do not know why the child should enjoy bringing joy to others. Do we even have anything approximating a serious understanding of "delight"?[136]

Sociobiology offered an answer. Supposedly there is an evolutionary advantage in being helpful to others, especially to those with greater status, whether measured by

---

[134] The extreme absence of caring appears in Cotard's syndrome when all of a person's senses are no longer linked to the emotional centers in the brain, and so "nothing in the world has any emotional significance, no object or person, no tactile sensation, no sound – nothing – has emotional impact. The only way in which a patient can interpret this complete emotional desolation is to believe that he or she is dead." V.S. Ramachandran, A Brief Tour of Human Consciousness (New York: PI Press, 2004), 91.

[135] Ramachandran uses the example of solving perceptual riddles to link puzzling images, attentive curiosity and insights ("A-ha" experiences) with emotion. See ibid. 48-49.

[136] Aquinas correlated "delight" with the "motion" of intellect seeking understanding and the state of being-at-rest when it reaches its goal. The intellect experiences enjoyment in knowing and a delighted will at rest. Summa Theologiae, Ia, 2ae, Q11, a. 3. c.

physical strength, economic resources or intelligence. So the delightful child, as a carrier of the species' history, will naturally, if not always consistently, try to please others.[137] Emotional attachments and affect-inspired actions have their genesis in biogenetic imperatives or demands. But how do biogenetic demands condition higher-order operations? Again, are we making any progress in understanding our puzzles in a theoretical way? Perhaps the category of demand will prove useful in relating biogenetic demands to data suggesting that the nervous system "demands" feelings, the psychic system "demands" images, and human intellectual functions "demand" insights or intelligible orderings of feelings and images. Specifying these multiple types of demands and identifying their proper objects are tasks for the next two chapters.

For now, a third step was promised in speculating about how sensibility and intelligence are mutually conditioning. One supposition is that, as a matter-of-fact, we develop in understanding and improve our deliberate acting by raising and answering questions about puzzling images and sensitive presentations. From a "bottom-up" perspec-tive, we would have nothing to question without the lower-order contents of human sensibility, and so intellectual and practical development would not occur. From a "top-down" perspective, actual developments in understanding and practice can alter the contents of sensibility. Recall the previous examples from Kolers' famous experiments in apparent motion and how the professional training of engineers altered the usual results.

But intellectual development is not guaranteed since all sorts of obstacles can block unwanted images and so defer

---

[137] The experience of what happens "naturally" but "not always consistently" is evidence of non-systematic relations between human actions and their preconditions, thereby leading to talk of probabilities governing those actions. Here is the basis for one line of criticism of at least those popularizers of sociobiology who confuse correlations with complete explanations.

questioning, and without questioning new under-standing is unlikely. Thus, intellectual development requires images which support our caring about understanding and doing the right thing. This brings us back to Henry Adams' question about effective symbols. Now, however, we can formulate his question more precisely. Under ideal conditions, our best judgments about what actions we should take are matched by sufficient care or a desire to follow through, but how do we increase the frequency with which this match occurs? Presumably one measure is to order lower-level conditions, e.g. images and sensitive presentations, so that they support the matching desire against interfering variables. But how do we achieve this "match"? The deliberate control of images to achieve desired results is one instance of the general puzzle: how do deliberate acts "order" lower-level biological and neuro-chemical states?

To summarize the inquiry up to this point — a theoretical handling of our puzzles first drew upon research in neuroscience. Rather than exploring that enormous field in any detail, we focused on an explanatory account of paying attention as a step toward asking how emotion, image and action are related. Asking this question has led to further questions: (1) Why do <u>images</u> play such a key role in evoking <u>emotions</u> and <u>actions</u>? (2) How do biologically rooted emotional <u>demands</u> condition higher-order operations? (3) How might higher-order operations, in deliberately selecting images, cooperate with those demands and support a person's desire to understand and to do what is good?[138]

---

[138] Should we expect easy answers to these questions? Consider some of the prior conditions to arriving at such answers. Does anyone care enough about the questions? Whose orientation in inquiry is such that that they delight in pursuing these questions for years with no expectation of easy answers? What are the lower-order conditions favorable to the emergence and survival of similar orientations in the face of competing demands for job security, popular acclaim or easy answers? What images and symbols can effectively promote such favorable conditions?

These questions identify the four key variables or categories for sketching an explanatory account of the dependency of action on emotion and image.

IV Shifting the Puzzles into a Theoretical Context

Spinoza lived close enough to the classical tradition of Western Philosophy to assume that *conatus* or "striving" has priority in talking about human intelligence. What symbols can evoke from sensibility cooperative support for intellectual *conatus*? Perhaps we have met embodied symbols, i.e. persons who inspired us by their love of learning and virtue. If that has been true in our lives, can we generalize about what might be effective in future cases? At least we might state the problem: The desire to understand and to do what is good competes for attention against a variety of wants and demands, many of which we may not recognize.[139] What images can effectively appeal to sensibility to cooperate with intelligence in trumping the competition?

Part II surveyed a few descriptive responses from literature (Adams), popular culture (Feynman's public lectures and the practices of commercial advertisers), clinical psychology (the case studies of Ramachandran and Damasio), and philosophy (Plato, Aristotle, Aquinas and Lonergan). We could consult any number of other sources. What would be a fair and up-to-date sample of the diverse "researches performed, the interpretations proposed, the histories written..." about our original puzzles?[140] Presumably any sampling begins with focused questions and a prior

---

[139] Recall the shift from epistemology to depth psychology as part of the West's cultural journey in the study of human action.

[140] Bernard Lonergan. Method in Theology (New York: Herder and Herder, 1972), 250. Even brief attention to this question should lead to demands for a division of labor and practical puzzling about how to distinguish and distribute the tasks. The Epilogue will take up this question and comment on how difficult it is for any one scholar to provide a "fair" sample.

orientation of curiosity about them. We attend to what interests us. Yet attention to data and interpretation of those selected for attention have prior conditions, from conventions within a profession to neural "alert systems" on guard against possible dangers. Thus, Chapter One was preparatory for understanding such conditions by asking what we mean by "attention".

The accidents of birth, early education and traumas along the way may "fix" initial orientations and interests. This is the meaning of the second part of the remark: "as the higher perfects the lower, so the lower disposes to the higher...."[141] But the first part affirms that deliberately designed projects of intelligence may "perfect" or complete initial tendencies and interests. Thus students will deliberately give their attention to some images and puzzles rather than to others because of their career plans.

What does "deliberately" mean here? Suppose someone is writing an essay on the dependency of action on inspiring images. The writer has at least a personally interesting question and proceeds to find authors who wrote something <u>about</u> it. Next are some interpretative efforts, perhaps comparing and contrasting the selected texts. There may even be some judgments on the coherence and sophistication of the selected texts. The writer is reaching some understanding <u>about</u> what others have understood about the question. But maybe the writer asks a new question: How am I going <u>about</u> making sense of what these texts claim? The three "abouts" are worth noticing.[142] The third one is the issue at this point. How do we go about shifting the discussion of images and emotions into a new key, into talk about things in relations among themselves? And more to the point – do we know what we are "about," what we

---

[141] Bernard Lonergan. "Finality, Love and Marriage," in <u>Collection</u> (New York: Herder and Herder, 1967), 29.

[142] I am indebted to Philip McShane for the use of these three "abouts" and for much else in this book that remains unacknowledged.

are doing? Is it a deliberate operating or simply mimicry of conventional practice?

Moving into a theoretical context begins with the further why-question and then goes on to identify basic categories and to work out correlations among them in order to achieve a relative independence from highly variable descriptions of how things are related to us. Part III provisionally identified categories relevant to the two puzzles formulated at the beginning of the Chapter. Four of those categories are where we begin: emotion (or feeling), image, demand, action.

The refinement of terms is part of the working out of correlations. Regarding the category "emotion," we can follow convention and offer no single definition of the term, at least not in the classical sense of *omni et soli*. Instead, we will begin by adopting a descriptive classification of emotions and go on to work out an implicit definition of the category in relation to the three other categories of image, demand and action. The first step is easily taken; the second requires most of the remainder of this chapter.

Damasio provides a useful classification of emotions under three headings: (1) primary or universal emotions (e.g. anger, fear, sadness, surprise); (2) secondary or social emotions (e.g. shame, jealousy, guilt, admiration); (3) background emotions (e.g. uneasiness, serenity, tension).[143]

Is the category emotion interchangeable with the term feeling? Damasio argues against this identification.[144] He

---

[143] The Feeling of What Happens, 50-51. Notice that he excludes from this classification what others often consider to be emotions. "I will refer to drives and motivations and pain and pleasure as triggers or constituents of emotions, but not as emotions in the proper sense. No doubt all of these devices are intended to regulate life, but it is arguable that emotions are more complex than drives and motivations, than pain and pleasure." (341, footnote 9.) For his distinction between moods and emotions, see 286.

[144] Carter adopts a similar distinction between feeling and emotion though she conflates "feeling" and "recognition of a feeling." "Emotions are usually thought of as mental events, which we might

distinguishes among emotion, the feeling of an emotion and knowing (recognizing) that one has a feeling of an emotion.[145] Since emotions and feelings can both be unconscious,[146] he distinguishes them in terms of the privacy of feelings, which are inner states unobservable by others, and emotional responses which, in many cases, are publicly observable. In short, feelings are internal and emotions are mainly external.[147]

This less than satisfactory distinction is the author's response to linguistic difficulties. While some languages conventionally distinguish between emotion and feeling, others do not; and, even in the former cases, usage often interchanges the terms.[148] An additional linguistic deficit is the absence of a distinct word for feelings that are not conscious.

---

imagine could be experienced as well by a brain in a vat as by a brain in a body. But in fact the conscious mental effect of emotion is secondary to bodily changes, which in turn are primarily designed to bring about bodily action. The 'feeling' of an emotion is the conscious recognition of a 'bad' or 'good' brain state, not its cause." Exploring Consciousness, 196.

[145] The Feeling of What Happens, 8.

[146] While Damasio acknowledges the difference between consciousness and attention (e.g. ibid. 15 and 18), I find he sometimes uses "unconscious" when what he should use is "unattended to" (e.g. 36, 318-319). His reference to "a running polyphony [of emotions and feelings] that underscores and punctuates specific thoughts in our minds and actions in our behavior" (43) is a useful metaphor for thinking about the difference between consciousness and attention. Dominant and recessive voices alternate without either type being unheard. Less metaphorically, the distinction in Chapter One between objective and apprehensive types of abstraction may be of some use in tracing the difference.

[147] Ibid. 42 and 291.

[148] Ibid. 340, footnote 6. The author attributes such interchanging of the two terms to "carelessness."

Still, if common usage has its problems, the search for explanatory correlates may avoid them.

Suppose, then, that, in keeping with the findings of neuroscience, we understand emotions as initially capacities within various brain locales that internal or external stimuli can activate and so begin the patterning or ordering of otherwise disordered neural impulses. Once activated an emotion becomes detectable as both a neural event and an alteration in organic or brain activities. Notice that an external observer can detect these changes by artificial means, e.g. PET, fMRI, EEG, or by inferences from gestures, facial flushing, changes in voice. However, the person experiencing the change can consciously feel the consequences of such activation without being conscious of either the neural events and chemical alterations giving rise to the feeling or the bodily manifestations others notice. So the emotion may be observed by external parties, but the feeling of the emotion remains private. Exhibiting the emotion is one thing; feeling it another. Then, given the difference between being conscious of something and being attentive to something, we can add a further distinction between feeling an emotion and recognizing one is experiencing or feeling it. How might these distinctions contribute to understanding links between images and actions?

Perhaps the earlier categories of orientation, arousal and focus can help track the relations among these new distinctions. As orientation was first understood as a general capacity for attending, so emotion is initially understood as a general capacity for responding affectively. As arousal was understood as a response to a determinate stimulus, so feeling is understood as a biochemical and psychological response to internal or external stimuli. As focus was understood as the recognition of a determinant object, so recognizing one is feeling an emotion is consciously attending to a determinate inner state. In sum, we have emotions as capacities activated by determinant stimuli producing feelings that sometimes we recognize ourselves as having. But is this sequence of parallel descriptions transcribable into explanatory correlations?

Suppose the general capacity (emotion) has its correlate in fields of potential internal and external stimuli. The capacity can be activated (a determinate emotion is possible) relative to some potentially activating subset of either of those fields. For a specific emotion actually to be aroused, there must be an actual stimulus evoking a response.[149] A feeling as an inner state is a correlate of such a determinate stimulus. In regard to actual emotions and feelings, we can say they are what actual stimuli evoke and the stimuli are what the former respond to. Of course, the interaction is more complex than this. As Proust noticed, certain smells and tastes (stimuli) can evoke feelings that in turn evoke a flood of remembered images, but these can in their turn evoke or reawaken feelings associated with them.

What of the third term: recognizing a feeling that one is experiencing? Recall the remarks in Chapter One on "focus" as "recognition (i.e. apprehensive abstraction) of a determinate something due both to prior adaptations in sensibility and understanding and to the data which evoke their response." If recognizing ("feeling" one's feeling) occurs in a "complete" act of attending to an inner state, then the third term involves a relation between operation and state-of-mind (object for consciousness) in which a person, to varying degrees, is (1) conscious of a state of feeling and (2) attending to it as an object, i.e. a feeling as an inner state. Again, some language deficits are present here, but to say, "I feel my feelings" is not necessarily redundant if the intentional relation between an act of attending and its object is familiar.[150]

---

[149] As in the case of "arousal" of attention, a specific emotional response to a stimulus may be biologically preset or the result of prior experiences, including deliberate training.

[150] Damasio asks why consciousness (recognition?) of our feelings should occur in addition to just having them. He speculates about the evolutionary advantages of being able to attend to our feelings. (Cf. The Feeling of What Happens, 285.) One could go on to

How does any of this contribute to the puzzle about the link between images and actions? If we understand "image" as any potential object of a possible act of attending, then this term can substitute for "stimulus" in the penultimate paragraph. Damasio uses "image" in such a broad way, i.e. not limiting it to visual representations.[151] One advantage of following his example is that it allows a single term to cover all the diverse sensible presentations and psychic representations (e.g. dream images) that are known to evoke emotional responses. To parallel the treatment of the earlier categories, we can stipulate that images are a field of possible representations potentially evocative of emotional responses. Images are actually able to evoke responses relative to determinate capacities in organisms (either biologically preset or "trained") for responding affectively. Images actually evoke responses when determinate capacities are aroused.[152]

But why do specific images evoke specific feelings? Again, as was the case with "arousal," only a general answer is possible. Emotional responses to images may be due to biological make-up or be the result of prior experiences, including training. Hence, our third category, "demand," will also be broadly understood so as to include both biological demands (e.g. for food, sex, play, rest) and psychosocial

---

speculate about the biological advantages of reflexive intentional acts whereby persons can deliberately attend to and evaluate their own acts of intentionality. Such reflexive acts make possible methodical procedures that have made a difference in human development.

[151] Ibid. 318.

[152] The category "image" was already treated in this way in Chapter One. "Similarly, images or phantasms are potentially intelligible prior to someone attending to them. They are actually intelligible (though only potentially understood) relative to someone attending to them as puzzling or interesting objects, i.e. someone engaging in objective abstraction. They are understood in act relative to someone having a preconceptual understanding of them, i.e. someone engaging in apprehensive abstraction."

demands (e.g. for status, revenge, community).[153] Both types of demands are correlates of images. That is, psychic demands are understood as spontaneous or "trained" reachings for images, and images are what respond to these demands. To connect this correlation to the preceding remarks about images and emotions — it is because demands are present that images are evocative of emotional responses and that emotional attachments are made to certain types of images. For example, when persons are hungry (a type of demand), the image of dinner being prepared can prompt emotions of happiness or anticipated satisfaction. When persons are in search of social status, the commercial ads associating ownership of a luxury item with such status respond to the demand. Actually eating the dinner or purchasing the luxury item becomes the action fulfilling the demand, thereby creating a determinate neural pattern intensifying the link between demand and emotionally charged image.

Beyond this general correlation among the three categories, we can hypothesize that "affective attachments" or associations occur between particular types of images and neural patterns such that the presentation of the former begins a cascade of neural activities and chemical releases producing organic changes that are the immediate substrate for psychological experiences of emotion and feeling.[154]

---

[153] Caring about understanding and about others belongs to the latter type of demand without, however, being independent of human biology as a capacity to "internalize environments." This capacity is most obvious in eating, but it is also a precondition to forming images, guesses, plans and fantasies. Chapter Three will pursue this topic further. There the focus will be on the varied demands of intentional acts, their "operators" and the dialectically related principles of assimilation and completion.

[154] Damasio acknowledges that contemporary neuroscience has not explained how images emerge from neural patterns. (The Feeling of What Happens, 322) Neuroscience has, however, made progress in

But which images have which cascading effects? The variables in answering this question are an indefinite range of cultural, biographical and biological conditions. Recall how Ramachandran's clinical cases exhibited abnormal reactions to images due to organic deficiencies. In addition, comments in Chapter One on expectations indicated how selected sensitive presentations are rarely independent of orientations (latent patternings) in those experiencing them. In other words, a person's orientation as a determinate capacity has a history of patterned results due to prior experience. Such histories establish probabilities that some types of images will more often evoke certain types of emotions in some types of populations. For example, feelings of hunger in today's teenagers will more likely be evoked by an image of a hamburger than by the sight of a feral pig. The malleable capacity to attend to and to respond affectively to something is made determinate through exposure to what has been frequently imaged in one's culture and biography. In other words, the range of possible evocative images is narrowed by contingencies of place and time.[155]

Such variable patterning is one clue to understanding how the process of attending "selects" some images from among the flood of sensible presentations surrounding a person. In Chapter One the question of selection was answered in terms of reflex and trained responses to stimuli. Now we can expand that answer to include (1) emotional

---

linking emotions with different brain locales. Cf. Carter, Exploring Consciousness, 115, 196-197, 210.

[155] In identifying various effects culture and biographical history have on which images evoke which emotions and on their subsequent expression, Damasio mentions three types of consequences. "In all probability, development and culture superpose the following influences on the preset devices: first, they shape what constitutes an adequate inducer of a given emotion; second, they shape some aspects of the expression of emotion; and third, they shape the cognition and behavior which follows [sic] the deployment of an emotion." (The Feeling of What Happens, 57)

attachments to certain images and (2) conscious control over which images receive attention.

If we assume emotions are indicators of preference or evaluation,[156] then selective attention to some images out of a range of "competitors" may be due to biologically preset or learned patterns operating much like "biased referees." But can we get beyond these sports metaphors? One step is to search for evidence that emotions "weight" images. So neuroscientific research detects increases in activity in the limbic system when some images produce stronger emotional responses than others.[157] The increased activity occurs "when the process of emotion leads to the secretion of certain chemical substances in nuclei of the basal forebrain, hypothalamus, and brain stem, and to the subsequent delivery of those substances to several other brain regions."[158] Among the effects of such releases are changes in the speed with which images are produced (either slowing or accelerating the speed) and in the clarity of the images (either blurring or sharpening them). Everyday examples of these effects are found in athletic competition when attention to details

---

[156] "Emotions are inseparable from the idea of reward or punishment, of pleasure or pain, of approach or withdrawal, of personal advantage and disadvantage. Inevitably, emotions are inseparable from the idea of good and evil." Ibid. 55.

[157] "Emotional reactions are the result of processing along the parallel neural pathway that goes through the limbic system. A familiar face, for example, creates more activity in these regions than an unfamiliar one, and a lover's face, or one that looks threatening, sets the circuitry zinging with excitement. As well as producing instant, specific reactions, such as running or reaching, emotional excitement brings about peripheral changes in the body state which prepares the body generally for 'flight, grab or flight' behaviour. These changes – mediated by hormones and neurotransmitters such as adrenalin and cortisol – feed back to the limbic system and amplify activity there...." Carter, Exploring Consciousness, 196-197.

[158] Damasio, 80.

increases. So professional tennis players learn to speedily anticipate opponents' moves, but the latter adjust by deliberately feigning moves to deceive the expectations of their opponents. To exemplify the blurring of images, consider how the emotionally "flat" world of chronic depression conflates the varied details of everyday life, so that there are no moments of elation and none of great sorrow.

But why do emotions and their cascade of neural and organic changes occur at all? Any answer will have multiple parts. First, emotion plays a fundamental role in directing attention by signaling that an image is significant, e.g. something dangerous. By helping "select" significant images, emotion provides the "drive" for greater attention. On the other hand, when emotional response is low or indifferent, the signal sent is "irrelevant," and so neural and organic systems save time and energy by inattention. In effect, emotional responses prove useful, for example, in alerting persons to dangers, to opportunities for eating and mating, to signs of bodily and mental distress or pleasure. Here Damasio's distinction between feelings and recognized feelings helps track different roles for reflex and deliberate responses. Reflex responses tend to be stereotypical and serve to maintain biological routines and to improve the odds of survival without the need for time-consuming cognitive acts. In contrast, having feelings and recognizing them can be a step toward remedying any cause of distress, toward extending momentary elation and enjoyment, toward planning how to evade or repeat an emotionally charged event.[159]

So the question of why we have emotions may be answered, at least provisionally, in terms of their utility for human planning and acting. Thus, our fourth category, "action," appears already linked to demands, emotions and the images that respond to the former and evoke the latter. In the simplest cases of reflex responses, a sensitive organism acts toward or away from objects "represented" as good or bad for it. In time some spontaneous bodily reactions are subject to

---

[159] Ibid. 284-285.

greater control by higher cognitive operations (an explicit focus of the next Chapter). For example, stifling yawns and suppressing looks of disgust or signs of nervousness require interventions from top-down "operators."[160] All the same, suppressed emotional responses may still be detectable by skin monitoring sensors or by the trained observer, e.g. a police interrogator. If the suppression of a reflex emotional response becomes habitual, the low-intensity emotion may be undetected by the conscious actor. Again, not all emotions and feelings are objects of attention.

But the second of the two questions above was about deliberate control over which images receive attention. As a step toward answering this question, we noted how there can be at least partial control over emotions and their expression. Further descriptive examples are easily supplied. We can deliberately distract ourselves from disturbing images so as to avoid feelings of sadness. The nervous public speaker focusing on a spot behind and above the audiences' faces is employing a strategy of avoidance to control an emotion. The veteran actor can turn on the tears by drawing on personal memories of grief, thereby using private feelings to exhibit the more public face of manipulated emotion.

That such control over emotions occurs is not in dispute, but understanding how it occurs is puzzling.[161] The general puzzle is how mental acts can effect organic changes. One clue to solving the puzzle may lie in studies of how emotional states (e.g. anxiety) can have effects on organic systems (e.g. the immune system). With the discovery that the nervous system and the immune system are not separate but interactive, it is now reputable to explore how a mental

---

[160] The notion of "operator" will be discussed in Chapter Three.

[161] The literature on the "cognitive awareness hypothesis" provides empirical results of "bias correction" when decision-makers become aware of how irrelevant emotions are affecting their judgments. See S. Han (162) for examples of test subjects exercising higher-level control over their moods, reactions to weather conditions and anger.

condition (e.g. depression or anxiety) can bring about organic changes. Carter summarizes some of the intriguing findings.

> The knock-on effect, from one system to another, of molecular changes explains why a condition such as depression – normally thought of as an illness of the 'mind' – may also have profound effects on many other parts of the body. For example, one common bodily change in depression (and dementia) is a drop in the levels of the excitatory neurotransmitter noradrenalin. This manifests as mental sluggishness because noradrenalin stimulates brain cells in the cortex, helping to generate thoughts and perceptions. However, reduced levels of nora-drenalin also cuts [sic] down activity in the nerves which stimulate the tissues that keep certain immune cells circulating. So instead of moving around the body, seeking out and fighting invaders like bacteria and viruses, the immune cells sit around in the body tissues, allowing infections to flourish.[162]

Descriptions of how all these interactions occur usually mention events at the cellular level.

> Some branches of the peripheral nervous system have been shown to extend right into immune system organs and tissues such as the spleen, lymph nodes, thymus and bone marrow. Signals sent from the brain to these areas may stimulate or inhibit them directly. [...] Neurotransmitters, hormones and cytokines (proteins which help defend the body against disease) used to each be associated with just one system – endorphins and neurotransmitters with the nervous system, hormones with the endocrine system and cytokines with the immune system. But now they have been discovered to be part of a single family of messenger

---

[162] Exploring Consciousness, 198.

cells which mediates between the systems as well as working within them.[163]

Besides references to depression and dementia, Carter also cites linkages among anxiety, cellular events and the suppression of the immune system. More to our purpose, she notes how positive emotional states can support the immune system in combating illness.[164] Her conclusion is relevant to our question of control. "Thus things that happen at the very 'highest' level of the nervous system — thoughts, beliefs and perceptions — can affect individual molecules in the furthest reaches of the body, and vice versa."[165]

The key clue to understanding how conscious acts may exercise control over images lies in how systems once thought separate are found to be interactive.[166] Suppose that deliberate attention to some images and deliberate avoidance or blocking of others require similar interactivity among systems. Some general assertions about system interactivity occurred in Chapter One. There human understanding was said to operate as "the higher integration of the sensitive flow of percepts and images, emotions and feelings, attitudes and sentiments, words and deeds."[167] At the same place, it was acknowledged that images provide the puzzling objects for questioning without which higher-level operations would not occur. To these generalities we can add that deliberate intentional acts (occurring as a structure or system of

---

[163] Ibid.

[164] "Positive mental experiences, on the other hand, can stimulate the immune system, helping to keep illness at bay. Laughter, for example, brings about profound changes in many parts of the body – it relaxes the muscles, increases blood flow to the peripheries and stimulates the production of 'feel-good' neurotransmitters which in turn affect other glands." Ibid. 199.

[165] Ibid. 200.

[166] The next chapter will replace this language of interactive systems with a more complex notion of dialectic.

[167] Insight, 585.

operations)[168] are themselves not separate from the interactive organic and neurochemical systems providing the flow of images that evoke questioning.

The notion of interactive systems begins the shift to talking of "action" in an explanatory way, and so on a par with the treatment of "emotions," "images," and "demands." Descriptive accounts of action and emotion are as old as the debates in Classical Philosophy over conflicts between reason and the passions and between intellect and will. The debates usually proceeded using a "faculty psychology" according to which separate powers jostled for control or precedence.[169] But what if the category of action refers to an understanding of linked operations among interrelated systems, occurring as matters of probability?[170]

---

[168] Details about the structure of intentional acts appear in the next chapter.

[169] The experiential basis for talk of conflicts among faculties is retrievable today in common-sense views of human agency. Some of our actions seem well considered, others impulsive, e.g. carefully selecting a birthday present for a friend versus filling up a plate at a buffet line or overlooking a faux pas by an acquaintance versus enjoying a rival's humiliating gaffe. We tend to esteem the former types of actions more highly and "own" them as more representative of us. Still, actions of the latter type sometimes "trump" our better judgments. How do we account for such lapses? A division of "powers" or faculties within us that can war with one another was part of a traditional response.

[170] Carter comes close to talking in this new way about what faculty psychology described as a battle between reason and the passions. "One reason that emotion has such an overwhelming effect on us is because there are more upward neuronal pathways from the limbic system, where emotional salience is evaluated, than there are pathways going down from the cortex. Where you have a connection between two brain areas which process information in conflicting ways, they act rather like a seesaw – the one that sends out the strongest signals inhibits the other. With more outward-leading pathways, the limbic system can more easily overcome

From a bottom-up perspective, the previous remarks about interactions between the nervous system and the immune system exemplify how the probability of illness can vary according to emotional states. These claims are relevant to understanding action: emotional states can effect changes in organic and neurochemical processes that are preparatory to action.

> Fearful stimuli, for example, produce muscle tension, adrenalin release, and an increase in blood pressure and heart rate; while attractive stimuli stimulate the release of neurotransmitters like dopamine or oxytocin. These internal 'motions' produce activation in the 'intentional' areas of the brain, where actions are prepared. These may in turn 'knock on' to the motor cortex itself, producing either those faint muscular twitches, or – if the activation is strong enough – overt action.[171]

While talk of "preparing actions" is fairly vague, a promising line of inquiry would be to work out the probabilities for certain types of actions among certain populations given exposure to certain types of images and the emotional "cascades" they tend to evoke. Such an inquiry would be easiest when dealing with reflex actions. The variables would increase rapidly for inquiries into non-reflex actions. But recall that the sequence from demand to image to emotion to action is reversible. So deliberate actions manipulating images may evoke emotions and so "move" others to act because of already established patterns among demands, emotions and actions. Commercial advertisers and political campaign directors appear to have some success in doing "rough estimates" of what types of action they can influence by what types of images they use.

---

cortical activity than vice versa." Exploring Consciousness, 200-201.
[171] Ibid. 199.

Diagram 2.1 portrays this two-directional flow among the four basic categories. It depicts both bottom-up and top-down "determinants" of action.

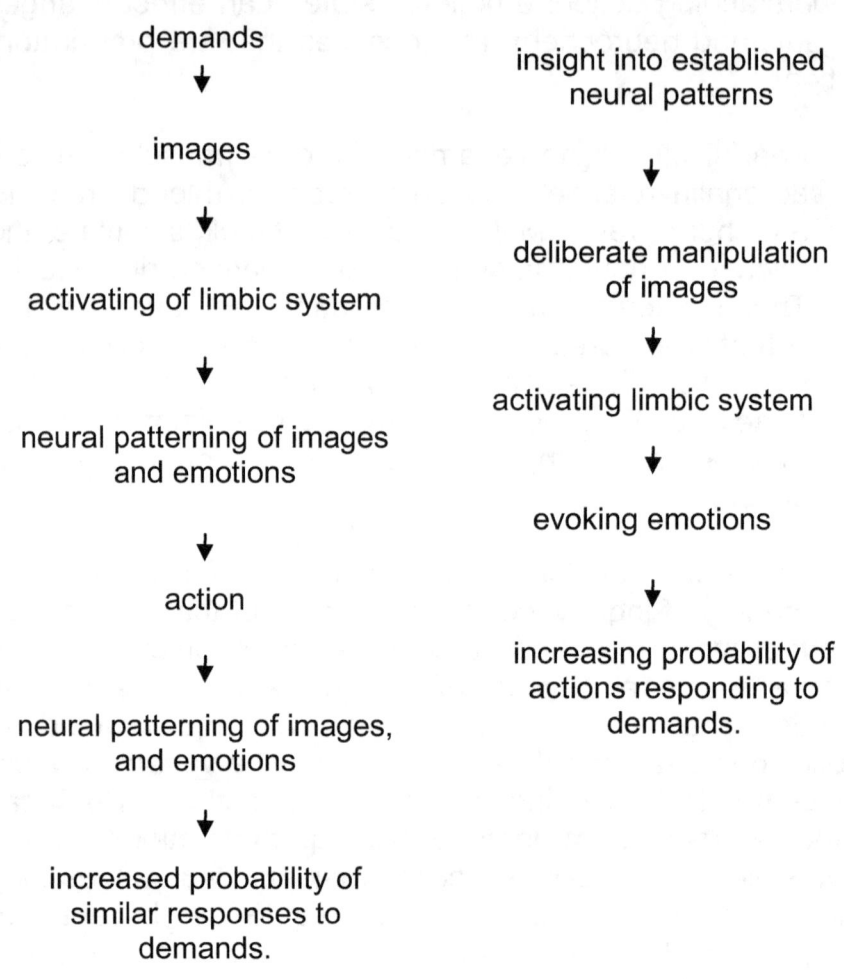

(Diagram 2.1)

Chapter One took a step toward a top-down perspective on action by describing attending as an "intentional act." Now, perhaps, the term has more meaning. In the first place, paying attention and the fourth category, action, are not separate types of events if we recognize that a "completed" act of attention involves not only the passivity (*motus*) of arousal but also the selectivity or active "movement" (*movens*) of focus. An action is something that not only happens to or "moves" a person; it is also something that a person does. What is assumed here, and previously, is that human sensibility is partly receptivity and partly an active "orientation" for internalizing and potentially manipulating environments.[172] One implication for an explanatory account of the fourth category, "action," is that it is bipolar. From a bottom-up perspective, action is a determinate response to antecedent demands, images and emotions; from a top-down perspective, it can precipitate new images, emotions, demands and further actions, even going so far as to alter its own antecedent conditions.[173]

The argument for an active orientation that revises its own conditions can be made both in pragmatic terms and by reference to "higher-order" operations of fantasizing and creativity.[174] First, pragmatic actions that respond to environmental dangers and that exploit available resources contribute to the survival of an organism. What prompts them

---

[172] To speak of human sensibility as "internalizing environments" assumes that images are parts of sensitively integrated environments which are part of our central nervous system. Contemporary psychology of perception easily defends this stance with clinical cases and experimental results.

[173] This claim will reappear in later chapters as part of a refining of the provisional meaning of liberty.

[174] Ramachandran's view of free will expands beyond what we mean here by "active orientation." "Free will – the capacity to plan open-ended scenarios and try out even improbable scenarios entirely in the mind by juggling images and symbols – if linked with episodic memories, enables you to see yourself as an active agent doing things in the future (or past) and thereby generating a full-fledged sense of self." A Brief Tour of Human Consciousness, 111. In the next chapter this description of active agency will reappear as a first approximation of the meaning of creative understanding.

is in part the biologically preset or trained orientation of sensibility toward images associated with such threats and rewards. But as available resources change, so must the actions that promote an organism's survival if it is to survive. The fact of survival in the face of significant environmental changes is evidence of an active orientation. Second, images as representations of inner and outer environments can provide direction for planning and potential actions. So, while images may signal danger and reward, they also may be the fantasies presenting "different options of action, different scenarios, different outcomes of action. We can pick and choose the most appropriate and reject the bad ones."[175] In sum, sensibility is both a receiving and a doing, and so images are the products of both receptivity and activity. The benefits of images lie in evading dangers and pursuing rewards but also in inventing solutions to problems and, through fantasy and action, creating new environments.

V Summary

This chapter has worked out explanatory correlations among emotions, images, demands and actions. It began with descriptive examples drawn from a variety of fields that identified two puzzles: How do emotions and images prompt actions? Why are there relations of dependency among actions, images and emotions? Along the way note was made of how the relations are reversible since deliberate actions can manipulate images and emotions. This reversibility set up a parallelism between this chapter's account of emotions and images and the previous chapter's inclusion of a top-down perspective on acts of attending.

To reconstruct the steps to solving the first puzzle from a bottom-up perspective: psychic demands of two types (reflex and trained) are a reaching for images which, when responsive to demands, produce increased activity in the limbic system and evoke emotions. Repeated links among

---

[175] Damasio, 24.

demands, images and emotions lay down neural patterns or expectations so that some affect-laden images become the "inspiring symbols" or motivating signals for overt actions. From a top-down perspective, deliberate acts manipulating images (e.g. commercial advertizing strategies) can evoke emotions already associated with those images because of their previous responsiveness to demands. In other words, the manipulated images are already part of neural patterns or expectations in some audience. To complete the circuit -- such deliberate acts, through the mediating images, emotions and demands, can prompt new actions, e.g. purchasing the advertized items.

Both perspectives can be translated into talk of interactive systems, e.g. neurochemical, biological and psychological schemes of recurrence. The model for such talk has been the interdependence of human sensibility and understanding. In brief, understanding presupposes questioning, and questioning presupposes sensitive presentations that are the "puzzling data" prompting inquiry. To reverse the sequence -- understanding can question how to improve a situation, and the exercise of creative fantasy can produce new imaginative possibilities that, through action, can become new sensitive presentations, e.g. the designed and constructed playground where once there was a garbage-filled lot.

Reviewing the interdependence of sensibility and understanding was a step toward "deepening" Henry Adams' question: What images can effectively appeal to sensibility to cooperate with intelligent planning and acting? No effort was made to find a specific answer to this question since the limited purpose was to consider again the puzzle from Chapter One about a top-down "ordering of lower-level conditions. A demonstration of such "ordering" followed in the deliberate shift from describing images and emotions to treating the four basic categories as explanatory correlates. In doing so, the previous accounts of orientation and selectivity in attending to things were "deepened." For example, psychic demands for appropriate images ground fluctuating activities in the emotional centers of the brain; with repetition neural patterns emerge linking types of demands, images and emotions, patterns that provide increasingly reliable signals for appropriate actions. In addition, talk of a reversal of this sequence and of interactive systems marked an advance over previous accounts of how mental acts could effect changes in an organism and its neurochemical processes. Deliberate manipulation of images can initiate a predictable "cascade" of neural demands linked to emotional responses increasing the probability of certain types of actions.

How have the preceding pages been relevant to the questions of liberty and intentional acts? As was noted in the Introduction, a historical and methodological strategy dictated these two brief surveys of some findings of neuroscientists. Historically the priorities in studying human action have shifted from metaphysics (Aristotle on motion) to epistemology (Descartes' puzzle on motion between separate types of "substances") and from cognitive psychology (including twentieth-century depth psychology with its latent determinants of understanding) to intentionality theory and neuroscience with its discoveries about the neurochemical and biological conditions for conscious operations. Methodologically it seems appropriate to acknowledge this cultural journey and to begin an account of liberty and intentional acts at the level of current scientific achievement. Thus, these first two chapters have identified and tried to understand some of the basic conditions for human actions: neurochemical and organic processes in Chapter One and, in Chapter Two, neuropsychological and biographical variables interacting with those processes.

Throughout this inquiry there is an ongoing effort to "deepen" the analysis of the puzzle about top-down control over lower-order conditions. The "turn" called for in the neurosciences (and its absence lamented by Posner) marked the first statement of the puzzle. The descriptive notion of interactive systems provided a clue as to how we might reformulate the puzzle. Eventually more will be said about a flexible range of a series of schemes of recurrence operating according to probabilities. What will guide changes in how the puzzle is formulated is the model of interdependency between human sensibility and intelligence.[176] The model offers three advantages: (1) it is verifiable in the performance of inquirers; (2) it is presupposed by whatever conclusions scholars reach about decision-making (i.e. they will have made judgments about their understanding of some data); (3) it keeps open the possibility of reversed sequencing of the pattern beginning with neurochemical processes and achieving completion with deliberate planning and acting.

So far there have been only descriptive examples of reversed sequencing or top-down control. No attempt has yet been made to explain how this might be possible. Still, the examples by themselves amount to more than an appeal to folk psychology. Consider how the interactivity of the nervous system and the immune system affects the probabilities of illness and health. Similarly the probabilities of good decisions and bad decisions vary with the relations among prior conditions, e.g. attentiveness, images, demands and emotions. The question, then, is whether deliberate, even if only partial, control over these variables can alter the probabilities of certain decisions being made.

To some readers this may all seem a belaboring of the obvious. Clearly cultural phenomena such as economic markets, political institutions, the various arts, sciences and speculative systems require, but are not reducible to, basic capacities for sensory representation, attentiveness, emotion and action. After all, other species have such basic capacities without producing such cultural realities. If these basic capacities studied in the neurosciences do not account for the latter, we must add to the list. Yet to name and to describe these "higher" capacities (e.g. language, reason, reflexive consciousness, creative understanding) is far from explaining

---

[176] In the next chapter this model (indebted to faculty psychology for its terms) will be translated into a dialectic between related but opposed principles of development (completion) and stability (assimilation).

what they are and how they form differentiated systems interacting with lower-order ones. The next chapter pursues an explanatory account of the last capacity, creative understanding.

In keeping with the claim in Chapter One that explanatory accounts require "increasingly complex series of images or diagrams to track insights into complex relations," this part of the chapter concludes with a "mapping" of its basic categories and their relations.

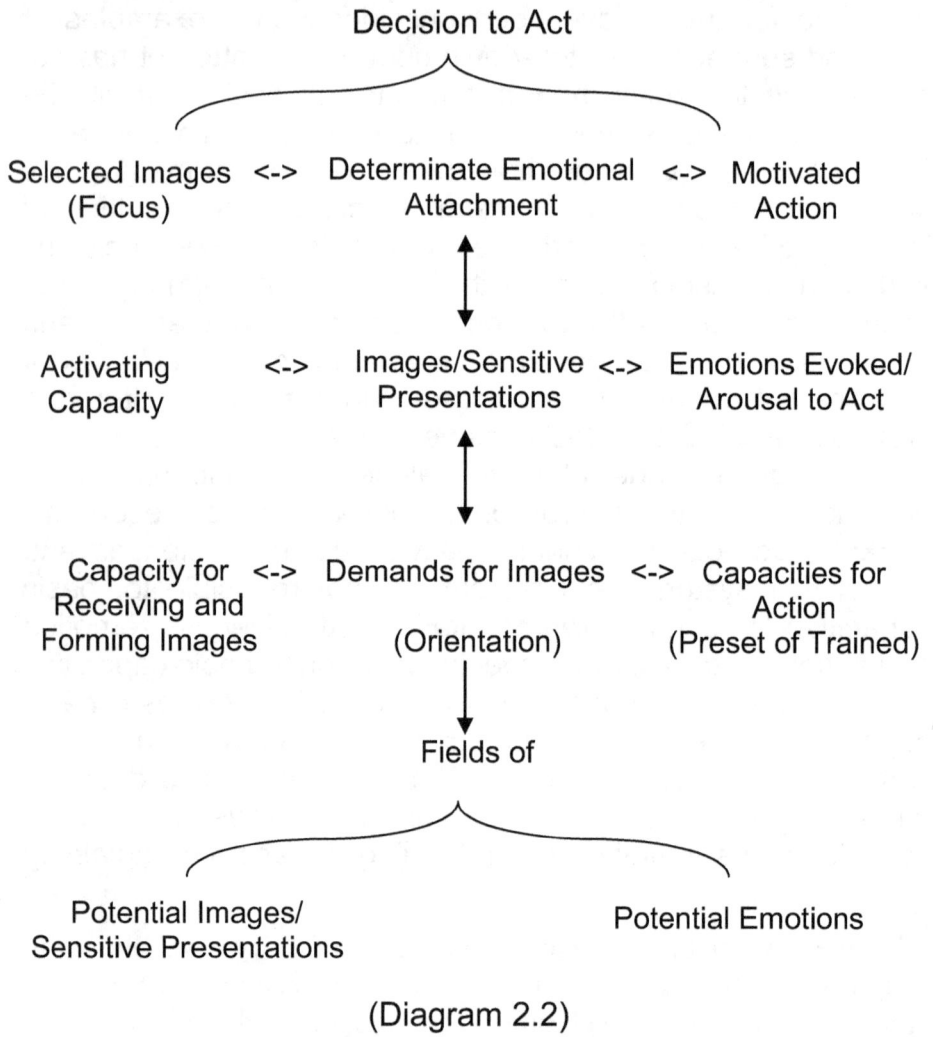

(Diagram 2.2)

VI A Puzzle from Neuropathology

Do philosophers have anything to say that is worth the attention of neuroscientists? Perhaps the test lies in whether they can offer a few new insights into puzzles already familiar to specialists in these fields. Thus, Chapter One ended with an analysis of Libet's Puzzle suggesting, first, how an oversight of the mixing of theoretical and common-sense perspectives and their terms led to the puzzle and, second, what it would take to reconcile theoretical conclusions and common-sense objections. This chapter concludes with a puzzle drawn from neuropathology and applies to it some of the preceding insights into relations among acts of attention, emotions and images. The limited purpose in doing so is to test the utility of explanatory correlations for more precisely wording this type of puzzle.

The general pathological condition is prosopagnosia, i.e. " the inability to recognize faces despite intact visual recognition of most other stimuli."[177] Our puzzle appears within this general disorder and is conventionally labeled "covert face recognition in prosopagnosia." Damasio presents the general clinical description.

> When a face-agnosic patient...is shown, in random presentation, faces of people whom she has never met as well as faces of close relatives and friends, and when we simultaneously record her skin conductance with a polygraph, a dramatic dissociation takes place. To her conscious mind, the faces are all equally unrecognizable. Friends, relatives, and the truly unfamiliar generate the same void, and nothing comes to mind to permit the discovery of their identity. And yet, the presentation of virtually every face of a friend or relative generates a distinct skin-conductance response, while unknown faces do not. None of these

---

[177] Martha J. Farah, Visual Agnosia, 2nd ed. (Cambridge: MIT Press, 2004), 92.

responses is noticed by the patient. Moreover, the magnitude of the skin conductance response is higher for the closest of relatives.[178]

The diagnosis is straightforward. The patient is able to distinguish faces from other objects, so the relevant images are understood to be those of determinate objects, i.e. faces as opposed to hands. Yet the faces are not recognized in the sense that the patient does not differentiate between familiar and unfamiliar ones. Nevertheless, the patient does differentiate them at some lower level given the evidence of skin-conductance responses.

At a descriptive level, the inference is that some sort of "monitoring" of images is occurring beneath the level of conscious operation. Such monitoring is no surprise to those familiar with twentieth-century depth psychology. But speculation about unconscious processing of images usually has few "controls" over its language. Jungians appeal to a universal unconscious and its archetypes. Freud had his metaphor of a censor approving some images for admission to consciousness and deleting or disguising others. His thesis in regard to dream construction is unexplained but undeniable: some of the most creative achievements of the human mind go forward without the aid of consciousness. But how are these amazing dream images with their masks and improbable combinations explainable?

The question invites endless speculation, but the puzzle of covert face recognition may offer some clues on how to handle it. A first step was taken in Chapter One when a complete act of attending was understood as having three distinct phases: orientation, arousal and focus. While a complete act of attention occurs in "focus," i.e. with the recognition of an object as something determinate, the prior category of orientation refers to an understanding of how established neural patterns provide a determinate capacity for guiding acts of attention. That is, such neural patterns make it

---

[178] The Feeling of What Happens, 300.

more probable that, from amid the flood of potential images, those of significance will receive attention. If arousal is dependent on stimuli and so an instance of receptivity, focus is both a receptivity and an activity. Stimuli (images in the broad sense) evoke attentive responses, but orientation, as sedimented neural patterns, actively directs attention to some images rather than to others. In addition, the preceding analysis of the category of emotion suggested how neural patterns could be "weighted" in favor of some images over others.

How do these earlier findings make a more precise analysis of our puzzle possible? In cases of covert face recognition, patients show no awareness of one face being more significant than another, but attached skin sensors indicate some subliminal recognition of differences. If we think of orientation as neural patterns capable of directing attention and if we understand that emotional "weight" attaches to some images rather than to others, then what is occurring in covert recognition is a latent linkage of neural patterns with images. Under ordinary circumstances the result would be explicit recognition of a close relative's face by the viewer. This would happen because the image of a familiar face would "fit" the established neural pattern (or expectation) already disposed or emotionally weighted to single out and attend to such an image. Additionally the viewer would actively integrate the image with the pattern and so "complete" the act of attention, and, thus, the "fit," much like a feeling, would be recognized. Notice this does not mean the viewer will report any emotional response or any awareness of having been guided to the recognized image. Such a response and linking are not objects of attention. Again, we are normally inattentive to many of our emotional states and expectations though both affect our selection of and attention to images.

What are the implications of the preceding summary? Clearly covert face recognition in prosopagnosia represents a deviation from what normally happens in the presence of familiar, emotionally weighted images, i.e. recognition;[179] Still, these cases reflect a continuance of the usual state of inattentiveness to most orientations and emotions and a continuance of the usual, unconscious neural processing of images for their "fit" with established patterns or expectations. What the skin conductance results indicate is that the "usual state of inattentiveness" and the "usual, unconscious neural processing of images" are present in the test subjects without the act of attention being completed.

Without using the metaphors of "monitoring," "censor" and "mask," these comments indicate how a complete act of attention does not occur even though some of its prior conditions are fulfilled, namely, the presence of a familiar image (arousal) and a prior neural pattern for registering it (orientation). What is missing is the final component of attention, focus, ordinarily occurring because of a recognized "fit" between an image and an established neural pattern. In its absence, the patient cannot report a "fit" between the image and an established neural pattern, i.e. cannot recognize the familiar face as familiar.

What prevents the linkage? Farah surveys a variety of hypotheses.[180] She includes her own position which "posits that covert recognition reflects the residual processing capabilities of a damaged, but not obliterated, visual face recognition system."[181] I suggest these "residual processing capabilities" may be those described in Chapter One as being routinely activated by stimuli within the orienting and arousal networks of acts of attention. By themselves they do not complete an act of attention.

What prevents the completion? Perhaps the damage is not, as Farah suggests, to the "visual recognition system." Much as in Ramachandran's case of Arthur, the disorder may

---

[179] "Prosopagnosic patients who manifest covert recognition appear to lack the subjective experience of recognition, at least for many of the faces for which they show covert recognition." Farah, 111.
[180] Ibid. 111-118.
[181] Ibid. 112.

be in the limbic system or in the linkage between the two systems. Ordinarily a familiar face generates more activity in the limbic system than an unfamiliar one. As noted above, when affective attachments or associations occur between particular types of images and neural patterns, the presentation of the "weighted" images begins a cascade of neural activities and chemical releases producing organic changes that are the immediate substrate for psychological experiences of emotion and feeling. In covert face recognition, there are electrochemical indicators that such a cascade begins; however, the subliminal integration of image and affect is not completed in a conscious act of attention or recognition.

Noted above was that emotion plays a fundamental role in directing attention by signaling that an image is significant. By helping "select" significant images, emotion supplies the "drive" or demand for greater attention. On the other hand, when emotional responses are low or indifferent, the signals sent are that something is irrelevant or unimportant, and so neural and organic systems do not respond further. Apparently what happens in covert face recognition is that neural activity relevant to feelings is insufficient to demand greater attention and so to prompt further responses from neural and organic systems. As a result, a familiar face is not recognized because its significance has not been felt. The failure here is more likely to be due to some breakdown, not within the visual recognition system, but in the limbic system or in the pathways between the systems.

CHAPTER THREE

What Is Creative Understanding?

I Introduction

The preliminary map for this inquiry was a sequence of four questions. The first was the question of diagnosis and led to the study of what it means to pay attention. The second was the question of motivation and led to a study of the role of emotion and image in motivating action. This chapter takes up the third question, the question for deliberation. When deliberating over options, or possible ends and means, we are engaging in intentional acts, i.e. mental operations that have as their objects possible actions and outcomes or possible means and ends.[182] How such operations are linked to images and emotions is not totally obscure.[183] For example, intentional acts operate on images since the latter are what prompt questioning, and, as concluded in previous chapters, persons attend to images depending on their emotional

---

[182] The broad meaning of "object" here is "the referred content of an intentional act...." Bernard Lonergan. Philosophical and Theological Papers: 1965-1980, Collected Works Vol. 17 (Toronto: University of Toronto Press, 2004), 22.

[183] Obscurity does surround how images are a prerequisite to understanding. Aristotle taught that insight into phantasm or image was a psychological fact grounding his alternative to Plato's Forms. (De Anima, III, 7, 431b, 2) What this inquiry has found so far is that intentional acts involve (1) an intelligent organism relating to images, and (2) the latter causing a change in the former (Damasio, The Feeling of What Happens, 133). As a result, we were able to talk of attention and action as both activity and receptivity. Obscurity remains, however, regarding how images contribute to the "construction" of ideas and how acts of understanding "abstract" the meaning of images to form ideas. If we reject the "obscurantism" that denies such puzzles exist, a realistic appraisal of contemporary cognitive psychology is that the discipline is still in its infancy.

"weight" or salience for those persons. Again, responsiveness to salient data may be reflexive or trained. Caring about some things more than others can become habitual so that one's orientation is highly alert to certain sights and sounds already associated with the objects of one's care, e.g. a parent's sensitivity to the sound of a child's voice. Contrary to a notion of consciousness as only receptive, the evidence is that the contents of consciousness are largely due to the orientation of consciousness itself.[184]

The objects of deliberative acts are usually imagined scenarios or anticipated possibilities. Thus, there is an element of creativity or fantasy in even the most routine planning. But, it did not require twentieth-century depth psychology to alert persons to the ambiguity of fantasies, dreams and imagined futures. As correlates of demands and emotions, images are intertwined with cultural, biographical and biological variables. As a result, all sorts of bizarre links between images and subsequent actions can and do occur. Psychotherapists record some of these; the last century showed the brutal consequences of political fantasies acted upon to the detriment of millions. Thus, the objects of deliberative acts are in need of criticism. How is such criticism possible? This question was already implicit when, after noting that emotion-laden images can support or impede intelligent planning and acting, we went on to ask what images "matched" our best judgments about what to do. One of the difficulties in answering this question is that we are largely unaware of the latent demands and their correlates,

---

[184] "Consciousness is not determined simply by the object. We have spoken of *Sorge*, concern, as the root of one's world, and also of a selective inattention that ignores what lies beyond one's horizon. Consciousness itself has a fundamental freedom; it is independent of biological and neural determinants. It is in that sense, it seems to me, that Heidegger speaks mainly of freedom, the freedom of the flow of percepts, the determination of one's world by one's *Sorge* or concern." Bernard Lonergan. Understanding and Being CW 5 (Toronto: University of Toronto Press, 1990), 228.

emotionally weighted images, that make up our own orientations or established neural patterns. How are we even to access these orientations, not to mention criticizing and perhaps changing them?[185] Even if we access them, there remains the added difficulty that they tend to be "stored" in the limbic system rather than in the cortex and so are less readily open to correction by new insights.[186] Hence, we experience the resistance of acquired prejudices and phobias to subsequent correction. By extension, we can account for some people's blindness to available options because of prior dispositions or habits rooted in links between images and emotions.

A first puzzle, then, about the relation of creative understanding to planning and action will be the question of how the former can overcome latent, emotionally weighted dispositions that block some images and so evade some insights and options.[187] Pursuing this puzzle and others will begin, as before, with descriptions of some basic terms and examples and then move toward translating them into explanatory categories and accounts. Part II will begin this process, and Part III will work out three approximations as to what we mean by "creative understanding." In doing so, a notion of dialectic will emerge modeled on but surpassing the previous correlation of human sensibility and intelligence as

---

[185] "Whatever one might think of psychoanalysis, it has at least made one great contribution to the world – the recognition that you have to access unconscious beliefs if you want to change them. This is the basis of nearly all psychotherapy." Carter, Exploring Consciousness, 202.

[186] Recall the remarks in Chapter Two on the implications of the priority of sensibility over intelligence.

[187] The assumptions here are: (1) the recognition of options requires insights; (2) insights are into images; (3) to avoid unwanted insights, persons block the images that could prompt the insights. Cf. Insight, 216-217.

well as talk of interactive systems.[188] Part IV will use the developed meaning of creative understanding to introduce a dialectical notion of liberty. All of this is background for Chapter Four where the complex institutional settings for deliberation and action appear for the first time.

II Descriptions of Creative Understanding

Relating the earlier category of orientation to creative understanding is a way of specifying a provisional meaning of the latter. Adding descriptive examples of both terms will further specify this provisional meaning. First, creative understanding is a capacity for innovative thought and action or for new insights and performance; and, second, a person's actual orientation is a historical determination of what initially are largely indeterminate capacities. As a general capacity, creative understanding is first an indeterminate potential for pursuing an indefinite number of possible means and ends. Repeated performance gradually "trains" this capacity so that it becomes a determinate, even skilled, capacity for future performance. Eventually a person routinely performs tasks at a particular level of skill and is predisposed or orientated to act at that level. Orientation becomes a relatively stable and predictable pattern for handling familiar tasks. For example, training and skill-acquisition allow one to dispense with explicit deliberation and to perform with ease and efficiency tasks that previously required concentration and delay. So the "saves" by a professional tennis player seem miraculous to the average viewer but simply evidence of skill to veteran players and courtside commentators.

Instead of the "training of orientation," we more commonly speak of the "forming of habits." Habits contribute to the experience of psychological continuity in the sense that

---

[188] The language of "sensibility" and "intelligence" has been used to this point despite its link to faculty psychology. Only gradually will a new terminology appear along with arguments for its superiority over more traditional language.

certain actions become more likely once patterns among types of actions are routine. However, creative understanding and habit may seem an ill-fitting pair. Usually we expect a creative person to break the "crust of convention," to depart from routines, to surprise us with novelties. However, these expectations are compatible with habits. First, by "habit" we mean an orientation to act in some ways rather than others because repeated acts have developed previously indeterminate capacities in determinate ways. To use an analogy, once rains have carved out passages down a hillside, the next rains are likely to produce flows down those same pathways. In decision-making, future choices that are consistent with past choices are more probable than inconsistent ones. For instance, in deliberating creative persons will predictably review options beyond the short list occurring to less creative persons. Random deviations can occur, but, if creative persons were to settle for purely conventional options, they would be acting contrary to their habitual performance. Thus, talk of habits becomes talk of probabilities, and so prior training can make it more predictable, more probable, that one population will continue to be more creative than another.[189]

    Still, there is a more complex puzzle here about creativity, habits and action. To introduce it, consider the distinction between a snapshot and a film clip. The former captures a single gesture or act while the latter covers a range of antecedents to and consequences of a single action. We tend to applaud the creative gesture and credit the one making it. Yet, in acting, persons presumably control what they do here and now (the snapshot), but the antecedents and consequences (the film clip) are largely beyond their control. To shift back to the language of orientation and habit – actions occur in "context" or are dependent on an indefinite number of prior and current conditions affecting what actions will occur

---

[189] The talk here of "populations" is intentional: probabilities and predictions based on them are applicable to "runs of cases" or populations, not to individual cases.

and what consequences will follow from them. Some of these conditions will be personal and vary with biographical contingencies; others will be impersonal and vary with sociohistorical circumstances. Both types of conditions supply creative persons with their concrete contexts for acting. One person's context may include the personal dispositions cited previously as the refined sensibilities of the artist, the detective or the medical diagnostician. But another person's context for operating may include the inclinations of the sociopath or the habits of the inveterate liar. Among the impersonal conditions of someone's context may be stable economic and political institutions allowing persons to take reasonable risks in investing and signing contracts. However, another social context might be anarchic, and actions taken with one set of consequences in mind might often produce wholly different outcomes.

Such variable conditions are the basis for two insights about creative planning and actions. First, both occur as matters of probability. That is, which options persons think of and which ones can be realistically pursued are dependent on non-systematic relations among an indefinite number of variables. Second, actions, as some medievals noted, are instances of agents being both moved and moving (*et motus et movens*); or as the previous chapter phrased it, action is both receptivity and activity.

To link these two insights in responding to the opening puzzle about "creative control" over or ordering of latent conditions, consider how even bad habits are no more than one type of antecedent to current action. Admittedly, repeated past acts "fix" present orientations, and the latter predispose persons to think of and to choose some options rather than others. But the anticipated intelligibility of actions they might take will be in the form of probabilities, i.e. <u>ideal</u> frequencies, and the intelligibility of actions they do take will be in the form of <u>actual</u> frequencies.[190] Again, non-systematic deviations

---

[190] Recall the discussion in Chapter One, Part IV on non-systematic relations, schemes of recurrence and emergence.

from well-established, highly probable patterns do occur. If someone asks why this happens, the answer requires insight into the difference between systematic and non-systematic relations among variables. If someone asks for evidence that this does happen, a re-spondent could cite examples of how divergences from habitual ways of choosing and acting occur because of changes in knowledge, e.g. learning about their new health problems leads some persons to change their eating habits. What begins as a departure from entrenched patterns may in time become a new pattern or habit. The key insight is to note how changes in knowledge may depend upon someone raising and answering new questions. But new questions and new answers occur as matters of probability and have as much claim as old habits to being potential antecedents to planning and action.[191]

This talk of probabilities governing the relations among deliberating, choosing and acting is a way of: (1) introducing a new category, "historicity," and (2) abandoning use of the descriptive category, "mechanism."

"Historicity" is a further specification of the terms "context" and "latent conditions." If we understand biographical and sociohistorical conditions affecting choices to be largely unrecognized, the claim that "history goes on over our heads" will make sense. First, we are born at a place and time that antecedent events have already molded beyond anyone's complete understanding. The details of individual biographies are mostly lost to memory. Which of those personal details and antecedent events have the greatest influence over current deliberating and acting will remain guesswork for even astute historians. Someone once remarked about English-speakers that, when they talk about themselves, they are indebted to William Shakespeare. What

---

[191] This claim will reappear several times as part of a key thesis that (1) actions are responses to demands; (2) along with neural, biological and psychological demands, persons experience the demands of the intentional operators that (3) can be determinate conditions for planning and action.

is true of our speaking is true of our imagining of possibilities, our deliberating over options and our responding to images. All along the line, we operate largely unaware of the degree of our indebtedness. Descriptively, then, historicity refers to an understanding of how our thinking, speaking and acting are situated in biographical and sociohistorical contexts, about which our understanding is always incomplete.[192]

Why should talk of probabilities lead to abandoning talk about mechanisms? As a variation on Descartes' "evil genius," some have held that the historical conditioning of human thinking and acting is a type of latent control over both. In speaking of such control, they have employed metaphors from an eighteenth-century deterministic worldview which recognized only systematic relations among events. Even today talk of mechanisms survives in accounts in neurobiology, psychology and sociology, perhaps because we lack a well-developed language for talking about non-systematic relations among types of objects and events.[193]

The absence of such a developed terminology was part of the earlier difficulty in talking about the "turn" to a top-down analysis of intentional acts and their effects on biological and neurochemical processes. The first response to that difficulty was in terms of "interactive systems."[194] Evidence of how interactions between the nervous system and the immune system affected the probability of illness provided an empirical basis for this alternative language. Still, showing that psychological states (emotions) can have effects on biological processes (immune responses) is not the same as showing higher intentional acts can "control" lower-order processes. To remedy this deficiency, Chapter Two introduced a model of

---

[192] Some have argued from the incompleteness of our understanding to an epistemological relativism. The claims above are not an endorsement of this conclusion, but the debates over this issue are beyond the limits of this work.

[193] See footnotes 82 and 90 in Chapter One for further conjectures about the longevity of the term "mechanism."

[194] See Chapter Two, Part IV.

interactivity based on the relation between sensibility and intelligence. The supposition was that, as a matter-of-fact, we develop in understanding and improve our deliberate acting by raising and answering questions about puzzling images and sensitive presentations. From a "bottom-up" perspective, we would have nothing to question without the lower-order contents of human sensibility, and so intellectual and practical development would not occur. From a "top-down" perspective, actual developments in understanding and practice can improve the operations of sensibility. Some of the evidence was from Kolers' famous experiments in apparent motion. The professional training of engineers made them more alert and attentive and less likely to report the mistaken readings of apparent motion given by other test subjects.

While these earlier pages discussed at some length the role of images and sensitive presentations in evoking attention and emotional responses (as part of a series of correlations among demands, responsive images, emotional attachments and evoked actions), little mention was made of the role of acts of understanding in evoking these types of events. Before moving toward an explanatory account of creative understanding, we can survey a few descriptive accounts of such acts.

In the 1980s Howard Gardner presented his theory of multiple intelligences, partly in criticism of conventional views of intelligence as some single capacity (measurable by standardized I.Q. tests) and partly in response to research suggesting intellectual competences were multiple and relatively independent of one another.[195] The varied examples he cited (e.g. navigating by the stars, composing music on a synthesizer, memorizing and teaching the Koran) seem to assume that intelligence is a matter of demonstrable

---

[195] Howard Gardner. Frames of Mind (New York: Basic Books, 1983).

skill or ability.[196] He contrasted these varied performances with a classical Greek view of rationality as the differentiating or essential property of the human species. The subsequent emphasis in Western civilization on rationality promoted the idea that intelligence was a singular and defining characteristic of humankind.[197] Opposing views emphasizing multiple modes of human understanding were not lacking over the centuries, and Gardner saw his task as one of confronting the classical view with mounting evidence in support of the latter. His sources were diverse: "studies of prodigies, gifted individuals, brain-damaged patients, *idiots savants*, normal children, normal adults, experts in different lines of work, and individuals from diverse cultures."[198] Additional findings from cognitive and developmental psychology bolstered his case for multiple intelligences as well as for his recommended educational reforms.

Gardner was the first to admit that "the idea of multiple intelligences is an old one, and [he could] scarcely claim any

---

[196] Ibid. 5-6. Damasio seems to assume the same identification of intelligence and skill when he remarks: "…intelligence pertains to the ability to manipulate knowledge so successfully that novel responses can be planned and delivered." The Feeling of What Happens. 198-199. The descriptive classifications that follow this review of Gardner's stance offer alternatives to the view that intelligence is equivalent to practical skills.

[197] The Classical Greek account was not unaware of multiplicity. "Intelligence" in operation had at least five distinct ends: "it is *nous*, grasping the point; *epistêmê*, grasping its implications; reflective *sophia* and *phronêsis*, understanding what is and what is to be done, and finally *technê*, grasping how to do it." Lonergan. Verbum, 193. It is this last usage (*technê*) that has come to dominate contemporary academic discussions of intelligence or understanding as "instrumental rationality." Outside the academy, usage retains some of the broader meanings. For example, "understanding" will sometimes occur in the sense of sympathy and even love as in, "I wish my friends were more understanding."

[198] Gardner, 9.

great originality for attempting to revive it once more."[199] Most of the competing theories of intelligence can be classified under three types. The easiest to describe are <u>pragmatic</u> theories of thinking. In keeping with Max Weber's notion of "instrumental rationality," these theories define intelligence as the capacity to use effective means to achieve preferred ends. Examples of problem-solving skills are abundant - everything from successfully changing a flat tire to improving factory productivity. Determining how intelligent a practice is requires measuring the efficiency of the means in producing the preferred outcome. By extension, then, creative understanding would be the ability to invent new and more efficient means for achieving selected ends.

A second type of theory of intelligence has become associated with what Paul Ricoeur called the "hermeneutic of suspicion." The shared thesis among the practitioners of this hermeneutic is that our thinking is under the control of latent conditions we scarcely recognize. As a result, we usually remain under the illusion that we are in charge of our own minds and are the masters of what we believe, say and do. Several varieties of this <u>illusionist</u> view of intelligence have reached a wide audience. Freud posited hidden traumas and repressed wishes as the real determinants of our thinking and acting. Access to these latent forces is possible principally through dream interpretation, but even then careful inquiry meets the resistance of the censor which masks painful memories and disturbing desires. In effect, intelligence seems divided against itself since its explicit desire to understand is repeatedly thwarted by subterfuges deployed in the service of other desires. In dreams, Freud noted, the most creative achievements of the human mind occur without the aid of consciousness. One implication for the meaning of creative intelligence is that its workings are partly latent and independent of deliberate control.

Two nineteenth-century figures, Marx and Nietzsche, offered variations on the Cartesian hypothesis of an evil

---

[199] Ibid. 11.

genius intent on manipulating mental operations. Marx held that class interests largely directed how persons thought about basic social issues of family, work, property laws and religion. Nietzsche proposed a will to power as the driving force behind all forms of life. In his critique of popular morality, Nietzsche argued that this amoral will was the source of doctrines of equality and justice as fairness. In effect, the high moral ideals of modern cultures had their origins in the will to power of the weak type of persons trying to control their natural masters. But then creative understanding appears to serve goals which usually remain hidden from consciousness, and so, again, its workings seem to be partly subterranean and independent of deliberate control.

A third type of theory of intelligence has had its philosophical proponents from Plato to Heidegger. The original meaning of *theoria* as contemplation is a clue to understanding this view of intelligence as fundamentally meditative. Humans are the type of beings for whom their own being is in question. That is, we witness the coming into being and the passing away of things and ask questions about all this transiency. Responses to these questions tend to be the "cover stories" or myths by which entire cultures define their existence.[200] Given the endless variety of myths, we might conclude that creative understanding is the ability to invent marvelous narratives about the meaningfulness of our existence in time. Quite a few commentators read such narratives as "instruments" for maintaining cultural identity and providing consolation in the face of life's hardships. However, this instrumental reading may be assuming that a pragmatic theory is the only realistic view of intelligence and its products. Perhaps a debate between the pragmatic and meditative camps would supply the illusionist viewpoint of intelligence with new evidence for its own stance.

---

[200] For this pattern of transiency, questioning and response, see Eric Voegelin, The Ecumenic Age, Vol. 4, Order and History (Baton Rouge: Louisiana State University Press, 1980), 75.

Such a debate may prove interminable. Henry Adams predicted as much when he commented on the experience of multiplicity in his time. The proliferation of different, often incompatible, theories, interpretations and worldviews has only accelerated since then. What has also grown is a healthy suspicion of "system building" and of claims to provide ultimate accounts of any part of human experience. The suspicion is perhaps born of the horrors in the last century perpetrated by those claiming knowledge of where history was going, of how an economy could be designed to benefit all or of which political order would provide every citizen with liberty and justice. Even without this record of killing for the logic of one's fantasy, our ignorance of so many basic things (e.g. how visual stimuli become recognized images) should incline us to tolerance of diversity.

This is at least one contemporary response to different and sometimes incompatible theories about intelligence and so much more. However, clues to another response were implicit in the preceding chapter when three "abouts" were mentioned. The third use of "about" referred to an understanding of how neuroscientists could make their own performance in studying the neurochemical processes of attention the object of their own attention. That is, they could ask how they were "going about" trying to understand these processes. Their focus of attention, then, would shift to their own intentional acts and their intelligently designed procedures made possible by those processes. To hypothesize: since answers (e.g. theories) proceed from questions, competing theories are products of inquiry; but, if the products are incompatible, perhaps a way of sorting through this multiplicity is to attend to the performance that precedes them. In particular, we might pay attention to the types of questions we raise and try to answer. What follows in Part III is a sketch of such a strategy of attention-to-performance and its implications. The prospects are: (1) to find unity amid multiplicity in regard to what "creative understanding" means, (2) to keep the promise made in Chapter Two to talk about a common structure of intentional acts, and (3) to offer an explanatory account of creative understanding.

III Approximations to the Meaning of Creative Understanding [201]

A first approximation of an explanatory meaning of creative understanding was implicit in Chapter Two. The clue was in Ramachandran's description of free will as "the capacity to plan open-ended scenarios and try out even improbable scenarios entirely in the mind by juggling images and symbols...."[202] The capacity to invent novel fantasies is usually thought the special ability of artists, but the claim here is that all persons exhibit this capacity to varying degrees. If we dream, we are inventing; if we deliberate over how to solve problems, we are fantasizing. Such diverse forms of creative understanding should not be surprising since every act of understanding is synthetic or constructive. The supposition here is that the data of the senses and the data of internal states (feelings and mental acts) provide no more than clues which an inquirer, much like a crime scene investigator, must assemble. In psychology of perception the conventional

---

[201] My use of "approximations" is third-hand. "Newton's planetary theory had a first approximation in the first law of motion; bodies move in a straight line with constant velocity unless some force intervenes. There was a second approximation when the addition of the law of gravity between the sun and the planet yielded an elliptical orbit for the planet. A third approximation was reached when the influence of the gravity of the planets on one another is taken into account to reveal the perturbed ellipses in which the planets actually move. The point to this model is, of course, that in the intellectual construction of reality it is not any of the earlier stages of the construction but only the final product that actually exists." Bernard Lonergan. "Insight Revisited, " in A Second Collection (Philadelphia: The Westminster Press, 1974), 271-272.
[202] A Brief Tour of Human Consciousness. 111; cited in Chapter Two, footnote 170.

reference is to a "principle of supplementation." Initial clues or cues as to what someone is perceiving need integration before they are meaningful. Massive research findings support the claim that mental acts, in ordering and representing data, involve a process of "filling in" and supplementing the data.[203] Simple examples are readily available. Casual reading of a newspaper involves skimming along, filling in and anticipating what the inks marks on the page mean.[204] Just as cases of breakdowns supply clinical psychologists with insights into what is ordinarily taken for granted and ignored, so picking up a text in an unfamiliar language can reveal that the ink marks are no longer "words" for us. What we tend to overlook is that words as meaningful symbols require the synthetic process of integrating the ink marks into intelligible patterns, a process guided by already established patterns.[205]

Motion experiments provide further evidence of supplementing operations in perceiving moving objects.

---

[203] Kolers' research has been cited above. There are also numerous experiments with perceptual illusions, e.g. the Frasier spiral. Oliver Sacks' popular works from his practice of clinical psychology contain examples of the principle of supplementation. See his "To See and Not See," in An Anthropologist on Mars (New York: Vintage Books, 1996), 108-152.

[204] To understand this process of making meaning, it helps to distinguish (1) the ink marks on the page, (2) seen print as a set of neurochemical patterns in the brain that can arouse attention, (3) "focused" on, that is recognized words, as intellectually patterned data-for-consciousness. These distinctions rest on insights preliminary to further puzzling about how we routinely make meaning. The preliminary insights presuppose one of the "displacements" discussed in the next chapter. A test of whether the relevant displacement has occurred, is to ask oneself, "Do I think there are words on the page?" For that matter, one could go on to ask, "Where is the 'page' on which the words seem to appear?"

[205] An easy test of this claim is available at any ATM machine with a braille pad. Are the "bumps" words for most customers?

When a moving target passes across the field of vision[,] it sets up a ripple effect in the visual cortex as edge-detecting neurons fire, one after another, along its trajectory. However, they do not fire when the edge passes across the bit of space they encode, but just before. (...) And so with a moving target – the brain responds 'as though' the object is passing across the space where it will actually be in a fraction of a second's time. If this response is then selected for consciousness[,] the experience will…be of a 'virtual object' – not the actual thing at all.[206]

For a determinate object to come into "focus," there is, first, a time delay between the arrival of visual stimuli in the brain and one's awareness of them, and, second, a constructive or creative process in that time interval by which fragmentary clues are integrated so as to allow recognition of a specific object.[207] The time lag between input and

---

[206] Carter, <u>Exploring Consciousness</u>, 152.

[207] "Consciousness is not immediate – it takes time to be fleshed out. There is a full fifth of a second delay, on average, between the time a visual stimulus arrives at the brain and the time it becomes conscious. And the gap between receiving information about a complicated stimulus and becoming conscious of what it means – that you are in the presence of a person wearing a blue coat, for example, rather than just being in the presence of a large blue form – is about half a second. During this split second, the brain does a phenomenal amount of preconscious work in order to turn a stream of electrical pulses into a conscious sight, sound, emotion, thought or perception. The signals that come into the brain from the sight of a person in blue, for example, are shunted to various parts of the brain where each element is separately dealt with before being put together to form the conscious recognition of the person." Ibid. 25-26. Might this view of consciousness be relevant to the time delays in Libet's puzzle? At least such findings make those time delays unexceptional, and a future explanatory account of consciousness will have to account for them.

recognition is well documented, but puzzles remain about how the creative process of integration occurs. One of these puzzles arises from experiments in apparent motion in which the mind not only "fills in" the object in motion but actually "backdates" the motion so that test subjects report movement along a line toward a new position when, in fact, the light signal from the new position preceded any apparent motion toward it.[208]

Solving such puzzles is a task for a new century of research. A purpose of this chapter is to generalize (find unity) amid the diverse forms of creative understanding. A first approximation, then, is that intentional acts impose unity on fragments; they create unity out of multiplicity. In doing so, they are acts of creative understanding. This is not to say such acts are unconditioned. The previous chapters described a variety of internal and external conditions for intentional operations. Some of these routinely support creative puzzle solving while others (e.g. neurological disorders, brain lesions or anarchic political conditions) prove to be impediments.

Without revisiting those earlier descriptions, we can summarize their general implication for a <u>second approximation</u> of creative understanding: it is a conditioned but flexible range of possible ways of attending to and diagnosing situations, of imagining possible improvements and of deciding on means and ends.[209] This generality is a way of expanding upon what the earlier terms "orientation," "context" and "historicity" meant. A diagram may help track the insights behind this generality about creative understanding, its preconditions and results.

---

[208] Nelson Goodman presented what he called "retrospective construction theory" to account for this ingenious but fictive rearrangement of clues to fit an expected order. See his <u>Ways of Worldmaking</u>, 81-83.

[209] Diagnosing, imagining and describing are instances of integrating, unifying or making sense of "fragments." The category "integrator" will appear in Part IV as part of a dialectical notion of ordered liberty.

$$H_2[H_1(n_j\ ;\ b_k\ ;\ p_l\ ;\ i_m)]$$

(Diagram 3.1)

"H_2" (History$_2$) represents the impersonal sociohistorical conditions for "H_1" (History$_1$), which stands for the details of an individual biographical history comprised of interactions with the former "H" and with the classes of processes and events listed in parentheses: (n) neurochemical, (b) biological, (p) psychological, (i) intellectual processes. The subscripts represent the indefinite number of variables under each class.[210] Thus, Diagram 1.2 in Chapter One can be read as specifying a few of the variables under psychological and intellectual processes (the three phases of an act of attention), under biology (the relevant brain locales for these phases) and under neurochemistry (the main chemical regulators of events at those locales).

A third approximation of creative intelligence will build upon: (1) the earlier insights into intentional acts as both creative and predictable because of non-systematic relations among relevant conditions and (2) the immediately preceding approximation of creative intelligence as a "conditioned but flexible range of possible ways of diagnosing situations, imagining possible improvements and of deciding on means and ends."

Since the alternative to distinction is confusion, we begin by asking how types of intentional acts differ from one another. Could some be purely active and others mostly receptive? Insights presumably follow upon reception of puzzling data that evoke acts of questioning. The insight itself is "active" in the sense that it synthesizes or integrates the

---

[210] I am indebted to Philip McShane for this approach to symbolization and for the use of semicolons to represent the irreducibility of one class of processes to another –- a not unimportant claim if "top-down" direction of lower-order conditions is to be plausible.

puzzling data. Still, many insights are experienced as something "received," i.e. things suddenly "fall into place." No matter how much desired, this is not something produced at will as if "catching on" were under a person's control.[211] So at least some intentional acts are not differentiated solely in terms of activity and receptivity.

Perhaps a differentiating characteristic appears in the different types of questions and answers that occur in inquiries. The medievals followed Aristotle in distinguishing four basic types of questions. Referring to Aristotle's <u>Posterior Analytics</u>, one author wrote:

> Any question, we are told – and so any answer and any item of knowledge – can be listed under one of four headings. Either one asks (1) whether there is an **X**, or (2) what is an **X**, or (3) whether **X** is **Y**, or (4) why **X** is **Y**. The superficial eye will pair off the first two questions together and the last two; but the significant parallel is between the first and the third, and between the second and the fourth.[212]

The same author later suggested a reduced classification of these four questions into two general types: questions for intelligence and questions for reflection.[213] Questions for intelligence ask, e.g. What? Why? When? How often? Questions for reflection ask, e.g. Is it an **X**? Is it real? Did it happen that way? Is it true? One way of distinguishing the two general types is to note what kinds of answers they anticipate. The first type calls for responses adding missing information about intended objects, events or frequencies. The second class anticipates responses of the sort: "yes," "no"

---

[211] This description of receptivity in understanding is consistent with artists' use of the term "inspiration" to convey their experience of being surprised by a sudden brilliant idea, a happy phrasing of words or sounds, a novel form emerging from stone or on canvas.
[212] <u>Verbum</u>, 26.
[213] <u>Insight</u>, 297.

or "I don't know."[214] If a customer asks the price of something, a clerk responding "Yes" will be unhelpful.

Perhaps by attending to question types we can differentiate intentional acts. Lonergan did so and, in works after *Insight*, identified four general types: questions for understanding, questions of judgment, questions for deliberation and questions of decision.[215]

Questions for understanding and questions for deliberation are subdivisions of his earlier class, questions for intelligence. The key difference between them lies in their intended objects. Questions for understanding ask, for example, what something is, when something happened, why something occurred. Questions for deliberation ask, for example, what can be the case, what acts are possible, what ends can be pursued. This shift in modality to possibilities provides a clue to a third approximation.

Before formulating that third approximation, we need to identify how these question types help differentiate intentional acts. We can begin by retrieving the earlier model of "interactivity" between sensibility and intelligence and then translating it into the language of intentionality theory. So sensibility becomes, for example, possible acts of looking, listening, imagining, smelling, feeling, i.e. possible acts of attending to sensitive presentations or inner states. All of these acts have correlates in possible objects of experience, e.g. sights, sounds, images, feelings, odors. Suppose we classify such operations as "empirical intentional acts."

What are the intentional operations of intelligence? Let the first type be specified by what questions for understanding intend. Again, they are a reaching for some intelligibility or meaning in the puzzling data of sense or data of internal

---

[214] A traditional phrasing of the distinction is that questions for intelligence anticipate synthesis while questions for reflection anticipate a positing or denial of synthesis.

[215] *Method* in *Theology* (104-105) presents a formulation of question types intermediate between that of *Insight* and later versions in popular lectures and essays.

states that are the correlates of empirical intentional acts. The intending may be haphazard and untutored and so yield little more than a hunch, a guess, a barely plausible solution to a puzzle. However, with training may come expertise; then the outcome is more likely to be an informed opinion, a technically sophisticated hypothesis, an expert's bright idea. Let us label the operations producing either type of result "intellectual intentional acts."

If the issue is significant enough, an audience may demand more from a glib responder and even from an expert. The audience may want to check the evidence or credentials of the responder by asking, "How do you know that?" The movement here is toward the distinct type of questioning called questions of judgment. The issue is whether the hunch or hypothesis, the understanding reached by guessing or by years of training, is warranted, justified, verified. Without venturing into the labyrinth of debates over the criteria for justifying truth-claims, we can simply note that this question type is asking whether something is real or true or an accurate account of what happened. The correlates of acts of judging are, thus, what we conventionally call "facts," "truth," real states-of-affairs or actual events. Suppose we label such operations of judging "critical intentional acts."

When it is not enough to know merely what is the case because the diagnosed situation calls for action, questions for deliberation follow.[216] Here the challenge of imagining

---

[216] Why does settling matters-of-fact not put an end to inquiry? One response is that biological demands (for food, mating, security) necessitate action and so prompt further operations. The strength of this response derives from the dependence of an animal species on flexible adaptations to changing conditions in external and internal environments. In the same vein, emotional linkages between images and demands are biologically useful in discriminating among possible responses to both demands and established preferences. When the species in question is both intelligible and intelligent, the range of possible demands and responses increases enormously. Fantasy becomes a source of novel responses and artificial demands,

alternative means and ends tests the range of a person's creative understanding. What persons deliberate over are possible purposes and courses of action, possible consequences and risks. This is when fantasizing can become a serious enterprise as one tries to play out various scenarios and calculate their preconditions and results. Let us call such operations "deliberative intentional acts."

The possibilities or options that deliberative acts generate become, in turn, objects for the fourth question type.[217] Questions of decision ask: What should we do? Which purposes are worth pursuing? Which option is the best choice under these circumstances? Such normative questions raise new difficulties in identifying the conditions for answering them. Once again, there will be internal and external conditions. For example, what are the concrete resources available to the one trying to improve a situation? Material limitations may make the best of intentions unfulfillable. Then, again, having the best of intentions may prove insufficient because of internal limitations. Perhaps the

---

e.g. what commercial advertising appeals to and can create. Even more dramatically, creative understanding can envision a history yet to be made, can fantasize about a past "better than it was" (i.e. counterfactual history), can imagine possible worlds that will never exist (e.g. the fabulous worlds of science fiction). This amazing range of deliberative intentional acts is, thus, a major clue to the meaning of creative understanding. An initial hint: What is the "demand" that evokes such a range of responses?

[217] Questions of judgment and questions of decision appear to be subdivisions of Lonergan's earlier classification, questions for reflection. Again a shift in modality, this time from what is the case to what should be the case, seems to be the basis for the distinction. Note that questions of judgment are usually part of the deliberative process, e.g. one should ask which of the imagined possibilities are realistic options given the circumstances. The linear description of question types here (and in Diagram 3.2 below) sacrifices complexity for the sake of clarity. Actual performance in questioning is usually a far more muddled and circuitous process.

one trying to decide on a course of action is too timid and prone to inventing frightening scenarios and so delays making a decision. Besides psychological barriers to effective action, persons may lack the technical expertise to use available resources, and so their good intentions are not followed by effective solutions. In addition, the ones making the decisions may be lax in considering how their acts might affect the well being of others, and so the range of options they think worth considering may be quite narrow and self-serving. Such added difficulties pertain, however, to answering questions of decision, and the limited purpose here is to distinguish the question types and then to use them to differentiate intentional acts. Suppose we call the preceding types of operations linked to questions of decisions "normative intentional acts."

The following diagram is one way of summarizing the immediately preceding paragraphs. It also suggests how intentional operations form a common pattern or structure of related but distinct acts. The implications of such a structure for talking about creative understanding follow below.

Intentional Acts	Question Types	Objects
Normative Acts	Questions of Decision	Best Option
Deliberative Acts	Questions for Deliberation	Possibilities/ Options
Critical Acts	Questions of Judgment	Fact/Truth
Intellectual Acts	Questions for Understanding	Guess/ Hypothesis
Empirical Acts	(Acts of Attending)	Clues/Data

(Diagram 3.2)

What are the implications of this structure of intentional acts? A few of them can be identified in a preliminary way, but later chapters will make others explicit. First, distinguishing between empirical and intellectual acts allows for a "complete" empirical act of attention (e.g. noticing a face) to include a minimal intellectual act, i.e. what Chapter One referred to as an instance of "apprehensive abstraction." Thus, cases of covert face recognition in prosopagnosia show that faces are distinguished from hands (the minimal act of understanding), but the further question of whether it is a familiar face is problematical. In cases of facial agnosia, there is a gap between the general classification ("It's a face") and the specific insight ("It's my brother's face"). What is missing is the further insight into, the recognition of, the specific instance with its differentiating and significant characteristics.[218] The study of covert face recognition at the end of the last chapter made this claim in different terms. An act of attention is not "completed" insofar as "focus" or a minimal insight into the significance of an image does not occur.

An implication of the distinction between questions for understanding and questions of judging is that established neural patterns or expectations are corrigible. While set neural patterns "favor" data that fit them, surprises do occur.

---

[218] This disorder reveals that, contrary to the conceptualist viewpoint in much of modern philosophy, intellectual intentional acts are the original sources of generalities and later mediate between generalities (e.g. concepts of faces and hands) and specific instances (a brother's face) that add variations to the generalities. If inquiries begin with only concepts/generalities, how do we ever identify differentiated instances of them? A Kantian maxim diagnosed half the problem: "concepts without experience are empty; experience without concepts is blind." But what is the middle term that allows one to recognize something as a particular instance of the concept and the concept as relevant to the instance? A plausible answer is that acts of insight are the middle terms between concepts and particulars. For example, insights must occur if doctors are to diagnose presented cases as instances of types of disease and if they are to determine the relevance of types of treatment for the presented cases.

Thus, persons admit mistakes, e.g. tapping on a stranger's shoulder while seeking out a friend at a crowded party. This simple case has a further implication. If guesses prove erroneous and are known to be so, then some operations must "trump" answers to questions for understanding. This is the critical function of acts of judging in relation to acts of understanding.[219]

Talk of one operation "trumping" another is far from precise. Perhaps a better form of expression is to speak of successive operations "completing" prior ones. For example, acts of attending evoked by puzzling sights come to a type of completion when acts of understanding ("a-ha" experiences) remove the puzzlement by making sense of the clues. Likewise, acts of understanding can give way to questions of judgment asking whether whatever sense has been made of something is in fact what that something is. Here the critical demand for more than a guess finds a completing response in the act of assent that is part of judgment.

This new language of operations completing one another provides clues to how we might reformulate earlier puzzles about "volitional control." To review previous references: volitional control supposedly occurs when test subjects give a wrong response, notice their mistake and try to adjust their answer.[220] It also occurs whenever a task requires sustained attention and maintenance of focus.[221] The same claim was made about spontaneous bodily reactions (e.g. yawns or signs of nervousness) being suppressed by top-down operators, and about deliberate

---

[219] Clinical psychology indirectly makes this distinction between functions of understanding and judging. For example, "schizophreniacs cannot tell the difference between their own internally generated images and thoughts and perceptions that are evoked by real things outside." (A Brief Tour of Human Consciousness, 94.) But, if their hallucinations are detectable, then acts of understanding must be distinct from acts that judge what has been understood.
[220] Cf. Chapter One, footnote 77.
[221] Cf. Chapter One, footnote 78.

efforts to control emotional responses by directing attention, e.g. by shifting one's attention from disturbing sights or by staying busy to distract oneself from painful memories. Chapter One labelled these instances of "executive acts."[222]

Describing such instances of top-down control has never been the problem. The question of how they occur was the puzzle Posner thought neuroscientists were neglecting.[223] The studies of action tend to formulate the puzzle as a barely understood interaction between cognitive systems (e.g. understanding the purpose of a hammer) and sensorimotor systems for employing that know-how (e.g. moving a hand holding the hammer in the correct direction and with the needed force). But how does the first "system" direct the operations of the second?

So far our efforts to answer this old question have been limited to reformulating the terms in which it is asked. We began by borrowing the language of an "interactive model"

---

[222] The label hides an ambiguity. Who is the "executive" here? Depth psychology has its Freudian censor that is intelligent, devious and resourceful. Clinical psychology has its cases of apraxia. In the extreme are cases of alien hand syndrome. "Often associated with apraxia, in this disorder the limb may perform movements not under volitional control, as if it has a will of its own. Severe alien hand on one side may result in intermanual rivalry, such as the anarchic hand trying to throttle the patient while the other hand under volitional control tires to fend it off...." J.D.W. Greene, "Apraxia, Agnosias and Higher Visual Function Abnormalities." Journal of Neurology, Neurosurgery and Psychiatry, 76 (December 2005), 33-34.

[223] The neglect has not been total. Studies of the organic/biological bases for deliberate action have identified relevant brain locales. "The formulation of an action requires the will and intention to do such a task, and is generated in prefrontal cortex. This signal is then used to activate left fronto-parietal systems that in turn activate motor engrams (for example, the pattern and sequence of movements needed to light a match) in premotor cortex. This is then fed down to the primary motor cortex and by the corticospinal tracts to muscle, with modulation from cerebellum and basal ganglia." Ibid. 31.

and used it to describe the relation between sensibility and intelligence. The goal, however, is to talk eventually in terms of dialectical relations. To that end, the first move was from the language of faculty psychology to the terminology of intentionality theory. The second move was to differentiate intentional acts and to identify, in summary form, some of the functional relations among these distinct acts. Here the language of "completion" suggested how successive acts creatively integrate what prior acts supply.[224] There is, still, a further question. What moves this process toward completion along?

This further question is key to understanding the next approximation to creative understanding. What has led up to this question is worth reviewing. Descriptively, creative understanding is the capacity to invent scenarios, no matter how improbable, by manipulating images, generating fantasies, having dreams. This initial description and some examples were followed by a first, and very general, approximation of creative understanding as a capacity to impose unity on multiplicity. After noting determinate limitations on this capacity, we offered a second approximation in terms of "a conditioned but flexible range of possible ways of attending to and diagnosing situations, of imagining possible improvements and of deciding on means and ends." Recall what "conditioned" means here. The prior terms "context" and "historicity" expressed how intentional acts have antecedent conditions. But the analysis of intentional

---

[224] The appropriateness of the language of "completion" for speaking about intentional operations is detectable in criticisms of defective performances. For example, when medical personnel overlook easily diagnosed symptoms, the complaint is they were not sufficiently attentive. When persons advocate policy changes but use contradictory arguments, the complaint may be that they have not completely thought through what they are saying. More commonly we all have complained, "You knew better than to do that." What we expected was that decisions and actions would complement or be consistent with prior understanding.

acts did not sidetrack into a study of those indefinite and multiple conditions. Instead, the focus was on differentiating the acts and their objects by distinct types of questions. Among the latter are deliberative questions that reach beyond both the objects of empirical intentional acts and the boundaries of fact. Why does such "reaching" occur?

A general response spoke of basic demands that evoked action.[225] In Chapter Two, the category "demand" meant "a spontaneous or trained reaching for images," and images were the correlative responses to demands. That earlier analysis focused on a study of how images, emotions and actions were related. Now the inquiry has expanded to a broader focus on different types of intentional acts, their interrelations and objects. The hypothesis is that dynamic interactions among the distinct acts form a process "moving toward completion."

In order to shift talk of acts moving toward completion into an explanatory framework, let acts of deliberation be one type of intentional operation linked to other types, all occurring as matters of probability.[226] In the first place, which deliberative acts occur within a population, given exposure to certain types of images or stimuli, will be dependent on an indefinite number of variables.[227] But, secondly, the multiple variables are correlates of acts having a definite order or structure, that is, the sequence in which the acts occur forms a pattern in which later acts supplement or integrate the results of earlier acts. Thus, the acts occur in response to non-systematically "received" variables, but they are parts of a dynamic structure assembling and ordering the parts toward greater completion.[228]

---

[225] Cf. footnote 212 above.

[226] This stipulation is consistent with the preliminary account of the category of "action" in Chapter Two, Part IV.

[227] The earlier reference to Golden Arches and feral pigs represents the range of these variables.

[228] This wording recalls the earlier effort to reconcile talk of creativity and habit. It also is consistent with previous descriptions

Why does this "creative assembling" of acts occur?[229] Evidence of movement is found in the question types. But what impels them? Spinoza appealed to *conatus*; neuroscience and psychology appeal to neural and biological demands. Aristotle appealed to a basic desire to know. This author is appealing to a gradually emerging notion of creative understanding. Employing the category of "demand," we can hypothesize that, just as there are spontaneous and trained demands for images relevant to biological and psychosocial functioning, so there are intelligent demands for understanding what is true and what would be good to do.

Such demands are not separable from emotions and images. For example, Aristotle recognized that acts of understanding proceed from desire and operate on phantasms or images.[230] In keeping with the broad usage of "image" in the previous chapter, we can identify images with an indeterminate field of possible objects of intentional acts potentially evocative of emotional responses. Images potentially meet intelligent demands and so can prompt intentional acts relative to determinate capacities in perceivers. Images actually meet demands and so evoke actual responses when determinate acts (e.g. specific acts of attention or questioning) occur as a result of both activity and receptivity. Again, it is because of intelligent demands that persons attend to images as worth understanding, and it is because of images that perceivers respond with operations.

---

of action as both receptivity and activity, as being both moved and moving (*et motus et movens*).

[229] What is true of the acts is also true of their objects. If this were an essay in metaphysics, the inquiry would investigate how distinct operations have correlates in compound objects, i.e. objects having empirical, intelligible and actual components.

[230] In more contemporary language, children are spontaneously curious, want to make sense of things and respond to puzzling experiences with questions. Why this native wonder and incessant questioning are less in evidence among adults is a puzzle for a different inquiry.

Previously we noted that repeated conjunctions of demands and emotionally weighted images establish determinate neural patterns intensifying the links between the two. We went on to hypothesize that such neural patterns, when presented with relevant images, set off a "cascade of neural activities and chemical releases producing organic changes that are the immediate substrate for psychological experiences of emotion and feeling." A question followed about which images had which cascading effects, and we noted that any answer would confront an indefinite range of cultural, biographical and biological variables. To repeat an observation from Chapter One: sensitive presentations and images are rarely independent of the "orientation" of the one perceiving them. That is, images are "received" according to the capacity of the receiver, a capacity with a history of patterned responses to previous images.

So we have highly variable patterning in the persons receiving puzzling images but also common patterning or structure in how intentional acts respond to puzzling images. This mix of variables and structure is an instance of multiplicity and unity, of highly variable images and ordered processing of them. Suppose the processing of variable images by structured acts is due to dynamic "operators" that reach for a synthesis of clues, puzzling images, fragmentary data.[231] The vagueness of the term "operator" may diminish if we understand how question types represent development toward anticipated ends. For example, suppose a demand for understanding is what moves one to anticipate answers by asking questions for understanding. Or let a demand for knowing what is the case be what moves one to anticipate settling issues of fact by asking questions of judgment. The meaning of "operator" is descriptively what moves one to act

---

[231] This talk of an operator or a dynamic principle of development was anticipated in the earlier description of understanding as constructive or synthetic. It also is consistent with the common references in cognitive psychology to a "principle of supplementation."

in inquiry. To shift this term into an explanatory context, we need to fix its meaning by its relation to a correlate. Doing so requires talk of multiple operators "fitting" each type of intentional act. For example, the operator for intellectual acts is a demand for an intelligible integration of clues, puzzling images or fragmentary data, but the integrator is the answer that meets the demand. The operator for critical acts is a demand for what is true, factual or accurate, and the integrator is the answer of assent that meets the demand. The operator for deliberative acts is a demand for new goals or possible solutions to problems, and the integrator is the creative option that responds to that demand. Questions mediate between demand and response, between operator and integrator, as the means for expressing demands and for satisfying them.

This new terminology[232] (replacing that of "interactive systems" and of faculties of sensibility and intelligence) expresses an understanding of intentional operations as receiving (*motus*) fragmentary clues, operating (*movens*) on them by selecting, questioning and integrating them by insights that respond to the demands mediated by questions. Since the concern of this chapter is with deliberative intentional acts, we can concentrate on the operator for such acts.

Suppose the relevant demand is for an understanding, not of what is the case, but of what possible states-of-affairs would be good to produce. Already noted was the dramatic range of responses to such a demand: fantasizing about a future better than the past, counterfactually imagining a past "better than it was," dreaming of possible worlds that will never be. This range of invention makes a plausible case for identifying creative understanding with the operator for deliberative acts. Still, the case is flawed since all intentional operations are creative – from the selectivity of attention in

---

[232] The terms are "new" only in the sense that they appear here as replacements for the earlier terminologies of interactive systems and of faculty psychology. I am indebted to Lonergan for the terms. Cf. <u>Insight</u>, 489-494.

empirical intentional acts to the decisive implementing of plans in normative intentional acts. All the same, the capacity to invent and to fantasize about an indefinite range of possibilities is evidence creative understanding contains a principle of development reaching beyond settled patterns of imagining, thinking and acting. This claim brings us close to a third approximation.

This is a good place to review the previous clues we have been following in trying to reach a new approximation. The first clue was the shift in modality appearing in questions for deliberation. Since the realm of possibility is far more extensive than reality, deliberative intentional acts potentially have far more intentional objects than those that actually exist. This amounts to an amazing degree of independence in its operations from actual cultural, biographical and biological conditions. Witness the fantastic worlds, super-human powers and bizarre life forms invented by writers of science fiction.

On the other hand, any independence from one's culture, historical context and personal psychological conditions will be limited. Discovery of the incredible range of creative understanding does not eliminate the neurochemical, organic and psychological antecedents of one's intentional operations.[233] Diagram 3.1, as well, made room for impersonal sociohistorical variables (H_2) condition-ing personal operations. It seems that such conditions form a principle of limitation or dependence in relation to the creative capacity of deliberative acts.

How can we formulate this relation between what are usually opposed terms: independence and dependence? A first, descriptive effort would be to assign "movement" to the operator and "rest" to the integrator. That is, the operator prompts acts of questioning, and the integrator, or answer,

---

[233] Patrick Byrne has explored how neural antecedents allow for "some randomness within our perceptions, memories and imaginations" and so provide a basis for intellectual creativity. See his "Neuroscience, Consciousness, Freedom and Lonergan" (in manuscript), 7-11.

brings the inquiry to a conclusion. Movement should be more frequent than rest since our questions exceed our answers. This potential for movement, for questioning and imagining, was the second clue to a further understanding of creative understanding. In principle, we can ask questions indefinitely about whatever endlessly fertile imaginings we may dream up.[234] But what is true "in principle" is not in fact what occurs. Children ask questions incessantly and dream up imaginary friends. Adults ask fewer questions and hope for a few real friends. Perhaps what happens in the intervening years is that the integrator gradually achieves dominance over the operator. That is, neural, biological, psychological and cognitive patterns become habitual ways of responding to the demands of the operator, and the range of possible responses one actually considers narrows.

Since this narrowing occurs with some frequency, an understanding of creative understanding as it actually operates becomes more complex. A new approximation must include not just a principle of development (a principle of completion) reaching beyond settled patterns but also a principle of stasis (a principle of assimilation) favoring established patterns. "Historicity" represented acknowledgement of antecedent conditions for intentional operations (ranging from the latent demands and emotionally laden images of a person's orientation to the impersonal variables of one's actual time and place). Thus, intentional acts exhibit "receptivity" to or formation by prior conditions. In some cases this means images will be blocked so that unwanted insights do not occur, but then some creative possibilities will remain outside the range of a person's actual deliberations. On the other hand, since intentional operations are products of receptivity and activity, actual planning and deciding that are

---

[234] The examples of endlessly fertile imaginings usually include late medieval speculations about angels dancing on pinheads and conundrums such as whether an omnipotent deity can create a rock so heavy he cannot lift it. Do contemporary discussions of multiple universes provide updated examples of unrestricted imaginings?

subject to probability may deviate from antecedent patterns. This possibility rests in part upon the possibility of an operator prompting new questions.

Perhaps now the significance of an earlier claim may be apparent: "new questions and new answers have as much claim as habits to being potential antecedents to planning and action." In other words, both operators and integrators, as expressing principles of growth and stability, motion and rest, can be determinate conditions of acts of planning and deciding. Put another way, the principle of supplementation, so well documented in cognitive psychology, can be innovative or routine in how it functions. Images can be readily assimilated to established patterns (e.g. driving the usual route to home without explicit attention to many familiar landmarks) or they can be deliberately manipulated to suggest improved conditions for living (e.g. designing a new road system). To hold together both possibilities as features of creative understanding, a model of thinking conventionally labelled "dialectic" proves useful.

While the term dialectic has had various meanings over the centuries, our immediate goal of understanding creative understanding dictates the usage here. So dialectic for us means the determinate interactions between related but opposed principles of intentional operations; namely the principles of completion and assimilation.[235] Conflict between the two principles characteristically involves resistance to new questions in favor of already acquired answers and the patterns of feeling, imagining and acting they support.[236] The

---

[235] This usage is a variation on Lonergan's formulation of a general notion of dialectic as a "concrete unfolding of linked but opposed principles of change." Insight, 242.

[236] Extreme examples of conflict range from vicious forms of bigotry to clinical cases of self-destructive behaviors. An analogy for intense psychic and intellectual division is found in the rare cases of alien hand syndrome, especially those in which patients manifest the disorder by using one hand to throttle themselves and the other hand to prevent this. Cf. footnote 218 above.

basic model for understanding how a positive, cooperative relation between the two principles promotes development is the structured movement from puzzling images to the questions they evoke (which express the demands of the intellectual operator), and then to the answers which are the responses of the integrator. Such cooperation makes possible an expert's gradual accum-ulation of insights that heads toward mastery of some area of inquiry. The expert's learning process will involve both assimilation of new insights to previously acquired ones and also, on occasion, the correction of the latter by the former. Such correction is possible because the principle of completion includes the demands of the critical operator for correct understanding.

This thin sketch of dialectic moves us closer to a third approximation of creative understanding. A preparatory move was in guessing that creative understanding was the operator for deliberative acts. The next steps were to dismiss this guess, to generalize that creative understanding was part of every intentional act and to hypothesize that in operation it exhibits both independence and dependence, movement and rest. The related but opposed principles of completion and assimilation translated this insight into dialectical terms. The various operators and integrators of distinct types of intentional acts mediate the related but opposed demands of these principles. The introduction of dialectic permits the principles and their demands to be understood as related but opposed features of creative understanding. So our third approximation is that creative understanding is a conditioned but flexible range of possible intentional operations responding to the related but opposed demands of the principles of completion and assimilation.

Perhaps it seems the effort in arriving at such a general conclusion has been disproportionate to the outcome. However, there are some advantages in shifting the discussion of creative understanding out of a descriptive framework where it was first spoken of as the capacity for innovative insights and performance. At the beginning of this chapter that description left us with a puzzle about historically acquired orientations and how they might be subject to criticism and correction. This puzzle originated in the insights behind the category of historicity. We are largely unaware of the personal and impersonal antecedents of our current feeling, thinking and acting. More specifically, we are mostly in the dark about the latent demands and their correlates, emotionally weighted images, that constitute much of our actual orientations. There was the added difficulty that such correlations of demands and responsive images tend to be rooted in the limbic system rather than the cortex and so are less readily open to correction by new insights. So the puzzle was how it was possible to evaluate and to correct this largely hidden "background" of present deliberating and deciding.

The first steps in responding to the puzzle made use of two insights. First, creative planning and acting occur as matters of probability since the indefinite number of variables conditioning those acts are related non-systematically. Second, intentional operations are instances of both activity and receptivity. An implication of the first insight is that new questions and new answers have as much claim as prior orientation to being potential antecedents of present acts of deliberating and deciding. The addition of a dialectical understanding of intentional operations to the second insight expands the meaning of activity and receptivity. New questions responding to the demands of operators (an instance of activity) can challenge already integrated patterns of feeling, thinking and acting (instances of receptivity). Since the "received" objects which intentional acts operate on can, besides sensible presentations, be fantasies, prior judgments and habitual ways of acting, the demands of the critical operator ground an evaluative function in regard to such objects.[237] Thus, this dialectical understanding of creative

---

[237] "Function" here refers to an understanding of the critical operator as orientated toward a distinct end, namely, correctly understanding what is actually the case or what should be the case. To link this function to the principles of assimilation and completion is a matter of noting that the "end" may be reached by affirming something is

understanding combines both empirical and critical functions in regard to how persons reach answers and reconcile them with prior ones. Besides assimilating new answers to prior ones, the critical function allows for the possibility of revising or reversing already entrenched answers.[238]

Creative departures from routines do occur in the arts and the sciences. The same is observable in individual cases of psychic patterns: some addicts do recover; some persons do overcome racial prejudices; some trauma victims do master their fears and resume their daily lives. Of course, not all succeed. In some cases it is resistance to new questions that makes needed changes less probable, but, again, that will be an outcome of the tension between related but opposed principles of completion and assimilation.

IV Introducing a Dialectical Notion of Liberty

Previous chapters contained three promises about what this third chapter would achieve. The first was that a new language (new categories) would appear making it easier to talk about the "turn," i.e. about how intentional acts might exercise some control over lower-order conditions. A step toward keeping the promise occurred in identifying the

---

compatible with already accepted answers or by affirming it as a correction or surpassing of already accepted answers. Endorsement of experimental findings as consistent with the standard model of some discipline exemplifies the former. Artistic judgments about a new style of painting as a significant and creative departure from conventional models exemplify the latter.

[238] Variations on Descartes' "evil genius" typically overlook this role of critical reflection in intentional operations. The demands of the critical operator, expressed in questions of judgment, are the condition for the possibility both of achieving stable viewpoints and of raising further questions that may destabilize them. The "critical" (judgmental) function of the operator provides a basis for answering a question from Part I of this chapter: How is criticism of the fantasies or objects of deliberative acts possible?

wondrous range of deliberative acts - from pragmatic planning of roads to meditative reflection on humankind's place in the cosmos and on to the fabulous worlds of science fiction. This range of possibilities is evidence of a relative independence of creative understanding from the initial conditions for its own operations. But the key word is "relative" since, as depicted in Diagram 3.1, intentional operations have historical, neurochemical, biological and psychological antecedents. The language of dialectic was introduced to account for evidence of both dependence and independence in deliberative acts. The principle of completion was introduced to broaden the application of what psychologists call the principle of supplementation and to account for the dynamic structure of intentional operations. We then went on to recognize limitations on such operations. The principle of assimilation accounts for some of the internal limits on the range of operations.

How does this new language make a difference? The first difficulty in talking about the needed "turn" was in describing how biological processes could build upon neurochemical events and how psychological states (e.g. emotions) could emerge from both.[239] The second difficulty, beyond the puzzle of how higher systems emerge from lower ones, was how to talk about the possibility of higher systems modifying their antecedent conditions in lower-order systems.[240] Descriptive examples appeared: depression (p_l) can suppress chemical releases in the immune system (n_j) thereby increasing the odds of disease (b_k); meditation techniques (i_m) can alter blood pressure and heart rate (b_k); deliberate inattentiveness (i_m) to disturbing images is a way of controlling emotions (p_l). But such examples do not explain how deliberate acts can control neurochemical, biological and psychological processes and events.

---

[239] Comments in Chapter One on "supervenience" and "schemes of recurrence" were first responses to this difficulty.

[240] Talk of "interactive systems" and criticisms of the category "mechanism" were first responses to this second difficulty.

The language of dialectic addresses both difficulties. While the use of "dialectic" has been limited to relations between the demands of the two principles of intentional acts, the resulting model suggests how to think through the first puzzle about systems emerging from lower-order conditions. For example, images can be objects or correlates of questions. Questions mediate between the images and anticipated answers or insights. What acts of questioning anticipate are not further images but insights that integrate or make sense of the original images. As noted above, intellectual acts are synthetic or constructive; they "supplement" the original images and so provide an analogy for how a higher system or integration emerges from prior conditions.[241] More specifically, the answers emerging as insights into images are higher integrations of lower-level materials, e.g. after gathering fragmentary data on traffic accidents along a particular roadway, a statistician can integrate them as an ideal frequency per time interval. This patterning of the data, formulated as a probability statement, becomes a guideline for analyzing future data. Since future analysis will eventually uncover discrepancies between ideal and actual frequencies, new questions will arise, particularly if the deviations appear with some regularity.[242] New questions represent the principle of completion impelling operators to test previously achieved integrations and so to anticipate further developments in understanding and so new integrations.

How does this model shed light on the question about the emergence of one system from another? It can serve as an analogy in which the relevant similarity is in relationships. As images are to answers so neurochemical processes are to organic systems; as aggregates of data are to formulated statistical frequencies so organic systems are to psycho-

---

[241] Insight (492-493) is my source for this model.

[242] The use of "regularity" is a way of noting that random deviations from ideal frequencies will occur but will not usually be the basis for further questions unless the occurrence becomes "regular."

logical states. While the operator impelling development from images to answers is the demand for understanding (expressed in questioning), the operators promoting transitions from chemical functions to organic functions and from biological processes to psychological states are to be discovered through empirical research. What the model offers is a heuristic pattern for exploring how higher systems emerge and develop.[243]

The relevance of the analogy to the second puzzle may not be apparent, so consider how neurochemical activities in distinct brain locales make possible the emotional states of fear and delight. A bottom-up approach will conclude that the psychological states reflect changes in "brain states," changes originating in neurochemical events. But such changes, like traffic accidents, are dependent on non-systematically related variables. So, for example, organic functions (b_k) vary according to suppressed or non-suppressed chemical releases (n_j) occurring because of emotional states (p_l).[244] Emotions vary according to the presence or absence of certain brain lesions (b_k) (recall the cases of Arthur and Elliot), but also because of the deliberate manipulation (i_m) of evocative images (p_l) (recall the goals of commercial advertising). Emotional states can vary depending on whether

---

[243] "Clearly, though this specification of the operator is extremely general, it offers some determination of the direction of development. Its application to concrete instances may not only confirm it but also give rise to further questions. The further questions will lead to further insights and so to still further questions. In this fashion, one's understanding of the operator begins to be an instance of higher system on the move in the development of scientific knowledge of development." Insight, 492. The envisioned scientific knowledge remains a remote achievement, at least in regard to the specific operators effecting transitions from one type of system to another.

[244] Recall the evidence of depression suppressing functions of the nervous system thereby affecting organic functions of the immune system.

one understands or is ignorant of techniques (i_m) for controlling fear of public speaking (p_l). These examples reflect both how psychological states are dependent on events in lower-order systems (e.g. neurochemical releases and brain lesions) and how deliberate manipulation (e.g. the use of evocative images and refined techniques) can exercise some control over them. As a matter of probability, the psychological states emerge from chemical and biological systems, but they can have effects on those antecedent conditions while also being subject to operations of a higher system, e.g. intelligently deployed images and techniques for manipulating emotional responses.

To reverse the analogy based on similarity in relationships – as answers are to images, so higher systems (as operators) can be to the antecedent conditions of lower-order systems (as integrators); as emotions can affect organic processes so deliberate acts can affect emotions. Both versions of the analogy have their uses since emotions are at once both routinely dependent on integrators (e.g. the routine functioning of chemical and biological systems) and potentially dependent on the operations of a higher system. This general conclusion suggests the benefit of a dialectical understanding of systems that are related among themselves as both operators and integrators.

Understanding the relations among operators and integrators in this way also supplies a general solution to the second puzzle. The solution emerges from three insights. The first insight is a broad generality: in regard to routinely occurring events, if we change key variables, we can change what routinely occurs. The second insight is slightly less general. If departures from what routinely occurs within a system are due to interfering, non-systematically related variables and if the evidence is that some of these variables belong to a higher system, then the possibility of a higher system effecting changes in a lower one is a matter of manipulating the latter variables. Educational efforts (i_m) to lower teen pregnancy rates by emphasizing the burdens of childrearing manipulate variables such as the demands for play, security and status (p_l). Stiffer penalties for drunk driving effect changes in the frequency of violations. At least in some cases, neurochemical demands (n_j) for alcohol are overridden by psychological demands for freedom and security (p_l), demands targeted by deliberate legal threats (i_m).

The third insight requires further remarks on what it means to "internalize environments." The original context for talking about internalizing environments was the discussion of the basic category "demand." The claim was that biological and psychosocial demands were correlates of images. The further claim was that both types of demands were capacities to internalize environments.[245] Eating is an easy example of action responding to a demand for incorporating some part of an environment. Less noticeable may be how intentional operations do something similar. Empirical intentional acts have as their objects images of parts of environments. But the images are "inside," and the sensitively and intelligently integrated environments we talk about are originally neural patterns within the central nervous system.[246] With experience patterns multiply and tend toward increasing complexity. For example, a basic act of attention can recognize an image as that of a dog. The simple classification of the object depends on a prior patterning or integration of similar images. But persons develop more complex classification schemes - from ordinary ways of describing dogs as friendly or dangerous to the technical classifications of kennel societies and the novel types genetically "engineered" by breeders. Contemporary astrophysics exemplifies this shift

---

[245] Cf. Chapter Two, footnote 149.

[246] In Chapter One reference was made to how contemporary psychology of perception finds these claims to be uncontroversial because of massively supported research. Still, the question of whether such patterns are more than "constructs" leads to traditional puzzles in epistemology which are not part of this study. If the usual debates and their impasses are avoidable, it is likely a matter of understanding the distinct role acts of judging play in the structured process of intentional operations.

from commonplace patterns to quite remote ones. Laypersons see images of color variations, but astronomers recognize those images as terms in correlations allowing them to measure distances, speeds and chemical compositions of stars.

Through such patternings the complexity of the realities persons study is slowly revealed. What they are internalizing is some part of the intelligible universe. If they are to track their developing understanding of that part, the images they rely on, e.g. the diagrams they formulate, should become more complex. But such diagrams will, then, represent more complex patternings or integrations of the universe they study.[247] Two developments are, therefore, occurring. There is the development of increasingly sophisticated diagrams reflecting the complexity of the objects of inquiry; there is a corresponding development in the inquirer. The accumulating insights into those objects (dogs, stars or whatever) become part of the context that an inquirer brings to future operations. In other words, the internalized environments become integrations affecting how the inquirer operates.[248] Put in ordinary language, the experienced person has a more

---

[247] "The higher system of intelligence develops not in a material manifold but in the psychic representation of material manifolds. Hence the higher system of intellectual development is primarily the higher integration, not of the man in whom the development occurs, but of the universe he inspects." Insight, 494.

[248] The integrations can occur as neural patterns (n_j), localized in different but laterally connected brain areas (b_k), as psychological patterns allowing for retrieval or remembering of representations (p_l) and as intelligible and intelligent patterns, i.e. understood meanings of images and sensitive presentations (i_m). Thus, operators bring to any new puzzle orientations, memories and meanings that will guide how they attend to, question, conjecture about and first judge a puzzling situation. The key, if unexceptional, insight is that the more complex the antecedent integrations operators bring to complex situations the more probable will be diagnoses "fitting" or adequate to those situations.

nuanced grasp of realities. Put in the language of dialectic, the integrations that an inquirer has assimilated contain far more patterned variables than those employed by inquirers less attentive or responsive to the wondrous diversity of the universe.

What is the significance of the preceding remarks on "internalizing environments" for a study of liberty, intentional acts and how higher-order systems may modify their antecedent conditions? First, talk of liberty will have a history. That is, we are indebted to predecessors for what we think and say about liberty. The category of historicity (H_1 and H_2) is a condition for intellectual operations (i_m) and their objects. Second, the development of the "representations" of the integrated objects is a condition for any further inquiry regarding them.[249] For example, the historical recognition of non-systematic relations among events and of how probability statements formulate ideal frequencies among them was both a development in intellectual history and a prerequisite to understanding a universe in which liberty is possible.[250] A subsequently integrated universe open to talk of "conditioned but flexible ranges of responses to variable conditions" is an achievement of historical inquiry. In turn, it is a universe that does not require one to choose between determinism and indeterminism when talking about liberty. We evade this false disjunction, first, by using the language of dialectic and, second, by recognizing that intentional acts always have determinate conditions. Some of these conditions are external (and so receptivity is a characteristic of acts), but others are internal, and among the latter are the questions and the

---

[249] Again, questions anticipate insights; insights are into images; complex images invite more complex questions and so more developed insights.

[250] "Historical development" here refers to an understanding that rejects (1) a classicist dismissal of probable events as beyond scientific interest, i.e. as not suitable for *epistêmê*, and (2) an eighteenth-century worldview for which all events follow from systematic relations ultimately expressible in mechanistic "laws."

operators that prompt them. The puzzle, then, is whether the latter determinants are ever relatively independent sources of planning and action. That is, are some operators "self-determining"?[251]

This question brings us to the third promise about this chapter: to introduce a dialectical understanding of liberty as part of this inquiry into intentional acts. First, we need to deal with an objection. Some may object to how we have approached this third goal. The complaint may be that the inquiry has focused too heavily on intentional acts and in doing so has "intellectualized" processes that are more scientifically studied in terms of biochemistry or social conditioning. For example, folk psychology associates clinical depression and its effects on decision-making with various negative moods and advises sufferers to exert more "will power." However, scientists will study the origins of depression in the body's neurochemistry, and such studies prove their worth through practical applications. Thus, by manipulating biochemical or environmental variables, e.g. by pharmacological means, by changing the colors in a room or by introducing certain aromas, therapists can alter people's emotional states. As for the social conditioning of our intentional acts, there are numerous studies in social psychology documenting dramatic shifts in how people act because of either group pressure (e.g. studies of mob psychology) or the commands of an authority figure (e.g. Stanley Milgram's study of obedience to authority).[252]

This objection to an intellectualist approach is correct in what it includes, namely, our intentional acts are contingent, i.e. they are dependent on a variety of antecedent variables.

---

[251] Chapter Five will have more to say about the various meanings of "self-determination."

[252] Obedience to Authority: An Experimental View (New York: Harper and Row, 1975). The results of such studies are at odds with common-sense beliefs about liberty. The goal here is not to defend the latter but to work out an explanatory account of liberty that takes into account such empirical findings.

However, it is deficient in what it overlooks. In "reducing" intentional acts to either neurochemical conditions or the variables of socialization, the objection omits mention of commonplace schemes of recurrence in which higher-order operations are conditioned by but still achieve a degree of independence from lower-order conditions. To previous descriptive examples we can add new ones. Recurrent and flexible biological processes allow for the survival of a species. In their routine functioning, these processes supply the conditions for the development of even higher-order activities.[253] Thus, hunger (a biological demand) serves as a stimulus to food gathering (i.e. a routine means to a natural end), but in time eating may become the rituals of fine dining and gourmet cooking. What was once biological necessity becomes a cultural activity taking a variety of forms and serving non-biological ends. Human history as "culture building" begins to be distinct from nature when persons turn biological necessities into the varied forms of making dinner, buildings, clothing and war. Eventually persons construct elaborate meanings about their lives in time, and a few even make their own intentional acts the explicit focus of their inquiries.

To use descriptive metaphors - there is a horizontal process of biological schemes through which a species preserves and replicates itself. Think of the routines of a rabbit searching for food, a mate and security. But there is also a vertical process whereby routine schemes at a lower level provide the conditions promoting and sustaining higher-level schemes which, in turn, can modify those prior conditions. For example, biological changes in the adolescent give rise to opportunities for dating rituals, dance clubs, wedding planners and laws stipulating acceptable responses to biological demands. Institutions are not biological entities, so "culture" has meanings beyond the uses of the term

---

[253] The question of how this is possible takes us back to the remarks on operators and integrators and the earlier heuristic pattern modeled on the emergence of insights from images.

"nature." An analogy drawn from artistic creativity may solidify this basic insight. The raw materials for the sculptor, whether they be stone or metal, are sublated into a vertical ordering that could not be possible without them but which is not reducible to them.[254]

To summarize the preceding remarks: higher-order processes pursuing higher ends are based on lower-order processes which pursue their own proper ends. A previous analogy is relevant: the complex processes of sight provide data for intellectual inquiry. Seeing has its proper end in images, and images in turn can become the focus of questioning; but questioning has its proper end not in more images but in the event called insight when one orders, comes to some understanding of, what it is one is seeing.[255]

We have now assembled the needed clues for a dialectical understanding of liberty. To review them: we began by noting that new questions and their anticipated answers occur as matters of probability. But then they have as much claim as prior answers (e.g. habits, orientations or integrations) to being potential determinants of new plans and actions. In planning actions, deliberative acts can exhibit an astounding range of fantasy. This capacity for inventing new worlds indicates the possibility of a relative independence of creative understanding from its inherited conditions. Its actually "internalized environments" are historical evidence of development both in inquirers and in the "universe they inspect" and so demonstrate a relative independence from former conditions. What impels such development is a principle of completion expressed, for example, in questions about possible improvements one might achieve in a given state-of-affairs. Though resulting fantasies may remain utopian and quite remote, this is consistent with the general

---

[254] We might ask what does the "sublating"? This renews the interest in what we mean by "creative understanding" and what intelligible principle explains its endless reaching.

[255] Insight, 33-34 and 483-484.

claim that the operator for deliberative acts is an intending of an indeterminate range of possibilities.[256]

Part of the opening puzzle of this chapter about the ambiguity of fantasies, especially political ones, was how they might be subject to criticism. The claim was that the critical operator, expressed in questions of judgment, performed an evaluative function in regard to prior integrations and new answers. As such, it is an <u>internal</u> condition for or determinant of assent to integrations (i.e. new or old answers). It is an instance of potential higher-order control over the operations and products of lower-order systems and the established patterns of habits and orientations. But how are the various operators of intentional acts part of a unified process? The principle of completion formulates the intelligibility of a dynamic and structured process that begins with neural demands for images and proceeds through an intending of facts toward an envisioning of an indeterminate range of worthwhile means and ends. The principle becomes contextualized and determinate in the historically formed orientations of specific inquirers. However, their historicity is no "evil genius" or latent manipulator of thinking and acting if acquired orientations are subject to questioning and criticism and if revisions in response to the demands of the critical operator (expressed in questions of judgment) are possible.

Such have been the clues. To our third approxi-mation of creative understanding ("a conditioned but flexible range of possible intentional operations responding to the related but opposed demands of the operator and integrator"), we can now add a dialectical understanding of liberty.

We skip the description of "snapshots" or single intentional acts. The enlarged focus is on "film clips." So we are talking about what particular persons can do with their historically determinate orientations shaped by antecedents (receptivity) but open to the normative demands of operators

---

[256] This is one way of reading the second part of the medieval assertion that human intellectual capacity was *potens omnia fieri et facere*.

(activity). Liberty, then, is a capacity of intentional acts conditioned by three types of determinants: (1) prior integrations[257] providing the established context for, (2) the demands of operators evoking intentional acts (3) moving toward indeterminate ends in response to the demands of the related but opposed principles of completion and assimilation.

What are the implications of this complex meaning of "liberty" for understanding how institutions affect intentional acts? This is the primary question of the next chapter. A third diagram (3.3) on the following page may help track the insights preparing for this new puzzle.

---

[257] Diagram 3.1 can be read as depicting the range of prior integrations from H_2 to i_m that are background conditions for current decisions.

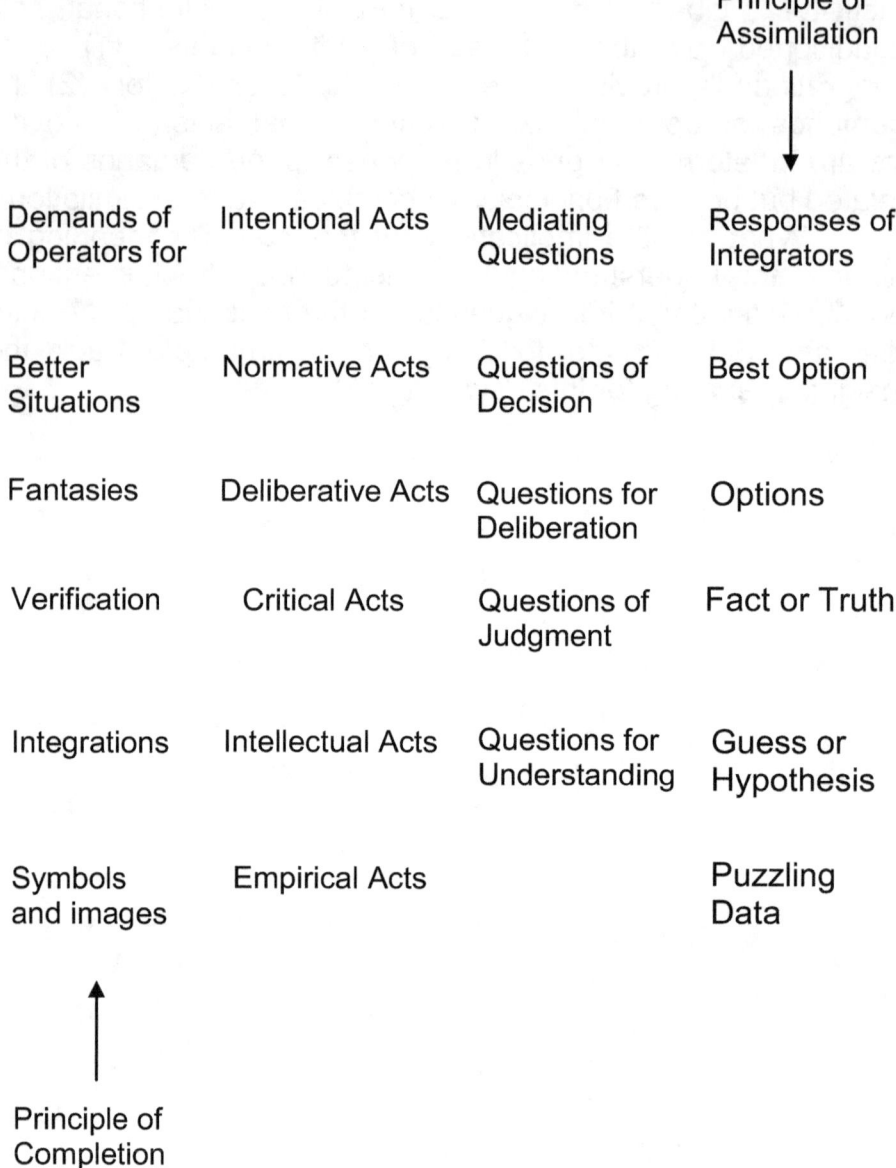

(Diagram 3.3 depicting variables under p_l and i_m)

CHAPTER FOUR

How Do Institutions Affect Decision-Making?

I Introduction

A variety of clues led up to a complex meaning of liberty at the end of the previous chapter. The insights integrating those clues have implications for puzzles in a number of different fields of inquiry. We have already noted a new way of understanding and talking about "volitional control" and "executive function" in accounting for top-down control of lower-order operations. As a result, we have a more precisely formulated and perhaps more resolvable puzzle about how to make the "turn" in neuroscience and cognitive psychology. Goals for the last two chapters will be to identify puzzles in economics and political theory and to discover what the previous understanding of liberty implies for those fields and their puzzles. To link those two fields with findings from neuroscience and cognitive psychology will be a goal of this chapter. The point of intersection for the diverse fields will be the question of how institutions affect decision-making.

Much as in the cases of creative understanding and liberty, the meanings of "institution" and "decision-making" will emerge slowly. Some clues have already appeared. For instance, the variables symbolized by H_2 and H_1 include sociohistorical conditions for the processes symbolized by p_l and i_m. So far the categories of "orientation," "demand," "operator" and "integrator" have specified elements in schemes of recurrence through which intentional acts occur. But a new goal will be to link social schemes of recurrence to the latter schemes. A clue to doing this is found in the earlier remarks on "internalizing environments." The general puzzle is explaining how socialization processes can make it highly probable that social beliefs and practices become internalized patterns or integrations for a new generation of inquirers.[258]

At first, the use of "institution" will be descriptive, but eventually the usage will "fit" the language of dialectic, and the term will be a correlate of other terms. Looking ahead, we will find that liberty has determinants in institutional set-ups but can also be a condition for either maintaining or disrupting them. To rephrase Berger and Luckmann's formulations: "Determinant acts of liberty are products of social orders and can act back on their producers."[259]

The language of dialectic is apt for talking about the moral ambiguity of possible relations between liberty and institutions. Liberty is a capacity made determinant in part by social conditions. If the latter include cultural decline and widespread institutional corruption, it will be more probable that the intentional acts of persons (e.g. their choosing of means and ends) will be far from ideal exercises of liberty. Likewise, there is always the possibility that persons will act contrary to their own "best judgments" even in social settings of cultural advance and institutional stability. In other words, social disorder can be a source of disorder in the exercises of liberty, and disordered liberty can be a threat to a relatively good social order.[260] On the other hand, liberty can be a source of challenges to existing social orders marred by corruption and systemic betrayals of human goods. It can also be a cooperative agent in maintaining and enhancing

---

[258] That socialization has this result is not debated, but explaining how it occurs requires a shift away from descriptions. Perhaps Freud's image of "a garrison in a conquered city" is the most famous description. <u>Civilization and Its Discontents</u> (New York: W.W. Norton, 1962), 71.

[259] For the various formulations of the authors, see <u>The Social Construction of Reality</u> (Garden City, N.Y.: Doubleday, 1967), 61.

[260] The meaning of "ordered liberty" will be part of the inquiry in Chapter Five.

institutional set-ups that consistently promote such goods.²⁶¹ In all these cases we can speak of "prior integrations providing an established context" for the exercise of a capacity. The context shifts the probabilities of which demands and responses will occur or not occur, but the capacity remains a source of possible deviations from those probabilities.

This dialectical understanding of the possible relations between liberty and institutions has a key implication for puzzles in economics and political theory. A first clue to this implication is a rephrasing of the old chicken and egg puzzle: Which comes first – institutions or individuals? If we think of individuals as saying and believing different things, where did they come by their languages and beliefs: family upbringing, schools, popular media? But, if we think of institutions as established, understood and accepted ways of doing things, who first does the establishing, understanding and accepting? Dialectic offers an alternative to an "either/or" phrasing of the question in the sense that priority need not be assigned to either term. Individuals are not the sole "primordial facts" nor are institutions. The "we" is <u>temporally</u> first in the sense that parents beget the child whose "I" emerges within the "we" of the family and some larger community. The differentiation of the individual from others emerges from interpersonal relations.²⁶² This much supports the claims that *mitsein* and ethical demands on individuals are primordial facts. However, capacities, as initially orientations toward an indeterminate range of ends, are characteristics of individuals. The "we" shapes such capacities and initially directs their probable line of development, but the capacities have a <u>logical</u> priority over such ordering by social conditions. Without the marble, the

---

[261] The range of possible relations between liberty (L) and institutions (I) can be symbolized as: (1) ~L and ~I; (2) ~L and I; (3) L and ~I; (4) L and I. This chapter will focus primarily on the mutually supportive relation symbolized in (4).

[262] Lonergan, "Lecture Three: The Relationship between Philosophy of God and the Functional Specialty 'Systematics,'" in <u>Philosophical and Theological Papers</u>, 210-211.

sculptor would have nothing to shape. This much supports the claim that individuals are primordial facts. But the meaning of "individual" here is hardly more differentiated than the simple negation: "I am not you."[263]

In more technical language, Heidegger wrote of several "equiprimordial" (*gleichursprünglich*) characteristics of human living. Perhaps, if we understand them as correlative terms, "individual" and "institution" refer to such characteristics; however, there are alternative ways of describing their relations. Usually when we talk of cause and effect, we are saying there is an intelligible relation of dependence of the latter on the former. But capacities depend on institutions for their actual formation, and institutions depend on individuals with capacities for their emergence and maintenance. "Interdependence" and "reciprocal causality" become the descriptive terms for how both are related. Put in the form of proportions – as prior integrations (e.g. habits) are to current choices and as determinate orientation is to a complete act of attention, so institutions are to individuals.[264]

This "thin" sketch of relations between liberty and institutions is background for the inquiry of this chapter. Part II focuses on decision-making. It begins by reviewing what has already been said about "normative intentional acts." It goes on to add further details about normative judgments and pays

---

[263] Cf. Hegel's Phenomenology of Spirit on the early stages of the dialectic of self-consciousness. The first understanding of "self" is relational but negative. A more developed understanding of self (one with a positive content) presupposes that liberty as capacity has become determinate through a decision to take risks in relating to others.

[264] Using the terminology of previous chapters, we can formulate an implication of these proportions: the second terms can stand to the first as both receptivity and activity (*et motus et movens*). That is, the causal relations between the terms are reversible: actual choices can modify prior integrations; complete acts of attention can modify initial orientations or expectations; individuals can reform as well as corrupt institutions.

some attention to traditional accounts of how virtues guide choices. Virtues as "habits" ground probabilities governing which decisions may be made, but, since liberty is a capacity with multiple potential determinants, virtues are just one class of potential determinants of decisions.

Part III opens with a diagram of the "Structure of the Good" as a heuristic mapping of categories relevant to understanding relations among liberty, institutions and their possible ends. Descriptive examples may prompt insights into those relations, but they are only preliminary to working out explanatory correlations among several of the most important categories. The dialectical relations of liberty and its determinants will reappear in that explanatory account. Part IV will make further connections among the accumulating insights into decision-making, institutions and liberty. These "integrations" will provide the background for a diagnosis in Part V of the political anarchist's dream of a purely voluntary social order. In subsequent chapters they will also be diagnostic tools for evaluating economic and political practices.

II What is Decision-Making?

This inquiry into decision-making begins with a review of previous remarks on "normative intentional acts" and then formulates an explanatory account of deciding. All of this is preliminary to linking intentional operators within schemes of recurrence to social schemes (institutions) that such operators produce and which "act back on" their producers.

Normative intentional acts are functionally related to other types of intentional operations.[265] Four question types provide clues for differentiating the types of operations and their intended objects. Questions of decision intend, first,

---

[265] The distinct acts and their intended objects are related not by similarity but by how they contribute to, perform functions in relation to, completion of a scheme of recurrence and its complex outcome.

possibilities or options generated by questions for deliberation and, second, the "best option" or what would actually be good to do. These related operations are parts of a dynamic structure responsive to the demands of a principle of completion. Talk of operations "completing" one another is an advance over talk of "volitional control" and "executive acts" since the former is tied to faculty psychology and the latter is a descriptive category. To identify questions of decision as events in a structured process of wondering that tends toward completion escapes these two problems. Decision-making about ends and means becomes a correlate and completion of prior intentional acts and their objects. In short, a normative intentional act integrates or completes what prior acts supply.

How are these distinct types of acts moved along toward completion? Reverting to the earlier categories of receptivity and activity, we can note again how creative understanding is "a conditioned but flexible range of possible intentional operations responding to the related but opposed demands of the principles of completion and assimilation." If reaching for an understanding of what would be good to choose is conditioned (moved) by an indefinite number variables, it still is a "moving." The category of "demand" appeared in Chapter Two as a way of expressing how biological needs necessitate action if they are to be met. But the category applies to more than biological needs and the actions they prompt. One significant expansion of "demand" manifests itself in human fantasies about "a history yet to be made," a past "better than it was," or "possible worlds that will never exist." If the demand to fantasize, to imagine "something better than what has been or is," moves deliberating, what moves deciding? The hypothesis in the last chapter was that, "just as there are spontaneous and trained demands for images relevant to biological and psychosocial functioning, so there are intelligent demands for understanding what is true and what would be good to do." Questions of decision manifest a demand for what would be good to do. In more complex terms, they express a desire for possible scenarios (images) that one will understand and judge as worthy of bringing about and, as imagined, will evoke emotions needed to support action. (Recall Henry Adams' puzzle of how to motivate a new century with images and symbols.) Effective action has its prerequisites, e.g. a capacity for fantasizing, emotions that "weight" options, images that evoke the needed emotions and so make decisiveness more probable.

With this abbreviated listing of prerequisites, a former scheme of recurrence reappears.[266] The correlative terms of capacity, demand, image, emotion and action are basic categories for explaining decision-making. To them we should add the category of "historicity" to acknowledge that all five categories, when applied to actual cases of decision-making, involve cultural (H_2) and biographical (H_1) variables. So decision-making "completes" a series of intentional operations that reflect capacities for responding to spontaneous and trained demands which are orientated by variable personal and historical conditions making emotional links to some images more probable than to others and so "weighting" the probabilities according to which decisions may be made. A diagram may help us track this complex meaning of decision-making.

---

[266] Most noticeably absent from this listing are the material or environmental resources that can make the difference between wishful thinking and a realistic option. Material limitations on liberty will be briefly considered at the end of this chapter.

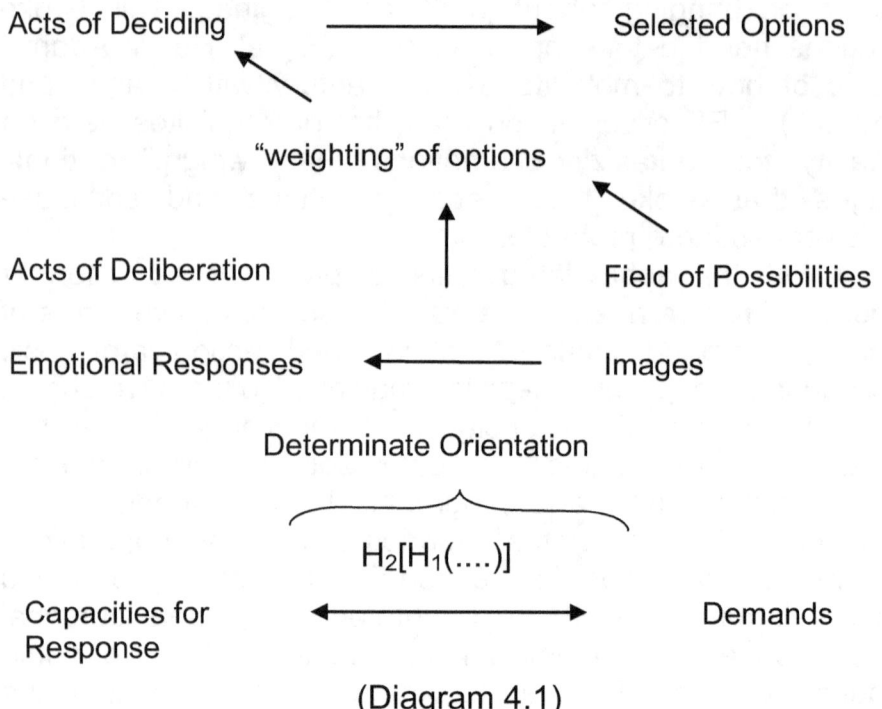

(Diagram 4.1)

Interrelating all these terms amounts to recognizing how we can have both highly variable antecedents to a decision while still having a common structure to actual choices. To incorporate both the receptivity of actors and the dynamic activity of structured operations, we shifted to the language of "integrators" and "operators." Briefly in review: we can distinguish operators because question types are distinct, i.e. we can posit operators for the distinct and functionally related intentional acts reaching for their proper ends in images, hypotheses, facts, possibilities and what is actually good to do. Integrators are the past and present responses that meet the demands of the operators while questions mediate between the demands and the responses.

Chapter Three focused on deliberative intentional acts and their operator, i.e. a demand for what possible states-of-affairs it might be good to produce. While the range of such acts and their intended objects was evidence of a relative independence of creative understanding from its initial conditions, the earlier insights into historicity and personal orientations qualified that independence. Evidence of both dependence and independence provided entrée to the topic of dialectical relations between operators and integrators and between a principle of completion and a principle of assimilation. The outcome of this shift to dialectic was the third approximation to the meaning of creative understanding: "a conditioned but flexible range of possible intentional operations responding to the related but opposed demands of the principles of completion and assimilation."

A normative intentional act is also an instance of creative understanding, so an explanatory understanding of decision-making will make use of the previous correlations. For example, actual decisions occur as matters of probability since an indefinite number of variables conditioning them are related non-systematically. Thus, since intentional acts are instances of both receptivity and activity, new questions and insights have as much claim as received opinions and habits to being potential determinants of new decisions. In the language of dialectic, the demands of the normative operator can challenge integrated patterns of deciding and acting. More specifically, since the question of decision (What should we do?) leads to a question of judgment (Is this really good to do?), the demands of the critical operator, if not blocked, can push inquiry beyond habitual patterns of response.[267] At least on occasion, new questions and answers to them can revise or reverse well-entrenched patterns.

This conclusion is consistent with earlier claims about the structured relations among intentional acts and their objects. As answers to questions for understanding are to images and as answers to questions of judging are to hypotheses, so answers to questions of decision are to imagined possibilities. Later intentional acts integrate or "supplement" what earlier ones supply. Even if established integrations "bias" a line of questioning (possibly revealing the demand of a principle of assimilation for what is compatible

---

[267] Cf. Chapter Three, footnote 212.

with prior beliefs and habits), this simply reflects the role of expectations (i.e. prior neural patterns) in guiding attention, the selection of images and emotional responses. But Chapter One discussed surprises as well as expectations, and Chapter Two noted how the deliberate manipulation of images can alter artistic tastes, consumer purchases and political allegiances. The subsequent generality is worth repeating: In regard to habitual, routinely occurring responses, if we change key variables, we can change routine responses. Educators make decisions to do as much with every new curriculum design.

The deliberate changing of key variables is an instance of decision-making acting back on existing initial conditions. Prior descriptive examples included efforts to lower rates of teen pregnancy, drunk driving and alcoholism. Behind such efforts are often imaginative strategies for encouraging populations to change how they make decisions. The usual goal is to change the "internalized environments" of a population so that persons consider a broader range of questions before acting. The alteration may be as simple as expanding one's horizon from the "snapshot" to the "film clip" so that one considers a broader range of imaginable consequences of single acts or habits.[268] As noted before,

---

[268] These photographic metaphors can be transposed into the language of schemes of recurrence. Parts of a basic scheme of intentional acts are the acts of deliberation yielding a range of options from which acts of decision make selections. Consider how adding reflective "sub-routines" can make the basic pattern a more controlled and effective way of operating. For example, to deliberative acts one could add the simple technique of "playing the devil's advocate," but one could also rely on "blue-ribbon committees" to escape some of the dangers of interest-group politics in generating policy options. To decision-making one could adopt some simple form of cost-benefit analysis, but one could also institutionalize judicial review of legislative decisions. Such are some of the ways of making a basic scheme more reliable. As part of a long-range fantasy, one could go on to imagine a transformed

such changes in internalized environments become part of the new context, the new integration, operators bring to future operations.[269]

An earlier example of a new integration was the historical breakthrough to an understanding of both non-systematic relations among events and how probability statements formulate their intelligibility as ideal frequencies. This development in intellectual history allows later generations to think of themselves as existing in and through complex series of internal and external schemes of recurrence and as having various capacities for conditioned but flexible ranges of responses to variations in those schemes.[270] From such an expanded context, we have gone on to talk about liberty and decision-making in dialectical terms and so have evaded a false disjunction between determinism and indeterminism. While intentional acts are dependent on "inputs" from neurochemical, organic and psychosocial schemes of recurrence, they also belong to higher-order schemes that exhibit their own flexible range of responses to such inputs.[271] The critical operator, expressed in questions

---

world of scholarship in which specialized schemes formed an ongoing cycle of operations in producing, interpreting, assessing and deciding upon diagnoses of problems and their possible solutions and in implementing and then monitoring the results of the decisions. The Epilogue will sketch such a fantasy.

[269] Cf. Chapter Three, footnote 244.

[270] The widespread use of the language of "mechanisms" is evidence that this development in understanding has not been matched by an adequate development in expression.

[271] Capacities for flexible and deliberate adjustments to such inputs are manifest in common experiences of planned responses to lower-order disruptions of higher schemes. For example, we are used to pharmacological interventions in neurochemical and organic disorders; individuals adjust their study habits when caffeine is no longer an aid to concentration; political dissidents employ new technologies to circumvent political censorship. Planning and deciding can flexibly and effectively respond to inputs that disrupt

of judging, belongs to such a higher-order scheme. It functions as an internal determinant of assent to actual states-of-affairs and of consent to bring about new states-of-affairs. In the latter case, it is functionally related to the act of decision-making which itself completes a scheme of recurrence.

The preceding review and expansion of the characteristics of decision-making lead to an understanding of a normative intentional act as a distinct type of operation correlated with other types of operations occurring within a higher-order scheme of recurrence that exhibits the three kinds of determinants already associated with liberty: (1) prior integrations providing the established context for (2) the demands of operators evoking intentional acts which (3) move toward indeterminate ends in response to the demands of the opposed but related principles of completion and assimilation.

Before focusing on the question of how intentional operations produce institutions and, in turn, are affected by them, we should take some notice of the conventional distinction between facts and values. As a matter of fact, the demands of operators evoke intentional acts. Persons experience spontaneous neural demands for images and affects, intellectual demands for answers to questions, rational demands for correct answers, normative demands for choosing options that are actually good. But what justifies believing that such demands are obligatory, i.e. persons should cooperate with them?

Chapter Three concluded that intentional acts formed a dynamic structure. Leading up to that conclusion were descriptive examples of persons attending to puzzling clues, asking questions and sometimes arriving at answers. The further question was why these acts occur as they do. Answering this further question led to studying these acts in relation to one another, i.e. beginning to understand them as distinct but functionally related operations forming a structure.

---

the pursuit of chosen ends, no matter whether they are routine ends or novel objectives.

The goal was an explanatory account of the intentional acts that were first experienced, named and distinguished in a descriptive context. Chapter Three formulated an explanatory account of the intelligibility of the processes of knowing and deciding, i.e. of what regularly occurs in raising and answering questions. In one sense this account is factual, i.e. what we find ourselves doing both in trying to understand what is true and in trying to do what is good. In another sense this account is normative since it explains an intelligible pattern among acts of intentionality. Ordinarily, once one has understood how some process regularly occurs, the intelligent thing to do is to act according to that pattern. Let the first meaning of "normative" (N_1) refer to this understanding of how a process regularly goes forward.[272]

Still, one can ask why persons should cooperate with the inner demands of their various operators even if they are the "normal" order in which acts move toward their proper ends. My reply is that the relevant evidence lies not in some theory of intentionality but in the performance of the one asking the question. The argument here is a performative one: Do I or do I not find the various demands occurring in my own practical, intersubjective and theoretical inquiries? Do I or do I not judge that cooperating with these demands distinguishes my careful performance from my careless performance in diagnosing problems, settling questions of fact, making plans and decisions? The appeal here is to what a reader may or may not have attended to in raising and

---

[272] For this usage of "normative," I am indebted to Fred Lawrence. Cf. "Editors' Introduction" to Lonergan, <u>Macroeconomic Dynamics</u>, lv-lvi. Bruce Anderson has supplied a useful example of N_1 and N_2 in questions about driving a car. Corresponding to N_1 are the questions: What are the essential parts of a car? How do they work together? What does it take for a car to work properly? Given how a car works, what must people do to drive intelligently?
Corresponding to N_2 are the questions: What traffic laws should we obey? What risks to ourselves and others should we avoid while driving?

answering questions. The supposition is that, after attending to one's own performance, one will judge that the inner demands of the operators are normative for one's self. Let this be the meaning of normativity symbolized as N_2.

The normative functioning of intentional acts (N_1) is a reaching for completion. Persons at liberty may or may not cooperate with the various demands of the operators contributing to this end. The normative notion of liberty emerging in this chapter identifies what persons ideally will do. Subsequent criticisms of less than ideal performance, of operations that are insufficiently attentive, insufficiently intelligent and morally undeveloped, will appeal to N_2.

III Decisions and Institutions

The reader may have noticed that no effort, as of yet, has been made to distinguish between moral and nonmoral decisions. Choosing a television channel or a favorite ice cream is a "value-laden" act but not one conventionally labeled a "moral choice." By way of contrast, choosing to be faithful to one's spouse and to be honest in one's business dealings are conventionally thought to be weightier matters and decisions of a moral kind. But what distinguishes such kinds of choices? A generic description of decision-making may help us detect the relevant differences.

Suppose decision-making is first an indeterminate capacity for choosing ends and means. Its correlate will be a field of possible ends and means. The empirical possibility of different ends and courses of action is one basis for the indeterminacy of the capacity.[273] But actual decisions are

---

[273] Another basis will be the non-systematic relations obtaining among images, sensible presentations, acts of attending and questioning, the demands such acts effectively express and the insights that occur as matters of probability. The use of "effectively" acknowledges that among the variables symbolized by the subscripts in p_l and i_m may be psychological and intellectual barriers to

eventually made from among the possibilities, and these add determinations to the capacity. The latter may be the impersonal determinants resulting from choices made by anonymous others (H_2), e.g. the cultural patterns new generations find already in place so that they uncritically believe that burning witches cures plagues or executing persons is a way of reducing violent crimes. They may be the personal determinants resulting from choices which, with repetition, become habits or established orientations. Then some will be predisposed to favor bright colors over muted ones, socializing over private reflection, cautious political policies over dramatic initiatives to improve lives.[274]

When the category "orientation" first appeared in Chapter One, we noted the development from an indeterminate capacity to a focused capacity through the forming of expectations or neural patterns. One puzzle was how acts of attention could select some stimuli out of a field of

---

attending to certain images and so to raising certain unwanted questions that would be responsive to a demand for further insights.
[274] Talk of historical and personal determinants of choice may raise a puzzle about liberty. Can we really be "at liberty" if, when we act "as we please," what pleases us is already determined by habits? One response to this puzzle suggests a notion of liberty as sometimes a characteristic of prereflective acts. "Acting out of habit" or routine need not mean one is not acting freely. Habitual acts can represent the demands of the principle of assimilation for psychological continuity and stability in living. One practical benefit of deliberately acting out of habit is found in increased efficiency. Recall the distinction between being conscious and being attentive and the relevant examples of driving familiar routes to work or carrying out routine tasks. In such cases explicit attention and reflection are not needed in choosing ends and means. The evidence is we proceed efficiently and voluntarily with our "business" without stopping to attend to other options and to weigh their merits. Lonergan takes up this puzzle in Grace and Freedom: Operative Grace in the Thought of St. Thomas Aquinas. CW 1 (Toronto: University of Toronto Press, 2000), 51-53.

competing alternatives. In Chapter Two a related puzzle was how emotions could "weight" certain images and so "dispose" or orientate persons to favor certain kinds of re-sponses or actions over others. Now our question is how a historically conditioned orientation affects decision-making.

Recall that one part of the process of making decisions is a question of judgment, e.g. asking whether something is actually good to do or is the best available option. Before answering such questions, we anticipate what relevant conditions first need to be satisfied. For example, if we are trying to decide on a large purchase, we may check the money in our wallets or our bank balance. If we are trying to decide whether to take an umbrella with us as we leave the house, we may look skyward for signs of approaching storms or may turn on a local weather channel. Without noticing what we are doing, we are intelligently checking whether an eventual judgment and a subsequent decision are going to have adequate support.

Let this intelligent anticipation of relevant conditions be labeled a "prospective judgment."[275] Again, the issue is what will count as relevant evidence for making a reliable decision. Here, then, is an initial intersecting of orientation with decision-making. The considerations or conditions that occur to persons as worth their attention will vary with differences in those persons, e.g. their habits and prior education. Consequently, their judgments about what is actually good to do will vary depending on what their prospective judgments have included or "counted" as significant issues. In short, the operating occurring in both types of judgments and in deciding may vary with the orientation of the operator.

This abbreviated sketch[276] of the role of orientation in decision-making has not been a digression from the earlier

---

[275] This terminology is borrowed from Insight, 304-306.
[276] Asking further relevant questions will lead to noticing how much is missing from this sketch. For example, granted decision-making has antecedent conditions in orientation, what are the formative influences on a person's orientation? Clearly biological age is a

question of how we can distinguish between moral and nonmoral decisions. If "determinate orientation" is understood as an integration or complex patterning of neuropsychological processes and psychosocial meanings (e.g. what counts as good manners or responsible uses of money), then to recognize its "influence" over judging and deciding is to accept part of the dialectical relation between the opposed but related principles of completion and assimilation. Determinate orientation represents habitual responses to the demands of the latter for continuity and stability. Suppose, however, that a "film clip" of moral decision-making notes development or expansions in understanding and caring about what is good to do. Then, there will be evidence that demands for stability have their counterpart in demands to expand beyond already achieved insights and emotional attachments.

Developmental psychologists in the last century proposed different schemata for such expansions of moral views. What follows is a very simple model of moral development in response to the demands for "completion." Suppose a child begins by assuming that what is good to do is what seems good at the time. Fairly quickly the child learns there often can be a difference between the two. The basic insight that "what seems good is not necessarily what is good" is not innate. Its sequel is also learned: "What is good for me is not necessarily what is good for others." The insight here may arise from noticing that other kids won't play with me if I always insist on getting my own way. Of course, a clever child may proceed to manipulate the other kids, but most children move on to a further insight: "What is really good is not

---

relevant condition for the exercise of capacity. Imagine neuroscientists studying the neurochemical processes of the six-week old infant's brain and then comparing their findings with those from studies of the brains of children who are twenty-four months old. What other kinds of formative influences are routinely at work shaping a person's orientation? Comments below on various "differentiations of consciousness" and "displacements" will return to this question.

measured solely by my wants and interests." A transition is perhaps occurring to thinking about how my actions might affect others. I may begin to ask a new question: "Would I want them to do to me what I'm thinking of doing to them?" What later in life may be learned as the Golden Rule or a version of Kant's categorical imperative will have its roots in these basic transitional insights.[277]

The limited purpose of this model of moral development is to identify the <u>minimal</u> and general considerations of prospective moral judgments. The hypothesis is that being moral in decision-making is, at a minimum, a matter of being careful in decision-making when "being careful" is usually specified by the preceding sequence of considerations. Thus, a person's orientation in acting manifests moral care (1) in distinguishing what is good and what merely seems good, (2) in distinguishing personal goods and the well being of others, (3) in considering a range of goods beyond personal wants and interests before making a decision. Note how the meaning of "what is good" is more "complete" by the end of this sequence of insights. Its meaning has expanded from what seems good to what is good, from what is good for one

---

[277] A further development and more precise wording of these crucial insights is a recognition that what I am justified in doing to others, others *ceteris paribus* are justified in doing to me. Why? Presumably because I am one among many, i.e. an instance of the general type "person." What I do to others, they, as instances of the same class, should be justified in doing to me under similar circumstances. Implicit here are the demands of the principle of completion. In seeking an explanation of why something is the way it is, we reach for an understanding of what is true of not just the single instance but of every relevant instance of a class of events or objects. Even vehement counter-claims about there being different types of people and so different "rules" for different types are an indirect acknowledgement of these insights. In effect, they are efforts to show that there are relevant differences among persons justifying differences in treatment among what would otherwise be similar cases.

to what is good for others and toward a further, as yet implicit, concern for what would be good for anyone to do in similar circumstances.[278]

With this minimal meaning of what moral decision-making generally has as it relevant considerations, we can distinguish between moral and nonmoral decisions. A choice will belong to the class of moral decisions when at least two of the three insights have some relevance to making it. In contrast, only the first insight will have any relevance to nonmoral decisions.[279] The two types of decisions do not differ in structure, i.e. in how the operations of deciding are related to other intentional acts, including that of prospective judging. The difference lies in what questions or considerations are relevant to the prospective judgments leading to moral or nonmoral decisions.

But concrete individuals ask or are unaware of the relevant questions and have or miss the relevant insights, and their prior orientations make one or the other alternative more probable. So it is that in debates over the death penalty, some participants will be predisposed to consider only the question of guilt; others will give priority to public security,

---

[278] The question of why others may have some claim on me for "due consideration" would lead to a broader discussion of equality and rights. A position on this question is implicit in the preceding footnote. The broader discussion is beyond the scope of this project though some of its issues will appear in subsequent chapters.

[279] Basing the distinction between moral and nonmoral decisions on these three insights is a further differentiation of the usual comment that moral choices presuppose effects on others, i.e. Robinson Crusoe needed Friday before he could act justly. While true, this generality is incomplete. Moral choices may involve effects on only the chooser. In such cases, the first and the third insights, but not the second, are relevant considerations in making such choices. Traditional discussions of prudence, temperance and fortitude sometimes focused on beneficial or harmful effects on the actor while the virtue of justice was thought relevant to how the actor's choices affected others and so involved all three insights.

while still others will be reluctant to condone executing even those guilty of heinous crimes. Yet orientations are not fixed but parts of the dynamic pattern of intentional operations. They are forms of integration and so exposed to the demands of the principle of completion expressed in further questions. These demands are one basis for changes in predispositions, settled judgments and favored opinions. Of course the demands meet limits in the determinate internal and external conditions of a person's actual living. Those conditions set up a flexible range of empirical possibilities within which a person's capacities for understanding and moral virtue can develop.[280]

The practical question, then, is how persons are to develop as moral agents within whatever ranges of empirical possibilities they enjoy. In traditional descriptive language, the question is how persons are to acquire "virtues." Suppose that virtues are habits that result when indeterminate capacities for acting (1) gain determinate direction through prior moral decisions and (2) are "completed" by gaining such direction. For example, a realized virtue of prudence presupposes (1) a capacity for judging and deciding, (2) a person's actual history of acts of judging and deciding, and (3) a preponderance of those acts being morally sound judgments and decisions. Within populations such established patterns of operation, or virtues of prudence, make sound moral judgments and choices more probable in the future. The analogy to skillful performance in a sport is apt. A capacity for performance becomes actual performance and, with repetition, can become skilled operation such that persons habitually display a high level of competence. Now suppose the performance is that of moral decision-making. Then the "skill" is a determinate orientation in choosing, a relatively stable pattern in how persons arrive at morally responsible choices. By exploiting earlier insights into expectations and

---

[280] So it was that historically many cultures witnessed no dissenting views on slavery or the death penalty. The emergence of moral objections to either practice was initially a matter of low probability.

habits, we can replace talk of "virtues" with talk of "flexible ranges of schemes of recurrent normative intentional acts." For instance, the virtue of prudence becomes a determinate orientation to make morally appropriate judgments and decisions such that prudent persons routinely respond to highly variable situations with a high probability of making morally appropriate choices.

The implications for "virtue ethics" of this shift in language are not the concern of this project. Instead, this brief response to the traditional question of how individuals are to "acquire virtues" provides a transition to the main question of this chapter: What role do institutions play in moral decision-making? The development of virtue may be thought of as a matter of altering the probabilities governing the conditions for the recurrent making of moral choices by some population. How do institutions make a difference in these probabilities?

Before exploring the relations between institutions and decision-making, we can take a quick look back at a problem of language first seen in Chapter One. In 1975 Posner worried that the neurosciences might develop a "research schizophrenia" regarding conscious acts. Sub-sequent decades have justified his fears. Unfortunately the same has been true in fields of genetics. Until the mid-fifties one could find writers asking how genetic materials could be organized by "top-down" operators to serve more complex organic operations. Since the middle of the last century, the focus in genetics has been almost entirely on "bottom-up" accounts of the genetic determinants of biological events. Thus, the descriptive language of genetic "blueprints," "mechanisms," "directives," "codes" and "information storage" has become commonplace in accounts of how genes provide the conditions for and "control" over biological operations.

While this study has not raised questions about genetic determinants and their links to the neurochemical processes sustaining organic processes, the question of the "turn" will someday have to be raised in the various fields of genetics. Whether the present inquiry, with its shifting from talk of "interactive systems" to talk of schemes of recurrence and of a dialectic between related but opposed principles of assimilation and completion, will prove of any use in making such a future turn remains an open question. At least the puzzle we now face, namely, how institutions affect moral decision-making, has a similar form and history.

Part of the history of this puzzle has been an non-dialectical understanding of institutional conditions ("nurture") which, when combined with p_i, c_j and n_k ("nature"), are assumed to be exhaustive of the data (1) in need of explanation and (2) relevant to understanding decision-making. Thus, bottom-up views have until recently predominated in sociobiology, social psychology and socioeconomics. In the last century behavioral psychology, with its rejection of introspective analysis and suspicion of "mind" as a four-letter word, adopted an equally non-dialectical perspective. With a later acceptance of cognitive psychology as a legitimate discipline, scientists were willing to talk about "mind" as a differentiated reality.[281] Still, technical language has lagged behind this change in perspective, and usage in neuroscience and cognitive psychology continues to default to the older terminology of mechanisms, and more recently to computer metaphors and talk of information systems.

We should not expect a new terminology to win wide acceptance anytime soon. What follows below will suggest some new terminology (e.g. "patterned resources" and "organizing principles"), but the primary focus will be on understanding the linkages among insights expressed in basic terms such as "capacity," "demand," "liberty," "orientations" and "institutions." The expectation is that, with sufficient descriptive examples grounding both insights and terms, an envisioned complex web of relations among correlates will pose a new challenge to future writers about liberty: How are they to talk adequately about the complex correlations among these terms? A first step is to display the categories as a "mapping" of complex relations. A series of descriptive

---

[281] For a brief history of this change in the views of "mind," see Jerome Bruner, "Nelson Goodman's Worlds" in Bruner, 93-95.

examples will specify the meanings and relations among the terms. Then the terms most relevant to this inquiry will shift into an explanatory context. We begin with the diagram.[282]

INDIVIDUAL		SOCIAL	ENDS
capacity, demand	operation	cooperation	particular good
plasticity	development, skill	institution, role task	good of order
liberty	orientation, displacement	personal relations	terminal goods

(Diagram 4.2)

    One clue to understanding this diagram is the earlier correlation between structured operations in inquiry and what those operations intend, i.e. their "ends." While questions of judgment ask what is the case and so intend "facts," questions for deliberation ask what can be the case and so intend possibilities that may be turned into realities. The first category, capacity, refers to an understanding of how persons spontaneously intend various goods and act in various ways to procure them. An easy example is someone shivering in the cold, wanting warmth and deciding to build a fire. The fire is a means, and warmth is the end or good that meets a human need or demand. Here is a clear instance of attention focused on or intending a particular good as its end. Next we can reflect on the history of human mastery of fire and other forms of energy as means of survival. The demands are recurrent, but the means for responding to them have changed. The operations or actions that expressed human capacity and produced heat for cave dwellers required modest skills, but over time both those operations and those skills

---

[282] This is an amended version of a diagram found in Lonergan's Method in Theology, 48.

became far more complex. The flexibility or <u>plasticity</u> of human capacities permitted <u>development</u> of new means (skills) for understanding and controlling sources of energy. Among the gradually developed means are <u>institutions</u> that now routinely supply energy on demand to paying customers. For example, city utility departments are humanly designed orders for delivering basic services (<u>particular</u> <u>goods</u>) so that customers have heating in the winter and air conditioning in the summer.

Reliable access to such services is possible only because of the ongoing <u>cooperation</u> among persons who fill certain <u>roles</u> and competently carry out assigned <u>tasks</u> with the required skills. The cooperative relations may be among anonymous parties, e.g. the persons who produce and those who consume energy from public utilities. A vast web of such anonymous relations links consumers as bill payers with utility plant employees, repair crews, managers of city departments and their staffs.

If all the related roles are predictably to yield energy for consumers, they must form a relatively stable order that people at least partially understand and repeatedly decide to maintain by carrying out their tasks in ongoing schemes of cooperation called "institutions." Such schemes in turn belong to more complex schemes. Institutions that distribute energy are dependent on the recurrent schemes supplying energy that continue so long as there are recurrent schemes exploring for new energy resources; and all of the preceding require the recurrent schemes of financing.

Particular goods will keep flowing as a result of such a complex <u>good</u> <u>of</u> <u>order</u> composed of so many diverse schemes of cooperation within and among institutions. But this order acts back on its creators. Institutional roles and tasks require certain types of skills, and this demand on human capacities favors the emergence and development of some operations over others. For example, in businesses the capacity for and the operations of counting will develop into professional accounting practices. The capacity for social interaction and subsequent social skills will, in corporate settings, become the policies of personnel departments. Even the child's capacity for daydreaming can, given the right market demands, become the skills used in making predictions about consumption rates and labor costs.

In review: operations express capacities and respond to demands; human plasticity makes possible the emergence of new skills, and institutional roles and tasks both presuppose those skills and evoke new ones. How is all this related to decision-making? The social orders that maintain a flow of particular goods flourish or decline depending on the degree of cooperation among persons willing and able to fill their roles in institutional settings. The vast network of interdependent operations continues to function because persons are able to do their jobs and actually decide to do them.[283] Let enough of them exhibit incompetence or a reluctance to play their roles and things begin to fall apart. At least this much can motivate executives to fund training and incentive programs.

The social orders that result from institutional networks sustained by the deliberate cooperation of largely anonymous persons are far from static arrangements. In the short run, institutions may seem unchanging, even inert, but their existence is rarely secure or stable. Internal and external conditions make possible their emergence and, if sufficiently altered, can threaten their survival. So there will be requisite skill-levels in an available workforce, but the latter experiences turnovers, and any replacements may be far less skilled. Investor confidence may launch an enterprise only later to vanish in a market panic. Consumer demand may expand and create new business opportunities, but it also may contract and leave some ventures high and dry. Besides cooperation in the workplace, there are the animosities that fuel office feuds and strikes. And then there are the external threats of political rivals, economic competitors and natural disasters, any of which can undermine the original

---

[283] Again, "function" is used here in the sense that acts are oriented toward their proper ends.

environment in which an institution first appeared and flourished.

So challenges to the survival of institutions and even to the survival of social orders are numerous, and a relevant question is why persons make sacrifices to meet these challenges. Classical Liberalism relied on an eighteenth-century psychology of the passions to provide an answer. People will sacrifice for a social order out of self-interest so long as they perceive that it provides a flow of goods to meet their needs. This appeal to self-interest has its doubters.[284] A social order can itself be a good that evokes passionate loyalty not simply because it provides particular goods to its members but because some members understand and admire it as worthy of their support. At least some instances of heroic self-sacrifice on behalf of social orders seem immune to ad hoc arguments asserting that all generous acts are traceable to self-interest.

In the first place, institutions and more complex social orders owe their emergence to intelligent plans and decisions to cooperate. In the second place, they owe their survival to the routine recurrence of both. Why, in particular, are the decisions recurrent? Threats to their recurrence may prove enlightening. If natural disasters can be accidental disruptions of institutional functions, systemic corruption and personal malfeasance are betrayals of trust. One difference here is that natural disasters do not proceed from intentional acts, but betrayals do. We assume people are at liberty to choose means and ends. They can cooperate for what they perceive to be the "common good," but they can also compete solely to advance private goods. However, whether they pursue common or private goods is not the decisive issue; rather, the question is whether what they routinely produce is not what seems good but what is good. In the latter case, they will, regardless of their intentions, be contributing to a good of

---

[284] Chapter Six will offer a genealogy of the psychology of "interests" and a criticism of its limits.

order that provides particular goods that are in fact good.[285] Thus, while a particular institution may function poorly so that its effects on a broader social order are largely negative, the offsetting benefits of other institutions within that more complex good of order may preserve the poorly performing member well past its useful lifespan.

There is no shortage of persons using liberty irresponsibly and of institutional practices harming human goods. Suppose a CEO is primarily intent on earning salary bonuses and amassing stock options larger than any rival's compensation package. Leveraged buy-outs and account-ing practices that inflate the company's annual earnings may be the means selected to gain these ends. Whether the company's "growth" is sustainable and whether employees' retirement funds and stockholders' investments are at risk are of little concern to the CEO. That concern has narrowed to gaining personal benefits and avoiding personal costs. But then the decisions that follow will undermine <u>personal relations</u> since they ignore the legitimate expectations of others for honesty and fair returns on their labor and investments. Instead of the good of personal relations, the CEO sees employees and investors simply as resources to be manipulated in pursuing private ends and particular goods.

Fortunately there are leaders who run private and public institutions differently and avoid such abuses of trust. They consistently make responsible uses of their capacities and skills. Executives and employees understand how their cooperative efforts meet both personal and communal needs. Feelings of loyalty to the institution, its personnel and customers guide choices. Despite occasional disagreements, they believe that what they are doing as a group is worthwhile, and so they sacrifice time, energy and self-interest to sustain their common enterprise. Why do they do this? Presumably

---

[285] The question of intention here is subordinated to the question of what actually results from one's actions. Actual goods may follow from self-interested pursuits; at least this much must be granted to Adam Smith's hidden-hand argument.

they are in agreement that some goods are worth the effort, i.e. are <u>terminal goods</u> worth promoting. These may be popularly labeled as the "values" of financial security for employees' families, the solid reputation of the firm and the professional integrity of its officers. Behind such talk are shared judgments about the goods of family life, of corporate responsibility to larger communities and of the ethical standards of a profession. When routine actions follow upon such judgments, the actors' decisions "complete" their best judgments about what is good to do. Operations, then, have as their correlates objectives that are actually good.

This correlation of personal decisions and their objectives is a step toward understanding the terms <u>orientation</u> and <u>displacement</u> as they occur in the diagram. If a person's orientation is toward understanding and doing what is good, then efforts to make moral decisions become a pattern or habit that witnesses few lapses. The old maxim was "the good is what good people do." On the other hand, if a person's orientation toward what is good is haphazard and episodic, decisions are inconsistent. Moments of clear moral resolve occur infrequently during longer periods of inattention to what one is making of a life. A momentary thought that one could be doing better by oneself and by others is met not so much by indifference as by a preference for comfortable routines in thinking and acting.[286] The tension between envisioned growth and a reluctance to shed old habits becomes a test of a person's liberty: "Will I move forward or rest where I am?" The test is personal: "What am I to make of my life?" While no one presumably can take away my responsibility for how I answer, others are part of the test since the question is also, "What are we to make of our community?"

The category "displacement" refers to an understanding of how persons sometimes dramatically reverse their habitual orientations. Addicts may reverse self-destructive

---

[286] The demands of the principle of assimilation, thus, override those of the principle of completion.

patterns of living; a new parent may reverse a narcissistic focus on personal convenience and decide to take more responsibility for parenting; an insider's loyalty to some group may become subordinate to new concerns for the effects that group is having on outsiders. Still, what comes first are the established orientations, and so the question is how persons are ever "displaced" from such prior integrations of thinking and acting. St. Augustine offered a succinct response: "*Incipit exire qui incipit amare.*"[287] Finding something or someone worthy of one's love offers a powerful antidote to the fears and rationalizations that sustain inadequately developed orientations.[288] But that is just a beginning, and a new "film clip" ideally will record new integrations of emotions and decisions yielding new orientations toward what is actually worth doing with one's life. Absent these new orientations, one wavers between moments of resolve and drifting along old paths.[289] The dialectic of assimilation and completion

---

[287] "One begins to leave who begins to love." Quoted in Eric Voegelin, "Eternal Being in Time," in <u>Anamnesis</u> (Columbia: University of Missouri Press, 1990), 140.

[288] For the criteria of a minimally adequate moral development in orientation, see the simple model of moral development at the beginning of this Part III.

[289] Rainer Maria Rilke's poem "Archaic Bust of Apollo" ends with the line, "You must change your life." (61) In "Requiem for a Friend," he identifies how much resistance any resolve to change may face:

> "We can so easily
> slip back from what we have struggled to attain,
> abruptly, into a life we never wanted;
> can find that we are trapped, as in a dream,
> and die there, without ever waking up.
> This can occur. Anyone who has lifted
> his blood into a years-long work may find
> that he can't sustain it, the force of gravity
> is irresistible, and it falls back, worthless.
> For somewhere there is an ancient enmity

reappears as a tension between a decisive departure from the past and the drag effect of old routines.

The preceding has been the promised descriptive exposition of the terms and relations suggested in Diagram 4.2. There was also a promise to offer an explanatory account of a limited number of those terms. Part IV offers such an account by correlating the category "institution" with the categories on line 3 of Diagram 4.2. Again, the primary question is, How do institutions affect decision-making? The framework for answering this question is a dialectical one. How do schemes of recurrence among intentional operations produce social schemes of recurrence that, in turn, act back on the former? This type of question appeared earlier. Then the puzzle was how schemes of recurrence among neurochemical processes made intentional acts possible, acts that, in turn, could deliberately alter those processes.

IV   A Dialectical Account of Liberty and Institutions

One way of exploring dialectical relations between intentional schemes of recurrence and social schemes is to revisit the question of how socialization processes make it more probable that group beliefs and practices will become the internalized patterns of thinking and acting of a new generation. Components of an answer have appeared in previous chapters. (1) The orientation of intentional acts is at first an indeterminate capacity. (2) Over time intentional responses give determinate content to this capacity. (3) *Mitsein* or social being is the first context for those early responses. (4) While individuals are capable of "acting back upon" their origins, the first "self" is a complex patterning of borrowed beliefs and practices.[290]

---

between our daily life and the great work."
The Selected Poetry of Rainer Maria Rilke. Stephen Mitchell, editor and translator (New York: Random House, 1982), 85-87.

[290] Recall the dialectic of institutions and individuals described at the beginning of this chapter. While the category "individual" has a

Among the first means by which institutions (e.g. family, church and school) evoke intentional responses and so shape early orientations are forms of public discourse, especially conversations about identities and social rankings, truth and falsity, right and wrong. In this sense others "talk me into existence."[291] This public discourse occurs at clan gatherings around the nightly campfire where a new generation hears the oral history of its people. It is part of elementary school education with its sanitized versions of a nation's history.

The modes of communicating accepted meanings to a new generation vary widely. If the modes and their contents vary, are there any common, even invariant, conditions for how the communication occurs? We can ask who routinely does the communicating. Commonly it will be individuals filling understood and agreed upon roles in institutions, e.g. clan elders, parents, teachers, clergy. These are the traditional authoritative voices, the socially approved sources of answers to questions. Still pursuing common features, we can ask, What do they communicate? A generic answer is "the shared meanings of the group." To be slightly more specific, they pass on the "intellectually and affectively patterned resources" of the group. In a word, they transmit to a new generation the "lore" of the group, i.e. its accepted understanding of its existence in time and how its members should feel, understand, evaluate, decide and act. Such a lore shapes the intentional acts of the next generation. It provides a determinate social context and content for exercising

---

logical priority over "institution," the latter has a historical priority over the former; hence, "historicity" is a fundamental characteristic of human understanding.

[291] A dialectic of "public word" and self-understanding begins here and remains open to the possibility of borrowed identities, beliefs and practices being disrupted. While actual disruptions arise from a variety of sources (e.g. personal tragedies, political crises, charismatic figures challenging conventional beliefs), this chapter will focus on how liberty, displacement and personal relations are sources of potential disruption.

capacities to think, judge and decide. It gives direction to and affects the probabilities with which habits in thinking, speaking and acting will develop in a new generation.

"Lore" may be an appropriate term for a clan gathered around a nightly fire, but is it apt for more complex societies? This question introduces a new topic, that of "differentiations of consciousness" and how they alter orientations in intentional operations. Perhaps the clearest case of such differentiation appears in the contrast between common-sense thinking and theoretical inquiry. The former is concerned with practical living and evaluates particular objects and events in relation to everyday concerns. So the question of whether some line of investigation is worth one's time will be answered affirmatively if, because of it, benefits are likely or harms are less likely. But persons can also ask further questions that ignore personal gains and losses; for at least a time, they can withdraw from the concerns of practical living and devote time and attention to solving intriguing puzzles for their own sake. Then attention is paid to understanding for the sake of understanding. One moves out of a practical pattern of experience into a distinct intellectual pattern with a different type of goal and different standards for what will be satisfactory answers.

The earlier distinctions between descriptive and explanatory accounts of attention, emotion and symbol were efforts to shift from a common-sense context into a theoretical one. Operating in the latter is not a matter of retrieving the "lore" of common-sense living but of exploiting and adding to "intellectually patterned resources" remote from ordinary living and its concerns. For example, speaking of dopamine releases and neural activities in various brain locales is remote from any personal expression of emotions and concern for how others will react. Is it possible to distinguish "organizing principles" for these distinct ways of operating and speaking? Suppose common-sense operating and speaking serve practical and particular ends. If the ends are to encourage certain types of actions in the new generation, the speaking may take the form of maxims, stories of heroes and villains, rules of thumb. The organizing principle is "Be practical," i.e. make effective use of whatever resources you have on hand to achieve the chosen end. Referring back to a principle of completion that "impels" questioning, we can surmise that both it and the organizing principle of practicality are satisfied when operations efficiently achieve their ends.

This surmise is perhaps premature. The principle of completion may give rise to further questions that have no clear link to the demand for practical solutions to particular problems. Those questions may push an inquirer beyond asking how something works or what technical skills are needed to do some job. Instead, the questions may be why something is the way it is or why some procedure actually "works" or turns out to be practical. These further why-questions may seem to serve no immediately useful purpose. The organizing principle of common sense is likely to be dismissive of them since they seem to delay action and to promise no compensating benefit. Thus, such further questioning must be responsive to some other organizing principle.

If the desire to understand for the sake of understanding can "trump" other desires in its search for answers, then perhaps the organizing principle of its searching is "Be comprehensive," i.e. one should pursue a line of inquiry to its end. But, then, the principle of completion and the organizing principle of theoretical inquiry will both have the same end, namely, answering all of the relevant questions, even if doing so delays action and so seems impractical.

In theoretical fields the means to this end will include "patterned resources" transmitted to a new generation through graduate programs, specialized journals, pro-fessional associations and their annual conferences. Graduate schools and research institutes represent institutional means for "inducting" trainees into the procedures, terminologies and accumulated understanding of various specialties. Where a clan inducts its new members by repetition of oral history, collaboration in hunting and rites of passage, specialized fields employ classroom hours, collaborative research projects and the "exit tests" of dissertations. In both types of cases, the capacities of a new generation receive training and then testing to see if candidates have successfully internalized the patterned resources of a community.

These descriptive remarks on socialization provide the materials for further comments on the dialectical relations between intentional schemes of recurrence and social schemes of recurrence. First, professional standards and procedures have a history. That history is not something "back there then" but is alive in the understanding and practices of contemporary members of the profession who, to varying degrees, are aware of the work of their predecessors and its effects on their own operating. Indebted to the latter, contemporaries proceed to operate more efficiently because of the work already achieved. But the expectation is that they in turn will add to the "patterned resources" or legacy of the profession for subsequent generations. So it is that, once internalized, professional resources and procedures are a basis for new questions and lines of research leading to new discoveries and so to expansions or revisions in the patterned resources of a field. The intentional schemes of predecessors set up social schemes that form and direct the capacities of new generations along determinate lines, thereby making it more probable that intentional schemes will continue to be effective in answering new questions, building the legacy of the profession and improving its social schemes.

In this account of socialization there is a mixing of commonsensical operations and theoretical enterprises. For example, designing graduate programs to shape the next generation of researchers will demand compliance with the principle of practicality. Similarly, obtaining funding and allocating space for research projects will require the practical skills of numerous individuals, from grant writers and accountants to program administrators and building custodians. But the operations of persons in these roles presumably are means serving the ends of actual research and discovery.[292] In intelligent practices, therefore, we find evidence of a principle of completion demanding that practical understanding serve more than immediate and particular ends. This offers a further clue to understanding institutions as forming a more complex good of order, one that supports a flow of goods not just for this population at this time but for an indefinite number of persons for an indefinite number of times.

The preceding pages have assembled a complex meaning of "institution." Through intentional acts an institution emerges as commonly understood and agreed upon ways of exercising capacities and developing skills for sustaining flows of goods, flows dependent on (1) the ongoing cooperation of individuals filling their roles in the agreed upon ways and (2) the recurrence of the intentional acts sustaining a good of order. A new generation will find such institutional set-ups and good of order an "objectivated" social context for developing their own capacities and intentional acts. It will demand of them internalization of various patterned resources so as to sustain the given social reality and its ongoing flow of goods. In diverse ways, demands of the principle of assimilation will take the form of tests of the competence of a new generation and its readiness to sustain a series of schemes of recurrence.

Before asking how liberty, displacement and personal relations can disrupt such complex schemes, we can review how such social schemes have analogs in what previous chapters discovered about expectation, orientation and

---

[292] Of course professions can make their own specialized ends final objectives. Thus, bureaucracies can stifle rather than support innovations. Rules and policies become inflexible determinants of how things are to be done simply because "these are the rules and policies." Scholarly routines sometimes exhibit a similar inertia. The common design of ethics texts with their reviews of competing theories is one example. For a parody of this rarely questioned practice, see the Preface to Shute and Zanardi, vii-viii.

decision-making.[293] Chapter One spoke of expectations as neural patterns that favored some stimuli over others in the competition for attention. But "expectation" is a subcategory of "orientation" which refers to an understanding of (1) a general capacity to respond to an indeterminate range of possible objects, but (2) one gradually acquiring determinate content by the forming of expectations as patterned results of prior acts of attending. It is the latter development in orientation that allows the shift from descriptive talk of competition among stimuli to talk of how prior acts increase the probability that some objects rather than others will receive attention.

The dialectical analysis of orientation was not explicit in Chapter One. Indeed, the remarks in Chapter Two on emotion and the weighting of images left that analysis implicit. All the same, the general capacities for attending and affectively responding were treated as correlates of the field of potential images. Thus, the capacities were said to be potentially determinate relative to some potentially determinate subset of the field, while the field set the range for any possible exercise of the capacities. To embed these correlates in the later dialectical analysis of Chapter Three, we can say that determinate orientations, particularly when they are longstanding expectations, are responses to the principle of assimilation, but they are also potentially responsive to the demands of the principle of completion. Thus, conflicts between images and expectations can give rise to new questions that may prompt new insights challenging established patterns in attending or responding emotionally. Thus, Chapter One claimed that "focus" should be understood as an ongoing conscious processing of determinate clues, one that may, in facing novel situations, "complete" itself by revising initial orientations.

---

[293] Again, a goal of this chapter is to link findings from neuroscience and cognitive psychology with later schemes in economics and political theory.

This review of neural patterns, affective responses and changes in orientations provides analogies for understanding the relations between institutions and liberty. Suppose institutions represent shared integrations of prior intentional acts, i.e. what persons have learned and agreed upon in living together. These are their institutionalized orientations toward handling a range of problems in a given environment. Thus, it is more probable that groups will first adopt tried-and-true responses to new problems than that they will rely on untested experiments. Institutionalized orientations are analogous to neuropsychological demands of the principle of assimilation for continuity and stability. Taken together they are integrations of neuropsychological processes and psychosocial meanings that become conventional guides to planning and acting. But, even granting the dominance of inertia in human living, we went on in Chapter Three to speak of "creative understanding" as a conditioned but flexible range of possible intentional responses. Its flexibility (human "plasticity") was evidence of the demands of a principle of completion. We can suppose that such flexibility remains a possibility in institutional settings both because human agents remain malleable and because novel conditions evoke adaptations if persons and their schemes are to survive.[294]

The dialectical understanding of liberty that slowly emerged in Chapter Three unified previous insights into sociohistorical and personal determinants of decision-making. Three types of determinants were recognized: (1) prior integrations providing the established context for (2) the demands of operators evoking intentional acts (3) moving toward indeterminate ends in response to the demands of the related but opposed principles of assimilation and completion. We went on to identify these types of determinants in relation to normative intentional acts. Normative acts first appeared as

---

[294] The reasons here are of two types. In theoretical inquiries human plasticity is responsive to the organizing principle, "Be comprehensive." Questions of adaptation, however, are more likely to be responsive to the principle, "Be practical."

one type of intentional operation correlated with other types occurring within a higher-order scheme of recurrence. Decision-making was said to "complete" that scheme but also to be responsive to spontaneous and trained demands which were orientated by variable conditions, including the prior emotional weighting of some scenarios, so that some choices were more probable than others. An analogy for such weighting is the preference within institutions for predictability and routine performance – often at the expense of creative understanding.

The neuropsychological and intentional patterns traditionally called "virtues" offer a further analog to institutional routines. Remarks above on virtues noted how a capacity for performance becomes actual performance and, with repetition, can become habitual performance. When actual performance is consistently one of morally sound judgments and decisions, then actual virtues become "flexible ranges of schemes of recurrent normative intentional acts" in doing what is good. In other words, established neuropsychological and intentional patterns make it more likely that a person will respond to highly variable situations with morally appropriate judgments and decisions consistent with past ones. Suppose, then, that institutionalized routines are a flexible range of responses to variable problems. The "range" has relative limits set by the routines; it amounts to a relatively stable pattern of responses that are available and more probably will be evoked by new situations. In some institutions this may mean there is a shared "culture" of creative and morally responsible ways of responding to new situations. Past decisions created and sustained the culture and so increased the probability that future decisions will be morally sound ones.

Of course, there can be institutionalized routines that systemically undermine a variety of human goods. Then the flexible range of responses will form a relatively stable pattern of morally defective judgments and decisions. In either case, responses to new problems are more likely to "fit" the established patterns and fall within the range of routine solutions to similar problems. When morally defective judgments and decisions have become routine within institutional settings, we can still speak of a "good of order." For example, a corporate culture of "closing the deal" no matter what it takes will form its own schemes of recurrence. Routine practices will "shade" the truth about a company's products, will ignore the legitimate interests of customers, will sacrifice personal relations within and outside the firm to monthly sales quotas, will use the most effective high-pressure sales techniques and will encourage intense and often humiliating competition among subordinates for upper-management's approval. All of this may contribute to a good of order, but it will produce a flow of particular goods to some and a flow of avoidable and unjustifiable harms to many others.

    Here we can return to the question above about how liberty, displacement and personal relations can disrupt such schemes. The category "displacement" refers to an understanding that persons sometimes radically reverse even well entrenched orientations. How this is possible is our first question. There is no obvious answer since "radical reversal" amounts to the occurrence of the improbable. That is, determinate orientations are habitual responses to the demands of the principle of assimilation for continuity and stability both in personal living and, by way of analogy, in institutional performance. Minor departures from habitual patterns in thinking and acting are not uncommon. For example, people change jobs, abandon old acquaintances for new ones, respond to mid-life crises with plastic surgery, changes in diet or home remodeling. But radical departures or displacements amount not to revision but reversal; they are discontinuous with previous patterns of thinking and acting. They go contrary to the demands of the principle of assimilation.

    Consider how a type of displacement can occur when one no longer expects that understanding what something is will be simply a matter of naming, describing or picturing what it looks like. Instead, further questions about what makes it what it is will push inquiry toward working out correlations among classes of events where the resulting answers or explanations are not of something imaginable. An earlier example of this was in the shift from calling rain a "form of precipitation" or describing imaginable droplets falling on parched fields to understanding how one class of events depends on and makes possible other classes of events forming the hydrological cycle. To everyday picture-thinking, such talk will seem "abstract" and remote from visible events. However, to one aware of the strangeness of the world of theoretical explanations, such talk will be quite "concrete"[295] since it contributes to a more comprehensive understanding of what actually makes rain what it is.

    The shift to explanatory relations in theoretical inquiries is a departure from familiar patterns of common-sense understanding and speaking. The neuropsychological patterns of images and affective responses that guide everyday living are not "at home" in a world where the principle "Be comprehensive" raises strange questions that common sense assumed were already answered. If the imperative of common-sense living is "Be practical," the demands which theoretical inquiry responds to will remove operators temporarily from its control. Institutions devoted to theoretical inquiry, however, are not entirely immune to such control. Their bids for funding will often contain promises that research will eventually return practical benefits.[296] Such is the price one type of understanding extracts from the other.

---

[295] Usage of the word "concrete" seems to have two opposed meanings: something is concrete if it is imaginable, but an understanding of something is also concrete if it approximates to a comprehensive account of what makes that something what it is. The latter usage implies that the former, more common usage, is "abstract" since it is so incomplete.

[296] Thus, budget requests for NASA are more likely to justify space programs in terms of technological breakthroughs than in terms of the human imagination slipping the bonds of earth.

Yet, in its operating, theory is irreducible to practical know-how with its attention to problems of the moment.[297]

Displacement also occurs in moral understanding and deciding. Above we identified a minimal meaning of moral development in terms of three basic insights: (1) what seems good is not necessarily what is good; (2) what is good for me and mine is not necessarily good for others; (3) before acting in ways that affect others, I should stop to consider whether I would like others to do to me what I am about to do to them. The movement, even at this basic level, is toward a more comprehensive understanding of what is actually good to do. The principle "Be comprehensive" impels the search for a "complete" understanding of what would be good to do. Absent personal or group bias, some portion of a population will eventually ask what anyone would be justified in doing under similar circumstances.

A type of political realism will resist this expansion of questioning. For example, departments within institutions engage in "turf wars" and defend them in terms of a zero-sum mentality: if we lose budget lines, staff or administrative responsibilities, another department will gain at our expense. On a broader scale, national leaders may endorse (usually in private) *Realpolitik* and its promotion of national interests regardless of the consequences to outsiders. Pushed to explain their policies, leaders may claim their primary obligation is to protect their own citizens. Of course, this rationale will often be obscuring the reality that only elite groups among those citizens are receiving protection. So some may assume the fundamental realities guiding public

---

[297] Lonergan identified the limits of practical know-how bereft of theory when he wrote: "The sum and substance of the whole issue is that ideas in the concrete will build you a shanty but not a house and still less a skyscraper." "Essay in Fundamental Sociology" quoted in Michael Shute, "'Let Us Be Practical!': The Beginnings of the Long Process to Functional Specialization in the Essay in Fundamental Sociology" John Dadosky, (ed.). Meaning and History in Systematic Theology (Milwaukee: Marquette University Press, 2009), 1.

decision-making are the demands of interest groups, voting blocs and vocal constituencies. Further questions about what would be good for anyone to do will seem impractical and idealistic. Schemes of recurrence may remain in place that resist radical departures from what is accepted as "just how things are done around here."

On occasion, however, someone appears on the scene to challenge the realist's assessment of the full range of human understanding and deciding. The prophetic voice of a social reformer raises further questions that those in power have been ignoring or censoring. Discontinuity in the orientations of the parties will be manifest in how each "reads" the other. The realist may well read the critic as simply a rival for power whose opposition, despite its façade of moral idealism, originates in a common *libido dominandi*. The critic, on the other hand, may understand that realists operate to protect their particular goods but may also judge their unwillingness to consider a more comprehensive perspective a sign of intellectual or moral failure.

Displacement can occur, then, when the imaginable benefits to "me and mine" become subordinate to further questions about what anyone would be justified in doing. Attention shifts from particular and describable goods here and now to reflection on classes of cases and what should be true of all similar cases. While all sorts of variables may account for such a shift, we can ask whether the principle of completion energizing intentional acts plays a key role. The argument above was that normative intentional acts complete prior intentional acts. Yet any integration is still subject to the dialectic of the principles of assimilation and completion. So, for example, every act of deciding has its correlate in some good affirmed as worth achieving. With repetition both the operation and its end become an entrenched pattern of acts responding to affect-laden images. As already noted, the principle of completion is potentially disruptive of such patterns or orientations in thinking and acting, but it is in need of assistance. Chapter Two read Henry Adams' search for new cultural symbols as recognizing that intellectual demands by themselves may prove ineffective in revising entrenched patterns. Feelings evoked by emotionally weighted images are needed if there is to be a resolute change in deciding and acting. This insight is consistent with the remark above about finding something or someone worth loving if one is to offset the fears and rationalizations that sustain inadequately developed orientations.

Personal relations, thus, can play a decisive role in disrupting individual and institutional patterns of operations. A commonplace remark is that, to those newly in love, the world seems a brighter place. Their reactions to other persons and to daily routines reveal a new delight and sense of well being. What poets praise in verse, neuroscience of attention explains prosaically. In Chapter One "to focus" meant to recognize something determinate both because of prior adaptations in sensibility and understanding and because of the data that evoke a response. Chapter Two explained the role of emotion in weighting or selecting some data out of a field of potential competitors for attention. In less metaphorical terms, neural correlations among images and emotions make it more probable that some images rather than others will be objects of attention. But to attend to some is to be inattentive to others. Put another way:

> Attending to an event in the visual world improves its processing. However, this benefit comes at a cost; namely the inability to detect other events in that same visual scene. [...] Inattentional blindness is thought to result from the inability of unexpected, task-irrelevant stimuli to attract attention, thereby preventing them from reaching awareness.[298]

Talk of inattentional blindness is a clue to understanding how personal relations may alter both perceptions of others and daily routines. When being in love "colors" the rest of one's world, the neuroscientific conclusion

---

[298] Fougnie and Marois, 96.

is that stimuli irrelevant to the emotionally weighted thoughts about a loved one will be less likely to reach awareness. By the same token, any stimuli relevant to those thoughts, and so potentially evoking memories of the loved one, will be more likely to reach awareness and evoke the affects associated with those thoughts. In effect, the cliché "love is blind" has a foundation in how acts of attending are always selective and in how links among affects and images routinely direct one's focus toward some images to the exclusion of others.[299]

The implications of the preceding comments for individual and institutional operations are worth noting. Insofar as personal relations foster attentiveness to the "other," the individual experiences a de-centering from self. This is one characteristic of moral development; namely thinking of others before making decisions affecting them. Insofar as institutional schemes recurrently promote personal relations, such de-centering becomes more probable in those filling assigned roles and making decisions. Then it is possible to find a corporate culture that enhances moral reflection and decision-making, one that depends on the interpersonal skills and cooperative relations of its members and acts back on those members by demanding even better skills and more cooperation. If we understand personal virtues as flexible ranges of schemes of recurrent normative intentional acts, we can understand institutions of the preceding type as flexible schemes of recurrence making morally appropriate judgments and decisions in variable situations more probable.

As a matter of fact there are corporate cultures that do not foster personal relations. In such cases established schemes make morally inappropriate judgments and decisions more probable. The example above was of a corporate

---

[299] The distinction between being conscious of something and attending to it is worth recalling. It is not that emotional states make one completely oblivious to some events; rather, they make it more difficult to focus on them. Studies of inattentional blindness that do not make this distinction can be misleading. See ibid. (98-99) for three hypotheses about why inattentional blindness occurs.

climate of opinion that prized "closing the deal" above all other goods. Since most employees have a life outside such climates, some at least will detect the absence of the good of personal relations in the workplace. As a result, they will experience cognitive and emotional dissonance in a work environment that breeds mistrust and self-centered competition. They will have "internalized environments" at odds with the demands of their work environments. The resulting tension between an integrated environment (that includes the good of personal relations) and institutional practices may have different resolutions. Some employees may changes jobs; some may compartmentalize their lives, i.e. meeting the demands of their pressure-filled jobs but acting differently with family and friends; others may try to alter the culture of their workplace out of loyalty to institutions that they believe can operate more humanely.

We have come full circle back to the possible relations between liberty and institutions.[300] If persons have acquired stable integrations of affective demands with intelligent moral responses, then their ongoing demands as operators evoking new intentional acts will favor, make more probable, intelligent moral responses.[301] If their workplace environment is at odds with this internalized environment, their demands as operators will repeatedly encounter resistance, i.e. their spontaneous impulse toward "completion" will meet established patterns of thinking and acting that resist assimilation to those already internalized.

What are the possible ways of responding to such conflicts? One option is moral resignation. The decision of the realists is to accept corporate or political practices as far less than ideal and to resign themselves to operating within the limits of narrow group interests. Perhaps they insulate their professional lives from their private living, i.e. they

---

[300] See footnote 257 for the range of these possible relations.
[301] This suggests that the symbolization of prior integrations should be expanded to include a category for moral integrations (m_n).
Hence the earlier diagram is amended: $H_2[H_1(n_j\,;\,b_k\,;\,p_l\,;\,i_m\,;\,m_n)]$.

compartmentalize how they act at work and how they relate to family and friends. This option, for all its immediate practicality, runs up against limits. The demand of the principle of completion is to make sense of and to achieve what is actually good in the full range of one's experiences. If some part of one's living, e.g. a role in a firm or institution, is at odds with this demand, then the demand is unmet, and so one's living is disturbed. The decisions one makes in one area of living will be inconsistent with the best judgments one relies on in another area. A temporary solution may be to blame others for the dissonance between one's living and best judgments. Here is a point at which liberty comes to the fore. The options of changing jobs or challenging accepted practices are sometimes available. There are risks, personal, familial and professional, in choosing either option, yet the evidence for liberty is that persons actually take such risks. In doing so, persons demonstrate that their demands as operators can "trump" the demands of social integrations.[302] However, is liberty experienced only in risky departures from established routines?

Within some institutions risk-taking is a job requirement. Pharmaceutical firms developing new drugs, venture capitalists scouting for new investments and exporters seeking new markets employ personnel adept at calculating risks and acting on uncertainties. Risk-taking need not, therefore, be always a departure from established patterns of deciding and acting. What remains constant is that social integrations shift the probability of which demands and responses will occur within a population. Institutions such as families, schools and churches may affect the orientations of members in ways that make risk-taking more probable as a response to novel problems. Parents may take their children to explore wilderness areas; schools may promote creative problem solving; churches may teach the parable that burying one's

---

[302] As noted above, in a dialectical understanding of liberty, liberty can be a source of deviation from the probabilities set by prior social integrations.

talent as a precaution against loss is a mistake. Such social messages make innovative thinking, deciding and acting more probable in persons whose orientations first become determinate within such settings.

As social context is a determinate of orientation, as orientation is a determinate of acts of deliberation and as the options generated by acts of deliberation are the first correlates of questions of decision, it is plausible to envision a range of cultural patterns (H_2) that routinely affect the probabilities governing decision-making by affecting these prior determinants of questions of decision.[303] For example, a culture that makes heroes of inventors, repeats stories of self-reliant individuals overcoming adversity, stresses self-determination and discounts talk of fate will convey its messages with emotionally weighted images and words.[304] Recall that possible acts of deliberation have their correlate in a field of possible choices, but actual acts of deliberating proceed from determinate orientations that include neural patterns or expectations already "weighted" toward some options over others. Reaching back to Chapters One and Two, we can repeat: attention to some images rather than to others is made more probable because of prior emotional attachments to them. But repeated cultural messages will "train" new generations so that some images will evoke stronger affective responses than others. By extension, then, what is true of selective attention to images can be true of acts of deliberation. Individuals can be socialized by cultural models and stories to ask further questions, to fantasize about

---

[303] Again, by changing initial variables or conditions, one can alter the probabilities with which objects will be attended to, deliberated over and made the actual objects of choice.

[304] Walter Rostow suggested how such cultural variables as belief in progress and the experience of success in scientific experimentation played a significant role in the emergence of capitalism in the West. See his How It All Began: Origins of the Modern Economy (New York: McGraw-Hill, 1975).

new options and to resist settling for conventional answers and solutions.

The point of this digression on institutional support of risk-taking and innovation was to envision how cooperation between the opposed but related principles of assimilation and completion may, in some social settings, become routine. The demand for stability and continuity is flexible enough to accept risk-taking when the "job" calls for it. In other words, a "trained" response to (or expectation of how to handle) novel situations can become an assimilated pattern or personal habit of calculating risks and acting under conditions of uncertainty. Since the principle of completion demands understanding and doing what is good, institutions that demand skills in imagining unconventional options and proposing novel solutions may be "instilling" public demands compatible with personal ones. As a result, there can be schemes of recurrence within a range of well-integrated patterns of institutional practices that encourage departures from established practices in favor of newer, more intelligent and moral practices. For example, personnel policies may include ongoing checks on sexual harassment and biases in hiring. Experiments with flex-time scheduling of work hours can be an intelligent response to the competing demands on busy parents and caretakers. These, at least, can be institutional efforts to remove old patterns of harm and to discover new patterns of cooperation that promote personal relations both within and outside a firm.

The opening question of this chapter was how institutions affect decision-making. The paragraphs immediately above have suggested an ideal case where social integrations, being assimilated by a new generation, are such that the demands of the institutions on those persons are compatible with the principle of completion evoking intentional acts in them. The various intentional acts proceed from distinct demands, one of which is a demand for doing what is actually good. Under ideal conditions, cultural messages, with all their affect-laden images, will support this demand by forming expectations or determinate orientations about responsible uses of liberty.

We can now modify the second notion of liberty. It remains a capacity shaped by prior integrations that form an established context within which the demands of operators evoke intentional acts.[305] Now, however, we can add that under ideal conditions those acts move toward completion with a higher probability because of supportive institutional integrations that are consistent with the demands of the principles of assimilation and completion.[306] Liberty ideally develops, (1) through social integrations originating in and sustained by intentional acts responsive to the compatible demands of the principles of assimilation and completion, and (2) through a moral operator's intentional acts responsive to those same demands.

The preceding focus on ideal conditions for the interaction between the demands of operators and the demands of institutions for suitable orientations and skills has been deliberate. It is a departure from a quite common approach to studying moral decision-making. Frequently ethicists begin by presenting morally defective patterns of activity and so-called moral dilemmas.[307] Then they invite

---

[305] For a symbolic representation of the range of these prior integrations, see footnote 297.

[306] We say "with a higher probability" because a dialectical understanding of the relations between institutions and liberty recognizes that individuals can cooperate with such favorable institutional integrations but can also act contrary to both the latter and their own demands as operators.

[307] What are presented as moral dilemmas are really just "hard cases" that fall short of what traditionally was meant by a moral dilemma, i.e. a situation in which a "forced choice" between mutually exclusive options meant that the chooser inevitably would do a moral wrong. For the strict meaning of "moral dilemma" and its impossibility, see Alan Donagan's explication of Aquinas' understanding of *perplexus simpliciter* and the exceptional cases of

readers to consider what decisions are normatively justified and what rationales or general principles support those choices. However, an alternate approach begins by envisioning cooperation between institutional practices and the demands of operators for doing what is actually good.[308] Doing so provides an ideal ordering of relations among the categories in a "structure of the good" and thereby supplies a normative framework for diagnosing how either exercises of liberty or institutional practices are defective. This framework will prove useful in the next two chapters that evaluate economic and political practices.

V Liberty and the Anarchist Dream

This chapter began with the question of whether individuals or institutions had priority over the other. A dialectical account of how both are related avoided an intellectual impasse regarding this question. One implication, as Hegel noted, was that law and liberty are not opposites. Institutional demands and the best judgments of operators may be compatible, at least on occasion. Just as prereflective habitual acts may be exercises of liberty,[309] so the routine functioning of institutions may support operators in their routine choosing of what they understand is actually good to do. The dynamic relations within institutions among demands for developing capacities, acquiring new skills and fostering new forms of cooperation to carry out new tasks have their parallels in the demands of operators for developing in understanding, altering initial orientations and promoting personal relations. Under ideal conditions, social demands

---

perplexus secundum quid. The Theory of Morality (Chicago: University of Chicago Press, 1977), 144-145.

[308] The focus, then, is on responses to those demands and the slow learning process of diagnosing situations, inventing options and assessing their merits. This process tends to vanish from sight in the conceptualist "deduction" of choices from general principles.

[309] See footnote 270 above.

and personal demands form a pattern of common expectations that is a shared orientation toward understanding and doing what is actually good.

But the ideal pattern of relations between institutions and liberty is neither always present nor ever secure when it is present. The probabilities governing its appearance and survival are low. Since the ways of doing something wrong are more numerous than the ways of doing it right and since historical examples of unintelligent and morally irresponsible acts abound, any ideal pattern of relations will be less probable than defective ones. If we ask why this is the case, we come face to face with an old puzzle about liberty. The why-question anticipates an explanation or reason for the occurrence of moral failures, but, insofar as such failures are due to deliberate refusals to cooperate with the demands of the operator of normative intentional acts, there is no reason to be found. Persons can rationalize and speculate about psychological constraints, but the brutal fact is that the search for intelligibility in unintelligible decisions is futile. It is as if one asked persons for their "better understanding" of why they had acted contrary to their "best understanding." In fact, they were unwilling to follow their best judgment and so have no explanation for not cooperating with their own demands as critical and normative operators. Here, then, is the old puzzle about liberty: we sometimes fail to exercise liberty in ways we know we should, and we sometimes exercise it in ways we know we should not. In the language of faculty psychology, we find in ourselves a volitional limit on our own rational decision-making.

As a matter of fact, liberty has various types of limits. Some of these were already recognized in the classes of determinants, i.e. the "prior integrations" ranging from H_2 to m_n. Among these conditions for moral decision-making, one can find legitimate reasons for failures to achieve certain goods and to prevent certain harms. For example, because moral decision-makers are physical, chemical and organic aggregates, they are liable to all sorts of material interferences with their exercises of liberty. Thus, floods, earthquakes and tornadoes can be dramatic intrusions into the routine operations of persons and institutions. Less dramatically, the minor illnesses that interfere with one's tasks at work and that undermine one's physical stamina can prevent one from doing certain good things one had every intention of doing.

In addition, existing social schemes of recurrence may be unable to provide a flow of material goods adequate for sustaining good acts or preventing harmful ones. For example, institutional resources may prove insufficient for saving victims of an epidemic in remote regions of a country. Shortages of medical personnel and supplies, impassable roads and a lack of regional airfields can translate into higher mortality figures despite the best efforts and intentions of those trying to assist. Natural disasters and economic constraints are often disproportionately experienced by the poor and politically voiceless, even in prosperous societies. For these populations, natural, social and personal limits on liberty often combine to threaten their very survival.

Distinctly personal limits can show up as deficits in psychic orientations and education. Noted above was that the variables symbolized by the subscripts in p_l and i_m may include psychological and intellectual barriers to raising certain questions, imagining certain options and making the right decisions. As a result the actual choices one makes may be far from what one would decide without such constraints. For example, legal aid clinics counsel indigent and mentally troubled clients who arrive confused and anxious because their government support payments, and so their medications, have been cut off. Such clinics also witness a stream of desperate parents seeking help to prevent their landlords from evicting them and their children.

In response to these and other sorts of crises, creative understanding, employing limited resources, invents social schemes of recurrence such as legal aid clinics, emergency service agencies, early warning systems, insurance companies, flood control programs, centers for disease control. These measures can be understood as defensive schemes set up to anticipate threats to human goods and to respond to them. In effect, they represent top-down controls, deliberate social integrations, to prepare for disruptions in lower-order schemes.[310] Since no one can anticipate every threat, these defensive schemes are apt examples of what is meant by a "flexible range of a series of schemes of recurrence," a range that has intelligently designed anticipations of risks and planned responses.

This final section's title is "Liberty and the Anarchist Dream." The relevance to it of the preceding remarks about limits on liberty may not be apparent. The anarchist dream is of a society without political authority, one in which no executive power coerces the decisions and actions of its competent members. Ideally all laws will be passed and enforced only if all those members have approved them. Dissent or subsequent non-compliance may occur, but there will be no need for a police force, criminal courts or prisons. All remain at liberty to dissent from a community's laws and to leave its confines for a community they find more acceptable. The primary norm is that each competent member should enjoy complete liberty in association and compliance.

The anarchist notion of liberty is non-dialectical. It assumes liberty from the start is something more than an indeterminate capacity. An even deeper assumption is that individuals are the basic realities while social relations are secondary phenomena. These assumptions seem at odds with the findings of contemporary psychology and sociology.[311]

---

[310] What societies develop as defensive schemes will have parallels in the deliberate planning of individuals. Parents instruct their children about how to react to a fire; recovering addicts try to avoid familiar haunts; those on tight budgets pay more attention to their spending habits and more carefully track their bank statements.

[311] One attempt to reconcile those findings with the deeper assumption is to distinguish between social relations and political relations. Suppose the former relations, e.g. those of family life, are equiprimordial with the notion of the individual, and so both are

Chapters Three and Four made different assumptions. Liberty as anything more than an indeter-minate capacity is not a "given" feature of human living, and individuals and institutions are equiprimordial correlates of that living. These alternate assumptions posited dialectical relations both between individuals and institutions and between the opposed but related principles of assimilation and completion that evoke intentional acts. One implication of these positions is that correlates in such dialectical relations are not separate realities; rather, the reality of each takes on determinate content only through its relation to the other. If we understand either correlate to be an independent entity, then we are understanding it abstractly, i.e., the part is being taken for the whole. Any resulting analysis of the correlate will have lost touch with reality.

Perhaps this is the reason many anarchist proposals, and those of their contemporary libertarian heirs, prove so feckless. While principled arguments appealing to general concepts of autonomy and heteronomy may be logically valid, they overlook that such conceptual contraries are real correlates of human living.[312] All the same, the anarchist

---

basic realities. However, political relations, e.g. contractual arrangements among citizens, are artificial and secondary constructs. This maneuver simplifies the issue of how liberty as capacity becomes determinate only through interaction with the prior integrations symbolized in H_2. For example, as used in the preceding argument, the distinction between social and political relations seems plausible since family life usually comes first as a determinant of an individual's development. However, should we assume that family life has not been shaped by political relations within a broader social order? This question may go unnoticed if dialectical thinking is not part of the anarchist's i_m.

[312] An example of a logically valid but unsound argument for the anarchist dream begins by making the concepts of heteronomy and autonomy mutually exclusive. To submit to the law of the "other" is to abandon autonomy; to be autonomous is to have a duty to follow one's best judgment about what one should do. Insofar as political

dream remains appealing since it promises deliverance from abuses of institutional powers.

Already noted was that ideal relations between institutions and liberty are never secure. Individuals holding public office and private citizens are all capable of refusing to cooperate with the demands of the principle of completion and so remain liable to harming themselves and others. While no explanation for such deliberate refusals is possible, we can anticipate moral failures and design defensive schemes to lessen their effects. The anarchist dream seems to underestimate the frequency of moral failures as well as the capacity of creative understanding to design political schemes of recurrence that mitigate the effects of such failures and

---

authority claims a right to command regardless of a subject's personal judgments, it is claiming persons under its authority have a duty to obey regardless of their own best judgments. But if all "duties" presuppose moral autonomy, then the claim to political authority ends in nonsense; namely, it amounts to saying that autonomous subjects have a duty to violate their duty. A version of this argument for anarchism is present in Robert Paul Wolff's In Defense of Anarchism (New York: Harper and Row, 1970), 8-10.

One problem with this argument lies not in the logical relation between the concepts of heteronomy and autonomy but in the fact that the experience of liberty is one of opposed but related principles of dependence and independence. Behind the problem is the hidden legacy of Scotus surviving in a conceptualist tradition within much of modern philosophy. For this tradition, there is no role for the act of insight in generalizing. We must somehow have concepts already, and a process of deduction is our only road to understanding our experiences. This tradition shows its presence when discussions of liberty begin with a general definition or concept of liberty that authors then proceed to "unpack." For example, defining liberty as the contrary of heteronomy is part of the anarchist's logically valid argument against any strict obligation for autonomous persons to obey political authority. But what is the empirical reality prior to conceptual definition? Do we find ourselves to be purely autonomous?

encourage their reversal by cooperative efforts to promote human goods. To the economic and political challenges creative understanding faces in doing either, the next two chapters turn.

CHAPTER FIVE: ECONOMICS AND LIBERTY

I Introduction

The structure of the good (Diagram 4.2) can serve as an "ideal type" for analyzing economic and political practices. Its categories form an ideal pattern of relations between operators and institutions such that the demands of each for intelligent and morally responsible decisions and policies are complementary. As an ideal type, the pattern helps one to detect if actually occurring practices deviate from the ideal pattern. A further question is how reforms of personal or institutional practices are possible. One author suggests an answer to this question:

> The first two lines point to the real situation. So, the good of order is the actual situation, even if we view it as massively disordered.... What, then, is the third line? Think of it as the untapped potential within that actual order, the liberty unreleased, the objectives unsuspected....[313]

---

[313] Philip McShane, "Lonergan's Educational Philosophy" (unpublished essay), 10. This reading seems at odds with what Lonergan wrote about the good of order.
> The good of order is not the institution; the good of order is the institution that works, that is working well. The same institution of marriage can be a source of misery or bliss. In one case you have the good of order, and in the other it is missing, something is missing. The same economy can mean prosperity or slump, depression. The good of order at one time is functioning. The good of order is the proper functioning, and it is something concrete, what actually is occurring in this society, in this group. "The Human Good" in CW 17, 343.

There is a puzzling ambiguity in the last sentence. The good of order is said to be both "proper functioning" and "what is actually occurring," yet the latter can easily be far from ideal. One way of

It seems there can be a good of order even if operations are sloppy, skills are in short supply, development of new ones is slow, the flow of goods is subject to breakdowns, cooperation is episodic and turf wars common. Institutions continue to function, but they squander resources, including human talents, and the actual rates at which goods routinely flow are far less than they could be.[314]

The third line, with its categories of liberty, orientation, displacement, personal relations and terminal goods, lists some conditions for the possibility of remedying defective practices. Of course, existing social integrations may be relatively immune to challenges "from below." For example, an educational bureaucracy can crush the initiatives of creative understanding, can breed a climate of moral resignation to the follies of classroom routines, can orientate teachers toward an ethic of survival so that "keeping one's

---

reconciling McShane's reading with Lonergan's text is to suggest that, while Lonergan introduced his "Structure of the Good" in the quoted article by referring to it as an "ideal type" and not "a description of reality" (333), his later comments mixed the two uses of the categories in the structure. Thus, the "good of order" is used normatively to refer to an understanding of ideal or "proper functioning" but also descriptively to refer to an understanding of "what is actually occurring."

[314] The performance of some school districts in educating students provides an example of such institutional disorder. It once was said that each new generation is a potential invasion of barbarians and education is the first line of defense. Some present educational practices seem to follow a revised maxim: "Each new generation is an invasion of potential barbarians, and educators help them realize their potential." The waste of human goods in schools is not irrelevant to this chapter's focus on liberty and economics. Those not understanding how an economy functions (and this probably includes most graduates of contemporary educational institutions through the university level), are hardly well prepared to make intelligent decisions about economic policies, whether personal or public.

head down" and producing passing scores on standardized tests become the measures of being a good teacher.

To talk of tensions between existing social integrations and "liberty unreleased" is consistent with what previous chapters presented as a dialectic between the principles of assimilation and completion. What this chapter adds to those previous pages is a normative understanding of liberty. Part II works out that understanding of liberty in relation to intentional acts, the demands of operators of those acts and the principles that evoke both acts and the varied demands of operators. Puzzles about failures to meet those demands (e.g. instances of incompetence or moral fault) are the basis for distinguishing between a normative notion of liberty and liberty as an insufficiently developed capacity. Part III applies the categories of line three to puzzles about competing economic viewpoints. In Part IV a case study focuses on a question in social economics: Under what conditions, if any, should consumers as "indirect employers" think they might be responsible for harms occurring to anonymous others? The purpose of this brief case study is to show the relevance of orientation, displacement and personal relations to understanding the origins of competing views of economic exchanges and their consequences. A further purpose is to suggest how ordered liberty is ultimately a matter of transcending limitations and undergoing various displacements in response to the demands of the principle of completion.

II   A Normative Understanding of Liberty

> The principle of progress is liberty, for the ideas occur to the man on the spot, their only satisfactory expression is their implementation, their only adequate correction is the emergence of further insights; on the other hand, one might as well declare openly that all new ideas are taboo, as require that they be examined,

evaluated, and approved by some hierarchy of officials and bureaucrats....³¹⁵

How plausible is this claim that the "principle of progress" is liberty? Classical Liberalism responded in terms of the practical benefits of free and open debate. New insights need to be aired and tested; those that survive scrutiny are more likely to have merit and be ways of improving a situation. With an improved situation, new insights will arise and, if subjected to free debate, will be similarly winnowed, so that some will point to further improvements in the existing situation.³¹⁶

But the claim is defensible in more theoretical terms. The preceding chapters have slowly assembled a theoretical account of the demands of a principle of completion. Chapter One investigated how a complete act of attention integrates prior states (orientation and arousal) and some subset of a field of possible objects of attention. The complete act of focus has its precondition in spontaneous or trained orientations toward that field. What initially "assembles" the acts is a demand for sensible presentations or psychic representations, i.e. demands for correlates corresponding to the capacities for seeing, touching, etc.³¹⁷

---

³¹⁵ Insight, 259.
³¹⁶ A pure cycle of progress can be described in terms of such an emergence, testing and implementation of insights. Cf. Lonergan, "The Human Good" in CW 17, 344.
³¹⁷ Sensory deprivation experiments and the hallucinations of test subjects provide evidence of affective neural demands for sensible presentations or psychic representations. The "intending" or spontaneous reaching of human sensibility is a capacity demanding completion in "objects" responsive to that demanding. Deprived of adequate sensible presentations, test subjects hallucinate, i.e. they fabricate objects to meet their neural demands. Oliver Sacks offers a case study of Mrs. C who, after the onset of deafness, experiences musical hallucinations. What makes her case unusual is that she eventually is able to exercise some control over them. See

Chapter Two pursued the question of how emotions made attention to some images more probable. In addition, since understanding and acting are distinct events, the integration of the two seems to require the "motivating" force of affect-laden images. Henry Adams was aware that to follow through, to complete one's intention to act, required the emotive power of images and symbols. So it is one thing to have a bright idea, but it is another thing to "complete" an action that brings the idea into reality. Images able to evoke emotions seem to be crucial to integrating the two and so to producing an act of deciding that completes a series of prior intentional acts.

In Chapter Three insights were described as integrating aggregates of sensitive presentations and psychic representations. What begin as puzzling and fragmentary data become unified, understood or recognized objects or events. But the question for judgment goes beyond this early integration to ask if what has been understood is in fact the case.[318] The act of judging is its own type of completion, i.e. it completes the search for correct understanding by discriminating between answers that are in fact not true and those that are. It denies or affirms integrations as existing independently of intentional acts.

Acts of deliberation respond to demands of a principle of assimilation for integrating possible scenarios with available resources, including current understanding. But the demands of the principle of completion may impel one's deliberating to expand beyond conventional views of means and ends and so to break with already familiar answers. A more satisfactory and complete answer may depend on the creative fantasies of the one deliberating. In turn, those fantasies will depend on cooperation with the demands of the principle of completion.

What deliberating produces as options, an act of judging will affirm as realistic or reject as irrelevant or

---

Musicophilia: Tales of Music and the Brain (New York: Alfred A. Knopf, 2007), 52-54.
[318] The focus here is limited to judgments of fact.

unattainable. The further act of deciding completes the series of demands for correctly understanding situations and making possible improvements in them by "moving" to integrate knowing and doing.

How do these summary remarks provide a theoretical basis for the claim that liberty is the principle of progress? The general claim is that intentional acts respond to the demands of distinct operators and in doing so form intelligible and intelligent patterns of operations. The intelligibility of the patterns can be specified in terms of the opposed but related principles of assimilation and completion. These general conclusions from intentionality theory are the basis for working out a normative notion of liberty, one that is a measure of progress. Doing so occurs in three steps. First, how is liberty related to intentional acts? Then, how is liberty related to the demands of the operators of those acts? Finally, how is liberty related to the principles of assimilation and completion that evoke both the acts and the demands of the operators?

In relation to intentional acts, let liberty provisionally mean a capacity of intentional acts to effect higher-order integrations of lower-order materials. For example, as acts of attention integrate sensitive presentations and psychic representations into recognized objects and events, so acts of deciding, following upon acts of deliberating, integrate recognized possibilities into new parts of the flow of sensitive presentations.[319]

This capacity for top-down integration or ordering has been a puzzle throughout the previous chapters. In Chapter One, there was a question about how to talk of deliberate selection of what one attends to (e.g. listening to a client and ignoring a ringing phone) and how certain neurochemical events (n_j) occur or do not occur depending on what selection

---

[319] Think of how the simple decision to paint a room one color rather than another alters the flow of sensitive presentations one receives once the room is painted. Similarly, choosing to smile at someone or to assist a person in need can alter the flow of sensitive presentations as either gesture evokes a response from the other person.

is made. Similarly, suppressing a yawn or deliberately increasing one's breathing rate affects biological operations (b_k) while controlling one's anger or ignoring fatigue affects psychological orientations (p_l). Less controversial but no less puzzling instances of top-down ordering appear when there is a deliberate ordering of one's questioning and judging (i_m) in double checking research results or playing the devil's advocate in regard to one's own conclusions. Then, there are cases where individuals subordinate their personal interests to concern for some greater good (m_n), e.g. acting fairly toward all parties in a dispute despite risks to one's reputation as a reliable team player.

Evidence of the capacity for top-down integration, in short, is present in all sorts of common experiences: attending to one thing rather than another, breathing deeply before going on stage, staying alert during a boring lecture, expressing anger in a controlled way, rejecting rest before a task is completed, pushing oneself to play the critic of favored beliefs, choosing to adopt a perspective on some issue broader than how one will be affected. Even if we infer the capacity from such common experiences, the neuroscientific evidence for its occurrence remains elusive.[320] Perhaps this is due to the research schizophrenia predicted by Posner. Still, the challenge is to imagine, design and conduct experiments that would determine: (1) if there are repeated correlations between deliberate intentional acts and otherwise

---

[320] Oliver Sacks reports on the case of Jacob L, a "distinguished composer in his 60s," who is able to exercise "at least some voluntary control" over the pitch distortions he experiences. Sacks' hypothesis is that the brain and ear form "a single functional system, a two-way system, with the ability not only to modify the representation of sounds in the cochlea but to modulate the output of the cochlea itself." He goes on to suggest that the "power of attention – to pick out a tiny but significant sound in our environment…seems to depend on this ability to modulate cochlear function, as well as on purely cerebral mechanisms." Musicophilia, 136-137.

not occurring organic and neurochemical events, and (2) if the experimental results allow neuroscientists to predict and to detect the recurrence of such patterns or correlations in future tests.[321]

In the absence of such research and its results, we can still speculate about the common empirical cases and the inferred capacity. We can ask, for example, how any such capacity for top-down integration might appear in intentional acts? This question introduces the second step: liberty in relation to the demands of the operators of intentional acts.

In traditional accounts, liberty is usually understood as a characteristic of some human acts that, while having antecedent conditions, are not wholly determined by them. In previous chapters remarks on non-systematic relations among events allowed for the gradual introduction of talk of intentional acts occurring as matters of probability. But, even if there are non-systematic relations between acts-at-liberty and their antecedent conditions, this does not say anything positive about what such acts are besides those prior determinants. In other words, the fact that there are non-systematic relations between regularly occurring types of conditions and subsequent acts is not sufficient to account for liberty in any positive sense. What usually happens is that writers proceed to talk about "self-determination," "self-regulation" or the exercise of "self-control" as linguistic expressions of their belief in some additional and distinctly independent determinant of these types of acts. But the terminology here may refer to no positive insights; instead, these phrases may mean no more than that "antecedent conditions are not totally in control of subsequent acts."

Anticipating these difficulties, we early on began talking of operators, integrators and their demands. In summary form:

---

[321] Patrick Byrne has identified the challenge here as one of detecting regularities in neural events that can be explained only by appeal to higher-order processes that integrate those lower-order events. Cf. Byrne, 17-18.

1. The capacity to pay attention proceeds to completion in response to the demands of the empirical operator for sensitive presentations or psychic representations as determinate objects of focus.
2. The capacity for understanding proceeds to completion in response to the demands of the intellectual operator for integrations of data as understood objects, events or patterns of relations among objects and events.
3. The capacity for judging matters of fact proceeds to completion in response to the demands of the critical operator for distinguishing between correct or probable integrations of data and those that are incorrect or improbable.
4. The capacity for deliberation proceeds to completion in response to the demands of practical intelligence for integrations of data into plausible courses of action and empirically possible outcomes.[322]
5. The capacity for deciding proceeds to completion in response to the demands of the normative operator for choosing the best available means to the best available end.[323]

The hypothesis here is that "liberty" is not limited to the final, complete act of deciding. Instead, the capacity for top-down integration is exhibited "all the way down" in the earlier intentional acts, beginning with acts of attention. As a

---

[322] Further acts of judging are assumed here in discriminating between logically possible and empirically possible courses of action.

[323] Further acts of judging are assumed here about the relative worth of different means and ends. While such judgments are acts of assent to the relative worth of either means or ends, the act of decision amounts to a selection or act of consent in choosing means and ends. It is this act of consent that brings to completion the process in the sense that the decision integrates "best judgment" with actual performance.

capacity for a "higher order integration of lower-order materials," liberty is present when one is carefully attentive (i.e. conscientiously selects what sensitive presentations to focus on); when one is diligent in diagnosing a situation in order to grasp relevant details more completely; when one double checks any diagnosis to see if any relevant details have been overlooked; when one deliberately presses for imaginative solutions to problems and deliberately compares them to available resources.[324]

In effect, the demands of the various operators call for cooperative responses that integrate "materials" in ways that meet the objectives of the distinct intentional acts. But then the old puzzle returns: persons sometimes act contrary to these demands or at least are careless in how they respond to them.

Diagnosing such failures to act carefully or according to one's best judgments can begin by relating liberty to the general principles of assimilation and completion. Faculty psychology described such failures as an inconsistency between what intellect recognizes as good to do and what the will consents to do. For intentionality theory the diagnosis is that a series of intentional acts is not brought to completion. For example, what acts of deliberating have identified as options, what acts of judging have narrowed to realizable possibilities and what judgments of value have affirmed as real possibilities worth achieving, acts of deciding do not proceed to adopt as courses of action. In terms of the principle of completion, what was affirmed as worth doing does not become the object of an act of decision, and so the last act in the series is not integrated with its predecessors.

---

[324] Any use of "deliberately" may seem to identify liberty with acts of deciding, i.e. with what one reflectively and deliberately does. However, the determinate orientations of persons, e.g. their habitual responses to images and puzzles, can be the basis for pre-reflective responses to the demands of the various operators. Without explicit deliberation, much like the tennis player returning a serve, a person may be at-liberty in giving "trained" responses.

Ideally the series should be complete, but in practice persons blunder: they are inattentive; they misdiagnose situations; they consider too narrow a range of options, and their judgments of value proceed from prospective judgments that exclude relevant considerations. The results are decisions that are inappropriate to the real situations because the latter are misdiagnosed or the selected options are unimaginative and overly simplistic responses to complex problems. Then there are the further cases of moral fault when all the preceding acts and their outcomes yield correct diagnoses and reliable judgments on ends and available means, yet the decisions to act do not complete the series.

In either type of case (intellectual blunders or moral fault), are the flawed decisions acts-at-liberty? To say that incompetent or morally irresponsible acts are never exercises of liberty would seem to have strange implications. Are only competent acts free? Are only virtuous acts free?[325]

To evade these implications, we need to identify liberty with something other than an adequate response to the demands of the principle of completion. The only alternative appears to be that an act can be an exercise of liberty if it at least responds to the demands of the principle of assimilation. That is, exercises of liberty, regardless of their degree of development, are acts that deliberately integrate operations with some already achieved understanding and practice. For example, persons can deliberately attend to some images but not to others according to their current understanding of what is important. Persons can proceed with limited attentiveness to diagnose a problem according to their present horizon of care, but the diagnosis may fall far short of including concern for parties actually affected by the problem. Persons can imagine possible solutions to a problem, but the resources they draw upon may be no more extensive than the practices

---

[325] This question is one source of the traditional distinctions between natural liberty and ordered liberty and between a negative understanding of liberty as the absence of restraint and a normative ideal of liberty.

with which they are already familiar. Liberty, in other words, can appear in performances that are far from sufficiently developed.

Recognizing that the capacity-for-performance may be followed by an actual performance that is quite defective, we can revise the understanding of liberty from Chapter Four to emphasize the demands of the principle of assimilation.[326] Prior integrations may provide a defective context for present performance, e.g. persons may not have outgrown an orientation that evaluates options solely in terms of personal consequences. Their current integrations skew the demands of operators so that the only questions raised are about personal gains or losses, but then the limited "ends" toward which the operator moves will be compatible with the demands of the principle of assimilation but at odds with the demands (and the further potential questions) of the principle of completion.

Still, a choice will be at liberty if it integrates an action deliberately taken with whatever present understanding a person has. In other words, a person's intellectual and moral orientation may be insufficiently developed, but the limited range of such a person's prospective judgments, imagined options and decisions will not preclude that a choice is freely made. Consider how one might have endorsed slavery in mid-nineteenth-century Alabama because it was consistent with one's religious beliefs and because its abolition implied a social order one could not imagine as a realistic possibility. In effect, the abolition of slavery was rejected as a revolt against God's order and as a fantasy leading nowhere. It was too "unthinkable" relative to prior integrations.

---

[326] Recall the meaning of liberty in Chapter Four: Liberty is a capacity of intentional acts conditioned by three types of determinants: (1) prior integrations providing the established context for, (2) the demands of operators evoking intentional acts (3) that move toward indeterminate ends in response to the demands of the related but opposed principles of completion and assimilation.

One general insight here is that cultural and biographical conditions may limit what insights occur to a person without implying that the person does not act at liberty. Again, prospective judgments that precede judgments of value will consider only those things thought relevant to answering whether an option is actually available and worth pursuing. Both custom and personal orientation affect which considerations are thought relevant and so set initial limits on subsequent judgments of value and choices.[327]

There is also the defective performance that shows up in a deliberate refusal to "complete" (in an act of deciding) the previously occurring acts and their outcomes. The general claim is that such acts-at-liberty are failures to respond to the demands of the normative operator. More specifically, one rejects the demand for integrating action with one's best judgment. Instead, one chooses to maintain an existing integration despite recognition of both its defects and one's capacity to remedy them.[328] Notoriously some will ask why a

---

[327] Again, such limits need not be fixed boundaries since further questions may occur to a person or changes in social circumstances may erode confidence in old answers. For example, dramatic changes in economic or political orders may increase the probability that missing insights will occur because previously unasked questions come to the fore as old schemes no longer function. Thus, severe economic recessions may undercut the "cover stories" by which groups (e.g. auto workers, textile workers, labor unions) justified their place in society. Prior integrations of meaning no longer answer the new questions as persons are literally displaced from their jobs and their former social identities. The demands of the principle of completion will generate further questions and, in time, may produce new practices and schemes to replace those that have failed.

[328] Plausible examples of such choices to maintain defective integrations appear in refusals to break bad habits, in efforts by elites to retain political privileges long after their leadership ceased to benefit society, in tolerance of economic practices that maximize profits for a few despite catastrophic harms to many others. The

person would make such a choice. Resisting the impulse to offer explanations of moral failures is perhaps dependent on having insights into how resistance to the demands of the normative operator in oneself is ultimately unintelligible. Giving in to this impulse to find reasons for irrational behavior tends to produce what once were called "rationalizations."

This digression on morally defective responses to the demands of the principle of completion underscores how liberty is a capacity with indeterminate ends and so a capacity that may serve to promote development or decline, both in individuals and in communities. But this generality introduces a new puzzle. If we are trying to work out a normative notion of liberty, will it be the measure of development and decline or will the consequences of an exercise of liberty be the measure of the moral worth of the act? In other words, will the normative notion of liberty be the criterion of good practice or will the consequences of practice be the measure of a good exercise of liberty?[329]

Previous chapters seemed to favor the second, consequentialist option. For example, Chapter Three explored how creative understanding was a capacity or potential for imagining both new opportunities and how to make effective use of them. But the proof lies in the doing, and so actual

---

issue here is more than a failure to act according to one's best judgment. There is a more basic failure to "grow," to allow oneself to be displaced from prior integrations. In this sense every moral failure is its own immediate punishment since it forestalls a development that would otherwise occur. The cliché that virtue is its own reward has its parallel in "vice is its own immediate punishment."

[329] The broader issue here becomes explicit in public policy debates. The good intentions of policy-makers are relevant in assessing their characters but irrelevant in evaluating their actual policies. For the latter, actual consequences are the measure, and using judgments about good character to excuse policy failures may make for "good politics," but the result is to confuse the issue of competence in performance with questions about personal character.

outcomes are the measure of how creative one has been. Chapter Four described skills as deliberately acquired modifications of spontaneous operations responsive to both personal demands and those of institutions. But, again, the measure of one's skills will be actual performance and not the prior capacity for operations. Similarly, Chapter Four described how intentional acts generate possible scenarios, judge some to be real possibilities and select those worth bringing about. Liberty was provisionally identified with this capacity both to select a new integration of what was first dreamt and to direct further acts to bring it into reality. But a "new integration" may be an instance of development or an instance of decline, and so we are back at the second puzzle about the measure of "good practice."

This puzzle remains unresolved as long as we understand "liberty" only negatively, i.e. as a capacity entirely unbound by antecedent conditions. It was important to specify a different meaning of liberty in relation to "lower-order" conditions and to indicate how prior integrations of neurochemical, biological and psychosocial conditions were non-systematically related both among themselves and to "higher-order" intentional acts. But can we say anything more about this "not entirely unbound" capacity?

Suppose that by "liberty" we understand a capacity of intentional acts to respond to the demand of the principle of completion such that they can develop or correct the antecedent integrations that initially shape their exercise. This may seem merely a repetition of earlier remarks on dialectic.[330] However, a normative position has been added. The new claim is that basic norms for human operations are

---

[330] Recall that, while prior integrations shape how persons think and act, the dialectical relations between persons and their environments allow the former some flexibility in how they respond to new situations. So it is that individuals can find creative solutions to new challenges (Chapter Three) and groups can modify their institutional practices to promote human relations (Chapter Four).

immanent demands that evoke those same operations.[331] Of course, the demands of prereflective performance may meet resistance from competing demands for preserving prior integrations that require avoidance of certain images, feelings, insights and decisions. Thus, we distinguish: (1) a normative notion of liberty as a capacity of intentional acts to respond to the demand of the principle of completion in ways that develop or correct the antecedent integrations that initially shape their exercise; (2) actual intentional acts that respond to the demands of the various operators; and (3) evaluation of these acts in terms of the normative notion.

So, in regard to the puzzle about the measure of "good practice," we can say that the immanent norms of the operators are criteria for evaluating both character and actions. Someone may quickly object that consequences are the measure in assessing actions, especially when they are public policies.[332] However, what do we mean by "consequences"? If the results of actions are at first simply new data to be integrated by new acts of attending, understanding and evaluating, then making any careful

---

[331] "To conclude, human authenticity is a matter of following the built-in law of the human spirit. Because we can experience, we should attend. Because we can understand, we should inquire. Because we can reach the truth, we should reflect and check. Because we can realize values in ourselves and promote them in others, we should deliberate. In the measure we follow these precepts, in the measure we fulfill these conditions of being human persons, we also achieve self-transcendence, both in the field of knowledge and in the field of action." Lonergan, "Self-transcendence: Intellectual, Moral, Religious" in CW 17, 319. The last four paragraphs of Part II in Chapter Four provided a fuller argument for the normativity of the demands ("built-in laws") of the various operators.

[332] See footnote 325 above for the standard distinction between judgments of character and judgments of policies.

assessment of practices, personal or public, is first a matter of meeting the immanent demands of the operators.[333]

Diagram 5.1 summarizes the role of immanent demands in evoking specific intentional acts and their objects.

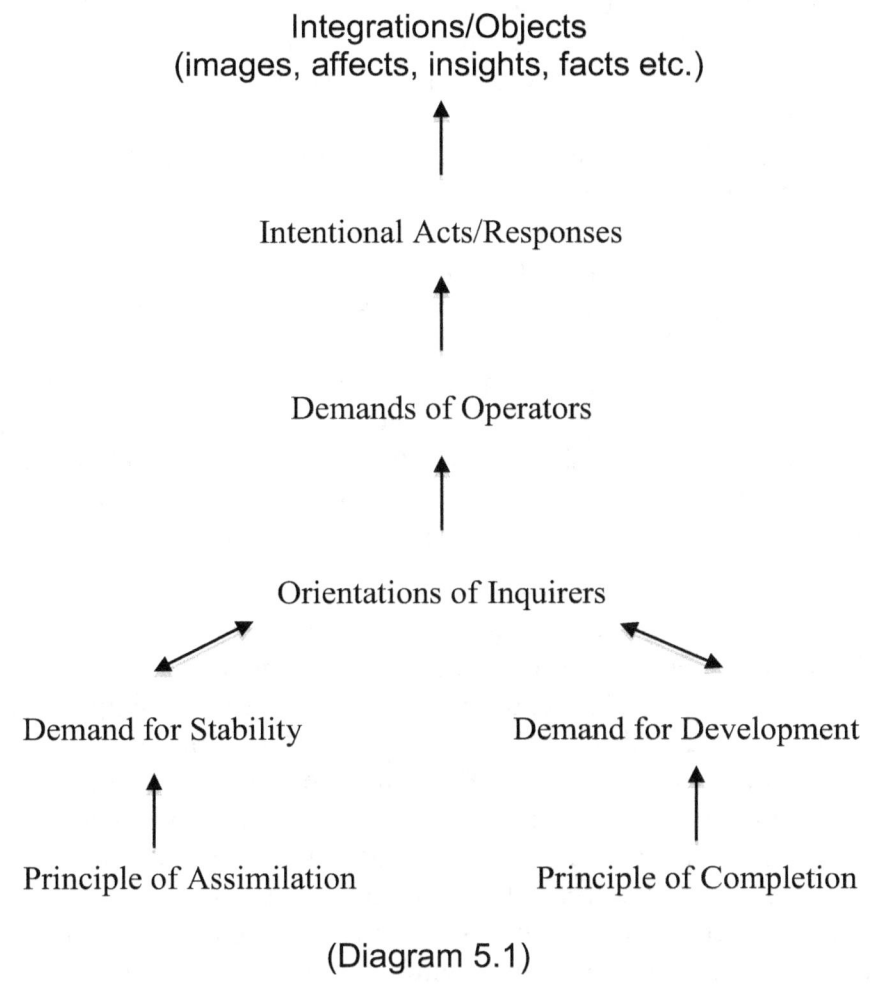

(Diagram 5.1)

---

[333] It may not have escaped the reader's notice that one implication of this position is that the conventional division of ethical theories into deontological and consequentialist types is not a fundamental distinction. Pursuing this insight is a task for a different inquiry.

III Implications for Economic Practices

What implications does this normative notion of liberty have for evaluating economic practices? To answer this question, we need to locate this notion of liberty within the broader explanatory framework of the "structure of the good." In particular, we need to relate it to the other categories on line three: "orientation," "displacement," "personal relations" and "terminal values."

Recall the understanding of decision-making as an act in a structured process of wondering that tends toward completion. The act of deciding occurs within a scheme of recurrence among intentional acts responsive to the demands of their varied operators for images, feelings, insights, plans and actions. The capacity to respond is made determinate, becomes a concrete orientation, through actual operations that, interacting with prior sociohistorical integrations, establish the personal historicity of the person making decisions.[334] Three basic insights specified a minimally adequate moral orientation.[335] To this minimum, we added a general account

---

[334] To cite the earlier text: "Suppose decision-making is first an indeterminate capacity for choosing ends and means. Its correlate will be a field of possible ends and means. The empirical possibility of different ends and courses of action is one basis for the indeterminacy of the capacity. But actual decisions are eventually made from among the possibilities, and these add determinations to the capacity. The latter may be the impersonal determinants resulting from choices made by anonymous others (H_2), e.g. the cultural patterns new generations find already in place so that they uncritically believe that burning witches cures plagues or executing persons is a way of reducing violent crimes. They may be the personal determinants resulting from choices which, with repetition, become habits or established orientations."

[335] The hypothesis is that being moral in decision-making is, at a minimum, a matter of being careful in decision-making when "being careful" is usually specified by care (1) in distinguishing between what is good and what merely seems good, (2) in distinguishing

of a "virtuous orientation."[336] Talk of "virtues" became talk of "flexible ranges of schemes of recurrent normative intentional acts." For example, a virtue such as prudence can be understood as a determinate orientation to make morally appropriate judgments and decisions such that highly variable situations requiring choices are routinely met by a patterned capacity to respond with a high probability of morally appropriate choices.

In Chapter Four talk of "displacements" suggested that some types of orientations were instances of determinate capacities that were more developed than others because they more readily met the demands of the principle of completion. For instance, a type of intellectual displacement is evident when a person moves beyond "picture-thinking" about institutions in terms of imaginable actors doing their jobs in imaginable edifices and, instead, understands that invisible acts of meaning sustain ongoing institutional activities. The

---

between personal goods and the well being of others, (3) in giving some consideration before making a decision to its effects on others.

[336] "Suppose that virtues are habits that result when indeterminate capacities for acting (1) gain determinate direction through prior experiences and (2) are 'completed' by gaining such direction. For example, a realized virtue of prudence presupposes (1) a capacity for judging and deciding, (2) a person's actual history of acts of judging and deciding, and (3) a preponderance of those acts being morally sound judgments and decisions. Within populations such established patterns of operation, or virtues of prudence, make sound moral judgments and choices more probable in the future. The analogy to skillful performance in a sport is apt. A capacity for performance becomes actual performance and, with repetition, can become skilled operation such that one habitually displays a high level of competence. Now suppose the performance is that of moral decision-making. Then the 'skill' is a determinate orientation in choosing, a relatively stable pattern in how one arrives at morally responsible choices. By exploiting earlier insights into expectations and habits, we can replace talk of 'virtues' with talk of 'flexible ranges of schemes of recurrent normative intentional acts.'"

visible activities in a grocery store recur because of the invisible and recurrent acts of understanding, promising, trusting, deciding and hoping occurring among suppliers, shoppers, employees, managers and so on.[337] Asking why any business is an ongoing enterprise will eventually lead to talk of such invisible acts of meaning and their recurrence, assuming, of course, the questioner is responsive to the demand for more complete understanding. With further insights into what sustains cooperation and the good of order, the questioner may be better able, more "at liberty," to revise or to develop any prior inherited views on what persons are to make of themselves and their personal relations.

     A type of moral displacement can occur when the questioning expands beyond consideration of effects on "me and mine" and takes into account the effects on "outsiders." A further development is evident when the questioning focuses on whether anyone would be justified in doing such-and-such a thing under similar circumstances. A more "complete" orientation in moral reflection is at work in the latter questioning since one's horizon of *mitsein* has expanded to include any person whatsoever. From this enlarged perspective, a questioner will more readily grasp the incompleteness of the idea that the individual-at-liberty is the basic moral category.

     Actual responses to the demands of the normative operator are decisions, and, as was seen in Chapter Two, affective responses to possible courses of action are crucial in decision-making. The cultivation and refinement of affects is often part of personal relations. How might such refinement occur in response to the demands of the principle of completion? Consider how personal relations may make a

---

[337] To transpose talk of these visible actors into an explanatory framework of interrelated functions has already begun with the references to operators and integrators and their varied demands. Pursuing a detailed account of one type of actor, e.g. a consumer, will be part of the following section of this chapter.

difference in what stance one takes in the usual debates about the merits of a free-market system.

The usual claim is that free markets promote ingenious solutions to problems, spur economic innovations and give rise to an improved standard of living in the aggregate. Since the intellectual talents and psychological aptitudes for making innovations are randomly distributed within a population,[338] a market system that provides equality of opportunity is a practical means for promoting economic goods. Critics of this set of claims commonly hold that voluntary economic exchanges do not provide or protect all human goods. They cite the legitimate interests of at-risk populations unable to compete in the marketplace, e.g. the very young, the incapacitated and the aged who lack adequate financial resources.[339]

One resulting question is what, if anything, can and should be done to offset the ill effects of the marketplace on such populations.[340] Two options seem incompatible with our normative notion of liberty. The first option advances a traditional laissez-faire argument that (1) individuals pursuing their self-interest will produce unintended social benefits and (2) in doing so will benefit more people in the long run than if we were to allow the moral agendas of political reformers to intrude on market decisions. One assumption here is that liberty in decision-making need not develop beyond an

---

[338] Here we have in mind both the intellectual gifts of inventors and the psychological aptitudes of entrepreneurs who bring the formers' discoveries to markets. Schumpeter's distinction is worth recalling.

[339] Examples of unintended harms or "third-party effects" on such populations are not difficult to find. Infants can go without adequate neonatal care because of the downsizing of parents' jobs. The disabled can lack access to private businesses because owners find it too expensive to retrofit older buildings. The elderly on fixed incomes can lose their homes because of rising property values and taxes in areas being "gentrified."

[340] Part IV of this chapter will pursue this question in relation to "third-party effects" in a global marketplace.

understanding and consideration of one's self-interest, at least when the questions are about economic exchanges with non-family members. Further questions about what range of relevant considerations should be part of our prospective judgments are left aside.

The second incompatible option is to rely on political power, exercised through bureaucracies, to direct economic activities toward some envisioned end. The end is usually some reduction or elimination of social problems, but the price tag is the reduction or elimination of liberty.

Why precisely are these options at odds with the normative notion of liberty? The laissez-faire stance appeals to the impersonal "mechanism" of the marketplace almost as a type of *fatum*.[341] In other words, progress will occur unintentionally and even despite defective schemes of normative intentional acts. Morally beneficial outcomes will occur even if the development of the normative operators is minimal. But, then, the demands of the principle of completion are presumably irrelevant to the making of a better history. Put in their place is a psychology of self-interest passing as a "complete" account of human operations. Smuggled into the account is belief in a providential order that produces virtuous results without virtuous actors and a hope that competing groups will ultimately check the abuses of each other. But this faith and this hope are usually left implicit while reliance on private charity is explicit as the remedy for those who fail to compete successfully.[342]

---

[341] The frequent use of "mechanism" in discussions of macroeconomics is open to the same criticisms voiced in Chapter Three about the use of this term in the neurosciences. In the background is an eighteenth-century worldview dismissive of moral issues as alien to science. Lonergan replied: "when physicists can think on the basis of indeterminacy, economists can think on the basis of freedom and acknowledge the relevance of morality." Macroeconomic Dynamics, 105-106.

[342] As an alternative to a positive defense, the usual defense cites the failures of "directed" economies and compares their results in raising

The second option makes a different act of faith. In relying on technicians to design programs to remedy the ill effects of a market economy, it trusts that such experts will themselves have adequately responded to the demands of the principle of completion for thoroughly understanding problems, creatively imagining remedies and correctly judging which are best and how to implement them. Even if the trust is warranted on occasion, it assumes that such responsiveness is a routine occurrence within a population of experts whose personal integrations are not liable to regular interference from competing demands. Even if such integrations were commonplace among economic technicians, most members of a society would not meet the demands of the principle. The message to them is: "Trust the experts who do the planning; you do not need to understand what is going on but just be compliant." In other words, pursuing a more complete understanding of what is good to do and then actually following through and doing it are not a task for the many but for the few. Still, the main criticism of this second option is that it assumes the determinate orientations of these few are as well developed as their plans.[343]

Is there a third option, an alternative to either a *fatum* or dependence on an economically educated elite? Suppose it is

---

average standards of living with the results achieved in market economies. This line of defense assumes a complete disjunction between market and directed economies and ignores empirical evidence of mixed economies achieving significantly higher average standards of living.

[343] Another way of criticizing the second option is that it is a non-dialectical reading of the tensions between integrations and operations. Insofar as the economic plans of technicians are efforts to maintain a given order, they are responses to the demand of a principle of assimilation. But the demand of the principle of completion is what spurs innovative departures from prior integrations. In contrast, bureaucracies are good at routine tasks, but their failures to anticipate and to respond creatively to novel situations are notoriously routine.

a slow "education of liberty." What might this mean? The earlier hypothesis was that liberty is operative in intentional acts "all the way down." As a response to the demands of the principle of completion expressed in distinct intentional acts, liberty appears in selective acts of attention, in questions of diagnosis about specific situations, in judgments about the adequacy of diagnoses, in creative fantasies about improving situations, in careful evaluations of options and in decisions about what is best to do. Ideally a series of acts comes to a relative "completion" in an act of deciding, the quality of which depends upon how well the previous acts have responded to the varied demands of their distinct operators. But how much education and what displacements will it take to make adequate responses to these demands commonplace within a large population?

What faith in an impersonal market mechanism or in economic technicians promises is a shortcut. One does not have to wait for such widespread developments in liberty. Instead, the advocates of automatic market remedies settle for underdeveloped notions of liberty and rationality, ones subordinated to the demands of sensibility for personal satisfaction. Insofar as the pursuit of their particular goods in open markets is thought inevitably to maximize aggregated social benefits, individuals need not "grow" beyond or experience displacement from this initial orientation of self-interest. In contrast, defenders of command economies acknowledge more developed notions of liberty and moral responsibility. However, they tend to assume that only a few persons will operate in ways consistent with these notions. They assume most people are incapable of intelligently and morally administering their own economic affairs. As a result, a few are to be free; the rest are to be regimented.

Trust in the impersonal "mechanism" of the marketplace or in the enduring benevolence and intelligence of economic planners is open to criticisms more directly based on a normative notion of liberty. As a capacity, liberty is the ability to respond to the demands of the principle of completion in ways that can develop or correct the antecedent integrations that initially shape its exercise. In practice, acts-at-liberty may fail to meet these demands but instead may meet the demands of the principle of assimilation for maintaining or retreating to some less developed set of integrations.[344] Normatively, however, acts-at-liberty responding to the demands of the principle of completion should meet the challenge of improving some prior integration. Such acts are then consistent with and complete the demands of the operators of intentional acts for reaching their objectives. Again, the claim is that the basic norms for human operations are immanent demands that both evoke those operations and are the criteria for evaluating any responses.

How are persons to recognize such immanent demands in themselves and their relevance to economic decision-making? The proposed answer in terms of the "education of liberty" promises neither shortcuts nor detailed plans.[345] However, some audiences may be eager to hear of any alternative to the intellectual and practical impasse of contemporary economic options. Over a quarter century ago, Alisdair MacIntyre described the impasse:

> On the one side there appear the self-defined protagonists of individual liberty, on the other, the self-defined protagonists of planning and regulation, of the goods which are available through bureaucratic organisation. But in fact what is crucial is that on which the contending parties agree, namely that there are only two alternative modes of social life open to us, one

---

[344] "Maintaining" occurs, for example, when a resolve to break a bad habit or to adopt a policy that would mitigate "structural evils" is not acted upon, and, instead, a prior pattern of operations is preserved. "Retreat" occurs when, in times of social upheaval, previously cooperative and law-abiding members of a distressed society withdraw to an ethic of survival that promotes private goods above all others.

[345] Remarks on functional specialization in the Epilogue will locate planning in a distinct specialty.

in which the free and arbitrary choices of individuals are sovereign and one in which the bureaucracy is sovereign, precisely so that it might limit the free and arbitrary choices of individuals. Given this deep cultural agreement, it is unsurprising that the politics of modern societies oscillate between a freedom which is nothing but a lack of regulation of individual behaviour and forms of collectivist control destined only to limit the anarchy of self-interest.[346]

Lonergan was trying to find a way around this very impasse when he wrote some forty years earlier of a need for new "rules" to guide persons in their economic decision-making. Political economists of a previous century had provided "a rule of *laissez faire* for governments and a rule of thrift and enterprise for individuals."[347] For a time faith in the automatic adjustments of the marketplace held these rules to be sufficient. If the Depression of the 1930s left that faith shaken, what new rules were individuals to follow? Lonergan formulated the stark options:

> Without [new and more satisfactory rules] human liberty will perish. For either men learn rules to guide them individually in the use of the economic machine, or else they surrender their liberty to be ruled along with the machine by a central planning board.[348]

If faith in the automatic adjustments of the market place and trust in an impersonal *fatum* are lost, then the question is what type of intelligent direction of the economy we will have.

> Is it to be absolutist from above downwards? Is it to be democratic from below upwards? Plainly it can be

---

[346] After Virtue: A Study in Moral Virtue (Notre Dame: University of Notre Dame Press, 1981), 34.
[347] For a New Political Economy, 110.
[348] Ibid.

democratic only in the measure in which economic science succeeds in uttering not counsel to rulers but precepts to mankind, not specific remedies and plans to increase the power of bureaucracies, but universal laws which men themselves administrate in the personal conduct of their lives.[349]

But how plausible is any alternative that requires widespread understanding of how a market economy works and widespread consent to act according to new precepts drawn from that understanding? Some will despair of the chances of success because they doubt large numbers of people will ever rise above an ethic of self-interest.[350] Others may question whether large numbers of citizens could ever acquire the needed understanding of economics. However, the envisioned education is not the training of professional economists, just as educating people about health care does not aim at making everyone a physician. Instead, just as most persons can learn which activities threaten their health and which benefit it, so most people can learn to recognize which activities threaten economic growth and which promote it.

Someone may quickly object by pointing out that large numbers of people ignore health warnings and avoid activities known to produce health benefits. Such, however, is the result of leaving people at liberty. The principle of completion makes its demands through the various operators, but inertia,

---

[349] Ibid.

[350] Amartya Sen criticized the liberal model of economic man for ignoring evidence that persons do routinely rise above this ethic in their economic and political decisions. In doing so, they must be irrational according to the views of rational agency adopted by the liberal model. Sen is blunt in his assessment of the model: "The purely economic man is indeed close to being a social moron. Economic theory has been much preoccupied with this rational fool decked in the glory of his one all-purpose preference ordering." "Rational Fools: A Critique of the Behavioral Foundations of Economic Theory." Philosophy and Public Affairs. 6(1977), 336.

human folly and accidents will always play roles in the human drama. The last century proved that the curtailment of liberty by a top-down direction of society produced neither a good order nor morally responsible uses of liberty. A more promising option appears to be some type of education of free individuals in the workings of a market economy and in what kinds of activities are compatible with its functioning as a genuine good of order.[351]

That the educational tasks are not impossible is suggested by how modern societies experience flows of traffic on their highways. First of all, most drivers know the difference between competent and incompetent performance behind the wheel. Because some are incompetent and others drive irresponsibly, regulations and the threat of penalties remain parts of social order. Still, most drivers go about their business without top-down supervision and without being motivated by threats. Presumably they understand what kinds of driving are required to maintain the good of order that is a traffic flow. They use their liberty to play their part in maintaining it while still driving defensively because they understand not everyone will cooperate in sustaining this common good. The analogy suggests that we might find a similar middle way between the options of an anarchic liberty in the marketplace and a regimentation of its participants.

The following case study sketches how someone might begin to meet the educational challenge that is a middle way. The study draws upon earlier accounts of schemes of recurrence and types of displacements. The revised accounts of both are part of the educational effort to expand

---

[351] A caveat is perhaps unnecessary regarding this educational option. An eighteenth-century dream of an enlightened age assumed that ignorance was the primary barrier to progress. As the previous chapter noted, there are multiple limits on liberty, including those that yield moral failures. In the last section of this chapter, talk of various displacements as prerequisites to more comprehensive understanding and better practices will implicitly correct the oversights of the earlier dream.

"horizons"[352] in thinking about economic decisions. Of course, such a case study proves nothing about the viability of the much larger educational experiment.   It amounts to an invitation to readers to fantasize about a long-term enterprise that may be the best hope for preserving an economy based on free enterprise. One possibility, of course, is that such an experiment would never be tried. Another is that it would be tried and found wanting. At least there is some incentive to make the attempt. If large numbers of citizens act like herds of cattle pushed along by screaming ads to consume as much as possible regardless of debt load and if they count on fantasies of stock market bonanzas or lotteries to rescue them from their debts and to deliver a grandiose standard of living, then any serious economic contraction will leave them disillusioned, desperate and eager to follow any charismatic figure who promises a return to prosperous times. But then the efforts to establish a society of free and responsible citizens will begin to seem futile.

Ordered liberty is not a given, and a society whose citizens cherish its attainment has remained a dream. The collapse of command economies near the end of the last century settled the debate about centralized control of an economy, but the further question is whether persons will use their liberty responsibly. As a global economy puts even more pressure on local social orders, the test of ordered liberty will be increasingly unavoidable: either large numbers of people will learn how a market economy works and will act responsibly in it or their defective uses of liberty will produce new disorders on an unprecedented global scale.

IV A Puzzle about Consumer Responsibility

In a global economy most consumers are "indirect employers" of the labor and productive activities of anony-

---

[352] Recall the earlier meaning of "horizon" as the range of questions one can raise and find significant or the range of considerations one can take into account and find relevant.

mous others. That is, by consuming they sustain the relationships between direct employers and employees. Put as a generality: without consumption production is pointless and soon ends. Let this sustaining relation (i.e. this necessary condition for ongoing employment and production) be the initial meaning of "indirect employer."[353] Why should anyone bother to make such an obvious point about the relation of consumers to usually anonymous employers and employees? For one thing, various puzzles have emerged about consumer responsibility for harms befalling third parties in market operations. This case study is an exploration of <u>three questions</u> about these puzzles:

(1) Why do consumers rarely think about their potential responsibility for actual harms occurring to remote others?
(2) What are the most common obstacles to thinking about acts of consumption from a broadened perspective that includes "indirect relations"?
(3) How might these obstacles be overcome?

Note that, while this study raises the question of potential consumer responsibility for harms to third parties, its purpose is not to determine if there is such responsibility; rather, the three preceding questions serve the limited purpose of this study, namely, expanding the horizons of consumers in relation to their economic decisions.

To begin with the first question, actual harms to remote others seem to be of two types: deliberate harms and unintended harms. The former include dangerous and avoidable working conditions routinely faced by laborers, e.g. the repeated exposure of migrant farm workers to pesticides. Two assumptions seem safe here: (1) some employers deliberately put employees at risk by allowing dangerous and

---

[353] For this understanding of "indirect employers," I am relying on the work of Professor Albino Barrera, O.P. "*Gaudium et Spes* and Catholic Ethics in Post-Industrial Economics: Indirect Employers and Globalization." The Journal of Catholic Social Teaching. 3:2(2006), 321-333.

avoidable working conditions to continue; (2) because of these risks faced routinely by anonymous others, consumers, at least in the short run, pay less than they otherwise would for some products. The question then is: Should consumers, or indirect employers, who benefit from these market arrangements, think of themselves as in any way responsible for harms done to anonymous "indirect employees"?

The second type of actual harm includes unintended consequences of market operations. Here we find the frequent discussion of "externalities" or effects on third parties that are not intended by the original parties to economic exchanges.[354] Examples of these sorts of unintended harms include the consequences of trade liberalization for once protected industries and for their workers[355] or the effects of "outsourcing" on domestic employee populations. Again, consumers may well benefit from lower costs for products no longer protected by tariffs or no longer made by more highly paid workers. But just because consumers benefit, does that mean they should think they are obligated to offset the losses experienced by foreign or domestic workers?

Suppose relevant questions here are: (1) What can be done about either type of harm? (2) Who, if anyone, has responsibility for preventing or remedying such harms? In regard to deliberately inflicted harms, most persons in the West have come to expect governmental action to prevent or to correct them. For example, a purpose of OSHA regulations is to prevent or to remedy workplace conditions that put employees at avoidable risk; legislation, often prompted by popular protests, imposes penalties on those inflicting avoidable damages to environments; courts routinely enforce terms of contracts; and new international bodies are playing

---

[354] Henry Shue supplies a detailed example of this sort of harm in his hypothetical example of a shift from subsistence agriculture to growing an export commodity. See his Basic Rights: Subsistence, Affluence and U.S. Foreign Policy (Princeton: Princeton University Press, 1980), 41-46.

[355] Barrera, 324-325.

roles in enforcing treaty obligations, particularly those involving trade. Notice, then, that, in regard to this first type of harm, consumers appear to have no direct role in rectifying harms; rather, the preventive and corrective measures are responsibilities of governmental bodies.[356]

What of the second type of harm? When unintended and adverse consequences befall third parties, who, if anyone, is responsible for remedying the situation? Barrera notes the difficulties in identifying whether anything ought to be done and, if so, by whom:

> To what extent are US consumers (greatly benefiting from inexpensive imports) liable for the plight of laid-off US manufacturing workers? And how about the fresh college graduates who are just entering the labor market and are unable to secure jobs because of international outsourcing and the transfer of capital to low-cost manufacturing sites in Asia and Latin America? Is there any obligation to provide them relief? If so, whose duty is it to provide such aid? [...]
>
> The decline in the value of the dollar has inflicted economic hardship on many EU exporters. Who has responsibility for providing assistance to those who have been unfavorably affected by a weakening dollar: the Chinese for undervaluing their currency relative to the US dollar, the US government for its uncontrolled

---

[356] Besides criminal and civil procedures, corrective measures by governments often include job retraining programs, unemployment insurance, workers' compensation programs, as well as international measures to ameliorate effects of global warming and overfishing of the oceans. Yet not all countries can afford adequate "safety nets" for their workers. When governments are ineffective in protecting their own citizens from harmful conditions, do consumers who benefit from those conditions have any obligation to offset or end the harms done? At least some consumers have answered affirmatively as witnessed in past boycotts of grapes and of products of child labor.

budget deficit, US consumers for accumulating such record trade deficits or the OECD countries who have simply relied on the U.S. economy to provide the necessary consumption demand to prevent the world from sliding into recession?[357]

A first response to such queries might well be puzzlement since most consumers would not think to ask such questions. If pressed for a response, some might assert that markets routinely advantage and disadvantage populations without any one person or group being responsible for the outcomes. The complexity of conditions that yield market outcomes for large numbers of people are neither designed by anyone nor under the control of particular groups; hence, when harms befall some, no one in particular may be responsible for remedying the situation.[358] This is one answer to the question about consumer responsibility, but there are other questions that serve the purpose of this study. Recall the first of the three focus questions of this case study: Why do consumers rarely consider whether they are possibly responsible for actual harms occurring to remote others? This question does not assume there is in fact such responsibility. Instead, it asks why consumers rarely wonder if they could have such a responsibility.

Perhaps a response is already present: the complexity of market conditions often makes it impossible to assign responsibility for harms done and for taking corrective measures. For example, imagine the division of labor presupposed by the laptop computer one purchases. Next, suppose environmental harms commonly occur in multiple countries either from producing microchips and other components or from disposing of used laptops. Yet who

---

[357] Barrera, 324-325.

[358] Friedrich A. Hayek's discussion of an economic order as a "catallaxy" arrives at this conclusion. See Chapter 10 of his <u>Law, Legislation</u> and <u>Liberty</u>, Vol. 2 (Chicago: University of Chicago Press, 1976), 115-120.

precisely is being harmed and by whom? The general label for the puzzle here is the "problem of indeterminacy."

Barrera's examples are indicative of the problems of determining what, if anything, is owed to whom and by whom. A similar difficulty appeared when an anti-drug campaign in the 1980s asserted that anyone who used illegal drugs was responsible for the violence and murders regularly occurring as part of the drug trade. Upon further analysis the question of complicity proved very difficult to answer. What if there is no one-to-one correspondence between a particular act of consumption and classes of events happening routinely elsewhere in the drug trade?[359] Then, all that anyone would be justified in asserting is that particular acts of consumption possibly put others at risk elsewhere in the drug trade. What is not justified is the assertion that a particular act of consumption is a necessary condition for the recurrence of the complex schemes of financing, producing, distributing and consuming illegal drugs. No single act of consumption inevitably contributes to violence regularly occurring in these schemes.

This minimalist claim about consumer responsibility may disappoint those campaigning against illegal drugs, yet advocates of "free market" capitalism may welcome the distance it puts between consumers and harms occurring elsewhere. But this assumes that both groups will even think about concrete acts of consumption as events within complex economic schemes. The meaning of "concrete" is itself a puzzle. For example, we commonly think of economic exchanges <u>descriptively</u>, i.e. we picture buyers and sellers, customers and clerks, borrowers and lenders engaged in transactions. Accordingly we tend to use "concrete" to depict something as an imaginable event or object, e.g. this buyer paying for this commodity at this store. But further questions will quickly expose the limits of this understanding of economic

---

[359] For the fuller analysis see William Zanardi, "Consumer Responsibility from a Social Systems Perspective," <u>International Journal of Applied Philosophy.</u> 8 (1990), 57-66.

exchanges. For example, what makes any business a business? What is a business as an ongoing enterprise? Why is it "ongoing"?

While it is easy to picture a grocery store or a bank and to describe what either looks like and what visible activities occur in it, the meaning of those activities is not visible or picturable. For example, the exchange between a borrower and a lender at the local bank can be filmed, but making sense of what later appears on the screen requires a shared understanding of the meaning of conventional gestures and signs of agreement. In particular, the <u>invisible</u> <u>acts</u> of promising and trusting, of judging and consenting, are what make the transaction what it is. In a very basic way such acts of meaning are what keep grocery stores and banks in business. They are ongoing enterprises, complex schemes of recurrence, because employers, employees and customers continue to share meanings, to extend trust and to elicit cooperation. What happens when trust erodes because promises are broken? Enterprises and schemes with their visible acts of exchange break down when the invisible acts no longer recur.

These remarks may seem to be a digression from the first focus question. However, they are consistent with the claim that most consumers are not accustomed to thinking of their acts of consumption as belonging to a class of events within ongoing economic schemes. Again, what is "concrete" commonly means what is visible, e.g. the checkout clerk and the shopper at the local market. But what if "concrete" means what a thing is and to understand what a thing is requires raising as many relevant questions as one can in pursuit of a comprehensive understanding of it?[360] Then, describing what something looks like is but a starting point; further why-questions will push the inquirer toward an explanatory account

---

[360] Helpful distinctions in the uses of "concrete" appear in the question-and-answer session recorded as part of Lonergan's third lecture in a series at MIT, later published as "What Are Judgments of Value?" in <u>CW</u> 17, 150-152.

that makes use of correlations among variable classes of events and objects.[361] But how obvious is all this to the casual shopper at a department store examining imported clothing? Or to repeat the second focus question: What are the most common obstacles to thinking about consumption from a broadened horizon that includes "indirect relations"?

The preceding remarks suggest that intellectual limitations are among the obstacles to a broader perspective on economic exchanges. Suppose these limitations often include oversights: (1) of externalities or third-party effects; (2) of personal capacity to prevent or to remedy harms, (3) of any potential obligation to do so.[362]

Ignorance or oversight of externalities is a plausible excuse when adverse consequences occur halfway around the globe. All the same, the mass media continually erode the plausibility of this appeal to ignorance. But perhaps the appeal still works when consumers ask what they can possibly do about distant calamities. Again, with increasing frequency the popular media report stories about international protest movements, boycotts, fair-trade campaigns, the aims of NGOs and the calls for new legislative initiatives.[363] So the efforts of some consumers to change the conditions under which others labor are on exhibit. Particularly for financially secure

---

[361] Consider the contrast between describing a car that is speeding up as a race begins and the physicist's interest in understanding constant acceleration, something that no one has ever <u>seen</u>. As noted before, the distinction between description and explanation is borrowed from Lonergan's <u>Insight</u>.

[362] Why these oversights? Tracing the sources of diverse viewpoints on economic exchanges is the task at hand in this section. What the following paragraphs will add, among other claims, is that the absence of a shift to the world of theory is a key obstacle to a "broader perspective on economic exchanges."

[363] Specific examples include: the fair-trade coffee campaigns, Amnesty International campaigns against the use of children in the military, the Nestle infant formula boycott, repeated demonstrations at WTO meetings.

consumers, requests for donations in time and money provide opportunities for them to exercise their limited capacity to prevent or to remedy remote harms.

Perhaps it is the third intellectual limitation (a failure to ask whether there might be any obligation to remedy or to prevent harm) that is the most difficult to overcome. Here there is no advertence to the possibility of consumer responsibility for remote and unintended harms. But suppose the question does occur. Advocates of a type of economic realism will be quick to dismiss any potential consumer liability. They will acknowledge that market operations often produce unintended harms, but, so long as no illegal acts occurred, they are not injustices; instead, they are unfortunate but "natural" outcomes. If someone claims that consumers who benefitted from market conditions are obligated to remedy harms befalling others under those same conditions, the response tends to be one of incomprehension or a demand for evidence of a contractual relation between the injured parties and particular consumers. Absent legal obligations, consumers may laudably exercise charity, but they are not strictly obligated to remedy harms that were neither intended nor the result of illegal acts by those consumers.

Here we have arrived at fundamentally divergent moral and political stances. Are the morally relevant relations among consumers and their indirect employees limited to those identified in contracts and legal statutes? While moral obligations of civility, respect and Good Samaritanism are usually acceptable features of non-economic exchanges, there appears to be little agreement on what obligations, other than those dictated by law and contract, apply in economic exchanges. Does this inquiry into potential consumer obligations end at an intellectual impasse? That is, are there incommensurable moral viewpoints on this issue, ones that no one can evaluate from some objective standpoint, and so they remain irreducible differences not subject to rational adjudication?

We suddenly find ourselves in a thicket of questions beyond the focus of this study. Still, in identifying some of the obstacles to thinking about acts of consumption in terms of ongoing schemes of recurrence, we have a clue to a way beyond this impasse. So-called incommensurable view-points and their supporting arguments are usually made explicit within the horizon of theory. If the analysis of their differences remains within that horizon, the differences will often be irreconcilable since they usually derive from deep-level assumptions that are unchallenged within the theories themselves. However, a third horizon of interiority may offer a way to identify and to criticize the origins of some of these differences.[364] This third horizon shifts the focus from the products of inquiry, e.g. competing theories, to the intentional operations that engender all theories. We previously saw one benefit of such a shift in attention by recognizing the limits of picture thinking. Whether imagining transactions between buyers and sellers or the observable features of plants and animals, one can go on to ask what makes any of them what they are. Then comments on complex correlations among classes of acts and events can become an introduction to non-imaginable schemes of recurrence. But just how are these two ways of thinking and speaking about economic activities or natural objects related? Longstanding debates have followed over which way of thinking is more concrete. Are what we see with our eyes the real things or are the intelligible patterns among acts and events what things really are? Different theories have arisen from different responses to such basic questions, and the result has been interminable debates within the horizon of theory. The way past these debates lies in focusing on the different ways of operating in relation to things.[365]

---

[364] The nomenclature for this horizon is borrowed from Lonergan. The focus of inquiry can shift to questions about the data of consciousness (i.e. intentional acts, relations among them and mental states) especially when theorizing generates equally plausible but incompatible conclusions.

[365] Sir Arthur Eddington's famous puzzle about his writing table is an example of both the longstanding debate and of its interminability

What proves beneficial in understanding differences between common-sense descriptions and theoretical explanations may help in understanding differences among moral and political stances regarding consumer responsibility. Operating within this third horizon proceeds not by listing different stances regarding obligations and economic practices but by asking why there are such differences. Any anthropology text provides a listing of cultural differences, and any survey of the history of political philosophy reveals competing political stances. But what if the question is how these variations originate? What differences in operators might account for some of these secondary variations?[366]

To begin with a general summary, suppose there are at least three general sources of diversity among moral and economic viewpoints.[367] First, the multiplicity of views may be due to differences in cultural-historical contexts; i.e., as "matters-of-fact," moral beliefs and economic practices vary according to place and time.[368] Differences in actual conditions at different times are the basis for different moral insights that support different economic practices. For example, moral norms for the care of the elderly may vary with the survival conditions of a group. A nomadic people in a routinely harsh environment may operate with a rule that prescribes abandoning the aged member who is no longer able to make the annual trek to winter feeding grounds. For less endangered societies, such a practice would be unjustifiable. In another case, usury may be condemnable or

---

if one overlooks the third horizon and so does not ask how one is operating in relation to an object and what one is assuming about what is real.

[366] The variations are "secondary" since questions precede answers; operations precede integrations.

[367] Lonergan. Method in Theology, 326.

[368] Many scholars hold that matters-of-fact are unexplainable and that cultural variability does not entail ethical relativism. Both conclusions are defensible but do not preclude making moral judgments about diverse beliefs and practices. See the next footnote.

acceptable depending on the economic development of the group and the purposes of usury within a given setting.

A second source of differences among moral views on economic practices will be the presence or absence of certain <u>differentiations of consciousness</u>. For example, concern for the outsider and a group's extension to non-members of rules protecting members become more likely after "tribal consciousness" has become capable of abstract generalizations that ignore some empirical differences as mere matters-of-fact. The general historical case is when group identity, while important, is no longer thought definitive of what it means to be human; then an understanding that other persons are deserving of respect and protection from harm will encompass more than group members. Historical developments in both religious and scientific understanding may have contributed to this shift toward a more universal perspective on persons as having worth independently of group identity. However, prior to that shift, conventional moral rules that protected insiders may not have applied to outsiders. The historical relativity of these rules need not be controversial. Just as differences in understanding, absent the negligent conscience, ground differences in moral culpability, so rules binding in one age or culture may be at odds with those binding elsewhere without the differences being evidence for ethical relativism.[369] The more "complete"

---

[369] The first two sources of diversity do not provide evidence for ethical relativism since the variable in both instances is the act of understanding. Because the act of judgment is distinct from the act of understanding, the fact that people at different times and places have understood differently does not mean they all made equally defensible judgments. If one's best current understanding is capable of further development, it is still normative, despite its incompleteness, in one's making morally responsible decisions. However, later developments in understanding may make earlier judgments no longer defensible. The demands of the principle of completion are for just such developments, and the normative notion of liberty is a measure of progress in meeting these demands.

viewpoint will comprehend the less developed one but not vice versa, and as more advanced it will find the earlier stance no longer justifiable. The history of debates over slavery in the West provides materials to exemplify these claims.

A third origin of diversity among moral views on economic practices lies in the presence or absence of various <u>displacements</u>. This is the most controversial of the claims about the sources of diverse beliefs and practices, but there is no avoiding the basic issue. Persons carrying out inquiries have the insights that later are the basis for generalized views. But persons may be more or less familiar with theoretical inquiries and their products, more or less developed in moral understanding, more or less at home in a world that contains manipulable resources as well as transcendent mystery. The degrees of intellectual, moral or spiritual development in the inquirer presumably affect the inquirer's understanding and evaluation of economic practices.[370] Since variable degrees of such developments occur across populations, we should expect differences in the demands of normative operators.

Rather than entering into a lengthy exposition of how various types of displacements are correlated with developments in understanding, one can cite performative differences familiar to many persons. For instance, if child psychologists are to be believed, intellectual development occurs when a child no longer evaluates the moral seriousness of an act solely in terms of the quantity of harm done but begins to count intention as a relevant measure of moral responsibility. Many will also accept that a type of intellectual displacement occurs when adults are able to think about what is good not solely in terms of immediate and tangible results (i.e. particular goods) but also in terms of the nonpalpable goods of social order, bonds of trust and personal relations. Instead of confinement in one's thinking to immediate and tangible goods, one affirms a good of order

---

[370] In terms of a social dialectic, one could rephrase the preceding remarks to substitute "tradition" or "culture" for "persons" and "inquirer."

that is due to the mediating but invisible operations of promising, hoping and trusting. Without this intellectual advance, one's moral judgments about economic policies and political programs are likely to remain focused on immediate consequences for oneself and others close at hand. As noted above, one result is that talk of "concrete" acts of consumption as occurring in and through complex schemes of recurrence will remain obscure.

How does something like moral displacement make a difference in economic viewpoints? In conflicts among nations or trading blocs, some will adopt a type of economic realism with its moral resignation to the evils that "must be tolerated." For example, in a world of competing nation states, the realist will assert that no nation is ever obligated to subordinate its economic interests to the well being of non-citizens. In contrast, moral displacement may broaden the horizon of one's concern beyond the interests of one's tribe. What secures the latter's good is at best a relative good that may, under some circumstances, be trumped by the good of the alien within one's borders or the good of some population beyond them. Have we met or heard of persons resisting political realism and the mantra of "My country right or wrong"? Did we find their actions admirable?

How does something like spiritual displacement make a difference in moral evaluations of economic practices? The pacifism of Quakers and their worldwide efforts to assist the impoverished have origins in religious convictions. The housing initiatives of Habitat for Humanity and their innovative approaches to financing home ownership originate from a similar source. Why do they make these efforts on the part of the indigent? Moral viewpoints that appeal to a calculus of utility or to reciprocal justice or to some balance of legal rights and duties do not provide adequate answers. These viewpoints do not capture the meaning of such cases because they are missing the prior insights and judgments of those who have experienced some type of spiritual transformation. Whether the insights and judgments accompanying such a transformation are superior to those preceding it is not argued here. All that is claimed is that persons reporting such transformations in their lives do report a difference in how they thought <u>before</u> and <u>after</u> the transformation. As well, they report the change has been for the better.

To sum up this mapping of some sources of moral diversity: we have variables in actual historical contexts, in differentiations of consciousness and in types of displacements. Even this brief survey can impart a sense of personal and historical relativity in how persons understand economic practices. But besides understanding there is judging, i.e. evaluating whether one's understanding is correct. To speak of "development" in understanding is to make some judgments, so hard intellectual work remains after assembling the diverse moral viewpoints or even after tracing the differences to their roots in any of the sources. The task is to evaluate, to judge and to decide among these differences. But how go about doing this?[371]

Our test case involves different responses to the question of how consumers as indirect employers are related to remote others. Advocates of the contractarian view of economic relations will insist that legal relations must exist between parties before specific obligations are legitimately claimed. Any legal obligations will be matters of doing justice, e.g. meeting the terms of contractual agreements. On the other hand, a theological view of social order may assume that all persons are related through a divine creator and so form a "family" prior to every legal contract. But then moral obligations are antecedent to legal ties, and consumers will have a broad range of obligations to many others as a matter of benevolence rather than as a matter of legal or contractual justice.

But how is any persuasive assessment of these contrasting views of social relations and obligations possible? Which views should one adopt as a guide in determining whether there could ever be consumer responsibility for

---

[371] In the Epilogue, this question will reappear in the discussion of the functional specialty "foundations."

externalities? One option is to play the skeptic or moral relativist by declaring that here is just one more example of "incommensurable worldviews" which exist side by side in contemporary secular societies. They reflect different cultural traditions kept alive within different communities of belief. There is no neutral position (a "view from nowhere") allowing assessment of such cultural differences, so one should not expect to find criteria outside of a particular tradition by which to evaluate or to judge the differences.[372]

This option actually reflects the first of the three sources of differences mentioned above. As a matter-of-fact, different cultural belief systems exist, and persons inheriting different traditions have internalized different worldviews. But is it possible to ask further why-questions or must the inquiry end with simply describing matter-of-fact differences? The shift to the third horizon is the promising alternative to ending at an impasse. As suggested above, we can go on to ask why different operators produce or subscribe to different, and sometimes incompatible, integrations of meaning.

Of course it is possible to ask further why-questions, but what is our capacity to answer them? Studies in social dialectic suggest that traditions and cultures are not boxes confining occupants to inherited worldviews. The descriptive mantra in dialectical analysis is that the "cause" produces the "effect" but the latter can act back on the former.[373] Hence, the cultural integrations that initially shape the thinking and acting of individuals can themselves become objects of investigation and criticism by those same individuals. How is this possible? At the heart of any social order is a principle of completion present in the indeterminate capacity of its

---

[372] Without attributing moral skepticism or relativism to his complex stance, I take the last two sentences to be a fair representation of H. Tristram Engelhardt's views of contemporary moral impasses. Cf. his The Foundations of Christian Bioethics (Lisse: Taylor and Francis, 2000).

[373] As noted before, I am indebted here to the work of Peter L. Berger and Thomas Luckmann, The Social Construction of Reality.

members to raise further questions. If we cannot anticipate all the questions that will occur to us next week, no prior indoctrination or socialization process can have the final say about our thinking and doing.

Granted the questions that in fact do occur to a person are partly dependent on prior experiences and understanding. Put in the form of a generalization: questions, answers and judgments are dependent on <u>context</u>. How do contexts vary? Again, to exploit the three sources of diversity reviewed above, an answer can mention three broad classes of variation. Non-dialectical analysis cites historical-cultural differences as evidence of incommensurable worldviews leading to impasses in trying to assess their differences. Still, the other two classes, or sources of variations, may offer exceptions to such impasses.

First, "context" in dialectical analysis is not something "out there" independent of "concrete"[374] individuals; rather, the demands of operators have multiple conditions. Social-historical relations constituted by prior judgments, decisions and their consequences, along with present interests and inquiries are some of those conditions. Such complex patterns can be more or less developed and more or less reflective of adequate understanding and reliable decision-making. For example, two hundred and fifty years ago David Hume had an insight about the mutually beneficial effects of trade between two nations.[375] While present in the culture, the insight was not an effective part of the "context" of recurrent judgments and decisions well into the last century. Even now calls for protectionist legislation continue, and the mindset of trade being a zero-sum game exists alongside more adequate views of economic exchanges. So we find

---

[374] Recall the two meanings of "concrete." The second use "fits" the pursuit of a comprehensive understanding of what an individual is and of what a social order is.

[375] David Hume. <u>Essays, Literary, Moral and Political</u>. (London: Ward, Lock & Co., 1817), 195-198.

varying degrees of intellectual development within individuals and entire cultures.

We are back then to the opening part of the earlier puzzle — but with a difference. Yes, the fact of diversity among worldviews is indisputable, but notice that we have been writing about views as more or less developed, more or less adequate. The terminology here presupposes evaluative judgments about advance and decline, about changes for the better or for the worse. But what are the criteria for these judgments? The criteria were implicit in remarks above about differentiations of consciousness and types of displacements. All sorts of complexities were overlooked earlier; however, given the limits of this study, perhaps no one will expect more than a sketch of how to move beyond the <u>fact</u> of historical-cultural differences to judgments about some of those differences. What follows is such a summary intended to return to the original focus of this case on (1) asking why consumers rarely think about their potential responsibility for what happens to indirect employees; (2) identifying obstacles to thinking about possible consumer responsibility for externalities, and (3) overcoming at least some of those obstacles.

While there are multiple types and combinations of types of differentiations of consciousness,[376] the focus so far has been on the contrast between descriptive (or pictorial thinking) and theoretical inquiry with its pursuit of correlations among variables. What difference does it make to be familiar with both ways of understanding and to know the demands and limits of each? There was the earlier example about businesses as ongoing enterprises. The standard textbook will mention a familiar cycle of classes of events, e.g. finance, production, distribution, consumption. A less conventional view suggests that even this familiar cycle has its preconditions in the recurrence of invisible acts of hoping, promising, trusting, agreeing. What might all this imply for

---

[376] Lonergan cites thirty two possible combinations of differentiated types of consciousness. "Doctrinal Pluralism" in <u>CW</u> 17, 98.

understanding consumers' possible responsibility for externalities?

A fundamental question is whether we understand human ontology more adequately, more comprehensively, as constituted in and through relationships with others or as only secondarily dependent on relations to others, e.g. as in the case of political association or contractual agreements. While evidence from child psychology and sociology seems to support a broad notion of the constitutive role of relations in human being, advocates of a more limited role would likely focus on how economic relations are dependent on political relations, as opposed to other types of social relations. For example, they could hold that political rights and duties derive not from human ontology but from specific contractual agreements. Then, by extension they could claim that economic relations have a similar source.

Even granting these claims, one can ask further why-questions about how persons actually relate to one another in political orders. So, for example, one may ask why persons ever heroically risk their lives to save political institutions from threats. Is it because they signed a contract stipulating that under certain conditions they would forego all private benefits and accept death rather than allow practices established by the contract to be destroyed? Or could it be that some set of political relations is held to be a higher good worthy of personal sacrifice? One could also ask, Why would anyone continue to be virtuous and law-abiding when illegal behavior would bring significant personal rewards, be undetectable and so occur with impunity? Perhaps a contractarian answer is: "Because one promised." However, the alleged promise was made under the expectation of a flow of reciprocal benefits. Why should one keep the promise when breaking it would instigate a new flow of significant personal benefits?[377] Does

---

[377] The queries here reflect standard criticisms of the eighteenth-century psychology "behind" Classical Liberalism and its contract theory of the state. If authority derives from the consent of the governed and the governed consent out of self-interest (i.e. because

the focus here on personal interests reveal too narrow an understanding of "rational agency"?

These further questions provide a transition to a sketch of how displacements can alter how one thinks about the effects of personal acts on remote others. Again, multiple types of displacements and combinations of them present a complexity beyond the scope of this study. One type, moral displacement, will suffice to exemplify a shift from an earlier to a later and, presumably, more developed way of thinking.

Suppose persons spontaneously care about understanding and about others, i.e., they are curious and exhibit a moral concern for others. Admittedly the range of caring about understanding and about others may initially be quite limited. But does expansion of caring occur and is such expansion an instance of development? Reflection on personal experiences of being careless and of being careful in research, in conversations, in driving a car may produce some examples of development.

As noted before, the <u>minimal</u> meaning of "being careful" in moral decision-making is captured in three basic insights: (1) what seems good is not necessarily what is good; (2) what is good for me is not necessarily what is good for others; (3) before acting in ways that affect others, I should stop to consider the effects of my actions on others. Most persons acquire this set of insights and so take the early steps in an expansion from caring about what is good "for me and mine" to a concern for wider populations. An analogous de-centering or displacement occurs when one learns to think about things not in their relation to oneself but in terms of their relations among themselves. That was in part the shift involved in understanding businesses as ongoing schemes of recurrence rather than as visible places, agents and events. A similar shift can occur when further de-centering allows a person to ask whether a course of action would be good for anyone to do under similar circumstances. Note the question

---

they anticipate future benefits), how do we account for heroic sacrifices and selfless virtue?

is not how will the action affect "me and mine." This decentering seems to be part of intellectual development as well. Recall the example of seeing something speeding up and only later puzzling about constant acceleration.

How do the preceding remarks help us evade the impasses of the second horizon of theory? Let's return to our earlier use of the word "context," but now its meaning may be less obscure. For example, study of a particular issue involves raising and trying to answer relevant questions. In doing careful research, a scholar ignores irrelevant and distracting questions; the focus is on puzzling out what pertains to the issue.

> To answer any one question will give rise to further questions. To answer them will give rise to still more. But while this process can recur a number of times, while it would go on indefinitely if one kept changing the topic, still it does not go on indefinitely on one and the same topic. Context, then, is a nest of interlocked or interwoven questions and answers. It is limited inasmuch as all the questions and answers have a bearing, direct or indirect, upon a single topic. Finally, because the context is limited, there comes a point when no further relevant questions arise, and then there emerges the possibility of judgment. For when there are no further relevant questions, there is also no opportunity for further insights to occur and thereby correct, qualify, complement the insights already attained.[378]

It may still be too easy to miss the relevance of this word "context" for the question about why some never entertain the possibility of consumer obligations to remote others. To whom does this "nest of interlocked or interwoven questions and answers" belong? The point is that some

---

[378] Lonergan. "Merging Horizons: System, Common Sense, Scholarship." CW 17, 61.

specific inquirer may have developed an increasingly more comprehensive understanding of some limited topic by raising and answering relevant questions. That inquirer, then, has become the more developed, the more adequate "context" that serves as the remote criterion of the truth of judgments about that topic.[379]

How plausible does this seem? With the passing of nineteenth-century positivism, it no longer is controversial to assert that there is an existential dimension to all theorizing, that there are limits to argumentation such that no amount of evidence and no argument "compel" assent to some fact or course of action. Put simply, facts do not speak for themselves, and deciding to assent is distinct from knowing what can be done or consenting to what should be done.[380] So the more differentiated the consciousness and the more advanced the multiple displacements in operators, the more reliable they are as criteria for judging different and competing worldviews. Of course some will worry that this conclusion makes "subjectivity" the measure of truth and moral rightness. But the issue is not whether decisions and commitments are decisive for judging but whether they are arbitrary.[381] Put another way, the issue is whether the decisions and commitments reflect ordered liberty or the disordered responses of persons living at odds with the demands of their own operators.

There is no "compelling" argument here. "Contexts" vary, and so some inquirers will be more advanced in some fields than in others; some will reflect the best of which persons are capable while others will reflect some of the follies of which all persons are capable. All the same, the native curiosity, the reach for further understanding, in persons is responsive to the principle of completion; so contexts can be

---

[379] "'The remote criterion, then, is concerned with one's overall development.'" Lonergan quoted by the editors in ibid., 64, fn. 25.
[380] "What Are Judgments of Value?" in ibid., 149-150.
[381] "Is It Real?" in ibid., 127.

destabilized "from within."[382] That is enough to hold the promise of further growth, even of radical displacement from one set of assumptions to another.

Diagram 5.2 represents an understanding of key variables affecting whatever integrations of meaning persons are likely to achieve.

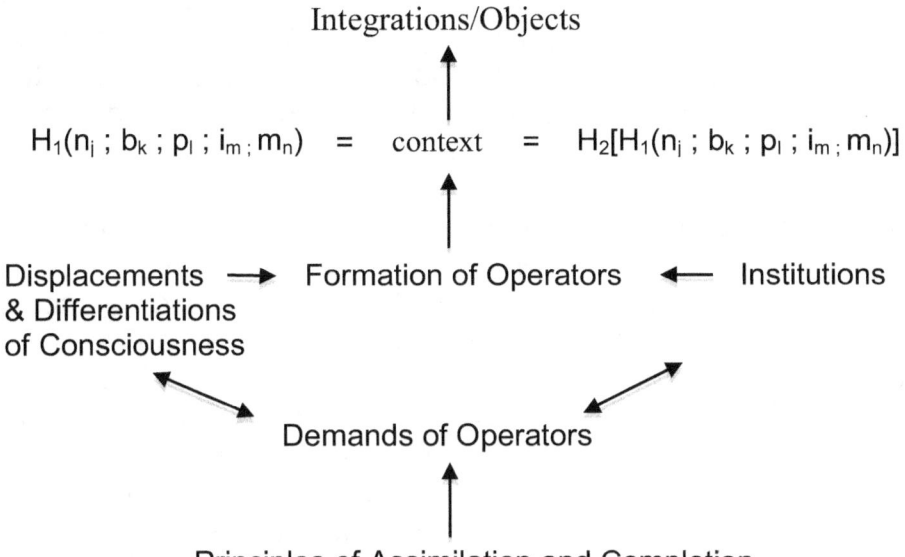

(Diagram 5.2)

Do the preceding comments answer the three earlier questions about potential consumer responsibility for externalities? The first question asked why consumers so infrequently think about such potential responsibility. The second question tried to locate some common obstacles to thinking about this issue. The third asked how we might overcome these obstacles. The responses to the first two questions cited the presence or absence of certain types of

---

[382] Keeping in mind a social dialectic, we should note that other persons are often external sources that destabilize established contexts; hence, Habermas can celebrate the benefits of public discourse for expanding one's initial horizons.

differentiations of consciousness and displacements. These responses are unlikely to make much sense to someone who is unacquainted with such shifts in thinking. In addition, they are not alterations that anyone can make for another. Partly for that reason this study does not take a stand on the question of actual consumer responsibility for externalities. Again, arguments are not by themselves compelling; an act of intellectual assent or judgment is distinct from acts of understanding. Therefore, we should expect ongoing disputes between, for example, advocates of neo-liberal economics and proponents of communitarian philosophies. But the hypothesis is that the origins of the ongoing debates lie not in variations in theories or arguments. Instead, the origins lie in varying degrees of development in human "contexts."

But then the third question (How might these obstacles be overcome?) receives a response. When hearing about seemingly incommensurable moral and economic viewpoints, we should ask further why-questions. The advice amounts to an invitation to exercise the principle of indeterminacy within ourselves. In more imaginable terms, it is an invitation analogous to Eric Voegelin's practice of anamnesis.[383] In this case the art of persuasion has an Augustinian precedent: *tolle et lege*, i.e. pick up, begin reading and thinking and see where they lead you. If the chief obstacle to raising relevant questions about consumer responsibility is the lack of development in those who should be doing the questioning, then a first step in overcoming the obstacle may be to invite audiences to consider further questions.

---

[383] Eric Voegelin's retrieval of the insights of Classical Greek Philosophy is summarized in "Reason: The Classic Experience," in Published Essays, 265-291.

CHAPTER SIX: POLITICAL LIBERTY

I Introduction

This chapter makes no attempt to formulate a political theory although previous remarks on the relations between institutions and individuals and on economic liberty presupposed elements of one. Instead, the narrower focus is on how the normative notion of liberty, developed in the previous chapters, might contribute to resolving several intellectual puzzles regarding political liberty. To anticipate those puzzles: When we endorse political liberty as freedom from interference in the pursuit of one's chosen ends, we are making a normative claim; yet specifying why we esteem this notion of liberty (and practices consistent with it) proves difficult. Is our endorsement due to the ends people can or actually do pursue? Is it due to the belief that persons can and should be "self-determining" or is it due to something else? Regarding the first possibility, contemporary talk of "ordered liberty" seems to presuppose some normative ends; yet, in the absence of agreement on such ends, speakers tend to talk in generalities about persons being free to pursue their "interests." In regard to the second possibility, contemporary efforts to specify a positive notion of liberty as self-determination likewise have trouble identifying any normative "content" that would distinguish self-determination from the freedom to pursue one's interests. Relating the normative notion of liberty to these puzzles is the primary purpose of this chapter.

Pursuing this limited purpose will follow the earlier pattern. Part II is a descriptive section detailing the puzzles and reviewing both pragmatic and teleological responses to them. Then the analysis shifts into an explanatory context (Part III) that applies the normative notion of liberty to the puzzles. Finally, the chapter ends with a case study as a way of testing the worth of an explanatory account of political liberty.

II Descriptive Context and Contemporary Puzzles

Most contemporary discussions of political liberty incorporate Isaiah Berlin's distinction between negative liberty (freedom from interference) and positive liberty (freedom as self-determination).[384] The latter means more than the absence of compulsion or interference by others. The talk is usually of "self-control" and sometimes even of a "higher self's" mastery over instinct and inclination. One modern precedent for the distinction is found in Adam Smith's distinction between a natural liberty and its formation by various institutions: family, church, school and even state.[385] "Character development" and "ordered liberty" are some of the variants describing the goal of these formative processes.

Our first puzzle in contemporary discussions of political liberty appears when we ask why persons esteem liberty. Traditional answers cited mastery over the passions and acquisition of virtues as the ends of liberty. For example, prudence was the acquired habit of judging what was good to do; its end was practical wisdom.[386] Fortitude was the

---

[384] Isaiah Berlin, "Two Concepts of Liberty" in Four Essays on Liberty (Oxford: Oxford University Press, 1969); revised and expanded, Liberty (Oxford: Oxford University Press, 2002).

[385] "Adam Smith is best known as an advocate of 'natural liberty.' But the understanding of what liberty means and of why it is worth having has changed radically from his day to ours. If Smith's association of liberty with institutionally fostered self-control sounds strange to us, it is because we have adopted the assumption that the most 'authentic' self is the self that is least inhibited by external standards, and so many have come to identify liberty with the absence of legal constraint, social constraint, and even self-restraint – with unbounded will and unconstrained desire; and imagine that Adam Smith offered the ultimate rationale for 'doing as one likes.'" Jerry Z. Muller. Adam Smith in His Time and Ours (New York: MacMillan, 1996), 2-3.

[386] Today even this traditional understanding of the primary "natural" virtue is contested or is just one of a number of ways of

acquired habit of being able to conform the will to one's best judgments despite resistance. Temperance was the deliberate cultivation of a character able to withstand competing desires that would thwart prudential judgments and their aims. To the degree that a theory of virtues was specific and was the basis for talking about liberty, ordered liberty had specific normative ends.

The situation today is that agreement on specific ends is in short supply. One symptom of the shortage lies in a modern psychology of human action that substitutes a language of interests for the earlier language of moral virtues. A distinctively modern response to the question of what specific ends liberty pursues (i.e. is ordered toward) employs a vocabulary of "interests." One author gave the following account for the change:

> The term 'interest' was selected by liberalism so that public discourse about politics and economics might avoid the limitations associated with the term 'opinion,' which the Enlightenment made synonymous with religious beliefs (read: fanatical superstitions) about the common good, and with the term 'passions,' which also carries a connotation of arbitrariness. The implication of the term 'interest' is that pursuing one's interest is more in accord with the public interest than acting in the name of the common good.[387]

Since they recognized that interests could be narrow or broad, modern writers spoke of "enlightened self-interest" as a

---

talking about prudence. "Prudence can be defined as a trait, virtue, norm, skill, mode of reasoning, and form of character." Robert Hariman, "Prudence in the Twenty-First Century," in <u>Prudence</u>: <u>Classical Virtue, Postmodern Practice</u>. Robert Hariman (ed.) (University Park: The Pennsylvania State University Press, 2003), 293.

[387] Fred Lawrence, "Editors' Introduction" in Lonergan, <u>CW</u> 15, lxx.

goal their writings on liberty were to promote.[388] But their purpose was not to elaborate a theory of virtues and moral development. Instead, the focus was on understanding how, under certain institutional arrangements (e.g. open markets), the pursuit of self-interest could yield unintended social benefits. In short, the promise was that one could have virtuous outcomes without virtuous persons.[389]

What are some consequences of limiting the "ends" of political liberty to talk of interests? Chapter Five raised questions about both the liberal model of economic man and its socialist counterpart. The critique began by noting that voluntary economic exchanges did not secure all human goods, something that is especially apparent for at-risk populations unable to compete successfully in the marketplace. What are the options for securing these further goods? One side argues that free markets do a better job than any other arrangement in increasing the aggregate wealth of a society and so in enlarging the pool of resources for protecting at-risk populations. Opponents cite the problems of maldistribution of resources under market conditions and argue that universal access to basic goods is more likely through the regulation of economic activities by

---

[388] What one perceives to be in one's interest and what actually is in one's interest may be at odds. Study of this type of conflict has a history. In Plato's *Gorgias*, Socrates depicts the tyrant Archelaus of Macedonia as so powerful that he is able to act with impunity. But Socrates asks whether this power is really anything admirable or worth having. If Archelaus ignorantly and blindly chooses what actually harms him, how is this an instance of power? Substitute the word "liberty" for "power" and you have an early case of the puzzle of why one should praise liberty.

[389] To be more exact, open markets do encourage a limited range of virtues, e.g. self-control (delayed gratification for the sake of capital formation?), reliability, honesty and reciprocity. However, the practical rationales for acquiring these virtues may leave self-interested actors content at a fairly basic level of moral development and indifferent to what further growth is possible.

state agencies. Chapter Five offered objections to both stances. The laissez-faire option appeals to a type of *fatum* that will produce good results without good persons, i.e. without the development of liberty beyond the basic concern for personal interest. But reliance on state agencies assumes: (1) those regulating economic activities will have adequately responded to the demands of the principle of completion in themselves; (2) they will routinely overcome to interference from competing desires, i.e. they will exhibit enduring benevolence as guardians of a common good; and (3) a social order guided by an elite can flourish even if the vast majority of its citizens do not meet the demands of the principle of completion in themselves.

Theoretical arguments are available for defending each option and for attacking its opposite. Perhaps the debate should shift to a study of historical outcomes produced by diverse types of political orders. Then the questions are what difference has it made if persons have enjoyed great discretion in ordering their own lives and what difference has the absence of such discretion made? This shift anticipates finding pragmatic reasons for esteeming liberty.

Some pragmatic answers are quite familiar. J.S. Mill provided the best known rationale for liberty as noninterference. The free circulation of ideas in open forums will eventually reveal the beneficial ones and expose the injurious. As a result, societies progress when individuals, free of unnecessary constraints, can speak their minds, have access to competing opinions and can make their own decisions.

Lonergan had his own version of a pragmatic argument. Improvements in local situations require insights into local conditions; the relevant insights tend to occur to the persons "on the scene;" therefore, those persons should be left largely at liberty to diagnose and to decide what their variable circumstances require.[390] To impose policies from the "top down" without close attention to local conditions: (1) is

---

[390] For a New Political Economy, 34-35.

to assume that generalities, abstracted from local variables, are a sufficient basis for sound decisions, and (2) is to overlook the diagnosis problem that requires insight into local conditions. If physicians proceeded to apply their medical generalities and skipped diagnosing individual patients, funeral homes would be much busier.

Richard Rorty had a further version of the pragmatic rationale for political liberty. He disparaged "foundationalist" efforts to justify the language of human rights and the liberal practices consistent with such rights. Instead he offered a pragmatic-historical defense of both. If a particular society finds that advocating universal human rights and promoting their protection "work" to its benefit, then that is sufficient justification for that language and those practices until someone provides adequate reasons for changing either of them.

A standard complaint against Rorty's stance was that his version appeals to "local" practices to justify a rhetoric that is universal in its claims. That is, the language of human rights applies to all locales, but the defense amounts to an appeal to what has been successful locally.

Critics cite at least three other problems with pragmatic arguments that appeal to the durability of a belief or a practice as reason enough to sustain either of them. The least serious of the three is that even the most durable practices rarely win universal applause. Public policies distribute benefits and burdens unevenly. While they may "work" for many or even for most, they usually "cost" some parties what they otherwise would not "pay." The rationales for the practices may be durable, but their defense may consist of dismissals of alternatives as "impractical," i.e. not what we are accustomed to doing. In effect, pragmatic arguments tend to be surprisingly conservative and dismissive of fantasy and experimentation.

A second problem is specifically relevant to defenses of liberty as noninterference. What are the limits of this liberty? For competent adults, the usual answer is that the liberty of the other person sets the limit on one's own. Hence, forbearance rights usually receive priority over substantive rights. In times of peace and prosperity, a social order can tolerate wide variations in how citizens choose to exercise their liberty. The very stability and economic success of the society supply evidence for the pragmatic defense of liberty. However, in times of political turmoil and economic distress, the same pragmatic calculus may reverse priorities. Restoring social order and prosperity may seem to require curtailment of liberty. In effect, if liberty is praised only because of its pragmatic benefits, its durability may be wholly at the mercy of *Fortuna* and the accidents of marketplaces and battlefields.

Perhaps the pragmatic response to such problems is a negative defense of political liberty; namely, we have seen how societies work under tyrants or elites exercising central control over public and private affairs. The historical evidence is that such social orders are not successful in distributing adequate benefits to most of their members, so we assume political arrangements favoring the diffusion of liberty will work better.

This pragmatic response can go on to defend its lack of any more positive or comprehensive rationale for praising liberty. After witnessing the horrors of the last century, many blamed those who dreamt of human perfectibility and believed that a temporary coercion of recalcitrant liberty could fulfill these dreams. From the monstrous misdeeds of totalitarian regimes, these critics concluded that persons are not perfectible and that efforts to coerce perfection will reveal not what is best in us but what is worst. What then is to be done? If the Leviathan is a failed option, tolerance may by default become the leading political virtue. As a rationale for the default, a pragmatic stance may assign liberty as noninterference and specific forbearance rights first place in the ranking of social goods. Individuals, within limits, should enjoy maximum discretion in their choices of means and ends, whether ordered or disordered lives result.

Perhaps we should conclude that praise of liberty as noninterference reflects a pragmatic, historical compromise, one that has produced definite benefits but at a cost. First, it presupposes a psychology of motivation that assumes the pursuit of self-interest or personal satisfaction is the origin of all human actions. This assumption is the basis for substituting *homo economicus* as a rational calculator of personal utility for older accounts of moral agents as capable of pursuing higher goods beyond their rudimentary wants and desires. Again, this change promises and delivers at least a temporary peace. But this may be because institutions are already in place and for a time continue to "form" or to educate self-interested persons so that they learn to desire higher goods. A durable traditional culture emphasizing the goods of family unity, civic responsibility, charitable acts and patriotism will check the potential abuses of a liberty no longer explicitly linked to high moral ends. But the "cultural capital" built up over centuries and invested in institutional set-ups may be draining away as new generations repeatedly hear that the good we cherish most is allowing individuals to pursue their own satisfaction.

Allaying such a worry at first was faith in the automatism of a marketplace that would, under non-monopolistic conditions, offset expected abuses of liberty through the competition among different interest groups. That faith reinforced the assumption that persons did not need to develop beyond the condition of rational calculators of their own interests for a social order to prosper. Presumably that faith has faded for most people; in turn, perhaps its assumption about rational calculators is also more questionable.

There is yet a further objection raised against almost every pragmatic argument. Someone may ask why a particular practice, technique or law works. This further why-question is not adequately answered by simply saying, "That's just the way things are." The question anticipates an explanation, and asserting a matter-of-fact is no explanation.

Historically a number of defenses of liberty offered explanations. Teleological theories argued that the ends that persons at liberty might pursue could justify political orders that offered opportunities for them to do so. If a virtuous life could not be imposed on persons, then social orders that fostered the pursuit of virtues and trusted individuals to undertake the pursuit in their own ways were an attractive option. Talk of inalienable rights to liberty and the pursuit of happiness presumed such trust in persons and disbelief that coercion could make persons virtuous, i.e. could force them to achieve their proper ends.

Theological defenses of liberty follow the same pattern. If the proper ends of human living are reached by spiritual purgation and growth, coercion might contribute to the former but not to the latter. Therefore, liberty is one of the necessary but not sufficient conditions for spiritual development, and as such it is to be esteemed.

Both types of teleological explanations evoke new problems. Historically theories of virtues have had metaphysical and theological roots that engendered endless debates. Overt appeals to theological assumptions in talking about the ends of human living have generated little consensus. Political penalties for actions inconsistent with such assumptions have generated strife and even wars. Thus, the language of "interests" and the psychology of rational calculation made their historical entrances as alternatives to a normative hierarchy of goods.

Still, esteem for liberty as self-determination seems to assume that persons are more than "rational calculators" of their own interests. Recall the second puzzle at the start of this chapter was how we were to distinguish liberty as self-determination from liberty as the unimpeded pursuit of one's interests. The esteem afforded the former is a clue to a difference. If self-determination always led to foolish choices or socially harmful acts, few would think it worth praising or defending. That self-determination is usually reserved for competent adults is a further indication that its defenders assume its proper end is something normative.[391] Those who

---

[391] "It is often suggested that the exclusion of minors, as well as lunatics and animals, is a limitation of liberty to those capable of being self-determining; but this seems not to be the case as

have not yet achieved competence or who are impaired are not thought to be self-determining in the sense of being able to choose means and ends wisely. So endorsement of self-determination must mean more than being left alone to make one's own decisions. Criticisms of competent individuals who choose to be vicious, cruel or exploitative seem to presuppose they have neglected some normative ends in their use of liberty. Their acts were self-determining in a very general sense; they were calculated, not thoughtless acts. They may even have foreseen harmful consequences to others, thereby making their acts all the more reprehensible. So praise of liberty as self-determination seems to assume more than the fact of making one's own choices. What is the basis for this praise?

Some have suggested that liberty as self-determination is valuable insofar as it allows persons to enjoy their rights, e.g. the right to acquire and to use property or to marry whomever they choose or to raise their children as they see fit or to voice unpopular political views.[392] Yet these rights are not the ends that liberty serves but the opportunities or means

---

adolescents seem completely capable of self-determination but are suspect on the score of wisdom, i.e. it is doubted whether they are capable of right self-determination. This is even more true of younger children who are capable of being self-directive in an obvious sense of that expression. (…) If it is claimed that self-determination in children is not real self-determination, the concept of self-determination then seems to come to be explained so as to be akin to rational, right, self-determination – at the very least rationality is being written more explicitly into the concept than it appears to be when stupid adults are considered and when self-determination is urged as a good which all adults should be allowed to enjoy." H.J. McCloskey. "A Critique of the Ideals of Liberty" in Self-Determination in Social Work. F.E. McDermott, ed. (London: Routledge and Kegan Paul, 1975), 171-172.

[392] For a discussion of this stance, see ibid. 175-176.

for expressions of liberty.[393] Perhaps rights and liberty serve further ends that are the basis for praising and defending both of them. Yet any extensive list of specific ends provokes interminable debates.[394] Perhaps shifting the question into an explanatory context in Part III will provide different results.

III Explanatory Context

The preceding section described puzzles arising when one tries to understand why we believe political liberty is so praiseworthy. Our hypothesis is that the way beyond those puzzles lies in understanding liberty-in-act as (1) remotely orientated by inner norms toward initially indeterminate ends and (2) as undergoing historical development because of "changing expectations" of what determinate ends are worth pursuing.[395] This section employs the categories of orientation, displacement and personal relations to construct an explanatory account of political liberty.

We begin with orientation.[396] Underlying any determinate orientation will be a tension between the related but competing demands of the principles of assimilation and completion. That dialectic is a condition for the possibility of developing beyond already achieved integrations of meaning and practice. But any such development presupposes some

---

[393] For example, a right of political dissent may be commonly recognized without anyone making use of it, i.e. actually voicing a dissenting view.

[394] Advocates of the "New Natural Law Theory" have encountered this reaction.

[395] The phrase "changing expectations" is intended to recall remarks in Chapter One on how assimilated patterns favoring attention to some objects over others are yet susceptible to "surprises" and so to revision. The dialectically related demands of the principles of assimilation and completion eventually explain how this is possible.

[396] Recall the meaning of "orientation" worked out in Chapter One: "the partially determinate context which an intelligent agent brings to acts of attending."

prior achievements to be surpassed. Speaking descriptively, we can talk of a tension between a desire to maintain familiar patterns and a desire for further growth. In moral terms, the tension may be an awareness of a fissure between what one is and what one ideally should be. How one responds to that tension in a single instance is an "event" that is either a responsible or an irresponsible use of liberty. How one responds to that tension over a series of similar instances is a "state" that reflects the habitual orientation one has in relating new means and ends to whatever integrations one has already achieved. To routinely resist the demands for development is one option; to repeatedly cooperate with them is another. One's determinate orientation, in other words, can either be a state favoring prior integrations or one adjusting the latter to integrate new means and ends. In either case, when thinking dialectically, we can recall how orientation remains only a partially determinate context, i.e. an indeterminate determinacy. Prior personal integrations [ranging across the complex series of interacting variables symbolized as $H_1(n_j ; b_k ; p_l ; i_m ; m_n)$] dispose new acts to assimilate their objects to already familiar patterns. Such is the "determinacy." However, prior integrations are subject to "surprises" on the side of objects and to the demand of the principle of completion on the side of the operators.[397] Such is the "indeterminacy."

Disruptions of established integrations do occur. The category of displacement refers to an understanding that radical shifts away from prior patterns of thinking and acting can and do occur. While there is no need to repeat examples of such occurrences, two diagnoses of intellectual impasses may indicate what can occur if this category plays no role in a theory of political liberty.

---

[397] The demand and the operators are also variables symbolized in $H_1(n_j ; b_k ; p_l ; i_m ; m_n)$. Recognizing the demand of the principle of completion as part of human living is the basis for the claim that liberty extends "all the way down," even to neural demands for feelings and to psychic demands for images.

In studies of competing theories of justice and rationality, one contemporary conclusion is that they arise from "incommensurable worldviews" that provide no common basis for adjudicating their sometimes incompatible differences.[398] By extension, studies of competing theories of political liberty will also lead to intellectual impasses. However, this outcome may not be inevitable, first, if one does not limit inquiry to the horizons of commonsense and theory, and, second, if one recognizes displacements can occur in efforts to understand. The first condition is met by shifting inquiry into the horizon of interiority and attending to the operations that produce concepts, worldviews and competing theories.[399] The second condition is met if one no longer assumes the classicist model of reasoning, i.e. demonstrative proofs proceeding from premises to conclusions. According to the model, if two inquirers begin with opposed premises (e.g. incompatible worldviews), they are unlikely to arrive at compatible conclusions. But what if some acts of understanding are marked by "leaps" or discontinuities? What if the insights that generate displacements are not deduced from prior premises but amount to departures from prior integrations of meanings?

This digression on incommensurable worldviews and their competing theories makes explicit two fundamental questions: (1) Are theoretical inquiries, whether their focus be justice, liberty or whatever you wish, deficient if the inquirers proceed without adequate attention to their own

---

[398] One source of this stance is in the debates surrounding Alasdair C. MacIntyre's Whose Justice? Which Rationality? (Notre Dame: University of Notre Dame Press, 1988).

[399] The distinction between the horizons of theory and interiority is marked by a shift in questioning from conclusions to the invisible operations that produce conclusions. For example, the critical remarks on a "classicist model of reasoning" assume one has paid attention to one's actual performance in making judgments.

performance?[400]   (2) If I attend to my own efforts to understand, do I ever detect that I move not from concepts (embedded in premises) to their implications but from questions to insights (some of which may disrupt prior answers) and then to concepts?[401]

Ironically taking a stand in relation to these two questions may occasion disruptions in prior integrations of meaning. For example, if one hopes that some method, theoretical framework or system of logic holds the key to resolving disputes among theories, eventual exposure to the multiplicity of such promising "keys" will probably undermine that hope. In the last century, the emergence of Quantum Mechanics resurrected the old debate between common-sense worlds of picture thinking and the strange worlds talked of by theoreticians. Which world is concrete and which is abstract? Are they incommensurable? Is one reducible to the other? Is one epiphenomenal? Presumably these questions ask one to take a stand, but perhaps a prior question should be about how inquirers operate in producing either common-sense descriptions or theoretical explanations. The focus of this question shifts to intentional operations and their different ways of relating to intended objects.

What of the second question about the origin of concepts? A conceptualist tradition is firmly in place in much of contemporary philosophy. How many texts begin by

---

[400] Chapter One noted that neuroscientific studies of acts of attention tended to proceed without those doing the investigations taking their own performance in attending as an empirical example of what they were studying.

[401] One's stance on the role of concepts in inquiry has consequences. If one assumes thinking begins with concepts and proceeds to work out their implications, then the discovery that there is no consensus on the meaning of key concepts leaves few options. As a result, the political options seem to be limited to coercion or "peaceable disagreement." In contrast, if one understands that acts of insight mediate between concepts and data, the further possibility of "displacement" because of new insights offers a third option.

announcing that the authors will "clarify the concept" of law, liberty, justice or mind? Authors often explicitly describe their works as exercises in clarifying concepts, "unpacking" the implications of premises or building conceptual bridges among different fields. But fundamental questions can intrude: Where do concepts come from? What are we doing in understanding and what role do concepts play in the process? Graduate students tend to answer such questions by citing theories they have studied. Their professors may do the same; in both cases they may not have personally explored the horizon of interiority. Still, a first displacement may have occurred when inquirers moved from the picture thinking of the common-sense horizon to the correlations of some theoretical field. But a second displacement may take place in recognizing that understanding how these two modes of knowing are different but complementary requires a third horizon distinct from both of them. The shift of attention to intentional acts begins to resolve old puzzles. In turn, this shift may produce a disruption in what one assumed about concepts, arguments and logic.

The possibility of such displacements is a condition for the possibility of new orientations in the study of political liberty, justice or whatever you wish. But both possibilities are the basis for making "incommensurable worldviews" and any theories dependent on them secondary issues. They are "secondary" in the sense that such products of inquiry presuppose intentional operations. Insofar as the context for those operations is an indeterminate determinacy, products of prior inquiries are not fixed boundaries for all subsequent inquiries.

What role does the third category of personal relations play in understanding either the social ordering of liberty or the latter's departures from prior integrations? Ideally family life and early education are the first institutional contexts for the ordering of liberty. Persons filling traditional roles induct the individual into the patterns of belief and practice that sustain various goods of order. In doing so, they model and sanction cooperative modes of living that precede and direct the development of the individual as a member of the group. Those patterns and modes of cooperation are antecedent determinants of the biography of the individual. A new generation experiences them as normative and affect-laden directives prescribing and proscribing how individuals are to think and to act. Thus, the first effect of personal relations is usually a conservative one: individuals learn to cherish established integrations, to internalize them and, when necessary, to correct departures from them.

Still, prior social integrations may be far from ideal. For example, misunderstandings, betrayals and the absence of love may mar family life. Social orders may experience rivalries and suspicion, structural evils and lingering effects of past injustices that leave in place practices generating new conflicts and further recriminations. Such may be one's first exposure to human relations and the determinate orientations of some community. The resulting "ordering" of the individual's liberty will be far from ideal. Indeed, the community may impart a rationale for its ways being all one can expect and so what one should accept. Even if the group is in need of liberation from various stupidities, factional squabbles, exploitative practices and festering grudges, it may tell a story that is a self-portrait of normality. The story may portray certain social ills as inevitabilities to which realists should resign themselves. Justice will be on display, but hidden from view will be its uneven application, usually to the advantage of those already benefitting from current distributions of power and privilege. Liberties and rights will evoke praise, but they are likely to be liberties and rights compatible with the existing political and economic order.[402]

---

[402] When political liberty is limited to "forbearance rights," one criticism is that this stance privileges an existing order such that disruptions of its current distributions of property, power and opportunity will be violations of others' liberties. It is as if the existing order had no history or at least its history was irrelevant to understanding present obligations not to interfere with others. One can read Robert Nozick as struggling (unsuccessfully?) with this

As noted before, any social ordering of one's orientations is but one of the determinants of liberty. The dialectic between the opposed but related principles of assimilation and completion is another. If one's own inner demands for security and continuity can conspire with a flawed social order to embrace a rationale "justifying" its ways, the demands of the various operators for understanding and evaluating current practices can be counterweights giving rise to doubts and even fantasies about better ways. Those demands are among the sources of disruption. Another source includes "surprising" or discordant data. These can take the form of satirical jibes by political cartoonists or dramatic revelations of previously hidden miseries within one's society.

But for now the focus is on personal relations as a source of potential disruption. As noted in Chapter Two, affect-laden images play a central role in "motivating" departures from routines in thinking and acting. Compatibility between responses to the demands of the empirical operator and responses to those of the intellectual operator seems to be a precondition to effective action when such action amounts to a departure from well assimilated patterns. The general insight here is hardly new. Free acts are not indeterminate since persons can have reasons for their actions, yet those reasons do not <u>compel</u> the actions. Reasons prepare the ground for action, but having them is not the same as acting upon them.[403] Plato's efforts to supplement his arguments with symbol and myth were an early recognition of how people needed more than arguments if they were to leave their caves.

---

criticism. See his <u>Anarchy, State, and Utopia</u> (New York: Basic Books), 1974, 152f. Would his struggle have ended differently had he begun with a understanding of "concrete" persons as symbolized in $H_2[H_1(n_j\,;\,b_k\,;\,p_l\,;\,i_m\,;\,m_n)]$?

[403] In the language of an earlier faculty psychology, intellect does not have an immanent end in action, and so the faculty of will has a function distinct from that of understanding. Lonergan, <u>Understanding and Being</u>, 227.

When they are in love, persons may experience an integration of affect and reasons promoting "daring departures" from prior patterns. While reasons may abound for changing the direction of one's life, it is usually when affective ties to others support such changes that they become highly probable. A charismatic leader or actual victims of institutionalized injustice may supply affect-laden images effectively liberating one from an inherited rationale of social practices and supporting one's search for a new integration of meanings and practices. The category of personal relations is therefore useful in understanding how persons may sometimes express political liberty in departing from initial orientations of self-interest and even of group loyalties.

Suppose that each new generation represents "lower-order materials" that established personal relations integrate into the common meanings and practices of some group. If the emergent orientations (e.g. habits) of those lower-order materials are in need of correction, personal relations are a condition for that change. Additionally, in responding to the inner demands of the various operators, individuals have the potential for a critical orientation toward communal beliefs and practices. The probability of that potential becoming effective increases when at least a few others are models of what initially is a lonely stance. A single dissenting voice is soon silenced, but a community of the like-minded can both amplify and sustain that voice.

To this point we have identified general conditions (1) for a social ordering of liberty and (2) for personal dissent from that ordering. But the earlier questions remain: Why do we esteem liberty as noninterference? If we go on to talk of liberty as self-determination, what normative "content" do we ascribe to this notion that makes it more than the pursuit of self-interest, enlightened or otherwise?

Some have thought the answer to the first question lies in the ends persons at liberty can and should pursue. If we take history seriously (regarding developments in understanding what is good), we should expect to arrive at no fixed or final list of good ends. Instead, liberty as an initially indeterminate capacity to pursue ends will exhibit a history, or better histories, of correlated acts and objectives or ends. In the case of an individual biography, repeated links between acts and ends will give a determinate orientation to a life, one conventionally referred to as a person's habits. In the case of a culture, the patterns extend beyond individual biographies in variety, complexity and durability. They supply materials for the research of ethnographers. In both cases historically integrated patterns take various forms, e.g. the values of a person, the cultural nomos of a society, the hierarchy of goods in a developmental theory of morality, the legal rights of persons.

    Such patterns, whether individual or social, are liable to disruptions, some of which may lead to further developments in understanding and practice. While little has been said of catastrophic disruptions (e.g. mental illness in the individual or foreign conquest of a society), those breakdowns in settled ways are not developments of capacities but potentially lethal blows to already developed capacities. Still, some "settled ways" are in need of disruption. For example, some persons may have determinate orientations hostile to new data, new questions, new insights; they may reject fantasizing about a better way of doing things and insist that choosing to preserve familiar patterns is just being realistic. We can describe such hostility and rejection as matters-of-fact but perhaps should not try to explain them.[404] Among the varied determinants of what orientation a person actually develops is the demand of the principle of completion mediated by the various operators. If one accepts this demand as normative, i.e. as how persons should respond, then one can fault or at least cite such hostility and rejection as defective.

---

[404] Assuming such hostility and rejection are at least sometimes at odds with one's inner demands, we should avoid trying to explain them. A listing of "motives" for them is possible, but to attempt to give "reasons" for them would be trying to find reasons for irrational responses.

What is the basis for judging that any self-determining acts are defective? As noted above, the remote criteria are the inner imperatives of intentional acts. Initially these norms have indeterminate ends; it is through actual operations that determinate ends emerge.[405] Just as the fields of possible objects of attention and of possible objects of acts of understanding are indefinite, so the corresponding possible intentional acts are indefinite in number. In effect, both possible operations and their corresponding objects are indeterminate terms in an indefinite series of possible correlations of acts and objects. One implication of this indefinite series is that there are no specific normative ends for liberty that are known *a priori*.

In a more positive vein, one can imagine the ideal case in which external conditions (e.g. institutions) and internal conditions are favorable to personal development. Then the social conditions (e.g. personal relations) may support the inner demands of operators for carefully diagnosing situations, fantasizing about improvements, judging among options and effectively implementing what one "feels" and knows to be worth choosing. As noted in Chapter Four, a condition for effective implementation is affective weighting of the options, and the category of personal relations seems to be a key variable in understanding how persons can choose an option that departs from defective meanings and practices. Again, historical examples of such "positive" departures are data to

---

[405] For example, the imperative to operate intelligently is a broad generality, but in time one learns to discriminate between promising and unpromising ways of operating. So as positive insights accumulate, one becomes skilled at efficiently handling certain types of questions or problems. A controversy relevant to this development of determinate content within what is initially a broad generality is the old dispute over the content of the natural law. Formal imperatives (e.g. "Do good and avoid evil") may be cited as principles of the natural law, but any determinate content they have is dependent on historical experience and insights.

be explained. They are the occurrence of the improbable since they are unexpected breaks with entrenched patterns.

Making personal relations a correlate of orientation was a way of explaining what was improbable, i.e. displacements away from settled patterns of thinking and acting and toward as yet unintegrated stances. What general characteristics of political order make such occurrences more probable? Two general conditions seem favorable. First, there is a need for "open spaces" if individuals are to meet the demands of operators. In descriptive terms, persons need to be at liberty to associate, discuss, make decisions, observe consequences and learn from them.[406] Hence, some set of forbearance rights would be a minimal condition in a political order favorable to allowing persons to respond to their own inner demands. Second, besides opportunities for personal initiative and self-correction, political orders need to perform "ordering" functions in regard to natural liberty. While other intermediate institutions (e.g. families, schools, religious bodies, professional associations) would take the lead in forming liberty, political institutions would have both prescriptive and proscriptive roles in determining what were responsible uses of liberty. Here, of course, the two hard questions about the "ends" of liberty (i.e. questions about the objectives of any ordering functions and of the standards of "responsible uses") reappear.

If the "ends" toward which institutions order liberty are to be more than the pursuit of perceived "interests," we can ask what some of those more specific ends might be. If the answer is that personal safety and public security are legitimate institutional ends, little controversy follows since most persons accept the legitimacy of governmental powers

---

[406] Progress, both personal and social, requires the accumulation of insights into concrete situations and practical experience with testing possible solutions. There appears to be no effective substitute for individuals "on the ground" accumulating the former and learning from the latter.

that promote these goods.[407] Controversies, however, proliferate when this short list of safety and security expands to include further ends. At the center of these disputes are historical memories of how disagreements about "higher" goods produced civil strife and war.[408] These memories turn up in current political debates over the agenda of the "religious right," over the so-called "culture wars" and over a strict separation of Church and State that some see as an attack on religious traditions. As noted in Chapter Five, such debates tend to proceed in terms of mutually exclusive alternatives: a laissez-faire option that grants individuals discretion in the ends they pursue and a regulatory option that restricts the range of options individuals pursue. But that previous chapter also suggested a third option: the education of liberty. What are its implications for identifying why we esteem liberty and political orders compatible with liberty?

Suppose political liberty assumes the capacity of adults (1) to cooperate with the demands of their own operators, and (2) to cooperate with one another in maintaining and improving social orders that are products of responses to those demands. Learning to cooperate both with those inner demands and with other persons begins with the tutelage of childhood, but, if that condition continues unabated for adults, the results will be not effective liberty but the rigidity of a planned social order. What such an order promises is

---

[407] The debates that do occur are usually about the means governmental agencies employ to achieve these ends.

[408] "Liberal democracy's original theorists, such as Thomas Hobbes, Baruch Spinoza, and John Locke, inferred from the factually controversial nature of the good, especially the highest good, that conscience and convictions about objective morality can all too easily turn into the chief causes of civil war. Peaceful human cooperation would consequently demand authorization by a democratic consent based on a lowest-common-denominator consensus that tends to overlook or neglect religious, personal, and cultural values." Lawrence, "Editors' Introduction" in CW 15, xxxvi-xxxvii.

deliverance from abuses of liberty and threats to social order. What it delivers are the rule of an elite and a stifling of initiative.

The fantasy of the education of liberty requires political orders that trust persons to be largely self-governing. The fantasy locates the remote criteria for judging whether self-governing actors are using or abusing their liberty not in laws or the terms of some social contract but in the inner norms of the operators.[409] Thus, the <u>primary political question</u> is how persons are to learn to respond effectively to their own inner demands. The claim here is that a regulatory option that relies on political coercion is not an adequate answer to this question. While coercive means may achieve some short-term ordering of public life, those measures tend to involve the few making decisions for the many who may comply but who, in doing so, need not undergo any displacement from long-term patterns of thinking and acting. In the long run, if the initiative remains with the few, no matter how benevolent they may be, they will become adept at repeating old solutions but less adept at inventing new remedies for new problems. They, in turn, will not risk needed displacements, and the populace they direct will be ill prepared to supply what the leadership lacks and never demanded of them.

What of the laissez-faire option? When adults enjoy great discretion in planning their own lives, there are no guarantees that they will make responsible uses of liberty. Still, there are opportunities for them to make their own decisions, acquire further insights through trial and error and potentially make better uses of their liberty as a result. This much provides a pragmatic rationale for the laissez-faire option. However, a more explicitly normative rationale can appeal to how intentional acts, as responses to the demands

---

[409] This locating of norms prior to the terms of any social contract points the way to solving an old puzzle of why contracting parties are obligated to keep the promises made in establishing the contract. We can say they are bound by their promises, but what makes promise keeping obligatory?

of the operators, are conditions for the possibility of further development. The regulatory option tends to frustrate this development. The laissez-faire option tends to neglect this possibility as an intrusion on personal discretion in choosing ends.[410]

The third option, the education of liberty, is admittedly a type of intrusion on doing whatever one pleases. However, its method is one of persuasion, and its assumption is that there is no shortcut to the democratic ordering of liberty.

How does this review of the three political "options" contribute to an explanatory understanding of political liberty? The earlier promise was to provide an explanatory account of political liberty that made use of a normative notion of liberty. Thus, a normative understanding of liberty replaced views of liberty as freedom from interference and self-determination in the pursuit of perceived interests. Previous chapters repeated the claim that the demands of the various operators are initially oriented toward indeterminate objects or ends. Institutions, as noted in Chapter Four, are "carriers" of historically assimilated and determinate responses to these demands. So it is that families, churches, schools and political institutions induct new generations into established integrations that provide them with determinate orientations. However, the social ordering of a new generation's orientations is but one of the prior conditions of liberty. The dialectic of the related but opposed principles of assimilation and completion and the mediating demands of the various operators are others. Thus, an explanatory understanding of political liberty will include both the capacity of intentional acts to respond to the various demands and institutional arrangements favorable to the exercise of that capacity.

---

[410] Insofar as advocates of the laissez-faire option adopt a skeptical stance in regard to questions of higher moral ends, they will be suspicious of talk of moral development and more likely to favor the virtue of tolerance and insist on the primacy of forbearance rights, especially in any "pluralistic" society.

What if the institutional arrangements are far from ideal and even unfavorable to the exercise of that capacity? As noted before, the prior integrations that set the context for responding to the demands of the various operators are themselves open to development or correction. Acts-at-liberty can be departures from assimilated patterns of thinking and acting. Still, an ideal case for the development of ordered liberty occurs when external conditions (e.g. institutions) and internal conditions are supportive of that development. Political arrangements that ensure some forbearance rights and that, with the support of other institutions, "order" natural liberty in responding to the demand of the principle of completion are compatible with a normative understanding of liberty.

With these conditions in mind, we can understand political liberty as a pattern of relations among intentional acts, inner demands and institutional set-ups that favor the recurrent meeting of those demands. In other words, if we esteem political liberty, it may be because we assume that some institutional arrangements, more than others, allow and encourage intentional operations to respond to the demand of the principle of completion in ways that develop or correct the prior integrations that provide the context for those operations.

A variety of political orders may be compatible with the normative notion of liberty. Just as the proper ends of ordered liberty are not a fixed list, so the types of political institutions compatible with ordered liberty may expand with further historical experience. In any case, the primary political question will remain how to "educate liberty" so that ever more persons respond effectively and routinely to the inner imperatives of intentional acts.

This formulation of the question invites the earlier criticism that the "Education of Liberty" is an option remote from current practices and accepted possibilities. What response can be made to the criticism?

In discussions of politics or economics, a type of realism, i.e. an entrenched set of viewpoints, often remains the final court of appeal for dismissing criticisms and evaluating new practices as daydreams or utopian fantasies. Liberating oneself from the hold of entrenched or conventional viewpoints requires more than the absence of governmental supervision and the availability of leisure time away from daily chores. Perhaps among the favorable conditions for this type of liberation is the appearance of rare individuals who win new and higher viewpoints on the issues of the day, but then only slowly and against the drudgery and inertia of their times and tribes. These rare cases offer a model for others.[411]

Suppose the model is not the visionary but the person who through years of effort gains some serious understanding of a limited part of reality. In fields such as economics and politics, the contrast is between the person who knows something well and the well-intentioned visionary whose proposals may wind up doing more harm than good. If we assume that progress in any field is a product of creative understanding, then the model is not the master of routines but the innovator.

How does the innovator embody liberty? In any stable good of order, routine ways (integrated patterns) of acting are usually in place and routine ways of understanding are commonly available. Innovation, in part, means finding a better way of understanding and a better way of doing something. Assuming the innovator is restless and uninspired by the routines, we can note a first, affective characteristic of liberty in the innovator's disdain for only repeating old answers and patterns of action. But an affective and positive meaning of liberty can also be part of this general description. The demand of the deliberative operator, exhibited in the imaginative curiosity of the innovator, is a basic source of liberation _from_ routine and so liberty _for_ new ways of understanding and acting.

To catch in ourselves this same demand requires a shift in attention from the puzzle to the process of puzzling,

---

[411] The word "model" might be treated in an explanatory way by recalling the correlations in Chapter Two among affects, images and actions.

from the answer to the process of questioning, from the assertion to the process of affirming. The challenge is to detect and to understand this demand in ourselves.[412] The repeated claim has been that the intentional operators are the experiential basis for affirming a positive notion of liberty and for formulating criteria for judging the uses of that liberty. With the required shift in attention to oneself, the question becomes: How have I experienced the demands of these operators? Another claim was that liberty at first is no more than a given capacity that subsequent intentional acts develop and make determinate. With the new focus, the question is: How have I experienced changes in the orientation of my liberty? Such changes can occur spontaneously in response to exigencies ranging from biochemical and physiological conditions to psychological and intellectual breakthroughs and breakdowns. But they may also occur more deliberately because I try to cooperate with the inner norms of my own operations.

    The supposition here is that human development occurs when the exigencies of the operators repeatedly meet with cooperation. Note the specifying of "development" in terms of cooperation with, for example, the spontaneous demands for understanding what is actually the case and for deciding to do what is actually good. In an older vocabulary, the mind-in-act becomes what it is through its intended objects or ends, i.e. through the realities it seeks to know and the possibilities it affirms as good and worth realizing through actions. In the vocabulary of this text, as one's orientation

---

[412] This shift in focus has implications for educational practices in the schools of the future. What if the educator's primary goal was to awaken in students a curiosity about their own capacity to make meaning and to fantasize? What if pedagogies were increasingly refined ways of asking students how they were going about trying to make sense of what someone had said about a particular object or event and to invent alternative views? What if theories of education became studies of how to go about generating such pedagogies and evoking such a focused curiosity?

becomes determinate through intentional acts, so the objects intended by those acts effect changes in one's orientation. Descriptively put, if one seeks to find the good in people, one gradually becomes more adept at finding it. More remotely, if one's further why-questions anticipate answers correlating yet-to-be-determined variables, those anticipated objects change how one proceeds to operate. One's intending develops beyond descriptive categories and images because the anticipated objects belong to explanatory understanding and its intelligible relations. One's orientation is toward the invisible.

The developments here occur in both the inquirer and the intended objects. The increasingly complex integrations that one is intending are requiring increasingly complex operations by the inquirer, and those operations are, in turn, providing more complex integrations of whatever one is investigating. For example, to study subatomic particles as wave functions requires increasingly more sophisticated mathematical operations by the student, but facility in those operations makes possible more sophisticated integrations of the relevant data. Both the universe one studies and one's operations are developing.[413]

How do the preceding remarks "move along" the question of what ends ordered liberty pursues? The hypothesis is that the ends or objects of normative intentional acts can make a difference in subsequent intentional acts. When Aristotle quipped that the good is what good persons do, might he have been thinking of how acts and their objects are correlates? In the language of dialectic, each "acts back" on the other. Analogously, facing first-rank opponents in playing tennis further enhances one's skills. In regard to moral actions, when one repeatedly intends objects that are actually good, further acts of understanding and deciding tend to be moral, and the range of goods one intends expands. As correlates both acts and their objects can affect the other's capacity for development.

---

[413] <u>Insight</u>, 494.

How precise can we be about this mutually supportive development between acts and ends? As mentioned above, there is no reason for assuming that there is a fixed and final list of ends of human development. Why not? The intellectual liberty we cited as basic to understanding human development is a reaching for the yet-to-be-known. In terms of its *telos*, our questioning is a reaching toward objects yet to be known and toward possibilities yet to be dreamed of, not to mention realized. So where the end of the process is not yet known, a complete account of the whole process and its ends will elude us. At best one has a notion of what will satisfy or complete our questioning. But neither the range of our possible questions nor the possible objects they might intend are known. This indefiniteness provides one reason for believing that economic liberty and political liberty are so important. On pragmatic grounds, economic liberty has proven effective in expanding material prosperity for more and more people and so in allowing them the leisure time to pursue other aims besides basic ones. On normative grounds, political liberty is a condition for further human development since the pursuit requires the engagement of operators in gaining insights and correcting prior patterns of thinking and acting.

To repeat: there is no reason to expect a fixed set of ends that defensible uses of liberty pursue. Put in terms of intellectual and moral forms of liberty, our understanding and deciding can be developing, and, to the extent that our best judgments guide our choosing, what we affirm as good (our ends) will be "on the move." Much the same point was made by Milton Friedman in the context of the earlier debate between economic freedom and governmental control:

> There is no formula.... We must rely on our fallible judgment and, having reached a judgment, on our ability to persuade our fellow men that it is a correct judgment, or their ability to persuade us to modify our views. We must put our faith, here as elsewhere, in a

consensus reached by imperfect and biased men through free discussion and trial and error.[414]

Are such generalities of any help in answering the question of the ends of ordered liberty? The general advice here seems to be that responsible uses of liberty are those conforming to "best judgments." But whose judgments count? The textbook response is "the community of informed opinion." This response is at first plausible since political understanding and practices have developed; both have long histories, and presumably some students of politics are better informed about past trials and errors than others.[415] Still, the textbook response seems less plausible when one reviews the current literature on political theories. Many voices claim expertise, but what they go on to assert amounts sometimes to a babble of contending voices. How then is one to identify which claimant is genuinely informed?[416] If the most reputable practitioners of a discipline produce plausible but incompatible accounts of the same materials, the suspicion will grow that the differences have less to do with evidence and more to do with background moral and aesthetic assumptions. To make any of these the varied criteria for evaluating choices or policies may turn the whole exercise of evaluation into

---

[414] Capitalism and Freedom (Chicago: University of Chicago Press, 1962), 34.

[415] One limit to relying solely on informed opinion appears in the description Niels Bohrs supposedly gave of the "expert" -- someone who can tell others what pitfalls or errors to avoid.

[416] The situation here is not unique to political theory. Since the nineteenth-century crisis of historicism, multiple disciplines have experienced crises similar to the earlier one in historiography. The seminal work on this is Hayden White's Metahistory: The Historical Imagination in Nineteenth-Century Europe (Baltimore: The Johns Hopkins University Press, 1973).

something very subjective.[417] But what is the alternative? If we are at the end of the "age of innocence" in regard to the subject's role in understanding and judging, then there is good reason to investigate how subjects develop and even experience radical displacements from previous ways of understanding and judging.

By default the education of liberty remains the long-term option consistent with prospects of further developments in human liberty. The description in Chapter Five of the challenge of understanding how an economy works is pertinent to the education of political liberty.

> In 1930 John Maynard Keynes wrote that "we have involved ourselves in a colossal muddle, having blundered in the control of a delicate machine, the working of which we do not understand." The true scarcity in his world -- and ours -- was therefore not of resources, or even of virtue, but of understanding.[418]

But understanding what an economy is and how it can develop is today one of the preconditions to ordered political liberty. Put another way, economic liberty for large numbers of people is unlikely to survive if they do not understand how markets operate. If sufficient numbers of citizens lack this understanding, then market economies may continue, but conglomerates and their advertizing campaigns are likely to dominate them and eventually to control political decision-making. Then the long struggle for liberty, both political and economic, will have had a brief victory.

---

[417] This worry perhaps betrays immersion in the conceptualist tradition which takes background assumptions or explicit premises to be the ultimate basis for intentional acts.

[418] Paul Krugman. The Return of Depression Economics. (New York: W.W. Norton, 1999), 168.

IV Case Study

The first section of this chapter began with a series of questions that the second section narrowed to two: (1) Why do we esteem liberty as noninterference? (2) Why do we praise liberty as self-determination? Talk of liberty as freedom to pursue one's interests seems an inadequate response to the first question. If talk of self-determination means no more than the pursuit of interests, it also seems an inadequate basis for praising liberty. The pursuit of interests is compatible with disordered uses of liberty and provides no criteria for distinguishing between uses and abuses of liberty.

A more promising approach was to relate the normative notion of liberty from Chapter Four to these two questions.[419] The category "orientation" refers to an understanding of how a capacity to respond gradually becomes a determinate, patterned way of assimilating new experiences. Prior to any such patterning is the demand of the principle of completion mediated by the demands of the various operators. These demands are a condition for the possibility of displacement from any determinate orientation. For them to be effective in radically altering the latter, some affective link between an envisioned change and a consent to change is needed. Personal relations commonly play a role in linking imagined possibilities and action.

The following case study presents a serious puzzle about how to effect such a linkage for large numbers of people in societies of mass consumption. It brings us full circle back to Plato's difficulty mentioned in Chapter Two. While the details of the case derive primarily from macroeconomics, the puzzle itself is one of political decision-making. It identifies a complex educational challenge for those advocating economic and political liberties. Meeting the challenge requires

---

[419] Again, that notion was summarized as "the capacity of intentional acts to respond to the demand of the principle of completion in ways that develop or correct the prior integrations initially conditioning their exercise."

displacements from various assumed "realisms" in social psychology, liberal economics and political theory.

We begin with some general comments about a market economy.[420] There is a conventional distinction between capital (or producer) goods and consumer goods. Shoe factories and the equipment in them, car assembly plants and the robots performing precise movements along an assembly line are examples of the former. Increasing the number and efficiency of capital goods yields an increasing rate at which consumer goods (shoes and private automobiles) flow into final markets. But such accelerations cannot increase indefinitely because natural resources and the ability of consumer markets to absorb what is produced are limited.

Still, such accelerations promise a rise in the standard of living, i.e. an increase in the rate at which goods and services enter consumer markets. The anticipated surge in consumer activity promises increases in profits, and so investors flock to ventures that generate or participate in economic accelerations. The major accelerations that are associated with the building of the railroads in the nineteenth century, the auto industry in the early twentieth century and computer technologies at its end were long-term affairs both in their emergence and effects. A general pattern for both their initial steps and their later consequences follows.

(1) The increase in capital goods occurs prior to the increased flow of consumer goods, e.g. it takes time to build factories and to design and assemble the machines that will operate in them. Thus, there is a time lag between an increase in capital goods and any new flow of consumer goods.

(2) During this lag, wages paid to employees in the producer sector will increase monies available for consumer spending prior to there being more goods to spend them on.

---

[420] The following remarks are heavily indebted to Lonergan's two volumes: <u>Macroeconomic Dynamics</u> (<u>CW</u> 15) and <u>For a New Political Economy</u> (<u>CW</u> 21).

(3) Absent an increase in savings and investment to absorb these added monies, consumer prices tend to rise. So, for example, during the high-tech surge of the late 1990's, dramatic increases in housing costs occurred in local economies tied to the computer information industry.

(4) Once the flow of new consumer goods begins to accelerate, a new problem appears. When the supply was short but demand high, the income to producers from investors and consumers was high; but, when the supply begins to meet demand, prices for the new consumer goods decline. As a result, there is less demand for producer goods, less incentive for further investment in them, and the earlier high incomes begin to shrink. Many producers respond by trying to find ways to protect their earlier incomes.

(5) One option is to cut wages and initiate rounds of layoffs. Choosing this option may generate a further problem. If this response is widespread, the economy experiences a significant rise in unemployment, but then there are fewer monies for consumption and so even less demand, which would seem to call for even more layoffs. What began as a promise of a rise in the standard of living may end in recession and even depression.

The preceding pattern describes what some call the normal "business cycle." In non-technical terms, the pattern formulates a conventional understanding of the rhythms of economic expansion and contraction in a market economy.[421] The crucial practical question becomes how to avoid a severe recession or depression. Historical answers have taken the form of colonialism (i.e. exporting surplus production to captive markets to offset inadequate demand in domestic markets while controlling production costs by importing raw materials at a discount from those captive markets); deficit spending (i.e. increasing demand in domestic markets by putting more

---

[421] "Conventional" is used here to indicate a puzzle beyond the limits of this study: Is the business cycle inevitable? In contrast to Marx, Schumpeter, Hayek and many other economists, Lonergan held that it was not inevitable. See his <u>Macroeconomic Dynamics</u>, 35.

monies in consumers' pockets); the manipulation of interest rates; and the various programs of the welfare state that, again, largely address the economic problem as one of insufficient demand.[422]

With this much as background, we can turn more directly to the case study. The hypothesis is that an as-yet-untested alternative to the preceding option of cutting the wage bill is worth considering. The alternative appears in two little-known works in economics by Bernard Lonergan.[423] The following is not an attempt to summarize his macroeconomic theory, but key parts of it will receive attention insofar as they shed light on the mentioned alternative.

Perhaps the central claim of his theory is that understanding a market economy requires a clear distinction between two levels of economic activity, which he labeled <u>surplus</u> and <u>basic</u> <u>stages</u> of production. These two stages roughly correspond to the conventional distinction between capital goods and services and consumer goods and services.[424] A complex series of productive processes make up the surplus stage. For example, the activities of program designers produce the software used in running the computer programs that control the movements of robots on assembly lines from which flow the cars that enter the basic stage when consumers purchase them for personal use.

The basic stage is the aggregate of rates at which goods and services move into the standard of living.[425] For example, part of the basic stage is the sum of rates at which so much new housing, private cars, toys and personal computers are being produced and sold per time interval.

---

[422] Ibid. 82-86.

[423] Cf. footnote 416 above.

[424] The correspondence is inexact since Lonergan's theory focuses on the monetary flows through and between these stages as opposed to theories that concentrate on other variables such as GNP, inflation rates, unemployment rates, the money supply.

[425] <u>CW</u> 15 (29) provides more technical and nuanced meanings of both the basic stage and the standard of living.

Part of the surplus stage is the aggregate of rates of production of capital goods and services.[426] Examples here are the rates at which machines, factories, malls and restaurants are being built per time interval. These means of production, as well as their maintenance and replacement, do not enter the standard of living but are the vehicles for sending goods and services into the basic consumer market.

The word "acceleration" can apply to processes in both stages. Surplus-level activities accelerate: (1) by <u>widening</u>, i.e. by increasing the number of producing units (e.g. more factories are built or more container ships are launched) or by using existing equipment to full capacity (e.g. by scheduling round-the-clock shifts); and (2) by <u>deepening</u>, i.e. by increasing the efficiency of producing units (e.g. building larger container ships or automating phone service), so that one is producing similar increases as in widening but with less labor. Now suppose that the key to significant economic development is an increase in output per labor hour. Three sets of distinctions can make this supposition more precise: velocity and acceleration, basic and surplus levels of the productive process, short-term and long-term accelerations.[427] The first two terms pertain to aggregate volumes of flow, i.e. "so much every so often" or the rates at which quantities of goods and services are produced per time interval. Let "velocity" be the routine flow in a set time interval, e.g. the normal rate of so many cars being produced every month. Let "acceleration" mean "going faster," speeding up the normal rate, e.g. producing so many cars + n every month.

---

[426] Ibid. 31-32. Lonergan uses the example of the railroad industry that produces new railroad tracks and boxcars (capital goods), but train passengers and shippers are the parties who consume transportation (a basic service).

[427] Ibid. 32-33, 116-117. Another set of distinctions which Lonergan employed identified three states of the "pure economic cycle." The "steady state" is the one missing from this summary since the puzzle in this study is how to complete a "surplus expansion" by bringing about a "basic expansion."

If the question is how to achieve economic development, the answer seems to be a matter of accelerating the rate of flows. This answer draws upon the second distinction between basic and surplus levels in the productive process. Think of how building more shoe factories eventually increases the flow of shoes to consumers. Again, surplus-level activities can accelerate by widening and by deepening. If those activities amount to the best use of existing equipment (e.g. no idle container ships or unused capacity on them), then this amounts to a short-term acceleration of productive processes. If, however, these activities improve the efficiency of existing equipment and/or add new, more efficient technologies (e.g. fiber optics go into old cable lines or check-out scanners replace manual cash registers), then these activities contribute to a long-term acceleration.

With this much said, we can revisit the earlier pattern of the business cycle and examine its dynamics. What happens when a promising innovation in the surplus stage attracts investments needed to fund its implementation? Assume that financial backers advance the needed funds and the project is underway. For example, checkout scanners are designed, machines are built to produce them, factories are set up to house the machines, employees are trained and so on.

As the process of transforming capital equipment in the surplus stage goes forward, what are its effects on consumer markets? As noted before, there is a time lag before anything new is being produced and for sale in the basic stage. During the time lag no new consumer goods are entering the basic level, but what does enter it is a percentage of the monies flowing into the surplus level as investment. Engineers designing the scanners and workers building the machines and constructing the factories are receiving salaries. Since they cannot eat machines and factories, they spend a portion of their wages on consumer goods and services. If the expansion of the surplus stage is widespread, then a significant number of wage dollars enter the basic level but pursue approximately the same number of goods and services, and so inflationary pressures mount.

What is the alternative to spending heavily on the basic level and so producing higher prices? If the monies are invested (e.g. in stock purchases), paid out in taxes, or deferred in terms of stock options, then they may return to the surplus level or at least not enter the basic market immediately. These responses may reduce the inflationary pressures during a surplus expansion and help support further expansion. But, as mentioned above, a new problem appears. Initial demand for the scanners is high, and significant financial returns (e.g. in the form of executive salaries, compensation packages and profits from IPOs) flow to producers and investors because what they are supplying is a product that is more efficient, promises cost savings to buyers and is in short supply.

These financial returns enjoyed by some are evidence of a successful expansion or lift in the surplus stage; but the next issue is how to bring about an expansion or lift in the basic or consumer market, i.e. raising the standard of living for the many and not just for inventors, entrepreneurs, investors and brokers. The first answer simply notes how a surplus expansion eventually increases the rate of flow of goods and services to consumers (e.g. more groceries checked out per time interval or more output per labor hour), presumably at a cheaper price. So initially the standard of living rises, e.g. consumers wait in shorter lines for service and so gain more time for other activities. But there is a new problem. As growing supply begins to match demand, profit margins decline since demand declines. Accelerations in productive capacity have begun to meet and even to exceed demand. The standard response of those used to the financial returns of a surplus expansion will be efforts to retain previous profit margins by cutting costs. Usually this means cutting labor costs ("downsizing" being the preferred option for many today). However, this response further depresses demand, and, if the response is widely adopted, an economy may enter a recession or even a depression.

Schumpeter envisioned economic accelerations as giving way to contractions but ones that left the average standard of living at a plateau above the starting point of the expansion.[428] Severe recessions or a depression amounts to a retreat below such a starting point. For Lonergan this outcome is a failure of creative understanding. The practical challenge in economics is to find ways to bring about the basic expansion and thereby to exploit the benefits made possible by the prior surplus expansion, but to do so without high inflation, significant unemployment, and a loss of confidence among investors and consumers.[429] How did he think it was possible to meet this complex challenge?

In summary form, he took a normative position (N_2) based on his understanding of the rhythms (N_1) of the productive process. The purpose of a surplus expansion is to produce a major basic expansion. While the former initially generates nonegalitarian results (e.g. unusually high financial rewards flowing to investors and entrepreneurs "behind" the take-off), eventually there should be a more egalitarian distribution of opportunities and benefits through a major basic expansion.[430] How did he think this was possible? He first distinguished between <u>normal</u> and <u>surplus</u> profits. "Normal" profits are income needed to maintain one's enterprise and to provide a reasonable standard of living for one's family. "Surplus" profits are income beyond what is required to maintain either the enterprise or a reasonable standard of living.[431]

---

[428] "The Analysis of Economic Change" in <u>Essays of J. A. Schumpeter</u> (Port Washington, N.Y.: Kennikat Press, 1969), 134-142.
[429] Lonergan, <u>CW</u> 15 (80).
[430] Ibid. 139.
[431] But who decides what is "reasonable"? Part of the education of liberty here is meeting psychological and moral challenges. As in traditional accounts of virtue and of ordered liberty, one must achieve self-control if one is to achieve fuller development. How well does such a traditional view survive in a culture of conspicuous consumption? The latter breeds artificial psychic demands that are antithetical to ordered liberty. How is effective resistance to such

The shift to a basic expansion faces its first test in what people do during the surplus expansion. Ideally they do not spend their surplus profits on the basic level because they understand that doing so leads to high inflation and a draining of investment monies needed to sustain the surplus expansion. That is the ideal case; it assumes large numbers of persons understand the rhythms of the economy and consent to play their parts in providing a higher average standard of living. Similar understanding and consent are needed as a surplus expansion slows. In Lonergan's terms, people need to treat surplus profits as a "social dividend."

What does this mean? The normative guideline for promoting a surplus expansion is "thrift and enterprise," i.e. accumulate savings and invest them in credible innovations. For a basic expansion the normative guideline is "benevolence and enterprise," i.e. use the same ingenuity and enterprise that produced the surplus expansion to devise innovative ways of allowing more consumers to participate in its benefits. Possible means are private and public investment in retraining those left behind by technological innovations, so that they may enter higher paying jobs; investing in community projects such as new parks or the restoration of historical landmarks; shortening the average work week, thereby increasing the number of wage-earners; launching low-tech industries to employ the unskilled. A practical objective of such innovations is to broaden the consumer base so as to absorb the increased production of the surplus expansion. This type of practical thinking may be more acceptable to many than the

---

demands to become commonplace? The education of liberty is a fantasy about widespread cultivation of attention to the inner demands of operators for intelligent and responsible decisions. Applied to economic choices, the tasks, beyond cultivating the habits of self-attention, include educating a populace about the rhythms of an economy and about intelligent ways of adapting to them. Of course, Plato's quandary presents a further task, i.e. supplying the affect-laden images able to evoke consent to intelligent adaptations.

moral reasons of equity and solidarity that also support the call for benevolence and enterprise.

We have finally arrived at our puzzle, and it amounts to a serious challenge in the education of liberty.[432] If most people assume ever escalating incomes and the conspicuous consumption they make possible are the criteria of personal success, then they will resist efforts to complete the cycle with a basic expansion. Treating "their" surplus income as a social dividend will seem at odds with their sense of economic realism.[433] What that realism dictates is preservation of the high incomes, profit margins and savings enjoyed during a surplus expansion. When the surplus expansion slows and the earlier high incomes decline, if cutting the wage bill fails, then "realists" will think the smart thing to do is to invest in safe securities (e.g. government bonds) that guarantee fixed returns. In the meantime the government probably will be embarked on deficit-spending programs as a way of stimulating economic activity and, in doing so, will be draining the economy of monies needed for the next surplus expansion.

The fantasy here is that there is an alternative consistent with the rhythms of a market economy: large numbers of persons are able to learn about these rhythms and

---

[432] "Now to change one's standard of living in any notable fashion is to live in a different fashion. It presupposes a grasp of new ideas. If the ideas are to be above the level of currently successful advertising, serious education must be undertaken. Finally, coming to grasp what serious education really is and, nonetheless, coming to accept the challenge constitutes the greatest challenge to the modern economy. We have had the great surplus expansion of the industrial and scientific revolutions. But we have yet to master the basic expansion." Lonergan, CW 15 (119).

[433] A political rationale will also be ready-to-hand in terms of the inviolability of legitimately acquired private property. What many people adopting this rationale fear are confiscatory taxes; what the education of liberty envisions is the fantasy of persons intelligently and voluntarily "spending down" their surplus income.

so are able to make informed decisions about how to act, and they will adopt a moral stance of <u>solidarity</u>, i.e. not each individual pursuing self-interest but intelligent subjects freely choosing to maintain and to develop their social order and its flows of goods.[434]

Some of the obstacles to realizing this fantasy are worth identifying. First, there is the challenge of having an economically educated population that knows not to spend excessively on the basic level during a surplus expansion but, instead, to invest and so fund further expansion.[435] Still, the issue is not simply one of educating those initially benefiting from a surplus expansion on how to act. There are also psychological obstacles to doing what one may well understand one should do. For example, during a surplus expansion the nonegalitarian financial returns to investors and entrepreneurs may evoke the "politics of envy" in some and result in calls for taxes on "windfall profits." This is especially likely since those living on relatively stable incomes will experience the inflationary pressures of a surplus expansion as threatening. In addition, there is a need to counteract a social psychology of conspicuous consumption that encourages extravagant purchases on the basic level. Especially liable to this pathology will be those benefiting the most during a surplus expansion.

Both of these psychological reactions can interfere with the two types of expansions. Taxes on what are alleged to be windfall profits may drain monies otherwise going to further investments supporting a surplus expansion. Persons

---

[434] Recall the remarks in previous chapters on the limits of "rational agency" as understood in Classical Liberalism. The earlier critiques can be posed as a question: Are persons able to transform an initial orientation toward self-advantage into a more "complete" understanding and deliberate choosing of the good of personal relations?

[435] Precedents for meeting this part of the challenge can be found in the widespread investment in war bonds by private citizens during World War II.

enthralled with conspicuous consumption will resist calls to distinguish between normal and surplus profits and to treat the latter as a social dividend. If the resistance is strong enough, any basic expansion becomes less probable.[436] But the ills of such a failure to complete a surplus expansion are predictable. The first stage will yield a new population of multimillionaires living lavishly and publicly alongside a larger population experiencing no such improvement in their standard of living; and, for those whose jobs were downsized or rendered obsolete, the visible prosperity of the newly enriched will seem to have been achieved at their expense. Desperate people will seek out villains when the real source of the difficulties has been a failure to understand how an economy works and how to adapt to its rhythms.[437] Political

---

[436] If the requirements for a basic expansion include transfers of the social dividend to populations unable otherwise to consume the increased flows of goods and services entering the basic stage, a further obstacle appears in a popular misconception that the profit motive is also the criterion of how one ought to behave in economic activities. A "realist" may assert that all non-individualistic norms may be praiseworthy, but they have no standing in a scientific account of economic behavior. Additional obstacles will be fears of how stock markets will react to declining corporate profits, how restive a board of directors may become, how foolish one may look to them if one voices moral concerns that seem at odds with attaining impressive quarterly reports. The fears are real, but psychological, moral and intellectual displacements are possible.

[437] "The fact…is that no difficulty is experienced in financing the surplus expansion. It is the first step towards increasing the standard of living of the whole society, and there seems to be little evidence that entrepreneurs, financiers, engineers, workers commonly are hesitant about taking that step. The difficulty emerges in the second step, the basic expansion. In equity it should be directed to raising the standard of living of the whole society. It does not. And the reason why it does not is not the reason on which simple-minded moralists insist. They blame greed. But the prime cause is ignorance. The dynamics of surplus and basic production, surplus

instability may soon follow upon economic difficulties, but at a minimum the surplus expansion will have ended without Schumpeter's lift to a new plateau.

Marx called capitalism a "progressive" economic order because he saw that for the first time it was possible to overcome the historical scourge of scarcity and to produce sufficient surpluses, so that the gain of one person need not be at the expense of another. In the terms used in this section, market capitalism manages the surplus expansion well. While Marx's remedies for the failings of capitalism have themselves failed, it remains true today that market capitalism has had no similar success with the basic expansion.

What are the chances of doing better in this century? Solving the problem of the transition from a surplus expansion to a basic expansion requires a serious educational effort and widespread cooperation with the demands of the various operators. Again, the failures of creative understanding, not of the economy, are the root of ongoing problems in distributing the benefits of market economies. Lonergan offered no legislative agenda or specific policy proposals. He did offer an alternative understanding of the dynamics of a market economy, one that does not make it the master but the servant of human flourishing. He also avoided the illusion that impersonal market forces can eventually solve all our problems and the equally illusory stance that a benevolently minded elite could succeed in imposing the required solutions. There are no substitutes for the educated liberty of persons who have experienced personal displacements[438]

---

and basic expansions, surplus and basic incomes are not understood, not formulated, not taught. When people do not understand what is happening and why, they cannot be expected to act intelligently. When intelligence is a blank, the first law of nature takes over: self-preservation. It is not primarily greed but frantic efforts at self-preservation that turn the recession into a depression, and the depression into a crash." Lonergan, CW 15, 82.

[438] In his early works Marx asked whether, in producing a good social order, one first needed a moral revolution in persons before

transforming them and, with the cooperation of likeminded persons, potentially transforming economic and political orders.

---

attempting a political revolution in institutions. He ceased to ask this question in his later works and opted for reliance on institutional changes and, more fundamentally, on the impersonal laws of historical development. Both he and Classical Liberalism seem in agreement that some impersonal mechanism and not personal displacements will ultimately make history better than it has been.

EPILOGUE: BOOK(S) NOT WRITTEN

An Epilogue traditionally is a looking back at what previous chapters have accomplished. This concluding section is no exception, but it also is a looking forward. As mentioned at the beginning, a fantasy about better practice would appear at the end. Before keeping that promise, I will review what other promises previous chapters tried to keep and the view of historical progress those promises presupposed.

I Anamnesis

A number of purposes motivated this book. There were problems with language, i.e. how both philosophers and neuroscientists continue to talk about liberty. Adopting the hypothesis that liberty "extends all the way down" to even the most basic of intentional acts, I promised to work out explanatory accounts of intentional acts and liberty. Those formulations suggest a new way of speaking about liberty, a new vocabulary that may make talk of free will and determinism obsolete. That this new way of speaking is an improvement over more traditional terminology first depends on whether descriptive categories and the understanding they formulate fall short of answers to further why-questions. In addition, correlating significant variables and under-standing them as basic terms explaining dynamic processes can result in an analytic structure contributing to further inquiries and to developing a powerful theory about such processes.[439] Thus,

---

[439] "An analysis leads from what everyone knows to significant variables that are mutually dependent – preferably dynamically dependent – on one another. In that way, you have your primitive terms and the source of a basis for developing a science as an analytic structure. Since your basis is analytic, whenever you apply it to anything, you'll have the analysis of that thing." Bernard Lonergan. Interview quoted in Caring about Meaning. Pierrot Lambert et al., eds. (Montreal: Thomas More Institute, 1982), 226.

the explanatory account of "orientation" in Chapter One became an analytic pattern for under-standing intentional acts besides those of attention.[440] As an example of explanatory understanding, it provided clues on how to evade some of the intellectual impasses in contemporary discussions of liberty. It also supplied clues for how to work out an explanatory account of liberty.

That explanatory account proceeded by way of three approximations. First, liberty is a capacity for higher-order integration of lower-order materials.[441] The relation between acts of understanding and the puzzling clues that evoke questioning was the model for understanding how acts synthesized lower-order materials. A second approximation was that liberty is a capacity for decision-making conditioned by three types of determinants: (1) prior integrations providing the established context for (2) the mediating demands of operators evoking intentional acts (3) moving toward indeterminate ends in response to the mediated demands of

---

[440] To quote one attempt to fix the meanings of basic terms in relation to one another: "The general capacity (orientation) has its correlate in the field of potential data; but the capacity is actually exercisable and so potentially determinate relative to some potentially determinate subset of that field. The capacity is actually exercised (aroused) relative to one of the three ways of responding to an actually determinate (focused on) subset of that field. These relations can be reversed such that one begins with the field as what sets the range for any possible exercise of the general capacity (orientation) and goes on to define a potentially determinate subset of the field as what can evoke (arouse) a potentially determinate exercise of the capacity. An actually determinate subset will be the correlate of a specific act of attention."

[441] For example, liberty in this sense appears in acts of attention. A complete act of attention, in selectively focusing on some subset of the field of data, minimally orders or recognizes that subset as something determinate. A puzzling sight or noise is minimally determinate as an image or sound and so already an instance of selection and integration.

the related but opposed principles of completion and assimilation. There were two objections to this complex notion: (1) if liberty extends all the way down, it is more than a capacity for decision-making; and (2) since morally defective responses to the demands of the two principles occur, we need to distinguish between normative and non-normative meanings of liberty. In a non-normative sense, exercises of liberty respond to the demand of the principle of assimilation by integrating operations with what are already suspected to be inadequate integrations of understanding and practice, and so they fail to meet the demand of the principle of completion to surpass prior inadequate integrations. In the normative sense, liberty is a capacity of intentional acts to respond to the demand of the principle of completion such that they can develop or correct the antecedent integrations that initially conditioned those acts.[442]

---

[442] Someone might ask if habitual acts of honesty that assimilate or integrate new operations with already achieved moral practices are acts of liberty in the normative sense even though there is no development or revision of antecedent integrations. In response, I would first point out the two parts of the non-normative sense of liberty. Besides assimilation of new operations to established patterns, there is a failure to meet demands for further development. Habitual acts of dishonesty satisfy the first type of demands but not the second. Habitual acts of honesty satisfy the first type, but how are they instances of further development? Perhaps the simplest answer is that habits and new moral acts are related non-systematically, so the demands of the operators are met not as a matter of necessity. On each occasion a prior disposition to be honest makes subsequent acts more likely to conform to the pattern, but the intentional acts that actually occur may deviate from the pattern. Thus, the acts may or may not respond to the demand of the principle of completion. If they do not, there is a moral failure; if they do, there is a further development in virtue. Recall the earlier shift in the meaning of virtue: "a flexible range of schemes of recurrent normative intentional acts." A determinate orientation to make morally appropriate acts routinely meets variable situations

Some further distinctions appeared. (1) Actual exercises of normative liberty may respond only somewhat adequately to the demands of the various operators mediating the general demand for completeness; they may at the same time involve compromises with competing demands. (2) Evaluation of actual exercises should consider the complex relations among, for example, concrete situations, the intentions of actors, their psychological make-up, what they actually do and the consequences that follow. (3) An understanding of liberty as having multiple types of determinants, including the related but opposed demands of two basic principles, assigns a heuristic role to a normative notion of liberty. That is, it prescribes what persons ideally should become or do. Falling short of the ideal is not the same as acting immorally. It may be acting humanly, all too humanly as Nietzsche said.

Implicit in this brief summary is the original hypothesis that orientation as a "determinate indeterminacy" is a multi-layered dynamism of various types of intentional acts with antecedent conditions ranging from neurochemical and organic patterns to sociohistorical integrations mediated by institutions. Neural patterns within individuals and institutional practices beyond them "favor" familiar integrations of meaning (e.g. attending to some data or questions and ignoring others) and make significant departures from them improbable. Yet displacements do occur. Creative understanding was understood as one source of such departures. The roles of affect-laden images in inspiring decisive action and of personal relations in supporting risk-taking were additional conditions favoring the occurrence of the improbable. Ultimately, the hypothesis was that positing a principle of completion was a way of making sense of the human capacity

---

with a developing capacity to respond in morally acceptable ways. Each time this recurs the capacity to respond in a similar way is a more secure scheme or pattern. The earlier analogy was to practice and the development of skills.

to do more than assimilate new "materials" to already established patterns.

What was the evidence for this supposition? Talk of a principle of supplementation in psychology of perception is commonplace. The experimental evidence for a "rounding off" and a "filling in" of the objects of perception is massive.[443] The "binding problem" in neuroscience is a recurrent puzzle as old as Aristotle's common sense and the medieval speculations about various inner senses. Perhaps more telling is the dynamism of questioning and the experience of restless efforts to "add" intelligibility to puzzling clues. Such clues are far from being "complete." Acts of understanding that could integrate clues do not necessarily occur. Despite a plethora of evidence, an inquirer may not have the insights that unify them into a meaningful solution. In addition, since different readers bring different orientations to the integration of clues, they can "read" the same clues in a variety of ways. On both counts, the higher-order acts and the lower-order materials are sources of indeterminacy in what integrations actually occur.[444]

The rationale for introducing the horizon of interiority was to invite attention to one's own orientation as an inquirer. As a matter of fact, am I a reaching for discoveries about what is the case and about what is good to do? How central to my

---

[443] The seen print of this sentence is an easy example of such supplementation. The ink marks become meaningful patterns when readers assimilate them to linguistic patterns with which they are already familiar. However, we are far from adequately understanding how this happens. How are neurochemical patterns in the brain linked to linguistic meaning? How do we make the transition from fragmentary brain signals to understood and so integrated symbols?

[444] The flexibility of lower-order materials is evident in botanical and biological evolution insofar as similar chemical environments have given rise to different species. The flexibility of higher-order acts is evident in the diversity of institutional orders that human beings have created.

living is a desire for making sense of things? The desire is not an invariant in actual human living since determinate orientations are variable contexts of possible and actual intentional operations.[445] So there is good reason to raise a basic question about personal orientation: Am I interested in living a comprehensive life? That is, is the demand of the principle of completion central to my living? Do I pursue further why-questions about some area of interest and have I detected the limits of nominal understanding and descriptive expressions?

Without affirmative answers to these questions on the part of large numbers of persons, the fantasy about the "education of liberty" will remain a very remote possibility, and its two defective rivals (the laissez-faire and regulatory options) will likely remain the sole contenders for directing human history. But what if we take a longer view of history and suppose that the desire for comprehensive understanding is a primary datum to be integrated into our stories about our times, our tribes and our futures? The promises contained in this text presupposed such a longer historical view, and it is worth making explicit.

Aquinas observed: "The human species is a capacity to understand which proceeds to its perfection by way of incomplete acts of understanding."[446] Suppose the "incomplete acts of understanding" are classifiable as <u>types</u> of

---

[445] Aristotle's famous remark that all persons by nature desire to know would seem to be at odds with this claim. However, he was well aware that what was a capacity in the infant and in the species became actual under varying conditions. Hence, when he remarked that "we are busy that we may have leisure," he was citing one of the conditions for the development of this capacity, namely, liberation from the pursuit of basic necessities. <u>Nichomachaen Ethics</u>, 1177b, 5-6. One might also argue that Aristotle was generalizing from his own experience in developing his capacity for inquiry and so not generalizing about what desires most persons actually pursue.

[446] Quoted in Michael Shute. <u>Lonergan's Discovery of Scientific Economics</u>, 107.

<u>understanding</u> occurring in a developmental pattern. For example, highly variable common sense is the type of understanding Socrates encountered among his Athenian audiences. In both their thinking and their doing, they were intent on the particular problems at hand and on how to remedy them. Socrates invited them to ask further questions that both exceeded the competence of common-sense understanding and required a disengagement from the immediate concerns of practical living. He asked them to enter a realm of theory and to think of general patterns of relations that would explain why everyday experiences were what they were.

No one has to accept such an invitation. For example, while knowing how to drive is useful in one's daily living, knowing precisely how a car engine runs is not required for a driver's survival. So common-sense living can give way to theoretical inquiry, but most civic leaders have better things to do with their time, and, besides, their common-sense thinking may not see any benefit in the effort. In the case of Socrates, the audience resented the invitation and condemned the inviter. In subsequent generations a few took up the challenge to enter into a world of theoretical reflection, but common-sense living remained resistant to theoretical inquiry. For example, despite the discoveries in psychology of perception, common sense has no doubt that seeing what is out there in front of us is the hallmark both of knowing and of what is real.[447] More troubling examples are common-sense estimates of foreign policy in terms of *Realpolitik* and of economics in terms of inevitably competing egoisms.

So we have two stages of incomplete historical development: (1) common-sense living and thinking, and (2) common-sense living and theoretical reflection alien to but occurring alongside of common-sense thinking. Can we anticipate a third stage in which theoretical reflection would

---

[447] One can read the history of modern philosophy as a struggle to relate these two distinct ways of understanding and the two realisms they imply. Cf. Lonergan. <u>Insight</u>, 11-12.

provide a guide to and intelligent control over common-sense living?[448] In other words, theoretical reflection, when required, would intelligently direct human practices. If this seems vague, consider how the history of politics or economics has been a distressing record of pre-theoretical activities randomly responding to challenges, sometimes with intelligent decisions but oftentimes under the dominance of transitory fears, ambitions and power games. Can one imagine a future in which theory and practice would be complementary, when the best available understanding was the widely accepted measure of what can and should be done? From this perspective, the political and economic realisms of recent centuries will seem adolescent rantings and inept adaptations of the human species to its problems.

From this standpoint, historical progress is the slow acceptance of the demands of operators for more complete acts, demands resisted by the inertia of unintelligible situations and the habitual solutions of prevailing common sense. Historical decline occurs because many ignore these demands and instead accept some inherited nonsense as the best they can do. In a political context, they accept *Realpolitik* and power games as the prevailing "wisdom." Then political history becomes a cycle not far removed from the bloody vendetta. What can break that cycle is not the appeal to political expediency, e.g. to "put the past behind us." Memories of injustices and losses are not so easily discarded. They will linger, fester and re-emerge as situations deteriorate and old animosities are rekindled by new misunderstandings and injustices. Here is the place in the human story to make a choice. By itself theory seems ineffective in moving persons to forego the cycles of violence. It needs the affect-laden symbols that stir persons to fantasize about a better way of living, but accompanying such fantasies should be both a

---

[448] One reason for the earlier introduction of the horizon of interiority was to sketch the standpoint from which to understand the differences between common sense and theory and so to track how one is operating in different inquiries.

desire to live a comprehensive life and effective ways of promoting that desire, that capacity, in more and more people.

What is remote in the infant and in the species is the actual development of this capacity. The obstacles to further development are numerous. Diversions from this barely felt desire are ever present. The exigencies of practical living lead many to conclude that all inquiry should serve immediate and practical ends. Human stupidity and not a little malice have made of history something far worse than it might otherwise have been. And accompanying this sorry record of achievements falling short of aspirations are political and economic ideologies that rationalize actual practice as the measure of good practice. Their mistake may be in overlooking that we have only a minimal understanding of our capacities for improvement.

To take a stand on what one means by historical progress says something about one's understanding of liberty. The normative notion of liberty refined in this text can be thought of as serving a heuristic function. It can guide empirical studies of how well individuals do their "personal best" in adapting to variable environments. It can also guide inquiries into how well different social orders have adapted to more complex environments. In the first case, suppose someone raises questions about what we mean by "adult growth." While theories of infant and adolescent development are plentiful, fewer theories are available about how adults survive and surpass the integrations of their earlier years. What the normative notion offers is a general heuristic for investigating how well adults have responded to the demands of the various operators.[449]

---

[449] One possible use of the heuristic is a questionnaire asking test subjects pointed questions about their attentiveness to the beauty or ugliness of their environments, their curiosity about new ideas, their care in making judgments about views at odds with their own, the frequency with which they fantasize about better futures for themselves and others, their record of following through with decisions to change their lives. Daniel A. Helminiak and Barnet D.

In the case of sociopolitical practices, Chapters Five and Six already raised questions about more comprehensive orientations in thinking about economic activities. Can large numbers of persons learn to think of their economic objectives as maintaining "reasonable" standards of living, improving the material conditions of entire populations through a basic expansion and liberating persons by increasing opportunities for participation in cultural activities? Realists sanction a less "complete" orientation. Instead of the flourishing of some good of order and its promotion of personal relations, the realists tell us that particular goods and the pursuit of self-interest are the actual objectives of the purportedly rational *homo economicus*. Amartya Sen already noted discrepancies between the alleged reality and actual performance. Again, the telling evidence may be closer: What is my orientation as a participant in economic schemes of recurrence?

The fantasy of the education of liberty presupposes that cooperation with the demand of the principle of completion can someday be widespread. It presupposes, then, that progress is possible in both economic and political practices, not as a matter of necessity or of some impersonal mechanism in charge of human history, but as a matter of deliberate and responsible uses of liberty. One author summed up the key condition that any economic and political order must meet.

> It cannot be a titanothore, a beast with a three-ton body and a ten-ounce brain. It must not direct its main effort to the ordinary final product of [the] standard of living but to the overhead final product of cultural implements. It must not glory in its widening, in adding industry to industry, and feeding the soul of man with an abundant demand for labor. It must glory in its deepening, in the

---

Feingold have been working on such a questionnaire and using it in counseling patients at Veterans Administration facilities in the United States. Initial findings have been promising but await publication and replication.

pure deepening that adds to aggregate leisure, to liberate many entirely and all increasingly to the field of cultural activities. It must not boast of science on the ground that science fills its belly. It must not glue its nose to the single track of this or that department. It must lift its eyes more and ever more to the more general and more difficult fields of speculation, for it is from them that it has to derive the delicate compound of unity and freedom in which alone progress can be born, struggle, and win through. Unity without freedom is easy: set up a dictator and give him a secret police. Freedom without unity is easy: let every weed glory in the sunshine of stupid adulation. But unity and freedom together, that is the problem.[450]

Evidence that this problem is unresolved appeared in the last chapter. Contemporary difficulties in identifying the ends of ordered liberty reflect disagreements on how to integrate liberty and order. Rather than take such impasses as permanent, this text has tried to find a middle way between skepticism and system building. Its thesis has been that inner norms order liberty and that liberty gains determinate content, becomes focused on specific ends or goods, through accumulating insights into the results of actual operations. But those operations continue, and so further insights may correct or revise prior integrations of meaning.

The puzzles and hypotheses of this text may prompt some further insights. Still, as the Introduction forewarned, the reflections on liberty that followed would leave many questions unanswered. For example, the diagnosis of Libet's findings at the end of Chapter One concluded that an explanatory account of consciousness was the missing piece of that puzzle; yet there was no effort to supply what was missing. Similarly, for all the talk of "top-down conditioning" of neural and organic processes, no detailed experimental results supplemented the descriptive examples of deliberate

---

[450] Lonergan, CW 21, 20.

acts to control lower-order events. What Posner anticipated as a deficit in neuroscientific research continues, and far more focus on "executive acts" is one of the challenges for a new generation of neuroscientists.[451] Even from a "bottom-up" perspective, there remains much research to be done on the neurochemical and organic conditions for experiences of curiosity, judging and deciding. As that research goes forward, we can expect that difficulties with language will be recurrent. For example, how are we to talk about neurochemical and organic conditions without adopting a reductionistic stance toward psychological states and intentional acts?

We need a new and more complex language flexible enough to track the dialectical relations between "materials" amenable to and setting limits on possible integrations and the intentional acts which can, within limits, order them in determinate ways. That language is not yet available. Still in use is the language of self-determining agency (causal agency), but can we seriously continue this usage without providing an explanatory account of "self" and how intentional acts "cause" neurochemical and organic events? Even to undertake this task is likely to generate the acute discomfort Jerome Bruner felt in talking about the "concept" of self.[452] Perhaps the discomfort is of a different sort when one begins not with concepts but with attention to the operations that generate them. At least this has been our strategy in trying to understand liberty.

---

[451] Cf. Chapter Three, footnotes 218 and 219.

[452] Bruner, 129-130. Perhaps discomfort should be a result of serious inquiry. Someone once observed that a failed text is one that does not leave a reader radically changed or displaced. Perhaps the same is true of serious inquiry. Goethe anticipated the resistance to displacement by remarking that sometimes the problem is not with the text but with the reader.

II Prolepsis

The Introduction promised that the Epilogue would entertain a fantasy about improved practice in future scholarship. What follows is an outline of the practice; next is an application of the practice to parts of the preceding text. One purpose is to suggest how this new practice could improve future studies of liberty.

Lonergan proposed a division of labor for theoretical inquiries that would make collaborative efforts individually more efficient and collectively more productive of cumulative results. His generic name for this practice was "functional specialization." He listed eight functional specialties: Research, Interpretation, History, Dialectic, Foundations, Doctrines, Systematics, Communications.[453] The labels "Doctrines," "Systematics" and "Communications" reflected his study of the distinct specialties in the field of theology. A more inclusive set of categories would be "Policies," "Planning" and "Applications," but more will be said about these categories below.[454]

The eight distinctions have an origin in the pattern of intentional operations that Chapter Three outlined. The labels for the patterned operations were empirical acts, intellectual acts, critical acts, deliberative acts and normative acts. An initial puzzle is how these five distinct types of intentional acts can provide a basis for eight functional specialties. The apparent asymmetry is resolvable if one distinguishes four of the intentional acts in terms of their relevant questions.[455] So

---

[453] Method in Theology, 127-133.

[454] Philip McShane first suggested the substitution of the terms "policies" and "planning." He was relying on Lonergan's references to "policymaking, planning and execution of plans" (ibid. 365) when the latter discussed how functional specialization could appear in fields other than theology. In what follows I will use the category "applications" in place of either communications or execution.

[455] Lonergan also distinguishes the four types of acts in terms of their proper ends or objectives. (Method in Theology 134.) The varying

intellectual acts find expression in what-questions, critical acts in is-questions, deliberative acts in questions about what options are available and normative acts in questions about which options are worth choosing. The asymmetry vanishes, first, if one supposes the initial four specialties are concerned with accurately understanding the past while the next four are concerned with future developments;[456] and, second, if one notices the duplication of the what-question in each set of four but with a shift in modality when it appears in the second set. Thus, there is the what-question pertaining to Interpretation (i.e. what is the meaning of the data interpreters receive from researchers?); then there is the what-question pertaining to planning (i.e. what courses of action are possible?).

The first functional specialty is research, and its objective is to identify or to collect data relevant to some inquiry. Examples are efforts to compile variorum editions of literary masterpieces and repeated calibrations of cyclotrons

---

ends or objectives are useful in distinguishing the specialties. Corresponding to research are the data and clues evoking empirical acts; corresponding to interpretation are the surmises and hypotheses proceeding from intellectual acts; corresponding to history are the judgments of fact occurring in critical acts; corresponding to dialectic are the worthwhile means and ends of normative acts. The next four specialties reverse the sequence of acts and objectives. To foundations correspond normative acts and intended goods; to policies correspond critical acts and affirmations of what general goods are worth pursuing; to planning correspond deliberative acts and possible courses of action; to applications correspond the empirical acts of attending to local conditions and to data emerging from adopted plans. Distinguishing the functional specialties in terms of their objectives makes it easier to recognize that, while the various types of intentional acts occur in each specialty, each remains distinct though related to the others because of its distinct objective.

[456] More specifically, the first four functional specialties aim at retrieving past achievements while the next four, relying on the results of the previous four, focus on guiding future actions.

to record the immense data they provide. A survey of the literature on the neuroscience of attention could be an instance of basic research preliminary to a broader project.

The relevant data that researchers assemble supply the materials for the second specialty of interpretation. The aims of the interpreter may be to reconstruct the common-sense understanding and modes of expression of an earlier era or to decipher what particular authors may have meant given their prevailing worldviews and the rhetorical devices of their times. Examples are studies of why Galileo assumed planetary motions were circular or why Darwin shifted from belief in a providential universe to belief in a universe governed by chance. Commonplace examples are monographs on particular poems, plays or novels where one objective is to suggest what artists wished a first-generation audience to experience through their art. Interpretation may also be the appropriate label for an inquiry into what Aquinas meant by "abstraction" or what neuroscientists mean by "executive function."

"History" has multiple meanings. Besides the German distinction between *Geschichte* and *Geschichtschreibung*, there are further distinctions in the types of historical inquiries scholars pursue. A basic type tries to settle questions about who did what, when, where and with what results. Broader inquiries will trace developments across entire cultures or eras. In the nineteenth century, some historians saw both types as serving to bring closer the day when they would have a universal history, i.e. a complete account of retrievable human affairs.[457]

History as a functional specialty makes use of the results of research and interpretation in pursuit of its aim, namely, understanding what was going forward, what was emerging, as the latest development within some field. Examples would include conference presenters whose purpose is to inform colleagues about their most recent

---

[457] Lonergan referred to the three types of historiographical projects as basic, special and general histories. Method in Theology, 128.

findings and to suggest what significance they have for the discipline. A paper that reviewed current theories on an issue in clinical psychology (e.g. how neurochemical, organic and psychological correlates help explain affective responses to images) and went on to suggest how recent findings might resolve old puzzles about the issue would qualify as an instance of this third type of specialty. A monograph that traced the use of terms from faculty psychology in accounts of mental acts and went on to note the changes in vocabulary due to intentionality theory would be an instance of history as a specialty.

Dialectic receives the diverse interpretations and historical reports as its materials and evaluates them in terms of how each may contribute to a comprehensive account of some issue.[458] But on what grounds does the dialectician decide how to classify or to order conflicting interpretations and incompatible historical reports? Neither are in short supply. Literary movements, philosophical schools and scientific fields exhibit external and internal conflicts. What the dialectician needs is a set of "basic positions" allowing for detection and diagnosis of the often obscure origins of such conflicts. While describing the conflicts is relatively easy work, explaining the differences is far more difficult. Comparing viewpoints will reveal similarities and divergences. Among the

---

[458] Lonergan remarks that the aim of dialectic is "high and distant. As empirical science aims at a complete explanation of all phenomena, so dialectic aims at a comprehensive viewpoint." (Ibid. 129.) As noted in the first part of the Epilogue, the evidence of a spontaneous reaching for a comprehensive viewpoint turns up when one takes seriously the further why-questions that exceed the limits of nominal understanding and descriptive expression. Of course, the envisioned comprehensive viewpoint would require that dialecticians operate in an explanatory context. This is a remote possibility. For example, a future author could transpose this Epilogue's descriptions of functional specialization into an explicit ordering of basic terms, correlations among them and among functionally related but distinct schemes of operations.

latter some will be irreducible while others will be complementary and perhaps reconcilable as "successive stages in a single process of development."[459] But what of the irreducible differences? These are challenging since they usually proceed from fundamental differences in assumptions about knowledge, morality and spirituality arising from the presence or absence of different horizons and displacements.[460]

Insofar as dialecticians have an adequate understanding of different horizons and have undergone various displacements, basic positions will be part of their "context" as inquirers allowing them to classify some divergences as rooted in inadequately developed horizons.[461] Thus, to answer the question above about "grounds" for deciding how to classify conflicting viewpoints, the concrete contexts of the inquirers are the basis for discriminating among stances compatible with and at odds with their basic positions.[462]

Examples of dialectic include classifying under one heading all views of liberty that do not go beyond descriptive accounts of imaginable individuals whose imaginable motions other individuals or circumstances either restrict or leave

---

[459] Ibid.

[460] Recall the example of Libet's puzzle at the end of Chapter One. Different readings of the experimental results will in some cases be attributable to the presence or absence in the reader of a differentiation of the horizons of common sense and theory.

[461] Examples of such positions appeared in earlier chapters in regard to moral and intellectual displacements and their implications for various theoretical impasses.

[462] Some may read this conclusion as endorsing a type of subjectivity as the grounds for dialectic. The issue is what one means by "subjectivity" and whether that meaning is expansive enough to include the demands of both the critical operator and the principle of completion. See below (especially footnotes 462 and 469) for further comments on the question of the criterion for the work of foundational specialists.

unrestricted.[463] Such views, despite other differences, share a common-sense horizon and so fall short of an explanatory context.[464] Dialectic could also be part of an inquiry that traced the origins of the Anarchist's Dream to an insufficiently developed understanding of how indeterminate capacities become determinate only through operating in relation to determinate conditions, including political institutions. Chapter Four explored relations between individuals and institutions and shed some light on how liberty-as-capacity becomes determinate in relation to various institutions. The goal was to explain how inquirers could be subject to prior determinations, both within and beyond themselves, and still be able to act-at-liberty.

A further exercise of dialectic could appear in criticizing talk of "mechanisms in the brain." The analogy to machinery ignores the key difference between systematic and non-systematic relations in complex processes. Non-systematic relations among lower and higher-order schemes of recurrence permit flexible adaptations, both internal (e.g. new neural linkages occurring after brain trauma) and external (e.g. using computer reading programs to assist dyslexic students). Such flexible adaptations are evidence of the need to think of liberty in dialectical terms.

The second set of functional specialties directs action by drawing upon what the first set has retrieved from the past. The general goal is the control of history. How do specialists pursue this goal in a methodical way? Lonergan's fantasy was that functional specialization could provide a controlled

---

[463] Hobbes' view of liberty appears to qualify as an instance of such "picture-thinking" about liberty.

[464] Note that the decision to categorize some views as deficient does amount to criticism. For instance, dialecticians do rule out views that are incompatible with already accepted levels of understanding and so not in need of careful attention. Easy examples would be astrology or alchemy as positions deserving serious consideration. Dialectic, then helps "narrow down" the range of positions in need of further reflection. <u>Method in Theology</u>, 141.

way of taking what was best from the past and applying it to the direction of future efforts.

The fifth specialty makes explicit what the inquirer takes to be basic positions and counterpositions. Recall that the operation corresponding to foundations is the normative act of deciding. Such an act is one of consent to what one has judged to be true and good. In effect, it amounts to taking a stand.[465] What are the grounds for such a stand? The question is not one of premises but of persons. That is, the "foundations" are not some initial set of propositions in an axiomatic system; instead, they are the inner norms of the various operators that give rise to inquiries, judgments, concepts, formulations and theories.[466] In practice these norms can be effective in producing reliable results only if persons carefully and consistently cooperate with them. This is why earlier chapters drew attention to various types of orientations, horizons and displacements. Talk of the inquirer as a "context" anticipated the claim here that what matters fundamentally is the person engaged in any of the specialties.

Since contexts vary, we expect inquirers to arrive at different conclusions. Some differences will be due to psychological variables, others to oversights of relevant questions and data; still others will reflect varying sociohistorical conditions that favor attention to some data more than to others. Of concern to the specialist in foundations are differences arising from different horizons and

---

[465] A famous example is Luther's: "*Hier steh' ich, ich kann nicht anders.*"

[466] Method in Theology, 269-270. This use of "foundations" is actually anti-foundationalist. In current usage the former is usually understood to be some set of basic assumptions or premises from which one deduces the further content of some theory. Lonergan's use of the term depends on his stand against conceptualism: concepts and theories arise from insights mediated by intentional acts that are responses to the immanent demands of the operators. A foundational question is which position corresponds to one's own performance in arriving at understanding.

from opposed basic positions. In such cases persons will be trying to make sense of the same phenomena but will be operating out of opposed contexts. The data may be the same, but what inquirers bring to the process of completion will yield contrasting results.

What one attends to as significant will depend on one's horizon.[467] For example, if the horizon of interiority is *terra incognita*, social psychologists may overlook the role of intentional acts or consider them epiphenomenal in accounting for economic and political activities. They are likely to limit their focus to psychic demands for satisfying needs. Any evidence of critical operators "trumping" egoistic needs will not fit their horizons. They are, then, likely to ignore it or to reinterpret it to fit their horizon.[468]

Clearly Lonergan's fantasy of functional specialization incorporates the problems of multiplicity both in theories and in their sources. How did he envision a way of sorting through intellectual and normative conflicts? His answer in part appears in the functional relation between the fourth and fifth specialties. Dialecticians presumably will manifest the differences noted above, including those arising from opposed horizons. However, one task of dialectics is to identify the roots of differences and especially to concentrate on differences arising from the presence or absence of various types of displacements. Dialecticians go on to work out the implications of what they take to be positions and counter-

---

[467] "The horizons that guide the performance of the tasks also guide the performance of the research. One easily finds what fits into one's horizon. One has very little ability to notice what one has never understood or conceived." Ibid. 246-247.

[468] A key hypothesis of this text is that we need not rule out one type of demand in favor of another. The question is whether explaining the complex determinants of human actions benefits from including the demands of intentional operators as well as the demands of neurochemical, biological and psychological processes?

positions.[469] In doing this they will reveal even more clearly what their own positions are. Both in identifying differences and in working out implications, dialecticians will be revealing their own horizons and whether or not they have experienced the various displacements.

This self-revelation proceeds in three steps. First, dialecticians are explicit in their judgments about which horizons the works they are investigating reflect. To the extent they go on to compare and contrast those works and their implications in terms of basic positions and counterpositions, they will be revealing their own positions. Lastly, if functional specialization is a dynamic collaborative enterprise, those comparisons, contrasts and positions will become materials for a new round of analysis by dialecticians. This last step is not unknown in current practice. Scholars and scientists routinely submit their findings to peer review and criticism. Suppose, then, that dialecticians "recycle" their findings within the specialty. What may come of this recycling?

Through this recycling and comparing of opposed positions, dialecticians may detect their own deficiencies along with those in works they review. Earlier remarks about the benefits of public discourse in revealing overlooked conditions for prospective judgments apply here. While the dialectical review process does not guarantee further development in the practitioners, it does have the merit of being an experimental procedure. That is, just as carefully conducted experiments may produce results that some refuse to accept or others misinterpret, so the circulation of materials among dialecticians may produce resistance and misreadings. Still, the process raises questions about basic positions and asks participants to reveal indirectly their own stands on these questions. It thereby provides multiple examples of peers

---

[469] Lonergan's specification of the meaning of "position" and "counterposition" appears at various loci in Insight. See especially 413-414 (for positions on knowledge and objectivity), 629-630 (for positions on ethics) and 702-705 (for positions on religious faith).

assuming different positions and makes basic assumptions and worldviews topics of discussion.[470] In doing so, the decisions that explicitly concern foundations will become a topic of discussion, i.e. what exactly one calls good and true and why will be the objects of reflection, perhaps leading to revision or re-affirmation.

It is worth noting that this approach to differences is a departure from much of current practice. Dialecticians are not intent on constructing arguments that prove their own positions and undermine opposing views.[471] Their tasks are to identify differences and to trace the origins of some to different horizons and opposed positions. In doing this much, they will be revealing their own level of development to astute readers. To the degree that others are responsive to the inner demands of their own operators, the self-exposure of the dialectician is an invitation for them to do likewise and so to confront their own commitments to understand comprehensively. Not all will be "up to the challenge." Again, displacements are radical departures from prior orientations, and the principle of assimilation favors views compatible with prior achievements. Yet the demands of the principle of completion are part of human reality, and the promise of the fourth and fifth functional specialties rests on the capacity of persons to cooperate with those demands. Liberty, in its normative sense, depends upon the same.

While dialectic identifies fundamental differences on moral, intellectual and religious questions, it is the fifth functional specialty that reveals in detail where a specialist

---

[470] Method in Theology, 253.

[471] Current practice often identifies philosophy with the construction of rational arguments. Despite the limits of this model, first criticized in Plato's Gorgias, it continues to control the imaginations of many philosophers. In the background may linger the conceptualist ideal of an axiomatic system allowing for a rigorous deduction of conclusions from a limited set of first principles. Here is an instance of a conflict between basic positions regarding understanding and so suitable material for the work of dialecticians.

stands on basic issues. Dialecticians take stands on basic issues, but foundation specialists focus on selecting and evaluating such stands as deficient and in need of improvement or as instances of advances in understanding basic issues. It corresponds, then, to the operation of deciding. Indeed, taking such an explicit stand can be an act of normative liberty since the decision may be an adequate response to the demand of the principle of completion for affirming as true and good what one currently understands to be so. Revisions will be possible since expanding horizons and developments in understanding are indefinite possibilities.[472]

But this openness to revisions in understanding and worldviews raises a question about what foundational specialists hope to achieve. Are they taking stands that are only personal beliefs? Are their commitments no more than individual preferences? If so, can they hope to advocate more than stances reflecting their own variable cultural and historical conditions?[473] To these puzzles, a first response is to recall that what is "foundational" is not a set of first

---

[472] Lonergan lists thirty-one types of differentiated consciousness. (Method in Theology, 272.) The number of possible combinations is an indication of the scope of potential development and of the need for some intellectual humility in what we claim to know.

[473] Again, there is no substitute for the subject-at-liberty who is responsive to the demands of the operators. Some may insist that there must be a criterion or measure of ordered liberty and, indeed, of truth independent of concrete subjects. Proposed candidates have ranged from principles of pure reason to primitive sense data. The earlier claims about orientation and displacement were subversive of such proposals. Ordered liberty is the result of responses to the demands of the operators. Objectively justified truth-claims and moral judgments are as well. Note that we are setting a high standard here. The type of subjectivity that exhibits ordered liberty and is the measure of objectivity appears in those who consistently cooperate with their own inner norms. In these claims, at least, are two instances of taking a stand.

principles, propositions or arguments but a structured pattern of operations responsive to normative demands. It is in this sense that foundation specialists can understand their work as having a transcultural basis. Of course, any formulations about their work will reflect linguistic and cultural variables and so not be transcultural. All the same, what the formulations about the operations and imperatives refer to is an understanding of the basic conditions for producing, preserving and developing any culture.[474] In this sense, functional specialists may hope to achieve something of validity for more than their own times and places.[475]

The sixth functional specialty is policies. Its materials come from tradition (e.g. the standard model of science at a given time) and from the reflections of contemporary scholars and scientists on the latest developments in their fields. New research, new interpretations, new histories will generate oppositions that dialectic will order and foundations will criticize. Thus, the materials for policies are fluid.

The aim of policy is to unify both the traditional insights and the latest discoveries on some issue that previous specialties have assembled and criticized. Unifying the results

---

[474] Ibid. 282. A more succinct version of the argument here is that, while formulations or expressions of meaning are subject to correction and development, the structured operations and their imperatives are the conditions for the possibility of any correction or development.

[475] Providing examples of transculturally valid positions that are open to variations in formulation and to diversity in locales and ages is not an insurmountable challenge. For instance, the normative notion of liberty in this text is open to a variety of different formulations. Its reference to "antecedent integrations" acknowledges the sociohistorical (H_2) and biographical (H_1) variables that shape the "contexts" for liberty-in-act. Still, the claim is that the demands of the principles of assimilation and completion are parts of the structured operations of intentionality that are the preconditions for all culture-building, including any theories of liberty.

will require reconciling differences. A first step is identifying the differences, and a second is selecting from among them whatever the specialists judge to be correct. As we saw, dialectic and foundations carry out both tasks. Dialectic assembles and classifies different stances on an issue (those of predecessors and those of contemporaries), and foundations distinguishes those that are true, those in need of further development, those at odds with fundamental positions. Policies, then, will employ both the assembled and distinguished differences to understand and to formulate what one is justified in asserting as true or probably true.

The formulations will reflect the linguistic and cultural variables among their authors. They will reveal the presence or absence of differentiations of consciousness and of various displacements in those authors. As well, ongoing research on an issue may provide new materials for consideration. For all these reasons, specialists in policies expect their understanding to be open to revision but also to be currently the "best available opinion."[476] Their expectation is legitimate. Descriptively the tension between tradition and new discoveries is one result of the dynamic and historical exchanges among the functional specialties. In explanatory terms, the demand of the principle of assimilation is for integrating new materials with accepted views, but the demand of the principle of completion is sometimes for more than simply adding refinements to traditional models and pouring new wine into old wineskins. Sometimes radical departures occur not just in individuals but also in fields. In those cases, policies will be the specialty aiming to produce new syntheses.

Examples may help pin down these generalities. The sixth functional specialty could take up the question of monetary payments to those who volunteer to give their non-essential organs to transplant recipients. The previous

---

[476] Lonergan described variations in the formulations of opinions under the heading of the "Ongoing Discovery of Mind." Method in Theology, 305-312.

specialties would supply the materials, and the further question would be if this shift in public policy was justifiable. The complexity of the issue quickly appears since traditional stances are at odds with more recent stances embracing a market mentality that endorses "freedom of choice" for both parties to any organ exchange. Reconciling traditional beliefs and such laissez-faire views or altering one in favor of the other would be an easy case of advancing no more than a best available opinion.[477]

Further examples could include an essay that applied recent findings in psychology and intentionality theory to traditional views of the motives "behind" economic decisions. A traditional model of "rational agency" may then seem quite incomplete and in need of further development. Similarly, what generations accepted as political realism may be subject to doubt if empirical evidence indicates that sometimes personal relations, orientations and displacements have modified institutional practices without violence or the threat of violence.

The seventh functional specialty is planning. It presupposes the materials of the earlier specialties and explores their implications for current and future practices. Consider how this might occur in regard to educational theories and their applications. Educational advances are possible because of research on past and current practices in the schools, interpretation of their results, reports on what

---

[477] For a close study of traditional and more recent stances on this issue, see Mark J. Cherry, Kidney for Sale by Owner: Human Organs, Transplantation, and the Market (Washington: D.C.: Georgetown University Press, 2005). While the author takes a policy stand in favor of a regulated market with monetary payments to donors, he does not pursue further questions about specific safeguards and implementation. Appropriately these hard questions belong to the specialties of planning and applications. It is worth noting that implementing a general policy position that is defensible "in principle" may be blocked because of practical difficulties in preventing serious and widespread abuses.

appear to be promising innovations, dialectical assembling of competing views and diagnosing of their origins, decisions on what in fact are best practices and judgments about what general lessons can be extracted from these practices to serve as guidelines for future practice. While it is the task of the next functional specialty, applications, to reflect on ways of implementing these guidelines in varying locales, planning formulates the general guidelines as materials for such reflection.[478] That is, acquiring and formulating a general understanding of best practices would be the primary task of planning specialists.

Proposing general guidelines will give rise not only to the contrast between certainty and probability but also to the contrast between logical proof and displacements. Argumentation can be logically rigorous within a theoretical system having explicitly formulated terms, correlations among them and secondary inferences from those terms and correlations. However, the formulations of systems are not independent of the orientations of theoreticians, and their orientations vary with the presence or absence of displacements. But a displacement "is never the logical consequence of one's previous position but, on the contrary, [is] a radical revision of that position."[479] So, for example, discovering the limits of nominal understanding and appreciating the "turn to the Idea" (*Wendung zur Idee*) in further why-questions can completely alter a view of educational practice as the transmission and testing of information and skills.

To one unfamiliar with such altered views, guidelines recommending that all students learn about the distinct horizon of theory will seem puzzling. Their initial judgments

---

[478] Guidelines as generalities require mediating insights into local conditions before use. The diagnosis problem as it occurs in medical fields makes clear the need for such mediating insights between the generalities of medical training and the symptoms of specific patients.

[479] Method in Theology, 338.

may be that the recommendations are impractical, elitist or at least not what the job market will demand of future graduates. This puzzlement over what such guidelines might mean is one of the challenges for specialists in planning. Most people recognize that contemporary educational practices need improvement. The problems of declining test scores and of high dropout and teacher-turnover rates are too apparent to allow most to think all is well.

What frequently occurs is that planning specialists generate different guidelines, some of which are incompatible with others. The response to this outcome is a return to dialectic: identify the different guidelines, classify them according to their origins, diagnose those arising from different horizons and opposed positions. From there the process continues by selecting guidelines compatible with one's foundations and by explicitly formulating one's judgments about which guidelines represent adequately developed horizons and basic positions and which ones do not.[480]

What does this built-in recycling of general recommendations accomplish? One should expect no more than what any science tries to achieve, namely, an incomplete, revisable understanding that is currently the best available understanding of some issue. Plans and recommendations of this quality are the materials for the next functional specialty.

Many will find innovative proposals baffling and just adding to the confusing multiplicity of recommendations already available. They will have what-questions in abundance: What do these guidelines mean? What results will they have? Which of them will fit our local conditions? Such questions pose the central challenge to the eighth functional specialty. Meeting the challenge will be a matter of answering the relevant what-questions about what can be done. Since the answer to one question may give rise to further questions, the work of application specialists is ongoing.

---

[480] Ibid. 347.

Specialists in applications labor both to communicate the achievements of the preceding specialties back to those distinct but interdependent fields and to adapt the guidelines they receive from planning to local conditions. In both labors the eighth functional specialty is concerned with data. First, it returns refined data to the other specialties for a renewal of their operations; second, in reflecting on local conditions, implementing detailed plans and monitoring their consequences, it is generating new data, a new flow of findings, for research.

This second function "completes" the cyclic operations of the specialties much as acting on a decision completes an inquiry that began with attention to some problem one wanted to solve. Since predicted con-sequences and actual outcomes often diverge, attention to and collection of the data flowing from implemented plans renew the cycle by supplying new data for research. Pilot studies of educational reforms and attention to their results in varying locales are examples of the eighth specialty. A further example would be implementing a program of payments for organ donors and tracking the effectiveness of the built-in safeguards against abuses in the program. In either case a new cycle of inquiries can begin with different specialists attending to empirical results, interpreting their significance, assessing them in relation to alternatives as promising developments or disappointments and then deciding which reforms or experiments yielded results compatible with foundational positions.

What may come of this ordered series of investigations? In completing and renewing the cycle among the specialties, applications contributes to the emergence of common understanding, shared judgments and common purposes. Insofar as functional specialists understand and accept the worth of their division of labor, they will be increasing the odds of reaching common understandings and judgments. But such shared meanings are the stuff of which communities are made.

Part of the fantasy of functional specialization is that institutional practices in academia and at research centers could become increasingly communal, collaborative enterprises as opposed to individual research projects. Imagine a group of specialists understanding their distinct aims, committed to explanatory understanding in their own fields, convinced that functional collaboration is the best use of their diverse talents, believing that such collaborative efforts are a way of making history better.[481]

What does it mean to speak of "making history better"? We can begin by describing history as the accumulation of meanings which intentional acts, with all their types of determinants, produce. A first order of reflection on the acts and their products occurs in the spontaneous recalling of a tribe's history by its elders and the telling of the tale to the next generation. A second order of reflection emerges later as historians take on the tasks of separating fact from fiction and producing critical accounts of the past.[482] A third order of reflection appears when thinkers focus on the second-order works in an effort to understand and to evaluate what their authors were doing and what objectives they were pursuing.[483]

---

[481] There is, of course, a further set of difficult tasks, namely, persuading others outside the circle of functional specialists to apply their explanatory findings to public practice. Lonergan noted the difficulties: "There is the far more arduous task (1) of effecting an advance in scientific knowledge, (2) of persuading eminent and influential people to consider the advance both thoroughly and fairly, and (3) of having them convince practical policy makers and planners both that the advance exists and that it implies such and such revisions of current policies and planning with such and such effects." Ibid. 366-367.

[482] The earlier distinctions among basic, special and general historiographical projects would be examples of second-order reflections.

[483] Speculative philosophies of history (e.g. Hegel) seem to be a mixture of both second and third-order reflections. Insofar as they

What if we think of functional specialization as both a product and an ongoing exercise of third-order reflection on history? That is, as a series of interdependent functions, the eight specialties form a methodological scheme of recurrence organizing third-order reflection in a more efficient way. The first four specialties are deliberate attempts to retrieve and to pass along what was best in the past; the next four deliberately use what they receive to make history better.[484] So the foundations specialists expect to learn from dialecticians what some of the best readings of the past are. From among those categorized and evaluated answers, the former go on to choose answers compatible with their basic positions. Drawing on the affirmed answers formulated as general policies, planning specialists can proceed to construct a genetic sequence of answers or views on how to improve history. Such a genetic sequencing of views would be a hierarchical ordering of previous answers. Just as foundation specialists take stands on basic questions about knowledge, morality and spirituality, so planning specialists take stands on what views are most progressive.[485]

Just how remote, even fantastical, is all this? To be more concrete, suppose a local improvement of history has to do with teaching practices. Past decisions <u>about</u> how and what to teach will be the object of second-order reflections as scholars ask questions <u>about</u> what earlier educators understood and attempted. Imagine that further questions

---

are methodologically naïve or unreflective about their own methods and those of their predecessors, speculative systems that claim to be critical works would belong to the special or general types of historiography.

[484] "The challenge of history is…progressively to restrict the realm of chance or fate or destiny and progressively to enlarge the realm of conscious grasp and deliberate choice." <u>Insight</u>, 253.

[485] Note that, while functional specialization is not a hierarchical ordering of the specialties, within the specialties themselves there will be rankings of data, interpretations, developments, positions, guidelines, options and ends.

arise <u>about</u> how scholars have gone about understanding and evaluating what earlier educators have understood and decided about educational practices.[486] Answers to these questions will require the assembling of materials, their interpretation, a gathering and classifying of the different interpretations and distinguishing between failed and successful experiments. But there are further objectives such as making decisions about best practices, formulating general guidelines about how contemporary educators should proceed, fantasizing about how to adapt these guidelines to local conditions, actually implementing some plan and monitoring what comes of it.

This concrete example may be helpful but deceptively simple. Recall that the ideal of a comprehensive viewpoint is a push toward operating in every specialty within an explanatory horizon. What might be the result of applying this ideal to the study of ordered liberty? Should we expect different results if the study were along the lines of functional specialization?

III Future Studies of Liberty

The Introduction contained a promise that this study of liberty would end with a look forward. What follows is a sketch of how future studies of liberty might proceed if functional specialization finds a wider audience in the academy. There are three purposes for this sketch: (1) detecting the "muddled" efforts of this present study of liberty that proceeded without a careful division of labor, (2) indicating how such a deliberate division of labor could avoid some of the detected deficiencies, (3) suggesting a series of future projects that could go forward efficiently if collaboration among distinct specialties occurs. The sketch, then, is both diagnostic and prescriptive. The general diagnosis is that current scholarly practices are far behind what often takes place in the natural sciences; the

---

[486] The three distinct "abouts" here refer to earlier remarks in Chapter Two, Part IV.

general prescription is that third-order reflections on those current practices yield insights that functional specialization formulates.

Chapter One exemplified the first two functional specialties. There was an incomplete survey of the recent literature of the neuroscience of attention and a limited effort to interpret findings relevant to the central question of what an explanatory account of acts of attending might be. Clearly further research is possible since the literature is ever expanding. The expanding range of research data will result in more work for interpreters, especially if they are committed to a comprehensive view.

What were some of the deficiencies and omissions in Chapter One? The focus on acts of attending was deliberate since they are the most basic type of intentional acts, and the emphasis on neuroscience was defensible since that broad field explores basic conditions for the occurrence of intentional acts. Since the hypothesis has been that liberty extends "all the way down" and is not a property solely of acts of deciding, this study should have gone on to survey the literature on the neuroscience of other acts, e.g. imagining, abstracting, questioning, guessing, judging, deciding. Admittedly the literature on these types of acts is less extensive than on acts of attending.[487] Even so the labor of surveying what is available is beyond capacity of a single researcher.[488]

---

[487] Chapter One noted a line of research worth pursuing. The question was what we mean by acts of inference. The electrochemical roots of expectations are in associated groupings of neurons. When some part of the grouping "fires," the conscious but prereflective response is to anticipate the whole. Can "training" lead to higher-level control over such responses? Can we deliberately modify expectations about how to make inferences? How is this top-down control possible?

[488] The literature on the neurochemistry of hearing is relevant to a comprehensive understanding of acts of attention. The same is true of the neurochemistry of taste and smell. As soon as one expands the literature survey to further acts such as those of imagining and

Collaboration among research specialists is already both a feature of neuroscientific practice and evidence of the practical necessity for a division of labor and of its benefits. Can scholars in other disciplines justify ignoring the necessity and the benefits of such a division of labor?

Assuming that neuroscientific research will generate further results on these other types of intentional acts, we can expect the labor of interpreters to intensify. Assuredly there will be reductionistic interpretations alongside of others that accept "top-down" formation of lower-order materials.[489] Specialists in history can take note of these differences and report the latest findings. It will be up to the dialecticians to begin the critical work of sorting out the conflicting accounts by identifying the sources of their differences.

Again, the ideal is that the various specialists will increasingly operate in explanatory contexts. The central puzzle of Chapter One, and indeed for the next generation of neuroscientists, requires this shift in horizons. The "turn" to explaining "top-down" direction of lower-order processes is the challenge. Descriptive examples are plentiful: deliberately ignoring a ringing phone, intervening medically in brain disorders, practicing meditation techniques to control stress, distracting oneself from painful memories. How do we move beyond descriptive examples of conscious acts affecting neurochemical and biological processes? Neuroscientists talk about feedback processes, selectivity in attention, training as

---

abstracting, the dimensions of the task are clearly beyond the reach of a single researcher. Then there is the further project of organizing all these diverse findings in relation to one another in a more comprehensive theory of intentional acts.

[489] The prevalence of reductionistic accounts will not soon wane. Consider how deeply entrenched information theory is in talk of brain functions and intentional acts. The metaphors of messages flowing along neural pathways and decoding centers that receive and transmit information are widespread. However, do we have a better language that respects the differences among organic, psychological and intellectual functions?

building upon and modifying automatic responses. More importantly, their performance in studying acts of attention is affecting in themselves the very neurobiological processes they are investigating. The "turn" can become an explicit focus of research by asking how their "conditioned acts" of attending to the data of attention not only lead to an understanding (integration) of those data but also determine what neurobiological processes are occurring as they attend to the data. Yet how are we to talk explanatorily about this top-down conditioning of lower-order conditions?

The language of emergence and supervenience made a brief appearance in Chapter One as a way of introducing the notion of schemes of recurrence.[490] The latter formulates an understanding of how initial conditions for the emergence of some integrated pattern of operations may change, but the pattern, if sufficiently flexible, may adapt to new conditions and so survive. There was the further question of how higher-order schemes emerge from lower-order ones. The relevant case was how psychological and intellectual schemes emerge from organic ones. There were two additional questions: (1) How does development from one ordered series of schemes to a new series occur without the latter being reducible to the former? (2) How do later series exercise control over more basic schemes that condition their emergence and survival? These questions outline a massive research project more anticipated than actually underway. Perhaps functional specialization will make its own practical contributions to the design and implementation of this project.

Chapter Two had its major questions: (1) What are the roles of emotions and images in prompting action? (2) Why are there relations of dependency among actions, images and emotions? Limited research produced examples of what a

---

[490] There is a missing step in this summary, namely, the commentary in Chapter One on systematic and non-systematic relations.

few major thinkers had written on these questions.[491] Interpretation of their remarks occurred within a descriptive horizon. The task, then, was to shift the questions and answers into an explanatory context.

Plato's cave allegory and the tension between sensibility and understanding provided a provisional framework for exploring reciprocal conditioning among emotions, images and actions. The introduction of the category "demand" was the crucial step in identifying basic terms and in beginning to correlate them. Biogenetic and psychic demands are sources of emotional attachments to images that can evoke actions, but, in turn, pragmatic demands can lead to actions deliberately manipulating affect-laden images to evoke or to block emotions. Commercial advertising provides descriptive examples of the latter.

These examples, along with experiences of suppressing yawns or signs of nervousness, were evidence for common-sense beliefs about a human capacity to control both emotions and the responses they tend to evoke. The question, however, remained of how to explain this reverse conditioning. Neural and organic processes are determinant conditions for feelings linked to images and for the responses (e.g. actions) those images evoke. To reverse the order of conditioning, we made use of Carter's survey of findings about interactivity between the immune system and the nervous system. Mental states and acts have their neurochemical and organic antecedents; however, those states and acts (e.g. depression and laughter) also bring about chemical and organic changes. Carter posited that interactivity among systems was a way to understand how mental acts could alter their own lower-order conditions.[492]

---

[491] A further clue to the necessity of collaboration among researchers appeared in the puzzle about a "fair sample" of representative views on these questions.

[492] The preceding examples and evidence had implications for later remarks on how a demand for comprehensive understanding could trump competing demands. They were also relevant to the later

The shift to talking about action in an explanatory context provisionally made use of the notion of interactive systems.[493] If the medievals understood and spoke of human action as *et motus et movens*, we might today speak of "both receiving and doing." Actions respond to demands and affect-laden images; they also precipitate new demands, assign emotional "weight" to new images and, by doing so, condition ("move") future responses to demands and images.[494] This understanding of action formed the transition to the dialectical perspective of Chapter Three and came close to being the first approximation of the meaning of liberty as a capacity to order lower-level conditions.

These shifts in language and perspective left many relevant questions about the four basic categories and their relations without answers. For example, the broad, stipulated meaning of "image"[495] in this text includes the role of language in meeting demands, evoking emotions and prompting actions. Does language require separate treatment? If so, further questions about aesthetic experiences, the demands they respond to, the sources of artistic inspiration, the release (liberation) from practical living that art and play provide – all these would prove relevant to expanding our understanding of the four categories. Clearly the work would be entering a new field. Again, the need for a division of labor is apparent.

In puzzling out an explanatory meaning for creative understanding, Chapter Three touched on aesthetics. It also took note of the ambiguity of the fantasies that modern depth

---

claim that personal relations could effectively change prior orientations.

[493] I say "provisionally" because a subsequent use of "dialectic" proved more adequate in talking about the relations among demands, emotions, images and actions.

[494] Commercial advertizing and political propaganda supply abundant evidence for both the receiving and the doing here.

[495] The stipulated use was of images as "an indeterminate field of possible objects of intentional acts potentially evocative of emotional responses."

psychology explores. Both fields presumably have much to offer in exploring creative understanding and its products. Again, the massive research and interpretations of both fields are relevant to investigating creative understanding; yet familiarity with all these materials is also beyond the competence of any single individual.

A minimal exercise in dialectic showed up in the critique of the language of "mechanisms" in understanding acts of deliberating and deciding. "Historicity" was the preferred category in talking about orientations or assimilated meanings guiding those acts. The larger issue was how it was possible to criticize prior orientations. The adopted strategy for answering this question was attention-to-performance. That is, given multiple theories of intelligence, we could focus attention on our own performance as a source of evidence for or against the competing views. Talk in later chapters about the horizon of interiority suggested how one might be able to sort through a history of the competing views. Describing intentional acts, differentiating them in terms of question types and suggesting that the dynamic relations among them form a process "moving toward completion" presuppose attention to one's own performance.

Chapter Three also took the conventional route of citing what already was commonplace in theories of perception, namely, the principle of supplementation. In part, this was to support the shift from the interactivity model of relations among "systems" to talk of later operations "completing" prior ones. Other purposes were to introduce a linguistic alternative to "volitional control" and to anticipate objections to talk of "executive acts" arising from puzzles about who or what was the "executive." The basic puzzle was how to understand interacting systems as a unified process. The old "binding problem" in regard to object recognition has its correlate in this puzzle about the unity of intentional operations. While complex problems (e.g. the meaning of "self" and the unity of consciousness) lurk behind these questions, the hypothesis was that the principles of assimilation and completion formulate the intelligibility of intentional operations as a dynamic and structured whole.

The language of operators and integrators specified how the principles of assimilation and completion are mediated by distinct types of operations that express demands for their proper objectives. Questions mediate between operators and integrators in the sense that they express the demands and anticipate the responses or answers that will meet the demands. Taking into account the conditioning of operations by prior integrations, we posited the principle of assimilation with its demand for assimilating new answers and practices to prior ones. The language of dialectic appeared as suitable for expressing this understanding of dynamic processes reflecting related but opposed demands for development and stability.

This hypothesis, with its basic terms and correlations, is "material" for the specialty of history. Is it a "going forward" in the sense of an advance in how we understand and speak about mental acts, their internal relations and relations to sociohistorical conditions? What the historian concludes becomes material for the dialectician. There will be opposed positions. The implications of this hypothesis for an understanding of liberty will be where some obvious conflicts appear. For example, the notion of liberty at the end of the chapter is dialectical, but other views assume one must choose between determinism and indeterminism in understanding liberty. Some of these views reflect confinement to picture-thinking and so ignore further why-questions that require answers in terms of intelligible patterns among related operations and principles that explain their ordering.

A number of claims near the end of Chapter Three invite foundation specialists to take explicit stands. First, do they hold that this universe contains non-systematic relations? If they affirm that it does, then their stand is compatible with the possibility of high-order systems changing variables in lower-order processes. Second, have they noticed that questions mediate between images and insights so that what is imaginable and what is intelligible are distinct? Again, an affirmative answer means they are more likely to assent to the claim that higher cognitive integrations emerge from simpler patterns through mediating acts of intentionality. Finally, are they acquainted with the differences between the intellectual operator and the critical operator in terms of their distinct demands and objects? Such familiarity will make it easier to understand how new questions could have as much claim as any prior integrations to becoming determinants of new insights, plans and actions. In other words, linguistic, cultural and historical integrations are not the sole determinants of what a person will always say, believe and do.

Counterpositions may be apparent when responses to the preceding questions are negative. A universe without non-systematic relations leaves lower-order conditions in charge of any systems dependent on them. A picture world contains only imaginable entities and events, and so talk of principles of completion and assimilation will seem no more than abstract speculation. Even if one is familiar with acts of understanding as synthetic, unfamiliarity with the distinct demands and objects of the critical operator may lead to the conclusion that intellectual constructs are all we can really know. Such contrasts dialecticians will formulate, and foundation specialists will explicitly evaluate.

The first three chapters drew upon research in neuroscience, psychology and intentionality theory. Chapter Four relied on sociology to expand the range of determinants of liberty-in-act. Given all the subspecialties in each field, no one is competent in any one, not to mention all four, of these fields. However, pursuing an adequate understanding of liberty cannot dispense with any one of the fields and its findings. Once more the need for collaboration and division of labor presses for changes in scholarly practice.

The practice in this study becomes even more questionable when, in addition to the four mentioned fields, it attempts to apply the developed notion of liberty to the fields of economics and political theory. The claim in Chapter Four is that the point of intersection for both sets of fields is in the relations between institutions and intentional acts. Thus, a general goal was to link social schemes of recurrence with patterns from fields that earlier chapters had reviewed. The central question was how socialization processes made group practices and beliefs (i.e. social integrations) part of the "internalized environments" of new generations. The language of dialectical relations was useful in understanding the four possible relations between liberty-as-capacity and institutions. An explanatory account of decision-making in Part II anticipated how institutions could both order liberty and be ordered by it.

Two conclusions from that account are indirect criticisms of alternative views. First, in regard to the fact-value distinction and the debates over the naturalistic fallacy, a performative argument concluded that the demands of the operators are normative in both senses of the word "normativity." The second conclusion was that distinguishing between moral and non-moral decisions depended on what types of considerations were relevant to the prospective judgments that precede either type of decision.

The literature on the naturalistic fallacy is immense, and the position in Part II appears with no prior review of the relevant materials that the first four functional specialties could supply on this question. Similarly, the position on the basis for distinguishing between moral and non-moral choices appeared without a prior summary of the less extensive literature on that issue. Neither stance, then, is more than an isolated hypothesis awaiting further testing. In both cases different views will supply dialecticians with more materials for their work. The same will be true regarding the understanding of "virtue" as a scheme of recurrence. These are three issues that could be the focus of three more books.

One purpose of this text has been to provide a new vocabulary to replace terms indebted to faculty psychology and an eighteenth-century worldview. Whether talk of schemes of recurrence and a dialectic among competing demands will replace talk of free will, mechanisms in the brain or the newer computer metaphors remains an open question.

A minimal hope is that future discussions of liberty will go forward with some understanding that among the determinants of human acts are the inner demands of intentional operators.

Chapter Four located those demands in relation to social determinants, many of which occur in ongoing schemes of cooperation, i.e. institutions. Such social realities place demands on the capacities of persons for various operations, including the development of new skills. Maintaining such schemes requires that persons are competent in their roles and repeatedly decide to fill them. Among the reasons for deciding to cooperate are the personal relations that institutional orders can foster and sustain. Feelings of loyalty to an institution, its personnel and customers, can survive personal disappointments and even prompt sacrifices of time, energy and self-interest to sustain a common enterprise.

The preceding descriptive passage is at odds with a descriptive psychology of "rational agency" that assumes persons act only out of self-interest. References to "terminal goods," to judgments that override concerns for "particular goods" or to "displacements" will be remote from the horizon of this psychology. The contrast will provide work for the dialecticians. The position here is that a basic insight (what is good for oneself is not necessarily what is good for others) can begin to disrupt any initial focus on particular goods and personal advantage. Other disruptions can arise from numerous sources, e.g. personal tragedies, political crises, encounters with charismatic figures challenging conventional beliefs. Chapter Four focused on how personal relations could redirect liberty-as-capacity toward new orientations, even to the point of abandoning prior integrations of meaning.[496]

Differentiations of consciousness are examples of disruptions of prior integrations of meaning. The shift from a common-sense concern for practical living to the intellectual

---

[496] For example, is the maxim attributed to Stephen Decatur, "My country right or wrong, my country" a final position for everyone?

pattern of experience with its further why-questions is one differentiation. The intellectual resources of the latter (e.g. correlations among dopamine releases and neural activities in different brain locales) will be remote from practical living. The text posited different ordering principles for both modes of thinking and speaking: "Be practical" and "Be comprehensive." This view will be at odds with the stance of ordinary language analysis as the primary function of philosophy. Ordinary language belongs to the horizon of common sense, but a more comprehensive philosophy will include the demands of theory for technical terms, their correlations and an understanding of things in their relations among themselves. Again, different views will supply materials for dialecticians and invite foundation specialists to make their own stances explicit.

Other positions in Chapter Four may produce the same results. One claim was that morally defective judgments and decisions routinely occur within institutional settings and still produce a good of order. A flow of particular goods to some and a flow of avoidable and unjustifiable harms to others may still be a good of order. All that is required is that some people recurrently receive benefits. This position presupposes that any good of order is subject to further evaluation. Controversy arises when someone cites either moral resignation ("That's just how people treat one another") or, on a broader scale, *Realpolitik* to excuse a significantly defective good of order. Either excuse provides an opportunity to detect and to classify opposed positions and orientations. To the "realists" their social critics are simply rivals for power, i.e. other players in the power game that is political life. Social critics may accept that the realists have a keen understanding of how to secure particular goods. What the critics may fault will be narrow perspectives on human capacities, oversights of the demands of the operators and failures to recognize how personal relations can disrupt flawed patterns of thinking and doing.

The dialectician can classify these opposing views as originating in different assumptions about human capacities. How does one go on to evaluate such assumptions?

Historical evidence of egoistic orientations and of departures from them will not be decisive for the foundation specialists. History supplies abundant examples of opposed orientations. What will prove decisive are the orientations of the specialists whose own "contexts" will reflect their social formation dialectically related to their actual responses to the demands of the various operators.

The locating of the grounds for evaluating conflicting views in the historicity[497] of persons is, of course, a view at odds with other conclusions about the criteria for evaluating differences. As such it becomes material for the fourth and fifth specialties.

The final remarks in Part V sketched a further set of opposed views. In a minimal way the critique of anarchism represented an exercise in identifying differences, tracing some of them to basic assumptions about liberty, persons and social relations and, then, formulating the fundamental oppositions. The next step was for this author to take a stand on these views and to give explicit reasons for that stand.

Chapter Five focused on the implications of the normative notion of liberty for economic practices. Two opposed views appeared at the beginning. If a laissez-faire stance has its defects, the opposed endorsement of a command economy has others.[498] The question, then, was

---

[497] To quote Chapter Five on the meaning of "historicity" – "The capacity to respond is made determinate, becomes a concrete orientation, through actual operations that, interacting with prior sociohistorical integrations, establish the personal historicity of the person making decisions."

[498] The major flaws of the laissez-faire stance are its underdeveloped understanding of liberty and rationality (an understanding indebted to a seventeenth-century psychology of motivation) and its belief in a *fatum*, i.e. a benevolent but impersonal mechanism governing markets. The main defects in the opposed view are the assumptions that the economic policy-makers will adequately respond to the principle of completion (i.e. they will habitually cooperate with their

whether a third option, a fantasy about the "education of liberty," was worth considering. The fantasy is not a dream of human perfectibility. Its modest hope is that what health education and driver education routinely achieve in large populations might someday be true of a population's understanding and practice of economics. The thesis was that there was no effective substitute for the development of ordered liberty in large numbers of citizens. In their economic activities, this development requires a widespread understanding of how a market economy works and a widespread consent to act according to the norms (N_1) that understanding uncovers.

Someone may object that this fantasy is politically naïve. If different economic views reflect the competing interests of different social groups, we should expect these groups to generate ideologies defending their interests and practices. Their rival stories of legitimacy will be as incompatible as their diverging interests. To think that anyone could arrive at an unbiased understanding and evaluation of economic processes and practices is to overlook the prereflective origins of views in economics.

The merit of this objection is its recognition of the prereflective origins of understanding. The determinants of intentional acts are multiple and often unrecognized. They influence the questions we ask and what considerations we include in our prospective judgments. Still, the objection proceeds from a non-dialectical understanding of intentional acts and so fails to envision the occurrence of displacements. But radical shifts from prior cultural integrations do occur, and one element in an explanation of those displacements has been the demand of the principle of completion. The fantasy is that large populations can cooperate with this demand and can experience the various displacements. To rule out this possibility is to despair of progress. But, then, why expect free markets to survive?

---

own inner demands) and that a good social order does not require a similar pattern of response among most of its citizens.

The case study at the end of the chapter was a minimal exercise in the fourth functional specialty of dialectic. As a fragment of the much larger project of the "education of liberty," its aims were to expand the horizons of readers regarding "indirect relations" and to shift the debates about economic decisions and their consequences into an explanatory context. Regarding potential consumer responsibility for "externalities," the case study identified two opposed positions, i.e. contractarian and communitarian views.[499] It continued with an analysis of the three sources of different positions and suggested how the two opposed positions may originate in the presence or absence of a differentiation of consciousness.

A minimal exercise in that fourth specialty also occurred in the critique of realists. The implicit stance was that, as questions of deliberation precede questions for decision, so fantasizing about improved practices should precede judgments about how realistic an option is. Realists tend to privilege current patterns in thinking and acting and to dismiss options that depart too far from those patterns. While responsive to the demand of the principle of assimilation, this stance may not be an adequate response to the demand of the related but opposed principle. From a broadened perspective, history is the ongoing activity of making meaning, and the results to date are far from complete. If we assume our "best practices" are relatively primitive, then we might give more attention to imagining better ways of operating. Expanding the horizons of consumers and dividing the labor of scholars among the eight specialties are such imaginings.

---

[499] As a "minimal exercise" in dialectic, the study was not an exhaustive listing of positions or of complicated stances that mingle parts of opposing views. Debates about justice exhibit the latter when some participants argue that fairness in economic exchanges is determined solely by legal statute and contractual obligations. Still, they applaud communitarian ends as objectives that moral individuals should pursue privately or collectively but always with the proviso that they do so voluntarily.

Will they receive enough attention or be dismissed as unrealistic?

Chapter Six pursued the critique of realism in both economics and political theory. There was a short history of the language of "interests" and of how its use in talking about the ends of liberty was unsatisfactory. The challenge was to find a better way of talking about "ordered liberty" and of understanding why we esteem self-determination.

A task for the specialty of history would be to expand upon this short history. What else was occurring in the culture to favor this substitution of "interests" for more specific ends? Why was an orientation toward higher goods no longer one of the common *topoi* of political theory? What shifts in ontology accompanied the demise of a strong theory of virtues and talk of ultimate ends in living?

Some historians may produce a story of eroding consensus, political conflicts, a slow acceptance of cultural pluralism and the practical necessity for tolerance of differences. Predecessors believed an ontology of the "lowest common denominator" was the key to civil peace. The historians may note that this compromise requires an understanding of rational agency remote from the original meaning of reason as the defining characteristic of being human.[500]

The language of "interests" fits this truncated understanding of human capacities, but then it also makes the esteem for liberty as self-determination puzzling. The puzzle is perhaps unsolvable without a normative notion of liberty, but what is the measure of liberty-in-act? The slowly emerging thesis in this text has been that a normative understanding of liberty appeals to the immanent demands of intentional acts as the measure. The responses those demands evoke make determinate the capacities of persons for operating and cooperating and so make history what it is. But this is one view among many, thus providing materials that dialecticians can compare, classify according to their origins and

---

[500] Cf. Voegelin. "Reason: The Classical Experience."

discriminate among in terms of opposed horizons and positions. The last step both prepares materials for foundation specialists and begins to reveal the basic positions of the dialecticians.

In criticizing talk of "incommensurable worldviews" and "conceptual constructs" as somehow beyond the reach of the critical operator, this text has revealed some things about its author's positions. A rudimentary study within the horizon of interiority makes both conceptual analysis and ordinary language analysis suspect as the purpose of philosophy. A few insights into the dialectic between social integrations and the demand of the principle of completion make suspect any talk of culture, history, gender or language as "evil geniuses" manipulating our every thought. The fact of displacements and of how personal relations can prompt them convinces this author of his incomplete understanding of the ends of ordered liberty. Explaining the tension between liberty and order in terms of the dialectic of the principles of assimilation and completion offers some hope that we can learn more about those ends and actually cooperate with the inner demands that intend them.

The case study at the end of Chapter Six incorporated these suspicions and this hope. While its primary question was economic, namely, how to achieve a basic expansion, the case was about overcoming a series of obstacles to the education of liberty. A deeply rooted psychology of conspicuous consumption, an economic realism that assumes the profit motive is a criterion of good practice, a politics of envy that opportunists manipulate in their power games – these are a few of the obstacles.

What are the odds of large numbers of citizens understanding and consenting to act according to the rhythms of an economy? Will they save and invest during a surplus expansion or spend lavishly in the basic circuit? Will those experiencing inflationary pressures during a surplus expansion wait for the promised basic expansion that yields more egalitarian results or will they succumb to the politics of envy? Will those prospering during a surplus expansion fulfill the promise by completing the cycle with a basic expansion by "spending down their savings" or will they protect profit margins and stock prices by cutting the wage bill?

If current practices are the best we can do, then the realists will accurately predict the answers. They will not be without rationales for maintaining current patterns of thought and action. In fact, their primary rationale will likely appeal to liberty, i.e. free markets, allowing "rational agents" to assess their own risks and to pursue their own interests, are best able to produce greater beneficial results than under any other arrangement.

The dissent of this text has been in the name of a normative or ordered liberty that is more than the pursuit of enlightened self-interest. Even to speak of the education of liberty as a further enlightenment of enlightened self-interest is an incomplete phrasing of the challenge. As early as Chapter Two, the further issue was how to evoke desired actions by affect-laden images. Overcoming the obstacles to the education of liberty requires moral, intellectual and spiritual displacements that arguments alone cannot achieve. Plato's puzzle, then, reappears. What can move people to turn around and to leave their caves? In more prosaic terms, what can so unsettle a prevailing realism that persons will entertain fantasies about better ways of thinking and acting? This text has offered a few fantasies about new economic and scholarly practices. It may take a major economic crisis to provoke doubts about a prevailing economic realism. Perhaps the fantasy of this text about improvements in current scholarly practice will require a similar crisis of confidence in the relevance of the academy to contemporary problems and their solutions.

BIBLIOGRAPHY

A. BOOKS

Adam, G., I. Meszaros and E.I. Banyai. Advances in Physiological Sciences. Elmsford, NY: Pergamon Press, 1981.
Adams, Henry. The Education of Henry Adams. Boston: Houghton Mifflin, 1961.
-- Mont Saint Michel and Chartres. New York: Penguin Books, 1986.
Adler, Mortimer J. The Idea of Freedom. Garden City, N.Y.: Doubleday, 1958.
Aquinas, Thomas. Summa Theologiae. Blackfriars 1970.
Balota, A. and Elizabeth J. Marsh. (eds.) Cognitive Psychology: Key Readings. New York: Psychology Press, 2004.
Bennett, Maxwell and Daniel Dennett, Peter Hacker and John Searle. Neuroscience and Philosophy. New York: Columbia University Press, 2003.
Berger, Peter and Thomas Luckmann. The Social Construction of Reality. Garden City, N.Y.: Doubleday, 1967.
Berlin, Isaiah. Liberty. Oxford: Oxford University Press, 2002.
Bruner, Jerome. Actual Minds, Possible Worlds. Harvard University Press, 1986.
Carter, Rita. Mapping the Mind. Berkeley: University of California Press, 1998.
-- Exploring Consciousness. Berkeley: University of California Press, 2002.
Cherry, Mark J. Kidney for Sale by Owner: Human Organs, Transplantation, and the Market. Washington: D.C.: Georgetown University Press, 2005.
Cushman, R.E. Therapeia: Plato's Conception of Philosophy. Westport, CT: Greenwood Press, 1958.
Damasio, Antonio R. Descartes' Error: Emotion, Reason and the Human Brain. London: Picador, 1995.
-- The Feeling of What Happens. New York: Harcourt, Brace and Company, 1999.
Donagan, Alan. The Theory of Morality. Chicago: University of Chicago Press, 1977.
Engelhardt, H. Tristram. The Foundations of Christian Bioethics. Lisse: Taylor and Francis, 2000.
Farah, Martha J. Visual Agnosia, (2nd ed.) Cambridge: MIT Press, 2004.
Flanagan, Joseph. Quest for Self-Knowledge. Toronto: University of Toronto Press, 1997.
Friedman, Milton. Capitalism and Freedom. Chicago: University of Chicago Press, 1962.

Freud, Sigmund. Civilization and Its Discontents. New York: W.W. Norton, 1962.
Gardner, Howard. Frames of Mind. New York: Basic Books, 1983.
Girard, René. Violence and the Sacred. Baltimore: The Johns Hopkins University Press, 1989.
Goodman, Nelson. Ways of Worldmaking. Indianapolis: Hackett, 1978.
Hariman, Robert. (ed.) Prudence: Classical Virtue, Postmodern Practice. University Park: The Pennsylvania State University Press, 2003.
Hayek, Friedrich A. Law, Legislation and Liberty. Vol.2. Chicago: University of Chicago Press, 1976.
Healy, Alice F. (ed.) Experimental Cognitive Psychology and Its Applications. Washington, D.C.: American Psychological Association, 2005.
Hume, David. Essays, Literary, Moral and Political. London: Ward, Lock & Co., 1817.
Jung, Karl. Memories, Dreams, Reflections. New York: Vintage Books, 1989.
Krugman, Paul. The Return of Depression Economics. New York: W.W. Norton, 1999.
Lonergan, Bernard. Caring about Meaning. Pierrot Lambert et al. (eds.) Montreal: Thomas More Institute, 1982.
-- Collection. New York: Herder and Herder, 1967.
-- Grace and Freedom: Operative Grace in the Thought of St. Thomas Aquinas. Vol.1 in Collected Works. Toronto: University of Toronto Press, 2000.
-- Insight: A Study of Human Understanding. Vol.3 in Collected Works. Toronto: University of Toronto Press, 1992.
-- Macroeconomic Dynamics: An Essay in Circulation Analysis. Vol.15 in Collected Works. Toronto: University of Toronto Press, 1999.
-- Method in Theology. New York: Herder and Herder, 1972.
-- For a New Political Economy. Vol.21 in Collected Works. Toronto: University of Toronto Press, 1998.
-- Philosophical and Theological Papers: 1965-1980. Vol.17 in Collected Works. Toronto: University of Toronto Press, 2004.
-- A Second Collection. Philadelphia: The Westminster Press, 1974.
-- Understanding and Being. Vol.5 in Collected Works. Toronto: University of Toronto Press, 1990.
-- Verbum : Word and Idea in Aquinas. Vol.3 in Collected Works, Toronto: University of Toronto Press, 1997.
MacIntyre, Alasdair C. After Virtue: A Study in Moral Virtue. Notre Dame: University of Notre Dame Press, 1981.
-- Whose Justice? Which Rationality? Notre Dame: University of Notre Dame Press, 1988.
Mathews, William. Lonergan's Quest. Toronto: University of Toronto Press, 2005.

McDermott, F. E. (ed.) Self-Determination in Social Work. London: Routledge and Kegan Paul, 1975.

Milgram, Stanley. Obedience to Authority: An Experimental View. New York: Harper and Row, 1975.

Muller, Jerry Z. Adam Smith in His Time and Ours. New York: MacMillan, 1996.

Nozick, Robert. Anarchy, State, and Utopia. New York: Basic Books, 1974.

Posner, Michael I. (ed.) Cognitive Neuroscience of Attention. New York: Guilford Press, 2004.

Ramachandran, V.S. A Brief Tour of Human Consciousness. New York: Pl Press, 2004.

Ramachandran, V.S. and S. Blakeslee. Phantoms in the Brain. New York: William Morrow and Company, 1998.

Rilke, Rainer Maria. The Selected Poetry of Rainer Maria Rilke. Stephen Mitchell. Editor and translator. New York: Random House, 1982.

Rostow, Walt. How It All Began: Origins of the Modern Economy. New York: McGraw-Hill, 1975.

Sacks, Oliver. An Anthropologist on Mars. New York: Vintage Books, 1996.

-- Musicophilia: Tales of Music and the Brain. New York: Alfred A. Knopf, 2007.

Shue, Henry. Basic Rights: Subsistence, Affluence and U.S. Foreign Policy. Princeton: Princeton University Press, 1980.

Schumpeter, J. A. Essays of J. A. Schumpeter. Port Washington, N.Y.: Kennikat Press, 1969.

Shute, Michael. Lonergan's Discovery of Scientific Economics. Toronto: University of Toronto Press, 2010.

-- "'Let Us Be Practical!': The Beginnings of the Long Process to Functional Specialization in the Essay in Fundamental Sociology" John Dadosky, (ed.). Meaning and History in Systematic Theology (Milwaukee: Marquette University Press, 2009).

Shute, Michael and William Zanardi. Improving Moral Decision-Making. Boston: McGraw-Hill, 2006.

Thoreau, Henry David. Walden. New York: New AmericanLibrary, 1960.

Voegelin, Eric. Anamnesis. Columbia: University of Missouri Press, 1990.

-- The Ecumenic Age, Vol.4 in Order and History. Baton Rouge: Louisiana State University Press, 1980.

-- From Enlightenment to Revolution. Durham: Duke University Press, 1975.

-- Plato and Aristotle. Vol.3 in Order and History. Baton Rouge: Louisiana State University, 1983.

-- Published Essays: 1966-1985. Vol.12 in Collected Works. Baton Rouge: Louisiana State University Press, 1990.

White, Hayden. Metahistory: The Historical Imagination in Nineteenth-Century Europe. Baltimore: The Johns Hopkins University Press, 1973.

Wolff, Robert Paul. In Defense of Anarchism. New York: Harper and Row, 1970.
Zanardi, William and Michael Shute. Improving Moral Decision-Making. Boston: McGraw-Hill, 2006.

B. ARTICLES and BOOK CHAPTERS

Barrera, Albino. "Gaudium et Spes and Catholic Ethics in Post-Industrial Economics: Indirect Employers and Globalization." The Journal of Catholic Social Teaching. 3:2(2006).

Beane, Melinda and Richard Marrocco, "Holinergic and Noradrenergic Inputs to the Posterior Parietal Cortex Modulate the Components of Exogenous Attention" in Cognitive Neuroscience of Attention. Michael I. Posner, (ed.) New York: Guilford Press, 2004.

Byrne, Patrick. "Neuroscience, Consciousness, Freedom and Lonergan" (in manuscript).

Bundsen C. "A Theory of Visual Attention" in Psychological Review, Vol. 97 (1990).

Cohen, Jonathan D. et al. "A System-Level Perspective in Attention and Cognitive Control" in Cognitive Neuroscience of Attention. Michael I. Posner, (ed.) New York: Guilford Press, 2004.

Colombo, John. "Visual Attention in Infancy" in Cognitive Neuroscience of Attention. Michael I. Posner, (ed.) New York: Guilford Press, 2004.

Csibra, G. et al. "Gamma Oscillations and Object Processing in the Infant Brain" in Science, Vol. 290 (Nov. 24, 2000).

Daly, Herman E. "Feynman's Unanswered Question" in Philosophy and Public Policy Quarterly, Vol. 26 (winter/spring 2006).

Deth, Richard C. et al. "Attention-Related Signaling Activities of the D4 Dopamine Receptor" in Cognitive Neuroscience of Attention. Michael I. Posner, (ed.) New York: Guilford Press, 2004.

Fougnie, Daryl and René Marois, "Executive Load in Working Memory Induces Inattentional Blindness" in Visual Cognition, Vol. 14, No. 1 (June 2006).

Funtes, Luis J. "Inhibitory Processing in the Attentional Networks" in Cognitive Neuroscience of Attention. Michael I. Posner, (ed.) New York: Guilford Press, 2004.

Hedden, Trey and John D.E. Gabrieli. "The Ebb and Flow of Attention in the Human Brain" in Nature Neuroscience, Vol.9, No.7, July 2006.

Greene, J.D.W. "Apraxia, Agnosias and Higher Visual Function Abnormalities" in Journal of Neurology, Neurosurgery and Psychiatry, 76 (December 2005).

Gruber, Oliver and Thomas Goschke. "Executive Control Emerging from Dynamic Interactions between Brain Systems Mediating Language, Working Memory and Attentional Process" in Acta Psychologica Vol. 115 (2004).

Han, S. and J.S. Lerner and D. Keltner. "Feelings and Consumer Decision Making: The Appraisal-Tendency Framework" in Journal of Consumer Psychology, Vol. 17 (2007).

Herd, Seth A. et al. "Neural Mechanisms of Cognitive Control: An Integrative Model of Stroop Task Performance and fMRI Data" in Journal of Cognitive Neuroscience, Vol. 18, No.1 (2006).

Lawrence, Fred. "Editors' Introduction" in Lonergan, Macroeconomic Dynamics. Vol.15 in Collected Works. Toronto: University of Toronto Press, 1999.

Libet, Benjamin. "Timing of Cerebral Processes Relative to Concomitant Conscious Experience in Man" in Advances in Physiological Sciences, G. Adam, I. Meszaros and E.I. Banyai (eds.) Elmsford, NY: Pergamon Press, 1981.

Logan, Gordon D. "Attention, Automaticity, and Executive Control" in Experimental Cognitive Psychology and Its Applications. Alice F. Healy. (ed.) Washington, D.C.: American Psychological Association, 2005.

Lonergan, Bernard. "Finality, Love and Marriage" in Collection. New York: Herder and Herder, 1967.

-- "Insight Revisited" in A Second Collection. Philadelphia: The Westminster Press, 1974.

-- "The Human Good" in Philosophical and Theological Papers: 1965-1980. Vol.17 in Collected Works. Toronto: University of Toronto Press, 2004.

-- "Self-transcendence: Intellectual, Moral, Religious" in Philosophical and Theological Papers: 1965-1980. Vol.17 in Collected Works. Toronto: University of Toronto Press, 2004.

-- "What Are Judgments of Value?" in Philosophical and Theological Papers: 1965-1980. Vol.17 in Collected Works. Toronto: University of Toronto Press, 2004.

-- "Merging Horizons: System, Common Sense, Scholarship." In Philosophical and Theological Papers: 1965-1980. Vol.17 in Collected Works. Toronto: University of Toronto Press, 2004.

McShane, Philip. "Lonergan's Educational Philosophy" (unpublished essay).

Naccache, Lionel et al. "Effortless Control: Executive Attention and Conscious Feeling of Mental Effort are Dissociable" in Neuropsycholgia, Vol. 43, No. 9 (2005).

Nobre, Anna C. "Probing the Flexibility of Attentional Orienting in the Human Brain" in Cognitive Neuroscience of Attention, Michael I. Posner, (ed.) New York: Guilford Press, 2004.

Pollack, Seth D. and Stephanie Tolley-Schell, "Attention, Emotion, and the Development of Psychopathology" in Cognitive Neuroscience of Attention. Michael I. Posner, (ed.) New York: Guilford Press, 2004.

Posner, Michael I. "Progress in Attention Research" in <u>Cognitive Neuroscience</u> <u>of</u> <u>Attention</u>. Michael I. Posner, (ed.) New York: Guilford Press, 2004.

Posner, Michael and Synder. "Attention and Cognitive Control" (1975), reprinted in <u>Cognitive</u> <u>Psychology</u>: <u>Key</u> <u>Readings</u>. A. Balota and Elizabeth J. Marsh, (eds.) New York: Psychology Press, 2004.

Robertson, Ian H. "Examining Attentional Rehabilitation" in <u>Cognitive Neuroscience</u> <u>of</u> <u>Attention</u>. Michael I. Posner, (ed.) New York: Guilford Press, 2004.

Ruz, Maria. "Let the Brain Explain the Mind: the Case of Attention," in <u>Philosophical</u> <u>Psychology</u>, Vol.19, No.4 (August 2006).

Sen, Amartya. "Rational Fools: A Critique of the Behavioral Foundations of Economic Theory" in <u>Philosophy</u> <u>and</u> <u>Public</u> <u>Affairs</u>, 6(1977).

Spratling, M.W. and M. H. Johnson. "A Feedback Model of Visual Attention" in <u>Journal</u> <u>of</u> <u>Cognitive</u> <u>Neuroscience</u>, Vol.16 No.2 (2004).

Swanson, James M. et al. "Clinical and Cognitive Definitions of Attention Deficits in Children with Attention-Deficit/Hyperactivity Disorder" in <u>Cognitive</u> <u>Neuroscience</u> <u>of</u> <u>Attention</u>. Michael I. Posner, (ed.) New York: Guilford Press, 2004.

Zanardi, William J. "Consumer Responsibility from a Social Systems Perspective" in <u>International</u> <u>Journal</u> <u>of</u> <u>Applied</u> <u>Philosophy</u>, 8 (1990).

Index

A

abstraction, 22-25, 29-32, 34, 68, 95, 97-98, 144, 339
academy, 130, 356, 373
acceleration, 262, 275, 314-315
Adams, Henry, 65, 197, 280, 375, 377, 379
adaptations, 49, 82, 84, 86, 88, 97, 141, 207, 213, 318, 332, 342
ADHD, 9, 56
Adler, Mortimer, 8, 375
administering, 250
administrate, 253
adolescent, 166, 332-333
advertizing, 82, 85, 111, 309, 360-361
affective, 99, 119, 207, 210, 215, 217, 230, 246, 296, 298, 304, 310, 340
affectladen, 295, 360-361
agency, 106, 109, 253, 274, 320, 336, 350, 366, 371

Agnosia, 115, 375
agnosia, 115, 144, 146
amygdala, 26, 28-29, 80
analogy, 47, 125, 154, 159-161, 167, 190, 208-209, 245, 254, 328, 342
anamnesis, 4, 199, 278, 325
anarchism, 225, 368
apprehension, 26, 34, 78
approximation, 109, 134, 137-138, 140, 147, 152-153, 155, 179, 326, 361
apraxia, 146
Aquinas, Thomas, 22-23, 26, 30-31, 42, 78-79, 84, 89, 92, 185, 219, 330, 339, 375-376
Archelaus, 282
Aristotle, 11, 26, 42, 77-78, 83, 92, 112, 121, 139, 149, 306, 329-330, 377
arousal, 25, 30, 38-41, 61, 66, 68-69, 96-98, 109, 116-118, 230

Index

assimilation, 99, 113, 153-158, 169, 176, 179, 182, 185, 187, 192, 198-199, 205-207, 209, 212, 215, 218-219, 224, 229, 231-232, 236-238, 249, 251, 289, 295, 302, 327, 346, 348-349, 362-364, 370, 372
autonomy, 224-225
Averroes, 42
awareness, 18, 40, 103, 117, 136, 213-214, 290

B

Barrera, Albino, 256-260
benevolence, 250, 269, 283, 318-319
Berger, Peter, 172, 270
biochemistry, 8, 17, 21, 42, 60, 165
biology, 36, 99, 138
biophysics, 21, 42
breakdowns, 135, 228, 297, 305
breakthroughs, 181, 210, 305
Bruner, Jerome, 20, 26, 192, 336
bureaucracies, 205, 248-249, 253
businesses, 194, 247, 272, 274
Byrne, Patrick, 152, 234

C

capitalism, 217, 260, 308, 322
Cartesian, 11, 131
categories, 10-11, 17, 22-25, 30-32, 36, 38, 49, 60, 63, 66, 69, 92, 94, 96, 98-99, 108, 111, 114, 123, 157, 171, 175-177, 192, 200, 220, 227-229, 244, 289, 306, 325, 337, 361
charismatic, 201, 255, 296, 366
classicist, 164, 291
coercion, 285, 287, 292, 301
cognition, 40, 100
collaboration, 13, 203, 354, 356, 360, 364
commonsense, 16, 291-292
commonsensical, 60, 71, 204
communitarian, 278, 370
communities, 198, 240, 270, 353
competence, 190, 205, 240, 245, 288, 331, 362
competition, 39-40, 44-45, 51, 92, 101, 206, 209, 215, 286
completion, 30, 41, 54, 99, 113, 118, 145, 147-148, 153-159, 167-169, 175-176, 179, 182, 184, 187-188, 190, 192, 198-199, 203, 205-207, 212, 215-216, 218-219, 224-225, 229-232, 235-242, 244-246, 248-251, 253, 266, 270, 276, 283, 289-290, 295, 297, 302-303, 310, 327-328, 330, 334, 341, 344, 346-349, 362-364, 368-369, 372
conatus, 92, 149
concept, 22, 144, 225, 288, 293, 336

Index

concepts, 27, 75-76, 78, 144, 224-225, 291-293, 336, 343
conceptualism, 343
conceptualist, 144, 220, 225, 292, 309, 346
conscience, 266, 300
consciousness, 12, 17, 22-23, 34, 43, 95, 97, 113, 116, 122, 131-132, 135-136, 174, 187, 202, 264, 266, 269, 272, 276, 278, 335, 347, 349, 362, 366, 370
consensus, 287, 292, 300, 308, 371
contexts, 9-10, 126, 128, 265, 269, 271, 276-278, 293, 330, 341, 343-344, 348, 358, 368
contractarian, 269, 273, 370
correlations, 13, 15, 17, 22, 24, 31, 35, 55-56, 58, 60, 62-63, 66-67, 90, 94, 97, 110, 115, 129, 156, 163, 175, 179, 192, 210, 213, 233-234, 262, 264, 272, 293, 298, 304, 340, 351, 363, 367
Cotard Syndrome, 89
curiosity, 13, 30, 89, 93, 276, 304-305, 333, 336

D

Damascene, John, 79
Damasio, Antonio, 29, 43, 52, 81-82, 88, 92, 94-95, 97-102, 110, 115, 121, 130
deficits, 55, 97, 222, 259
definition, 19, 47, 94, 225

deliberation, 16, 121, 124, 140-141, 148, 152, 176, 180, 193, 217, 231, 235-236, 370
Dennett, Daniel, 8
departure, 56, 127, 157, 200, 210, 216, 219, 295, 346
departures, 56, 157, 161, 209, 212, 216, 218, 249, 291, 293-296, 298, 303, 328, 346, 349, 368
dependence, 8, 34-35, 141, 152, 155, 158, 174, 179, 225, 249
dependency, 47, 72, 74, 78, 82, 84-85, 88, 92-93, 110, 359
Descartes, Rene, 11, 81, 112, 128, 157
description, 5, 17, 62, 66, 109, 115, 134, 139, 142, 147, 150, 155, 168, 172, 184, 228, 262, 304, 308-309
determinants, 108, 112, 122, 131, 165, 167, 169, 172, 175, 179, 182, 185, 191, 205, 207, 217, 221, 234, 238, 244, 294-295, 297, 326, 328, 344, 354, 364, 366, 369
determinism, 7, 79, 164, 181, 325, 363
deviations, 125-126, 159, 173
diagnostician, 19, 61, 126
dialectic, 87, 105, 113, 123, 154-155, 158-159, 164, 172, 174, 179, 192, 199-201, 212, 229, 241, 267, 270, 277, 289, 295, 302, 306, 338, 340-342, 346, 348-349, 352, 361-363, 365, 370, 372
differentiations, 187, 202, 266, 269, 272, 277-278, 349
dilemma, 28, 219
discontinuities, 56, 212, 291

Index

disordered, 96, 172, 227, 276, 285, 310
displacement, 10, 135, 193, 198, 201, 205, 209, 211-212, 228-229, 244-246, 250, 267-268, 274, 277, 289-290, 292-293, 301, 310, 336, 347, 351
dispositions, 10, 12, 38, 47, 123, 126
Donagan, Alan, 219
dopamine, 18, 39, 41, 62, 107, 202, 367

E

economics, 4, 12, 171, 173, 206, 228-229, 253, 256, 278, 281, 303-304, 309, 311, 313, 317, 330-332, 364
economies, 5, 248-250, 255, 309, 312, 322
Eddington, Sir Arthur, 66-67, 264
emergence, 45, 56-57, 59-61, 91, 126, 159, 166, 174, 190, 194-196, 217, 229-230, 292, 311, 353, 359
Engelhardt, H. Tristram, 270
entrepreneurs, 247, 316-317, 320-321
epiphenomenal, 15, 62, 65, 292, 344
epistemology, 11, 92, 112, 162
equality, 132, 189, 247
equiprimordial, 174, 223-224
equity, 319, 321

ethics, 191, 205, 256, 330, 345
evil, 11, 101, 128, 131, 157, 168, 298, 372
explanation, 6, 22, 24, 36, 45, 53, 66, 83, 188, 192, 221, 225, 262, 286, 340, 369
externalities, 257, 262, 270, 272-273, 277-278, 370

F

faculty psychology, 7-8, 11, 42, 49, 79, 106, 113, 124, 147, 151, 176, 221, 295, 340, 365
faith, 5, 73, 75, 248-250, 252, 286, 307, 345
families, 198, 216, 299, 302
fantasies, 10, 88, 99, 110, 122, 134, 141, 147, 156-157, 167-168, 170, 176, 231, 250, 255, 295, 304, 332, 361, 373
fate, 73, 77, 217, 355
fatum, 248-249, 252, 283, 368
feedback, 15, 43-44, 46, 51, 54-56, 358
feedforward, 45-46, 54, 56
Feynman, Richard, 74-75, 83, 92
Flanagan, Joseph, 45, 60
fMRI, 24, 36, 54, 96
fn, 276
forbearance, 285, 294, 299, 302-303
formation, 22, 153, 174, 280, 282, 358, 368
foundationalist, 284, 343

Index

foundations, 253, 269-270, 337-338, 343, 346, 348-349, 352, 355
framework, 10, 71, 87, 148, 155, 200, 220, 244, 246, 292, 360
freedom, 5, 8, 10, 122, 152, 162, 185, 248, 252, 279-280, 302, 307-308, 310, 335, 350
Fregoli Syndrome, 80-82, 84
frequencies, 56, 58, 126, 139, 159, 164, 181
Freud, Sigmund, 116, 131, 172, 376
Friedman, Milton, 5, 307

Heidegger, 122, 132, 174
heteronomy, 224-225
heuristic, 58, 160, 166, 175, 328, 333
hierarchy, 36, 230, 287, 297
historicity, 127-128, 137, 147, 153, 156, 164, 168, 177, 179, 201, 244, 362, 368
historiography, 308, 355
Hobbes, Thomas, 300, 342
horizons, 255-256, 277, 291, 341, 343-347, 352, 358
Hume, David, 271
hypotheses, 118, 178-179, 214, 335, 338

G

Galileo, 339
Gardner, Howard, 129-130
Girard, Rene, 5
Goethe, 336
Goodman, Nelson, 43, 50, 137, 192
Gorgias, 77, 282, 346

I

ideologies, 333, 369
imperatives, 90, 298, 303, 348
incommensurable, 263-264, 270-271, 278, 291-293, 372
incompleteness, 128, 246, 266
indeterminacy, 184, 244, 248, 260, 278, 290, 328-329
indeterminism, 164, 181, 363
inertia, 205, 207, 253, 304, 332
infant, 43, 187, 247, 262, 330, 333
inference, 80, 116, 357
inflation, 313, 317-318
injustices, 263, 294, 332
innovations, 40, 205, 218, 247, 304, 315, 318, 351

H

Habermas, Jurgen, 277
Hacker, Ian, 8
Hayek, Friedrich, 259, 312
Hegel, 174, 220, 354

Index

insight, 22, 84, 108, 121, 127, 138, 144, 155-156, 161-163, 167, 187, 189, 213, 225, 239, 243, 271, 284, 292, 295, 366
institution, 171-172, 174, 193, 196-197, 200-201, 205, 216, 227, 366
integrator, 49, 87, 137, 151-153, 155, 168, 171
intellect, 8, 23, 89, 106, 236, 295
intelligence, 48-51, 76, 82, 86, 90, 92-93, 113, 123-124, 129-133, 138-140, 147, 151, 163, 235, 250, 322, 362
intelligibility, 22, 74, 126, 140, 168, 181, 183, 221, 232, 329, 363
intentionality, 8-11, 49, 98, 112, 140, 147, 183, 232, 236, 340, 348, 350, 364
interdependence, 76, 111, 174
interiority, 264, 291, 293, 329, 332, 344, 362, 372
invariant, 58, 201, 330
inventors, 217, 247, 316

J

James, William, 17, 19
Jung, 84

K

Kant, 188
Keynes, John Maynard, 309
Kolers, Paul, 43, 49-50, 69, 90, 129, 135
Krugman, Paul, 309

L

laissez-faire, 247-248, 252, 283, 300-302, 330, 350
leisure, 304, 307, 330, 335
liberalism, 196, 230, 273, 281, 320
liberation, 294, 304, 330, 361
liberties, 5, 294, 310
Libet, Benjamin, 3, 12, 15-16, 43, 65-69, 115, 136, 335, 341
limbic system, 81, 101, 106, 108, 110, 119, 123, 156
Locke, 300
Lonergan, Bernard, 6-7, 22, 25, 33, 57, 75-76, 82-83, 85-87, 92-93, 121-122, 130, 134, 140, 142, 151-152, 154, 173, 183, 185, 193, 211, 227-228, 230, 242, 248, 252, 261-262, 264-265, 272, 275-276, 281, 283, 295, 311-314, 317-319, 322, 325, 330-331, 335, 337, 339-340, 342-345, 347, 349, 354
Luckmann, Thomas, 172, 270

Index

M

MacIntyre, Alasdair, 251, 291
macroeconomics, 248, 310
Marx, 131-132, 312, 322
McShane, Philip, 7, 93, 138, 227-228, 337
mechanism, 53, 61, 127-128, 158, 248, 250, 323, 334, 368
metaphysics, 11, 112, 149
Milgram, Stanley, 165
mitsein, 173, 200, 246
moods, 49, 86, 94, 103, 165
morality, 132, 220, 248, 297, 300, 341, 355
Muller, Jerry Z., 280
multiplicity, 130, 133, 137, 147, 150, 265, 292, 344, 352
myth, 77-78, 84, 295

N

necessity, 166, 327, 334, 358, 360
Nietzsche, Friedrich, 131-132, 328
noninterference, 283-285, 296, 310
normativity, 184, 242, 365
norms, 241-242, 251, 265, 289, 298, 301, 305, 321, 335, 343, 347, 369
Nozick, Robert, 294

O

operator, 56, 87, 103, 150-157, 160, 168, 171, 178-179, 181, 186, 219, 221, 235, 238-240, 246, 295, 304, 341, 364, 372

P

pathway, 28-29, 44, 101
perception, 33, 38, 40, 44, 62, 109, 134, 136, 162, 329, 331, 362
phantasms, 22-23, 98, 121, 149
Plato, 75-78, 81, 83, 85, 87, 92, 121, 132, 282, 295, 310, 318, 346, 360
Posner, Michael I., 18-19, 37-39, 47-48, 51, 56, 58, 62, 112, 146, 191, 233, 336
potency, 22-23
precepts, 242, 253
predispositions, 69, 190
preferences, 46, 141, 347
probability, 9, 18, 31, 45, 59, 100, 106-108, 112, 126-128, 148, 154, 156, 159, 161, 164, 167, 179, 181, 184, 190-191, 206, 208, 216, 219, 234, 239, 245, 296, 351
prosopagnosia, 12, 115, 117, 144
Proust, Marcel, 97

Index

Q

questionable, 286, 364

R

Ramachandran, V.S., 27-29, 33, 80, 84, 88-89, 92, 100, 109, 118, 134
rationality, 130-131, 250, 288, 291, 368
rationalizations, 199, 213, 240
realism, 211, 263, 268, 303, 319, 350, 371-373
Realpolitik, 211, 331-332
receptivity, 109-110, 117, 121, 126, 139, 149, 153, 156, 164, 168, 174, 176, 178-179
recurrence, schemes of, 15, 22, 40, 45, 57-58, 63, 87, 111-112, 126, 158, 166, 171, 175, 177, 180-182, 191, 196, 200, 204-205, 208-209, 212, 214, 218, 222-223, 225, 234, 244, 246, 254, 260-261, 264, 268, 272, 274, 334, 342, 355, 359
reductionistic, 53, 336, 358
reflex, 20, 25-26, 32, 39, 64, 72, 100, 102-103, 107, 110
regulators, 41-42, 64, 138
relativism, 80, 128, 265-266, 270
Ricoeur, Paul, 131
Rilke, Rainer Maria, 199-200

Rorty, Richard, 284
Rostow, Walt, 217
Ruz, Maria, 17, 37-39

S

schizophrenia, 48, 191, 233
Schumpeter, J.A., 247, 312, 316-317, 322
Scotus, 225
Searle, John, 8
selfdetermination, 217, 279, 287-288
Sen, Amartya, 253, 334
Shakespeare, 127
Shue, Henry, 257
Shute, Michael, 80, 205, 211, 330
skepticism, 270, 335
slavery, 190, 238, 267
socialization, 166, 171-172, 200, 204, 271, 365
sociobiology, 89-90, 192
sociology, 10, 128, 211, 223, 273, 364
Socrates, 76, 282, 331
soul, 42, 77, 334
specialization, 13, 211, 251, 337, 340, 342, 344-345, 354-357, 359
Spinoza, Baruch, 92, 149, 300
spirituality, 341, 355
stability, 113, 154, 172, 185, 187, 207, 209, 218, 243, 285, 363
Stroop test, 24, 34, 39
subjectivity, 276, 341, 347
substrates, 19, 39-40, 47, 57, 59, 64

Index

supervenience, 56, 158, 359
supplant, 49
supplementation, principle of, 135, 150, 154, 158, 329, 362

T

thalamus, 35, 38, 41
theorizing, 36, 264, 276
Thoreau, Henry David, 76
tradition, 92, 225, 267, 270, 292, 309, 348-349

U

unemployment, 258, 312-313, 317
unintelligible, 221, 240, 332
usury, 265-266
utility, 102, 115, 194, 268, 286

V

virtue, 76, 92, 189-191, 240, 245, 274, 280-281, 285, 302, 309, 317, 327, 365
Voegelin, Eric, 77-78, 132, 199, 278

volition, 8, 38, 62

W

whyquestions, 203, 261, 273, 286, 363
Wolff, Robert Paul, 225

Z

Zanardi, William J., 1, 80, 205, 260
Zeno, 66

www.ingramcontent.com/pod-product-compliance
Lightning Source LLC
Chambersburg PA
CBHW050329230426
43663CB00010B/1793